AFTER 1177 B.C.

OTHER BOOKS BY ERIC H. CLINE

1177 B.C.: The Year Civilization Collapsed: Revised and Updated

1177 B.C.: A Graphic History of the Year Civilization Collapsed, with Glynnis Fawkes

Three Stones Make a Wall: The Story of Archaeology

Digging Deeper: How Archaeology Works

Digging Up Armageddon: The Search for the Lost City of Solomon

AFTER 1177 B.C.

The Survival of Civilizations

ERIC H. CLINE

PRINCETON UNIVERSITY PRESS
PRINCETON & OXFORD

Published by Princeton University Press
41 William Street, Princeton, New Jersey 08540
99 Banbury Road, Oxford OX2 6JX

press.princeton.edu

Library of Congress Cataloging-in-Publication Data

Names: Cline, Eric H., 1960– author.
Title: After 1177 B. C. : the survival of civilizations / Eric H. Cline.
Description: Princeton : Princeton University Press, [2024] | Series: Turning points in ancient history | Includes bibliographical references and index.
Identifiers: LCCN 2023022187 (print) | LCCN 2023022188 (ebook) | ISBN 9780691192130 (hardback) | ISBN 9780691255477 (ebook)
Subjects: LCSH: Iron age. | Mediterranean Region—Civilization. | Mediterranean Region—History—To 476. | BISAC: HISTORY / Ancient / General | SOCIAL SCIENCE / Archaeology
Classification: LCC GN780.25 .C55 2024 (print) | LCC GN780.25 (ebook) | DDC 937/.01—dc23/eng/20231023
LC record available at https://lccn.loc.gov/2023022187
LC ebook record available at https://lccn.loc.gov/2023022188

British Library Cataloging-in-Publication Data is available

Editorial: Rob Tempio and Chloe Coy
Production Editorial: Mark Bellis
Text and Jacket Design: Karl Spurzem
Production: Erin Suydam
Publicity: Maria Whelan and Carmen Jimenez
Copy editor: Beth Gianfagna

Jacket Credit: Joseph Mallord William Turner (1775–1851), *The Decline of the Carthaginian Empire*, 1851. Courtesy of Tate.

This book has been composed in Arno Pro with Trajan Pro 3

Printed on acid-free paper. ∞

Printed in the United States of America

10 9 8 7 6 5 4 3 2 1

Dedicated to

Diane Harris Cline

Classicist and Cellist

Someone once said that his favorite times in history
were when things were collapsing,
because that meant something new was being born.

—JULIAN BARNES, *THE SENSE OF AN ENDING* (2011)

CONTENTS

List of Illustrations xi

List of Tables xiii

List of Maps xv

Series Editor's Foreword xvii

Preface. "It's the End of the World as We Know It" (. . . and I Don't Feel Fine) xix

PROLOGUE. Welcome to the Iron Age 1

CHAPTER ONE. The Year of the Hyenas, When Men Starved 7

CHAPTER TWO. Conqueror of All Lands, Avenger of Assyria 42

CHAPTER THREE. The Mediterranean Became a Phoenician Lake 80

CHAPTER FOUR. King of the Land of Carchemish 111

CHAPTER FIVE. In the Shadow of the Ruined Palaces 134

CHAPTER SIX. From Collapse to Resilience 157

EPILOGUE.
End of a Dark Age 195

Author's Note and Acknowledgments 201
Dramatis Personae 207
Notes 213
References 251
Index 305

ILLUSTRATIONS

FIG. 1. Coca-Cola vending machine in Rethymnon, Crete xx

FIG. 2. Tel Dan inscription with the words *Beit David* highlighted 23

FIG. 3. Replica of Gezer calendar inscription 28

FIG. 4. Tiglath-Pileser I clay prism 50

FIG. 5. Kurkh Monolith of Aššurnasirpal II 64

FIG. 6. Shalmaneser III at Tyre, from Band III of the Balawat gates 69

FIG. 7. Black Obelisk of Shalmaneser III, with the submission of Jehu 76

FIG. 8. Sarcophagus of Ahiram, with Phoenician inscription 102

FIG. 9. Pharaoh Osorkon I with Elibaal inscription, from Byblos 103

FIG. 10. Warrior vase from Mycenae 135

FIG. 11. Visualization of the adaptive cycle 161

FIG. 12. Reconceptualization of the adaptive cycle with the phases labeled in terms of the Late Bronze Age, LBA Collapse, and Iron Age 162

FIG. 13. Reconceptualization of the adaptive cycle specifically for Greece, from the Late Bronze and Iron Ages through the Archaic and Classical periods 163

FIG. 14. Intergovernmental Panel on Climate Change, *SREX* cover, 2012 165

TABLES

TABLE 1. Kings and regnal years mentioned in the text—northern area xxxii–xxxiii

TABLE 2. Kings and regnal years mentioned in the text—southern area xxxiv-xxxv

TABLE 3. Societal changes indicative of a system collapse and subsequent dark age 5

TABLE 4. Terms and definitions related to resiliency 169

TABLE 5. Broad categories of resilience for the various areas/ societies in the centuries following the Collapse 172

TABLE 6. Resilience, or lack thereof, by area/society and century BC, also indicating adaptive cycle phases 181–183

TABLE 7. Sequels of civilizations/societies in the centuries following the Collapse 189

TABLE 8. Societal lessons learned from the LBA Collapse and aftermath 194

MAPS

(following the preface, drawn by Michele Angel)

MAP 1. Overview of Iron Age Eastern Mediterranean xxvii

MAP 2. Egypt during the Iron Age, with sites and areas mentioned in the text xxviii

MAP 3. The Levant during the Iron Age, with sites and areas mentioned in the text xxix

MAP 4. Cyprus during the Iron Age, with sites and areas mentioned in the text xxx

MAP 5. Western Mediterranean during the Iron Age, with sites and areas mentioned in the text xxx

MAP 6. Aegean region during the Iron Age, with sites and areas mentioned in the text xxxi

SERIES EDITOR'S FOREWORD

In this, the fourth volume in the series Turning Points in Ancient History, Eric H. Cline continues the story that he told in its first volume. In *1177 B.C.: The Year Civilization Collapsed* (2014, rev. ed. 2021), Cline recounted the remarkable tale of the ruin of Bronze Age civilizations in place after place in the Eastern Mediterranean and Near East. The year 1177, as he demonstrated, was a turning point, but what came next? In the current book, *After 1177 B.C.: The Survival of Civilizations,* Cline turns his probing intelligence to that question. And a great story it is.

Cline is after big game in this book, and he pursues it with power and passion. He addresses one of the fundamental subjects of the historical profession—the rise and fall of civilizations. He does so, however, by taking a fresh approach: it's not rise and fall that he seeks to explain but fall and resurgence. How do societies respond to collapse or the threat of collapse? Why do some endure while others go under? What makes some civilizations resilient while leaving others fragile? To answer these questions, Cline proceeds to a panoramic survey of ancient societies from Greece to Mesopotamia.

In crystal clear prose enlivened with wit, *After 1177 B.C.* offers a fascinating mix of archaeology, history, climate science, and social theory. It ranges over a great variety of civilizations: Assyrians, Babylonians, Canaanites, Egyptians, Greeks, Hittites, Israelites, Phoenicians. This is a bravura performance, and one that few scholars would be able to match for its range. Cline draws on his vast knowledge of archaeology to bring the reader up close and personal with artifacts and sites, from inscriptions and obelisks to swords and from temples to tombs. There are dramatic moments, including a knife thrust to a pharaoh's neck and the discovery of the bones of what might represent a woman sacrificed in a warrior's grave. And a cavalcade of characters graces the book's pages, from ancient kings and conquerors to centuries of scholars who engage in more civilized, if no less ardent, battle over history and its cycles.

Cline reaches the intriguing conclusion that the centuries following the Bronze Age collapse were not, as the textbooks say, a "Dark Age." In fact, they represent a period of innovation. Mass literacy, the use of iron tools and weapons, the invention of coinage, and the emergence of the Greek city-state (*polis*) were among the revolutions of the era. Specialists in the period know this, but the message hasn't gotten through to the public yet. So, writes Cline, enough with the Dark Age: let's simply call this period the Iron Age instead.

This is a hopeful conclusion and a welcome takeaway, because *After 1177 B.C.* is not merely academic. Rather, it focuses on a theme that speaks to us today. In an age of innovation proceeding at a breakneck pace and a cascade of unsettling events around the world—pandemic, war, forest fires, artificial intelligence—it couldn't be timelier to contemplate how our ancestors coped (or failed to cope) with change and catastrophe.

Barry Strauss

PREFACE

"It's the End of the World as We Know It" (. . . and I Don't Feel Fine)

I began writing this book early one morning in February 2019 while sitting on the balcony of a rented apartment in Rethymnon, Crete. We were there for the beginning of my wife Diane's Fulbright grant to teach at the University of Crete. I had arranged to have the semester off from our own university so that I could accompany her, and we were enjoying the weak winter sun and visiting familiar archaeological sites before her classes began. We were also marveling at the ubiquity of antiquity in modern marketing, personified by depictions of Ariadne holding a ball of yarn and Minoans leaping over bulls. That wouldn't be particularly surprising except that the scenes were emblazoned on the sides of a dusty refrigerator full of Cokes outside a shop in an alleyway deep in the oldest part of the city.

That particular morning, it was peaceful and quiet, with the sun rising in front of me over Homer's beloved Mediterranean Sea and with the snow-capped White Mountains off to my left in the far distance. All seemed well as I sipped my coffee and surfed the Internet, reading various periodicals online while lending half an ear to the news on streaming audio.

Then I started listening more closely to what was being reported by the BBC. We were being warned about the possible collapse of our current civilization, courtesy of a multitude of interrelated factors ranging from climactic to economic. These, according to a study that had just

FIG. 1. Coca-Cola vending machine in Rethymnon, Crete. Photographs by E. H. Cline.

been published and was now being breathlessly described by the journalists, could soon result in "economic instability, large-scale involuntary migration, conflict, famine and the potential collapse of social and economic systems."[1]

It had been almost exactly five years to the day since I first published *1177 B.C.: The Year Civilization Collapsed*, which examined the causes of the Collapse that took place in the Aegean and Eastern Mediterranean at the end of the Late Bronze Age, more than three thousand years ago.[2] In it, I explained what life was like during the fifteenth to the twelfth centuries BC in those regions—from what is now Greece across to Iran and Iraq and from Turkey down to Egypt, to put it in modern terms. I described the G8 of that time—the Mycenaeans, Minoans, Hittites, Cypriots, Canaanites, Egyptians, Assyrians, and Babylonians—and then examined the possible causes of the Collapse that ended their internationalized world, though exactly why and how it happened so quickly and so completely is still very much a mystery.

Among the possible factors or causes that I discussed (including subsequently at greater length in the revised and updated 2021 edition) were climate change, drought, famine, earthquakes, invaders, and disease. I concluded that none of them would have been sufficiently cataclysmic on its own to bring down even one of the Bronze Age civilizations in the Aegean and Eastern Mediterranean, let alone all of them. However, a combination of all (or many/most) would have created a perfect storm of calamities, with both multiplier and domino effects, which could have led to the rapid disintegration of one society after another, in part because of the fragmentation of the globalized Mediterranean network and the breakdown of the interconnections on which each civilization was dependent. As I concluded there, "In short, the flourishing cultures and peoples of the Bronze Age . . . were simply not able to survive the onslaught of so many different stressors all at the same time."[3]

Crete is one of the places where civilization essentially collapsed and the advanced society whom we call the Minoans basically disappeared at the end of the Bronze Age, to be replaced by a new iteration. The Mycenaeans on the nearby Greek mainland, known as the homeland of Achilles, Odysseus, Ajax, and the Greek states described in the *Iliad* and *Odyssey*, didn't survive either—or at least their society/culture didn't. Nobody today claims to be Minoan or Mycenaean. So, the news that day did cause me a bit of consternation—striking home with a particular sense of "future déjà vu," one might say, as we worry in turn that a catastrophic collapse may lie ahead for us and our globalized world. It could be the end of the world as we know it, as R.E.M. once sang, but I really didn't feel fine about it. If there is another collapse coming, I wondered, is it too soon to start thinking about how we will rebuild? Will it even be possible?

My thoughts also turned to what it might have been like for them, back when their Bronze Age world was collapsing. What did each of these areas, or the survivors in them, subsequently do—or fail to do, as the case may be—about the situation(s) in which they found themselves? Did anyone at the time know that they were in the middle of a collapse?[4] How did they regroup and recover? Or did they? Were they resilient? Did they transform? Or did they simply go under, to be replaced by new states and new societies?

I am not alone in being interested in such issues. In recent years other archaeologists and ancient historians have begun to explore more fully the question of what happens after a collapse has occurred—not just in terms of the Late Bronze Age Collapse, but regarding any number of other societies and civilizations over the past millennia that endured a sudden disintegration, either total or partial. These cases range from the Harappans in the Indus Valley four thousand years ago to the Romans in Italy at the end of the classical age to the Maya in Central America in the ninth century AD, and many others as well. Some failed to survive, but others somehow made the transition and managed to successfully reestablish or reinvent themselves.[5]

The question is: how were the survivors able to endure and continue? Some of the terms now being batted around to describe survival of modern crises include "coping," "adaptation," "transition," and "transformation." The word "resilience" has become especially popular because it has become clear, as one pair of scholars have said, that "collapse and resilience are two sides of the same coin; collapse occurs when resilience is lost, and resilient systems are less likely to collapse." Princeton historian John Haldon and his colleagues have pointed out that the manner in which previous societies have responded to stress depends on three things: their complexity, their flexibility, and their systemic redundancy, "all of which together determine the resilience of the system."[6]

All of this was further driven home to me beginning about eight months after we returned from Crete, during the winter and spring of 2020, when the COVID-19 pandemic hit the United States and the Black Lives Matter protests spread across the country after the death of George Floyd Jr. The protests, some peaceful, but some erupting into violence because of counterprotesters and actions by federal agents, continued into the summer and fall.

A year later, despite a change in the US presidency, things were no better. In August 2021, the United Nations released an extremely pessimistic report on climate change, while the US National Intelligence Council issued a report on the pandemic, stating that it had "deepened economic inequality, strained government resources and fanned nationalist sentiments." At about the same time, wildfires erupted simultaneously in both California and Greece, and problems with the global supply chain began to emerge, creating troubles for consumers wanting items ranging from laptop computers to automobiles and everything in between.[7]

At that moment, my thoughts during our earlier time on Crete no longer seemed like just an idle academic exercise. To the previous list of stressors, we had now abruptly added a worldwide pandemic, wildfires more intense than usual, severe storms and other evidence of climate change, supply chain issues on a global scale, and serious societal fractures along political lines in the United States.

Nor did things improve with the new year. During the spring, summer, and early fall of 2022, we saw Russia invade Ukraine, new strains of COVID-19 spread rapidly around the world, and ongoing revelations about what happened at the US Capitol on January 6, 2021. I was worried before, but now I was very seriously wondering if another "perfect storm" of calamities has arrived and whether another collapse is just around the corner, as I described previously for the year 1177 BC. It has all happened with breathtaking speed—far faster than it had taken back in the twelfth century BC, which is my personal benchmark for civilizational catastrophes.

The questions that I was asking myself while on Crete, and which have been asked for some time by other scholars, are now being asked by the US government, as well as members of the media.[8] What happens after a society collapses? Is it gone forever, or does it bounce back? Can one simply pick up the pieces and begin again? Are there replacements called up from the minor leagues—new people and a new society? Or can the surviving people show resiliency and adapt to the new circumstances by transitioning and transforming to a "new normal"? As archaeologist George Cowgill said back in 1988, "the 'collapse of a civilization' . . . is a far less simple idea than we have been accustomed to think."[9] So too is the rebirth or transformation of civilization. That is what we will explore together in the following pages, by examining what actually took place in the Aegean and Eastern Mediterranean during the period after the Late Bronze Age Collapse.

—

A few words of warning are in order before we begin, however. As we will see, the situation after the Late Bronze Age Collapse was more nuanced than one might have thought. As the international network linking the entire Aegean and Eastern Mediterranean fell apart (and there is no doubt that it did), the individual societies each had to make their own decisions regarding survival. Their choices were simple: if they were to survive, they had to cope, adapt, or transform to the new normal. If they didn't, they faced extinction. This becomes clear when one studies the immediate aftermath of the Collapse and compares the situation of each of the ancient societies involved, which is exactly what I will do in the following chapters. I am interested in not only who survived and why/how they did, but also who did not (and why they didn't).

In addition, I should mention that the initial drafts of this book followed a chronological approach, much as I did in *1177 B.C.*, looking at what took place during each century after the Collapse. However, I subsequently decided that a geographical approach would provide a better sense of how each of the societies responded to the Collapse over time, as the inhabitants in each region attempted to work their way out of the aftermath of the catastrophe that had affected them all, though there will still be a certain amount of connectivity between the various chapters at a number of points. In essence, we have here eight examples of what to do, or not to do, after a collapse.

I will tell the story using specific objects as signposts for our journey—most often inscriptions written on stone, clay, papyrus, and other materials, but also other ancient artifacts. In presenting this underlying evidence, I am aiming for intellectual transparency: to show not only what we know, but how we know it. However, as will become apparent, especially for the Assyrians, Babylonians, and Egyptians, who left extensive written inscriptions, in many instances there is enough granular detail (perhaps too much, on occasion) to focus on some of the higher-ranking individuals and their accomplishments, but not always for those in the lower levels of society. Moreover, for some of these societies, such as the Mycenaeans, Minoans, and Cypriots, the specific details of most of the individuals who lived during this period, whether rich or poor, elite or insignificant, are now lost to history. My discussions will therefore vary dramatically from chapter to chapter, with deeper dives into specific details and stories when possible, depending on the amount and type of information that is available, but I aim for a common denominator of basic historical coverage wherever possible.[10] Who lived, who died, I'll try to tell their story (to reference the hit musical *Hamilton*). And, for those who have difficulty keeping the players straight without a scorecard, a glossary of the most important people and their details has been included as a "Dramatis Personae" towards the end of this book.

We also need to be aware that this will be a much messier story than that of the Bronze Age. In fact, we should think in terms of stories (plural) rather than a single story, for in examining the responses of the various societies during these centuries, we are looking at a Mediterranean realm that had been fragmented by the collapse of the intertwined world as they had known it. It will be a bit like looking into a kaleidoscope, with some connections and links but with the pieces often separated from each other or only tenuously connected, to be brought together again only at the conclusion of this tale. But we have a unique opportunity here to investigate what happens after a system collapse by examining in detail the history of not just one society, like the Maya or the Romans, but eight different ones. And that is exactly what we will do for the first five chapters of this book. Then, in chapter 6, we will take what we have just learned and analyze it, ranking the societies in terms of their resilience and their success or failure to adapt or transform, using criteria and definitions provided by the IPCC, and will be able to examine which of this is relevant to our modern world, with the hope that it might provide some guidance for us on how to make our own societies more resilient against the potential catastrophes that we currently face.

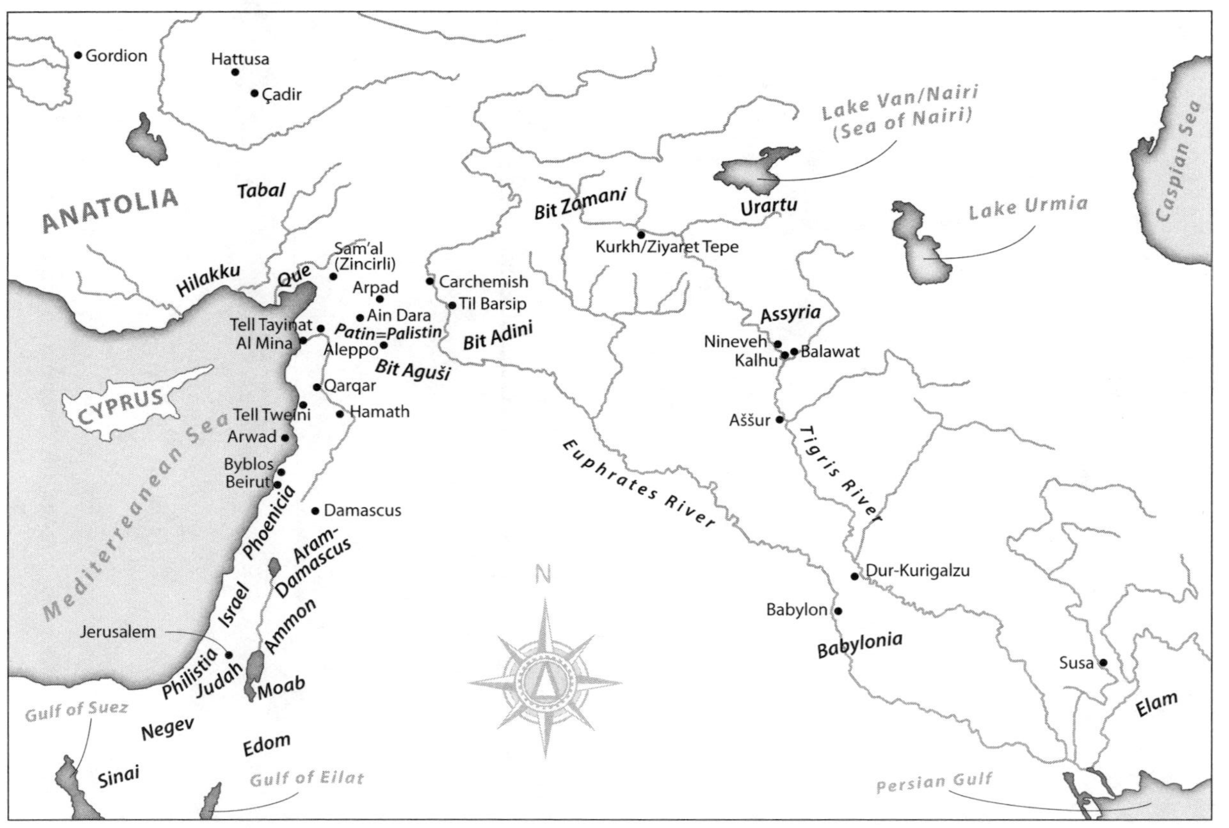

MAP 1. Overview of Iron Age Eastern Mediterranean, with Neo-Hittite, Aramean, and Mesopotamian sites shown, and with southern Levantine kingdoms identified (but not all sites listed).

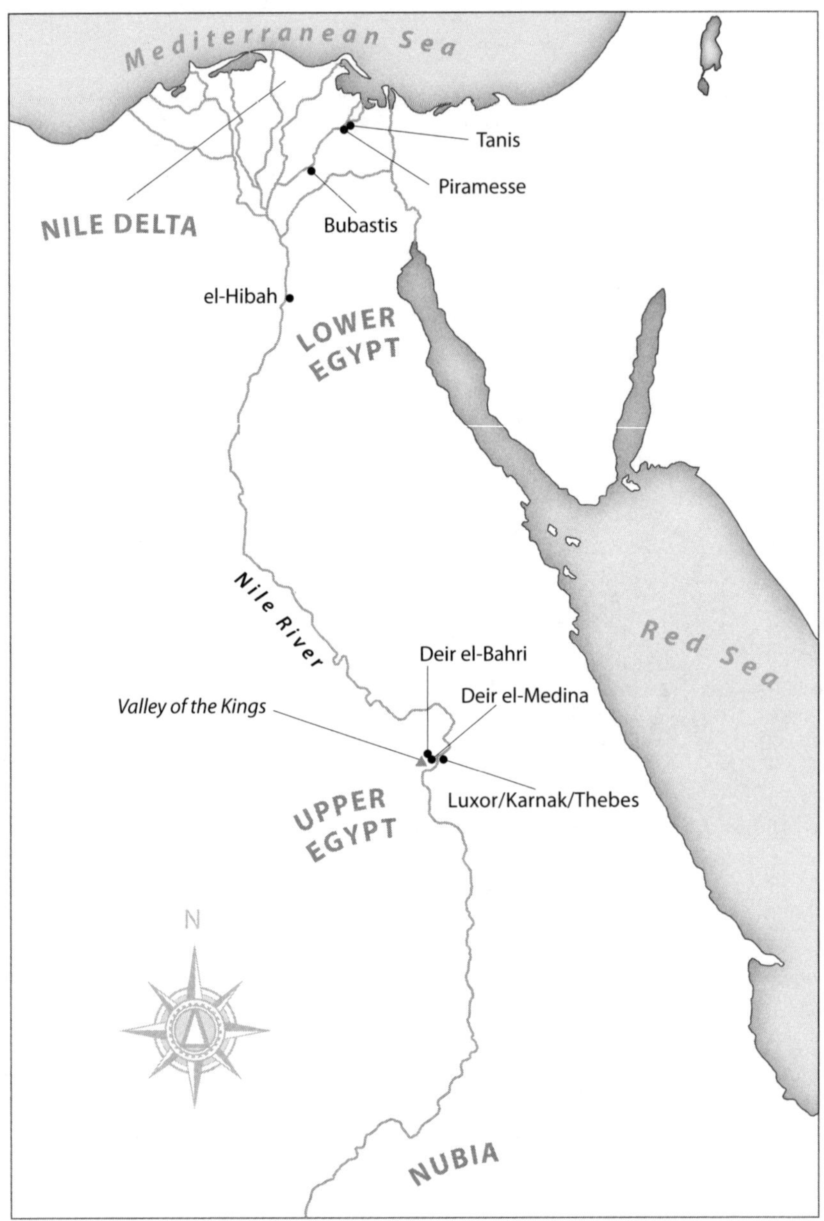

MAP 2. Egypt during the Iron Age, with sites and areas mentioned in the text.

MAP 3. The Levant during the Iron Age, with sites and areas mentioned in the text.

MAP 4. Cyprus during the Iron Age, with sites and areas mentioned in the text.

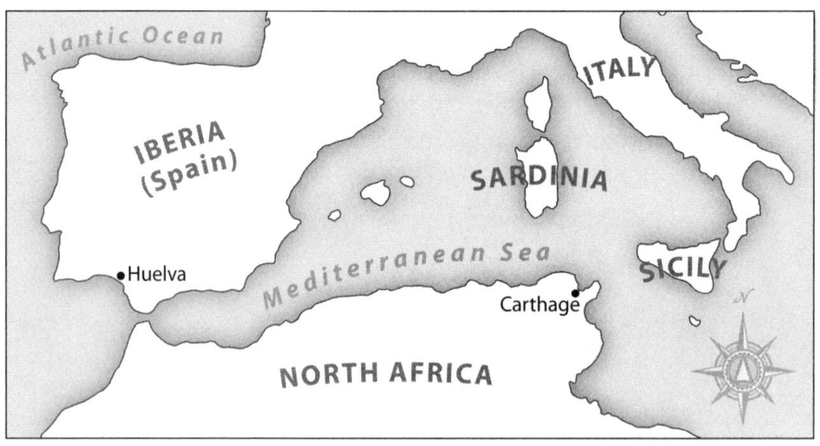

MAP 5. Western Mediterranean during the Iron Age,
with sites and areas mentioned in the text.

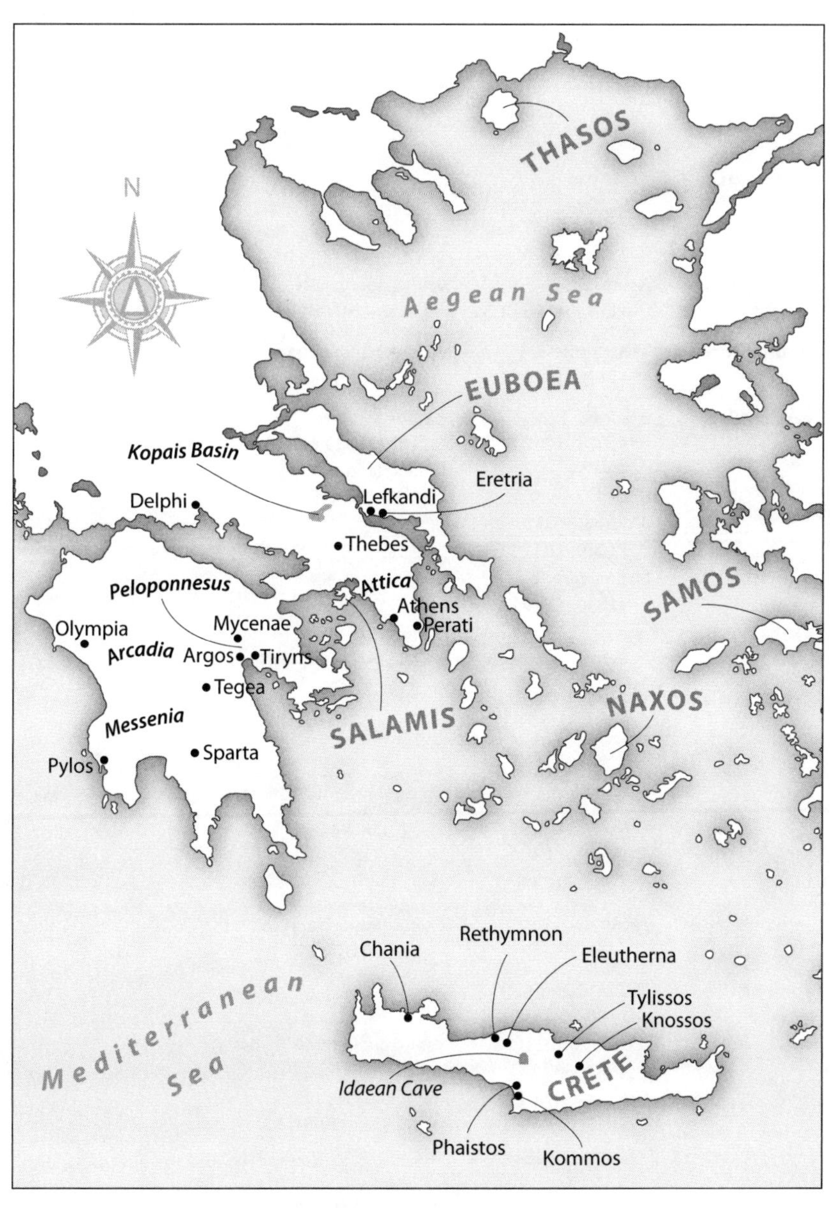

MAP 6. Aegean region during the Iron Age, with sites and areas mentioned in the text.

TABLE 1. Kings and regnal years mentioned in the text—northern area

	Assyria	Babylonia	Elam
13th century BC	Tukulti-Ninurta I (1244–1208 BC)		
12th century BC	Aššur-dan I (1179–1133 BC)		Shutruk-Nahhunte (1190–1155 BC)
		Enlil-nadin-ahi (ca. 1157–1155 BC)	Kutur-Nahhunte (ca. 1155–1150 BC)
	Aššur-reša-iši I (1133–1116 BC)	Nebuchadnezzar I (1125–1104 BC)	Hutelutush-Inshushinak (ca. 1120–1110 BC)
12th–11th century BC	Tiglath-Pileser I (1115–1076 BC)	Marduk-nadin-ahhe (ca. 1099–1082 BC)	
11th century BC	Aššur-bel-kala (1074–1057 BC)	Marduk-sapik-zeri (1082–1069 BC)	
		Adad-apla-iddina (1067–1046 BC)	
	Aššurnasirpal I (1049–1031 BC)		
	Shalmaneser II (1030–1019 BC)		
		Kaššu-nadin-ahhe (ca. 1007–1005 BC)	
10th century BC			
		Nabu-mukin-apli (ca. 978–943 BC)	
	Aššur-dan II (934–912 BC)		
10th–9th century BC	Adad-nirari II (911–891 BC)	Shamaš-mudammiq (ca. 900 BC)	
9th century BC	Tukulti-Ninurta II (890–884 BC)		
	Aššurnasirpal II (883–859 BC)	Nabu-apla-iddina (ca. 887–855 BC)	
	Shalmaneser III (858–824 BC)	Marduk-zakir-sumi (ca. 855–819 BC)	
	Shamši-Adad V (823–811 BC)	Marduk-balatsu-iqbi (819–813 BC)	
		Baba-aha-iddina (ca. 812 BC)	
9th–8th century BC	Adad-nirari III (810–783 BC)		
8th century BC			

Carchemish (Great King)	Carchemish (Country Lord)	Kunulua/Palistin (Tayinat)	Sam'al (Zincirli)	Urartu
Kuzi-Tešub (ca. 1200–1180 BC)				
Ini-Tešub (late 12th c. BC)				
		Taita I (11th c. BC)		
Sapaziti (late 11th c. BC)				
Ura-Tarhunta (early 10th c. BC)	Suhi I (ca. 1000 BC)	Taita II (early 10th c. BC)		
Tuthaliya II (10th c. BC?)	Astuwalamanza(s) (10th c. BC)			
grandsons of Ura-Tarhunta (10th c. BC)	Suhi II (10th c. BC)	Manana (mid 10th c. BC)		
	Katuwa(s) (late 10th c. BC)	Suppiluliuma I (late 10th c. BC)		
	Suhi III (ca. 900 BC)	Halparuntiya (early 9th c. BC)	Hayya (ca. 870/60–840 BC)	
		Lubarna I? (early 9th c. BC)		
	Sangara (ca. 875–848 BC)	Suppiluliuma II/Sapalulme (mid 9th c. BC)		Aramu (ca. 859–844 BC)
		Qalparunda II (mid 9th c. BC)	Sha'il (prob. co-ruler ca. 850–840 BC)	
	Isarwila-muwa (2nd half of 9th c. BC)	Lubarna II (late 9th c. BC)	Kulamuwa (ca. 840–810 BC)	Sarduri I (ca. 834–828 BC)
	Kuwalana-muwa (2nd half of 9th c. BC)			Ishpuini (ca. 828–810 BC)
	Astiru(wa) I (ca. 810 BC)			
				Menua (ca. 810–786 BC)
	Kamani (ca. 790 BC)			Inushpua (ruled with Menua)
				Argishti I (ca. 786–764 BC)

TABLE 2. Kings and regnal years mentioned in the text—southern area

	Tyre	Byblos	Kingdom/City Damascus
13th century BC			
12th century BC			
12th–11th century BC		Tjekkerbaal/Zakarbaal (ca. 1075 BC)	
11th century BC			
10th century BC		Ahiram (early 10th c. BC)	
	Hiram (ca. 970–936 BC)	Ethbaal (early 10th c. BC)	
		Yehimilk (mid 10th c. BC)	
	Baal-ma'zer [Baal-azor] I (late 10th c. BC)	Abibaal (mid-late 10th c. BC)	
	Abdi-Aštart [Abdastratus] (late 10th c. BC)	Elibaal (mid-late 10th c. BC)	
10th–9th century BC	Methusastratos [usurper] (late 10th c. BC)	Shipitbaal (late 10th c. BC)	
9th century BC	Iš-Aštart (early 9th c. BC)		
	Aštar(t)-imn (early 9th c. BC)		
	Pilles (early 9th c. BC)		
	Ethbaal (early-mid 9th c. BC)		Hadad-ezer (ca. 858 BC)
	Baal-ma'zer [Baal-azor] II (mid 9th c. BC)		
			Hazael (ca. 842–796 BC)
9th–8th century BC	Mattan I (late 9th c. BC)		
	Pumiyaton [Pummayon/Pygmalion] (late 9th-early 8th c. BC)		

ypt	United Monarchy	Israel	Judah	Moab	Edom
mses III (1186–1155 BC)					
mses IV-X (1155–1098 BC)					
Ramses XI (1098–1070 BC); 2) Smendes (1077/69–1043 BC); and 3) Herihor (1080–1074 BC); Panedjem I (1074–1036 BC)					
usennes I (1039–991 BC)	David (ca. 1000–970 BC)				Hadad (early 10th c. BC)
menemopet (991–982 BC)					
amun (979–958 BC)	Solomon (ca. 970–930 BC)				
susennes II (958–945 BC)					
heshonq I (ca. 945–924 BC)					
sorkon I (ca. 924–890 BC)					
		Omri (ca. 884–873 BC)		Mesha (9th c. BC)	
akelot I (890–872 BC); Sheshonq IIa (ca. 890 BC)		Ahab (ca. 871–852 BC)			
sorkon II (872–831 BC)		Joram (ca. 850–840 BC)	Jehoram (ca. 849–842 BC)		
			Ahaziah (ca. 842–841 BC)		
		Jehu (ca. 841–814 BC)			
Sheshonq III (831–791 BC); Takelot II (834–810 BC)		Joash/Jehoash (ca. 804–789 BC)			

PROLOGUE

Welcome to the Iron Age

Sweeping down from the north, wielding gleaming weapons of sharp iron, the fierce Dorian warriors brought a quick end to the Mycenaean civilization shortly after 1200 BC. Greece was plunged into the world's first dark age. According to the later Greek historian Thucydides, it was just eighty years after the Trojan War.[1]

Early archaeologists and historians working in modern Greece embraced the concept of a "Dorian invasion." According to their scenarios, the invaders brought with them new types of pins and brooches, burials, pottery, and—most important of all—swords made of iron.[2] This story became part of the established account in textbooks on ancient Greece and still figures prominently in various compilations, including the most recent edition of the *Columbia Electronic Encyclopedia,* which states: "The Mycenaean commercial empire and consequent cultural influence lasted from 1400 to 1200 B.C., when the invasion of the Dorians ushered in a period of decline for Greece."[3]

However, it probably never happened.

The existence of a Dorian invasion was questioned as long ago as 1966, by scholars such as Rhys Carpenter of Bryn Mawr, and it continues to be questioned today. It has been described as a "baffling situation of an invasion without invaders," "a scholarly mirage," and "an extraordinary and paradoxical situation, in which there is no sign of the presence of a hostile invader." Joseph Tainter, the preeminent scholar of collapse, put it nicely: "Quite simply . . . the Dorians have left curiously little archaeological trace," while Professor Gregory Nagy, the former director of Harvard University's Center for Hellenic Studies, has said that "there is no need to posit a 'Dorian Invasion' . . . if in fact the Dorians were already 'there' in the Peloponnesus, as a substrate population."[4]

In fact, none of the "evidence" mentioned above requires the arrival of a new people to explain its existence, and some of the so-called innovations are now known to have already begun in the Bronze Age, including Naue II swords and violin-bow fibulae. Other innovations, such as mastering the technology of ironmaking, only came about after the destruction of the palaces, rather than either previously or simultaneously, as we will see below. Moreover, Mycenaean-style pottery continued for another century and a half after things began collapsing, until the middle of the eleventh century BC.[5]

There is also significant evidence of continuity during this period, despite the sudden and total failure of the political and economic systems that had been in place on mainland Greece during the Bronze Age. For instance, linguistic specialists have suggested that some features of the Dorian dialect can already be detected in the language of the Linear B texts used by the Mycenaeans, which is an early version of Greek. Thus, the various dialects may simply have been spoken by different Greek-speaking groups who survived the great Collapse, rather than by invaders coming from farther away.[6]

Furthermore, there is no large influx of new populations. In fact, archaeological surveys have indicated exactly the opposite, for there was a dramatic drop in population on mainland Greece immediately after the Collapse. Initial estimates that the population had decreased between 75 and 90 percent from the thirteenth to the eleventh centuries BC are now considered to be a bit too high, but current assessments still hover between 40 and 60 percent for the decrease—with an estimated population of about 600,000 toward the end of the Bronze Age dropping to about 330,000 in the Early Iron Age on mainland Greece.[7]

Not everyone died, though; some survivors simply moved to new areas in Greece that had previously been unpopulated but that were perhaps now deemed safer places to live than where they had been before. Others may have moved even further away, migrating east to areas such as Cyprus or Canaan or west to Italy, Sardinia, or Sicily.[8]

Simply put, despite more than a century of excavation by this point, there has been no definitive proof uncovered of the Dorian invasion. It is a myth or literary tradition created by ancient Greek writers to explain, in part, how there came to be several different dialects of Greek spoken and written during the first millennium BC, but it is not backed up by any physical evidence.

If the idea of a Dorian invasion has been tabled, shelved, and discounted by scholars for several decades now, one can reasonably ask, why is it still discussed? The fact of the matter is that, despite the skepticism of scholars about a Dorian invasion, belief in it outside the small community of academics continues. Sarah Morris, a professor at UCLA speaking of "the persistent specter of the Dorians," says that "as much as the Dorians are now disallowed by professional specialists in history, language, and archaeology, they are still entrenched . . . in textbooks and classrooms. In other words, pedagogy—from curriculum to textbooks to course outlines—has not caught up with scholarship."[9]

Rather than the concept of a "Dorian invasion," Iron Age specialists now prefer instead to discuss the idea that some migrations may have taken place within Greece itself, as survivors of the Collapse moved to new areas and away from the Bronze Age citadels.[10] It may seem—quite literally—to be merely a matter of semantics, but there is a world of difference between the two types of movements—that is, migrations versus invasions—with the former often peaceful and sometimes stretching over significant periods of time and the latter implying a violent and much more sudden episodic event involving outsiders coming into the area. In fact, such a migration of surviving populations is actually quite common in terms of what happens following a system collapse such as took place at the end of the Late Bronze Age. Another good example occurred in the American Southwest ca. AD 1300, where the population emigrated en masse from the Four Corners area southward to the Rio Grande Valley following a dramatic climactic downturn.[11]

Was It Really a Dark Age?

If scholars' previous thinking about the Dorian invasion of Greece can now be demonstrated to be incorrect, then what else might we be wrong about in describing the centuries immediately following the Bronze Age Collapse, which has long been called by scholars "the first dark age"? In fact, we need to ask whether it really was a dark age. Is that an accurate description of what life was like across the entire region in the aftermath of the Collapse, especially if the Dorian invasion never happened?

Three decades ago, Nicholas Coldstream of University College London called this period in Greece "an age of total illiteracy and, in most Aegean regions, an age of poverty, poor communications, and isolation from the outside world." However, writing at almost the exact same time, archaeologist Willie Coulson agreed that while the general perception is that this era was "a low point in the quality of art and life . . . a primitive and poverty-stricken time," he also noted that we don't have a good universal definition on which all scholars can agree.[12]

Merriam-Webster's dictionary defines a dark age as "a time during which a civilization undergoes a decline." Two examples are provided: (1) "the European historical period from about AD 476 to about 1000" (which is not the topic of concern here); and (2) "the Greek historical period of three to four centuries from about 1100 BC" (which is my focus). It adds a general definition of "a state of stagnation or decline."[13]

In fact, the criteria that Cambridge University archaeologist Colin Renfrew used back in 1979 to define a system collapse can also be used as criteria to define a dark age (which Renfrew said almost always follows a system collapse), speaking strictly from a societal viewpoint. These include (1) the collapse of the central administrative organization; (2) the disappearance of the traditional elite class; (3) a breakdown of the centralized economy; (4) a settlement shift; and (5) population decline. To these, as additional symptoms specifically of a dark age, I would add

TABLE 3. Societal changes indicative of a system collapse and subsequent dark age

Aspect	During/after collapse
Centralized economy	Collapses
Central administration	Collapses
Traditional elites	Disappear
Settlements	Shift/move
Population	Declines
Writing	Lost
Impressive architecture	Disappears

(6) a loss of writing; and (7) a pause in the construction of monumental architecture.[14]

Joseph Tainter notes that a systematic collapse of a civilization or society is also usually thought to bring an end to "the artistic and literary features of civilization, and to the umbrella of service and protection that an administration provides." As a result, he says, "The flow of information drops, people trade and interact less, and there is overall lower coordination among individuals and groups. Economic activity drops . . . while the arts and literature experience such a quantitative decline that a dark age often ensues. Population levels tend to drop, and for those who are left, the known world shrinks." All of this is usually seen as a fearful event, "truly paradise lost." However, according to Tainter, sociopolitical collapse is quite a normal occurrence and even to be expected in the general course of the life of most complex societies.[15]

It is perhaps not surprising, therefore, that toward the end of the eighth century BC, the Greek poet Hesiod lamented the fact that he was living during just such a period. "Would that I were not among the men of the fifth generation," he wrote, "but either had died before or been born afterwards. For now truly is a race of iron, and men never rest from labor and sorrow by day, and from perishing by night; and the gods shall lay sore trouble upon them."[16] It is from him, along with the growing use of the new metal, that we get the moniker "Iron Age" for this period, as an alternative to the oft-used "Dark Age."

So, was this a dark age? Or should it now be seen as something else, especially if one is looking not only at societies, but also at the individuals who made up those societies? As James Scott of Yale University has recently asked, "'dark' for whom and in what respects?"[17]

This is the question at the heart of our explorations. What was it like for those living in the aftermath of the Collapse, and how was it different in each of the affected areas? What did it take to survive? That is what we will examine in the next several chapters, as we follow each of the societies and areas—sometimes superficially but often in great detail, as the evidence permits—through their twists and turns from the twelfth to the eighth centuries BC before we proceed to our analyses. So, let us begin.

CHAPTER ONE

The Year of the Hyenas, When Men Starved

(Egypt, Israel, and the Southern Levant)

A quick knife thrust to his throat by an assassin ended the thirty-two-year reign of Pharaoh Ramses III of Egypt in 1155 BC. Two decades earlier, Ramses had won an immense victory over the Sea Peoples, but now he fell victim to a sordid harem conspiracy set in motion by one of his own wives, named Tiye, and a lesser son named Pentawere.

The assassination, now known as the Harem Conspiracy, first came to the attention of modern Egyptologists about 150 years ago.[1] The details are contained on approximately six papyri, some or all of which may have originally been part of a single scroll that was cut into sections by an enterprising antiquities thief before being sold to various people and places. The longest of these documents is now known as the Turin Judicial Papyrus, housed (perhaps not surprisingly, given its modern name) in the Museo Egizio in Turin, Italy. It had originally been purchased by Bernardino Drovetti, the French consul general to Egypt in the early 1800s; he then sold it to the king of Sardinia; and it eventually came to live in the Museo Egizio.[2]

The papyrus contains many of the details of the four trials of his accused assailants. The conspiracy was apparently hatched by Tiye, who wished to have her son by Ramses III, Prince Pentawere, accede to the throne. There were as many as forty accused conspirators, both members of the harem and court officials, who were tried in four groups. A number of them were found guilty and received the death penalty; several were forced to commit suicide right in the court. Pentawere was among those sentenced to death, and it is assumed that was true of his mother as well, although no record of her trial survives.

Although it was known that Ramses III had died before the verdicts were reached in this case, it is not clear from these documents whether the plot had succeeded, and the question was left open by Egyptologists. But apparently it had, although this fact was only brought to light in 2012, when CAT-scans were made of Ramses III's body, which had been found more than a century earlier, in 1881, within the Deir el-Bahri cache of mummies near Hatshepsut's mortuary temple. It had been moved there by priests for safekeeping early in the Twenty-Second Dynasty, in the late tenth century BC, following a series of royal tomb robberies that had stretched back over more than a century.

As reported in the *British Medical Journal*, it was clear that Ramses's throat had been cut. The sharp knife that caused the wound had been thrust into his neck immediately under the larynx, all the way down to the cervical vertebra, cutting his trachea and severing all the soft tissue in the area. Death was most likely instantaneous, or nearly so. Subsequently, during the embalming process, a protective Horus-eye amulet had been placed in the wound, either for protection or for healing, though it was far too late to help the king in his corporeal life. In addition, a thick collar of linen was placed around his neck to hide the stab wound. It was only during the CAT-scan analysis that the scientists were able to see through the thick cloth and identify the injury that killed the king.[3]

A second body, of a male aged between eighteen and twenty and known only as "Unknown Man E," was found with Ramses III in the royal burial cache at Deir el-Bahri. Wrapped in a ritually impure goatskin and not properly mummified, the body has been suggested to be that of the guilty prince, Pentawere. DNA tests indicate that he could have been Ramses III's son, but this conclusion is by no means universally agreed within Egyptology. The forensic evidence, including facial contortions and injuries on his throat, suggests that he was probably strangled.[4]

The assassination set the tone for the coming centuries in Egypt, for the aftermath during the years that followed their victory over the Sea

Peoples was not pretty. For instance, we now have evidence that the megadrought, which can be traced via proxy data from Italy all the way to Iran (in modern terms) and which I believe was one of the primary stressors leading to the Late Bronze Age Collapse, finally hit Egypt at about this time. This occurred because the flow of the Nile was reduced when rainfall decreased on the Ethiopian plateau, a situation that lasted for approximately two hundred years. This, not surprisingly, led in turn to a food crisis and thus famine in Egypt, as well as to related economic problems, including nonpayment of wages, which culminated in a strike and demonstration by the workers at Deir el-Medina in Ramses's twenty-ninth year on the throne—possibly one of the first recorded pieces of industrial action in history.[5]

When Ramses III died, this era in Egyptian history also came to an end, although his sons and grandsons continued his dynasty for another four decades. Although Egyptian culture and society did not completely collapse, and Egyptians did not vanish from the face of the earth, neither was their transformation to the new world order particularly successful after the Bronze Age Collapse. While they did survive, it was at a much-lessened capacity; no longer would they have been counted among the "Great Powers" of the day, as they had been during the heyday of the Eighteenth and Nineteenth Dynasties.

Instead, for the next two centuries, the Egyptians were hobbled by a government riddled with intrigue, not to mention problems with succession and rivalries that occasionally resulted in two, three, and sometimes even four rulers in different parts of Egypt at the same time. On occasion, a strong leader would emerge, such as Sheshonq I, a Libyan ruler who founded the Twenty-Second Dynasty, but that would not be until ca. 945 BC, more than two hundred years after the death of Ramses III, and it would not last.

The eight pharaohs who followed Ramses III were all named Ramses (IV to XI), and their reigns witnessed a steady deterioration of the situation in Egypt. The first two kings, Ramses IV and V, were on the throne for just ten years between them and did little that merits mention.[6]

There are also intriguing questions surrounding the latter's death, for he may have fallen victim to yet another calamity—disease—which might be associated with the Bronze Age Collapse. His mummy has pustules still visible on his face, leading to the suggestion that he may have died of smallpox ca. 1140 BC, which might be corroborated by texts that mention new tombs being dug for himself and other members of his family. The men who did the digging were subsequently given a month's leave "at the expense of the Pharaoh" (i.e., with full pay), following which the Valley of the Kings was closed to visitors for six months, perhaps as an effort at quarantine.[7]

During Ramses V's rule, Egypt continued to control the copper mines at Timna, in the Sinai Peninsula, but he is the last Egyptian pharaoh whose name is found in that region. Similarly, his successor, Ramses VI, is the last pharaoh whose name is found at the turquoise mines of Serabit el-Khadim, also located in the Sinai. This is usually interpreted to mean that the Egyptians had lost control and/or withdrawn from the southern Levant almost entirely by about 1140 BC or so.[8] Interestingly, a small bronze statue base found at Megiddo by the Chicago expedition in the 1930s is inscribed with the cartouche of Ramses VI and is frequently cited as proof that Canaanite Megiddo was not overcome until this time, but it is in a disputed context and cannot be used to shore up any such arguments.[9]

When Ramses VI died in 1133 BC, the workmen constructing his tomb in the Valley of the Kings accidentally buried the tomb of Tutankhamun, which lay next to it, thereby leaving it for Howard Carter and Lord Carnarvon to discover in 1922. His son then came to the throne in turn, as Ramses VII. We don't know much about his reign, but texts from the ten years (or less) during which he ruled indicate that the price of grain soared and that the economy was unstable.[10]

Similarly, after a brief reign of just one year for Ramses VIII, who, as a son of Ramses III, was probably already elderly when he became pharaoh, the problems continued for the next ruler, Ramses IX (ca. 1126–1108 BC). He was on the throne for eighteen years, during which time trouble was increasing in Egypt, specifically in the form of tomb robberies, famine, and disruptions by "foreigners" near the workers village at Deir el-Medina. It may have been at this time that Egypt first lost control over Upper Nubia and the gold mines located there. It is also possible that the rule of Egypt was split during his reign, presaging a common occurrence over the coming centuries.[11]

Among the legal documents from this period are the Tomb Robbery Papyri, as they have come to be known. These are a dozen or more texts, spanning the reigns of Ramses IX through XI, which include the so-called Abbott Papyrus and the Leopold-Amherst Papyrus from Ramses IX's sixteenth year. Within them, we find detailed descriptions of tomb robbing within the royal necropolis as well as in private cemeteries. Most of the looting had apparently just taken place during this Year 16. A number of the tomb robbers were caught, and confessions were extracted during the subsequent interrogations and trials. The thieves were all sentenced to death, most likely by impalement, since that was the usual sentence for robbing a royal tomb.[12]

The robberies had begun even earlier, however, for we know that sometime prior to Year 9 of Ramses IX's reign thieves broke into Ramses VI's tomb. Again some of the thieves were caught. In a fragmentary papyrus in Liverpool, England, known as P. Mayer B, one of those arrested confessed specifically: "I spent four days breaking into it [the royal tomb], there being five of us. We opened the tomb and entered it. We found a basket lying on 60 boxes." He then described finding bronze cauldrons, bronze washbasins, and various other bronze objects. They also opened two chests full of clothing, which are described in detail.[13] The fact that bronze objects, rather than gold, are mentioned is especially interesting and may be a reflection of the decline in prosperity since the days of Tutankhamun.

Unfortunately, at that point the text breaks off, so we do not know what else they found and/or took, how their theft was discovered, or what punishment was subsequently meted out, though it was likely the death penalty. However, we do know that when Ramses VI's mummy was found in 1898, within the tomb of Amenhotep II where it had been subsequently moved for safekeeping, it was clear that it had been "savagely attacked by the tomb robbers, the head and torso having been hacked to pieces with an axe." As the British archaeologist

Peter Clayton notes, "The priests had piously rewrapped the pieces on a board in an effort to make it resemble human form. When Elliot Smith examined it in 1905, he found portions of at least two other bodies included within the wrappings: a woman's right hand and the mutilated right hand and forearm of another man. Where the king's neck should have been were his separate left hip bone and part of his pelvis."[14]

Some of the problems from Ramses IX's time continued into those of his successor, Ramses X, who ruled briefly at the end of the tumultuous twelfth century BC. According to the scanty records from his reign, principal among these problems were a continuing lack of food and a related reduction in work-related activities (presumably because of hunger) as well as the presence of additional unnamed foreigners in and around Deir el-Medina.[15] His successor was to be the last of the Ramses—Ramses XI—whose rule marked both the beginning of the new century and the ending of the Twentieth Dynasty.

Overall, the twelfth century BC in Egypt was marked by food shortages and political infighting, among other problems. How resilient were the Egyptians then? They were able to cope and continue to exist but really failed to make the transition properly, neither adapting particularly well nor transforming at all. As a result, not only do we see societal problems but also a rapid decline in Egypt's previous role as a major international power.

Where's My Mummy? Egypt during the Twenty-First Dynasty

Ramses XI ruled Egypt for nearly thirty years at the beginning of the eleventh century BC, from ca. 1098 to 1070 BC. He had by far the longest tenure of any pharaoh during the Twentieth Dynasty. His first nineteen years were relatively peaceful, though there were still tomb robberies and famine. One papyrus mentions a woman possessing gold looted from a tomb, who claimed she had received it in return for selling some food during "the year of the hyenas, when men starved." Worse was yet to come, for the second half of his reign was marked by fragmentation and civil war within Egypt, ending in rival rulers.[16]

Egypt had managed to retain most of its administrative structure until this point, but the system now began to break down when the high priests of Amun in Thebes began competing with the kings to rule the country. A high priest of Amun named Herihor, who is mentioned in the *Tale of Wenamun,* which I will discuss in chapter 3, claimed control over Nubia and Upper Egypt and assumed the title of viceroy of Kush as well as vizier to the pharaoh. By Ramses XI's nineteenth year, Herihor was ruling Upper Egypt and Nubia as far as Thebes. This now became known as Year 1 of the "Renaissance" (from the Egyptian *wehem meswt,* meaning "the repeating of births"), though it was hardly a renaissance as we now understand the term.[17]

At the same time, an administrator named Smendes took control in the north, that is, Lower Egypt, specifically in the region of Piramesse in the Nile delta. He too is mentioned in the *Tale of Wenamun,* along with his wife Tanetamon, who may have been a daughter of Ramses XI. Ramses himself remained as pharaoh but was essentially reduced to a figurehead. Thus, at that point, rulership of Egypt was split among the three men—Ramses XI, Herihor, and Smendes—with the latter two ostensibly owing allegiance to the former but actually operating independently.[18]

The fragmentation of Egypt did not help the country respond to the crises of the age. Tomb robbing remained enough of a problem that Herihor and the other priests moved some of the royal bodies from their original tombs in the Valley of the Kings. Ramses II's mummy, for instance, was temporarily placed into the tomb of Seti I in Year 15 of Smendes. The two were later moved again, ultimately into the cache at Deir el-Bahri, late in the tenth century.[19]

Immediately following Ramses XI's death in 1070 BC, Smendes became pharaoh, thus founding a new royal dynasty, the Twenty-First, and ruled for the next twenty-five years. This marks the start of the Third Intermediate Period, which was, as a whole, a time of dislocation, punctuated by periods of disorder—and a few of relative prosperity. He and his immediate successors ruled from the new capital of Tanis in the Nile delta region for the next century and more, until ca. 945 BC.[20]

For his part, Herihor continued to rule Upper Egypt from Thebes, meaning that the country was now split in two. The situation apparently continued into the time of Herihor's successor, Panedjem I, who was elevated from high priest to king following Herihor's death. He was most likely married to Henuttawy, probably a granddaughter of Ramses XI, thereby linking both of the new ruling families to the previous dynasty and beginning a reunification of Upper and Lower Egypt.[21]

The work of safeguarding the burials in the Valley of the Kings was continued by moving ten royal mummies into a side chamber within the tomb of Amenhotep II. Among these were the bodies of Thutmose IV, Amenhotep III, Merneptah, Siptah, Seti II, and Ramses IV, V, and VI. In 1898, French Egyptologist Victor Loret, who had just been appointed director of the Antiquities Service, discovered the tomb and all of its royal mummies, including that of Ramses VI mentioned above. Although he excavated the tomb with care and kept a journal at the time, he only ever published a preliminary report of his findings. Ironically, long after Panedjem died, his own mummy would also be moved for safekeeping to the cache at Deir el-Bahri.[22]

Meanwhile, when Smendes died in about 1043 BC, he was probably buried at Tanis in the first of a series of burials from the Twenty-First Dynasty. About five years after Smendes's death, after a brief rule by another sovereign, a son of Panedjem I named Psusennes I came to the throne and proceeded to rule for nearly fifty years (ca. 1039–991 BC). With his accession, Upper and Lower Egypt were reunited once more. His reign may also mark the first instance of Egyptian involvement with the Levant in nearly a century.[23]

The evidence comes in part from the gold and silver vessels as well as other objects, including *ushabtis* (small human-shaped statuettes that were placed in graves to accompany the buried person into the afterlife), found in Psusennes's tomb at Tanis. The French Egyptologist Pierre Montet discovered the tomb in 1939–40, just as World War II was beginning. What he found in the tomb was unexpected; it has been described as one of the richest burials ever found from ancient Egypt, surpassed only by that of King Tutankhamun.[24]

When Montet first entered the burial chamber, he saw a solid silver coffin in the middle of the room, surrounded by bronze vessels and other objects, with more items against the walls. The wall decorations confirmed that it was the tomb of Psusennes I. Montet alerted King Faruq, who was ruling over the modern country of Egypt at the time, and waited until the king arrived at the site before opening the coffin. As Egyptologist Bob Brier tells the story, "When the coffin was opened on March 23, 1939 . . . a gold mask was revealed, covering the long dead Pharaoh." However, it was not Psusennes. Instead, the hieroglyphs indicated that the mummy in the coffin was a previously unknown king, Sheshonq IIa. This was extremely strange, as on the basis of his name, this king belonged to the dynasty following that of Psusennes, ruling perhaps a century later, during the Twenty-Second Dynasty. Moreover, Sheshonq was not alone in the antechamber, for the mummies of the last two kings of the Twenty-First Dynasty, Siamun and Psusennes II, were found there as well; Sheshonq's coffin had been placed between them.[25]

As Brier notes, if Sheshonq IIa was in Psusennes I's tomb, then where was Psusennes? Was this another case of a royal mummy having been moved or hidden in antiquity? As it turned out, the mummy hadn't gone very far, and it didn't take Montet long to determine that fact, for the next year, starting in mid-January 1940, as Montet continued to clear what was actually the tomb's antechamber of the various grave goods, he noticed that there were two hidden doorways, barely visible in the west wall. As he later wrote: "We started with the northern opening. Small blocks were removed easily, but we then found ourselves stopped by a large block of granite which so exactly filled the corridor that for some time we did not believe it possible to extract it. Projecting through the very narrow slit the light of an electric lamp, inside we saw two metal objects, one shiny, the other green with oxide, and a massive stone."[26]

When he was finally able to remove the blocking stone, by wrapping a cable around it six times and pulling it out of position by means of a hoist, and continued down the corridor, Montet found himself in a narrow room. It was one of two burial chambers in the tomb, with a massive pink granite sarcophagus surrounded by gold and silver vessels, as well as canopic jars (which contained the mummy's preserved viscera) and other items. By this point, it had been nearly a year since Montet first found the tomb, but had he finally found the long-dead pharaoh? As Montet described it, "The inscriptions which framed it on the right and on the left and those which were engraved on the east face told us that we were, this time, at Psusennes."[27]

However, it was clear that the sarcophagus had originally been intended for, and used by, Pharaoh Merneptah, the first pharaoh to fight against the Sea Peoples and to mention "Israel," back in 1207 BC. The cartouches had all been erased and those of Psusennes substituted, although enough traces remained to make the original readings certain. Merneptah's mummy had recently been moved into the tomb of Amenhotep II a short while before, and thus this sarcophagus (the innermost of three) was now available for reuse. It had therefore apparently been moved from its original location in the Valley of the Kings to this tomb in Tanis.[28]

In late February, Montet lifted off the heavy lid of the pink sarcophagus. Inside, as he later wrote, was "a second sarcophagus, in black granite and in the shape of a mummy." By its style, this one had once belonged to a Nineteenth Dynasty noble. Without waiting any longer, Montet opened this second coffin. Within it lay a third coffin, this one made of solid silver. When its lid was opened, there were no additional coffins, only a gold mask and a gilded mummy-board. These covered the king's body, all its wrappings and flesh utterly decayed down to a bare skeleton but bedecked with gold jewelry. The hieroglyphs confirmed that he had finally found Psusennes I, who has since been nicknamed "The Silver Pharaoh." It took Montet a further ten days to carefully remove the gold mask and then the bones of Psusennes; they and other artifacts from the tomb were eventually transported to the Cairo Museum in an army truck.[29]

Meanwhile, behind the other hidden doorway lay yet another burial chamber. It had originally been intended for Psusennes I's wife, Mutnedjmet, but her body had been removed at some point and replaced by that of Psusennes's immediate successor, Amenemopet. It is not clear why this exchange took place, nor is it clear why Siamun, Psusennes II, and

Sheshonq IIa were all in the antechamber of Psusennes I's tomb rather than in tombs of their own. Siamun and Psusennes II may have been buried in the tomb from the outset, but Egyptologist Aidan Dodson has noted that plant remains found on Sheshonq's mummy "seem to have grown into the bones while the coffin lay in standing water," which would indicate that Sheshonq's original tomb may have been flooded, thus requiring his reburial here in Psusennes's antechamber.[30]

Although Montet had found an intact pharaoh's tomb, with some material as spectacular as that found in Tutankhamun's vault, the world's media was more concerned with the world war going on at the time than it was with a long-dead pharaoh. As a result, this amazing discovery has not received the notice and acclaim that it should, although the treasures were displayed in their own special room within the Cairo Museum and have now been redisplayed in rooms that all held treasures of Tutankhamun.[31]

Montet also found hundreds of *ushabtis* in Psusennes's tomb, as mentioned. These are now scattered, in various museums and private collections, according to Shirly Ben-Dor Evian, who served as curator of Egyptian archaeology at the Israel Museum in Jerusalem.[32] The museum has four of them in its collection—three were found in his tomb; the other probably comes from a looted tomb located somewhere nearby. All are made of copper. One has the name "Psusennes" inscribed on it; another has the name of his wife Mutnedjmet; and two more have the name of the general Wendjebaendjed, who was buried in a subsidiary chamber of Psusennes's tomb.

Ben-Dor Evian and her colleagues subjected the four *ushabtis* to lead isotope analysis, a technique that can help pinpoint the origin of the copper used to make the objects. Intriguingly, the copper in each of them comes from the Arabah region of the Negev highlands, on the border between modern Jordan and the Sinai. This is where the copper mines in the Timna Valley (in the Sinai), sometimes called "King Solomon's Mines," and Wadi Faynan (in Jordan) are both located. Clearly

Egypt, which had received much of its imported copper from Cyprus during the Bronze Age, was now getting at least some from this region. This is part of the evidence that suggests international trade had resumed between Egypt and the southern Levant after a gap caused by the Collapse.[33]

Israelites and Philistines

I am attempting to cover two areas in this first chapter, so by pivoting at this point to more fully introduce details about the southern Levant before returning to Egypt and what will become an ever-more intermingled story, we can learn a few details about the situation there at the time from a papyrus called the *Onomasticon of Amenemopet,* which was found in 1890 within a jar at the site of el-Hibah in Egypt. It is now known in fully nine different copies. One portion of this manuscript, which lists peoples and places, mentions three of the groups that made up the Sea Peoples—the Sherden (Shardana), the Tjekker, and the Peleset (Philistines)—along with three cities: Ashkelon, Ashdod, and Gaza.

The implication in the papyrus is that remnants of the three groups had settled in these cities or had been settled there by the victorious Egyptians, as Ramses III claimed. It is noteworthy not only that we see the Tjekker here too, as well as the Peleset, but also that the cities named are three of the five that belonged to the so-called Philistine Pentapolis: Ashdod, Ashkelon, and Gaza were located along a stretch of the coastline in southern Canaan at or near the modern cities by those names, while Ekron (Tel Miqne) and Gath (Tell es-Safi) were situated further inland. Archaeological evidence uncovered at four of these five cities (Gaza has not yet been excavated) indicate that they were all Canaanite cities during the Bronze Age but then began to exhibit the material trappings of Philistine culture beginning at about this same time, that is, during the late twelfth and into the eleventh century BC.[34]

Just under a decade later, by 1899, the site of Tell es-Safi was identified as Philistine Gath, and joint excavations by the American archaeologist Frederick Bliss and the Irish archaeologist Robert Alexander Stewart (R.A.S.) Macalister began. By 1914, Macalister had published one of the first books in English devoted entirely to the Philistines, titled *The Philistines, Their History and Civilization*. Renewed excavations at the site began under the direction of Aren Maeir of Bar Ilan University in 1996 and have yielded much new information; I will refer to some of this data below.[35]

As Carl Ehrlich of York University has said, it seemed at first that the Philistines were going to be "the legitimate heir to the ancient Egyptian empire in Canaan." However, that was not to be. Instead, the Israelites took over most of what had been Canaan and, after feuding with the Philistines from the time of Israelite King Saul, as well as with David and then his son Solomon, eventually "the status as Egypt's heir" in the region "passed . . . to Israel."[36] The Israelites were unique in this period as practitioners of monotheism. They are variably considered either newcomers to the scene or lurkers in the background for some time, for the date and means by which the Israelites came to establish themselves in the land of Canaan is a complex and controversial issue.

Numerous scholars have weighed in on this topic, including with hypotheses that involve the biblical story of the Exodus and a military conquest of Canaan by the Israelites, resulting either in a genocide or a more peaceful integration such as variously described in the Books of Joshua and Judges in the Hebrew Bible. Other possibilities have been suggested as well, envisioning the Israelites as nomads or semi-nomads peacefully infiltrating the area, or as peasants from the highlands who revolted against Canaanite overlords, or even as gradually developing into "Israelites" from within the local Canaanite population. These theories are known variously as the "Conquest" model, the "Peaceful Infiltration" model, the "Revolting Peasants" model, and the "Invisible Israelites" model.[37] The most recent discussions have revolved around more anthropological considerations of the ethnicity of the Israelites, especially in comparison to the other peoples who also emerged in the region during this same approximate period.[38] These include the Philistines, who took over the coastal region of the southern Levant.

No matter which theory individual scholars subscribe to, we know for certain that an inscription on a victory monument of Pharaoh Merneptah, found by Sir William Matthew Flinders Petrie in 1896, claims that the Egyptians defeated a people called "Israel" who were living in the land of Canaan by about the year 1207 BC. We also know that, regardless of the antecedent events and the means by which they entered the picture, the initial Israelite settlements were established by the end of the twelfth century or thereabouts, and quickly exploded in number during the early eleventh century BC. That much has been attested courtesy of a multitude of archaeological surveys that have been conducted in the region since at least the 1960s.[39]

Given those facts, and regardless of whether they had been languishing in the Sinai for several decades or were already present in the land but "invisible" or had been infiltrating the land slowly over centuries, the Israelites may have simply taken advantage of the havoc in Canaan that was occurring during the Collapse. The political and military vacuum created by the retreat of the Egyptians, and the destruction of the various Canaanite cities, would have meant that the Israelites could have moved into areas that they could not normally have occupied under their own power. As a result, they would have been able to take over all or most of Canaan by the end of the twelfth century BC.[40]

While still speculative, this scenario plausibly provides the "how" that is missing from most of the other hypotheses. For those who believe in the miraculous hand of God, there is no need to investigate further, but for the rest, it remains a viable question as to how else the Israelites could have possibly attacked and successfully captured the imposing Canaanite cities. Under normal circumstances, they are unlikely to have been able to do so, at least on their own. However, once the Sea Peoples invaded the Canaanite coast as part and parcel with the other calamities (drought, famine, internal rebellion, etc.) that brought the Canaanite culture to its knees, and once the Egyptians had retreated from the region, the Israelites may have been able to occupy the ruins of the larger cities and to take over some of the lesser towns all by themselves, thus completing the conquest of Canaan. It is likely that the later biblical writers subsequently gave complete credit for the capture and destruction of the Canaanite cities to the Israelites without even mentioning the role of the Sea Peoples because they only knew the latter in terms of the biblical Philistines who caused such trouble for Saul and David over the course of their reigns.[41]

Recent studies involving climate change by Dafna Langgut of Tel Aviv University and her colleagues indicate a possible link to the early Israelites and Philistines in terms of a temporary cessation in the severe drought. Starting perhaps as early as 1150 BC and certainly no later than ca. 1100 BC, there seems to have been an uptick in the available moisture in the southern Levant, creating slightly wetter climate conditions, which in turn permitted "intense olive and cereal cultivation."[42]

The more favorable conditions may have lasted in this region until ca. 950 BC, which corresponds to the same approximate time period as the initial emergence of the Israelites. As Langgut and her colleagues state, "The improved conditions in the highlands during the Iron Age I enabled the recovery of settlement activity, which is the backdrop for the rise of ancient Israel. . . . Similar conditions in other parts of highlands in the Levant could have led to the development of equivalent settlement systems which gave birth to other biblical nations—the Aramaeans in Syria and the Ammonites and Moabites in Transjordan."[43]

This idea has now been supported by another new study, which suggests that this area in particular was one of the only regions in which the population actually increased, rather than decreased, at the beginning of the Iron Age, that is, the period immediately following the Collapse. If so, the population increase could potentially be the result of the new kingdoms established in the southern Levant, including Israel and Judah, as well as Moab, Ammon, and Edom, though scholarly discussions continue about whether there were already inhabitants in these areas, quite possibly nomadic, as some have suggested, who survived the Collapse or if they were all newcomers to the region who migrated in during the aftermath.[44]

King David

Our primary source for what happened next is the Hebrew Bible, where—if we take the story at face value—we are told that the Philistines created problems for the fledgling Israelites and their newly anointed King Saul and his sons later in the eleventh century. Matters came to a head when Saul and his progeny fought the Philistines in the Jezreel Valley, not far from Megiddo (biblical Armageddon). There, in about 1016 BC on the flanks of Mt. Gilboa, according to the biblical account, Saul and three of his sons were killed in battle and their bodies hung from the walls of Beth Shean (1 Samuel 28–31; 2 Samuel 1; 1 Chronicles 10).

Soon thereafter, one of Saul's remaining sons, Ishbaal (or Ishbosheth), took over the northern half of the young Israelite kingdom while David declared himself king over Judah, the southern half of the kingdom (2 Samuel 2:1–4, 8). Eventually David took over the northern part as well, establishing what we now call the United Monarchy around the year 1000 BC.[45]

Unfortunately, we have no corroborating evidence from any archaeological or epigraphic sources to confirm these stories told in the Hebrew Bible, so we have no way of independently confirming their accuracy—but, though much debated, they seem plausible, especially given the other events taking place in the general area during this time period. Moreover, even until recently we had no evidence from outside the Bible attesting to the actual existence of David, strange as that might seem. All of that changed in 1992.

During that summer, Gila Cook was working as the architect for the archaeological expedition at the site of Tel Dan (ancient Laish), located north of the Sea of Galilee in modern Israel. The excavation was being directed by Avraham Biran, a longtime, well-respected archaeologist and professor at the Jerusalem campus of Hebrew Union College. He had been digging at Tel Dan for more than twenty-five years by that point, since 1966. The site itself is in the middle of a beautiful nature preserve that includes the icy-cold headwaters of the Jordan River and a great restaurant serving fish for tourists and locals.

Cook's goal that day was to accurately draw and record the stones in a wall that they had recently uncovered. However, her project was derailed when the raking light of the sun created shadows on one stone in particular, revealing the presence of an inscription that was carved on its surface, which nobody had previously spotted. It was written in

FIG. 2. Tel Dan inscription with the words *Beit David* highlighted. Photograph courtesy of Oren Rozen via Wikimedia Commons.

Aramaic, using Phoenician lettering. When it was subsequently translated, the text created a sensation, for it contained the words *Beit David*—the "House of David." This was the first time that an inscription mentioning the biblical King David had been found; in fact, it was the first time that any attestation to the existence of King David had been found outside the Bible.[46]

It turned out that the stone probably came from a larger monument that had most likely been set up about 841 BC, nearly a century and a half after David ruled (ca. 1000–970 BC). Additional fragments belonging to the same monument were subsequently found by the expedition the next year, although there are still many pieces missing. While it remains the subject of some scholarly debate and discussion, it seems that the inscription had commemorated the capture of Tel Dan by an Aramaean king named Hazael, whose home base lay just to the north at Aram-Damascus and who ruled ca. 842–796 BC. We shall meet him again below.

The fragmentary inscription, as it is currently extant, reads:

> . . . my father went up [against him when] he fought at [. . .]. And my father lay down, he went to his [ancestors]. And the king of I[s]rael entered previously in my father's land. [And] Hadad made me king. And Hadad went in front of me, [and] I departed from the seven [. . .] of my kingdom/kings, and I slew [might]y . . . kin[gs], who harnessed tho[usands . . . of cha]riots and thousands [of] chariot horses. [I killed Jo]ram . . . son of A[hab], king of Israel, and [I] killed [Ahaz]iahu son of [Joram, kin]g of the House of David. And I set [their towns into ruins and turned] their land into [desolation . . .].[47]

The discovery of this inscription put to rest a dispute that had been raging in academic circles, with some scholars doubting that the tenth-century BC rulers David and Solomon had ever existed, for no extrabiblical (i.e., outside the Bible) evidence for either monarch had been found until that point. Thus, the discovery of this inscription, with its mention of the House of David and the inherent implication that there had been a historical David (who had founded the dynasty), was extremely important. The reference to David and the dynasty that he founded also suggests that Solomon most likely existed as well, since he is David's son.[48]

As a side note, I should mention that a possible, though very much debated, second reference to the House of David can be seen on what is known as the Mesha Stele. The inscription, which is much better known for its mention of "Omri, king of Israel," was first seen and identified by an Anglican missionary named F. A. Klein in 1868 at the site of Diban in what is now modern Jordan. Even with a third of its text now missing, it is still the longest monumental inscription ever discovered in the Holy Land and is one of the first discovered extrabiblical inscriptions that names a person or place known primarily from the Hebrew Bible—for example, Omri, king of Israel, in addition to, possibly, the House of David.[49]

Edom and the Edomites

According to the biblical account, when David was establishing himself as king, the nearby kingdom of Edom was among the territories that he conquered. This was located to the south and east of David's original territory, in the general area of Wadi Faynan in what is now modern Jordan.

The biblical stories of David's conquest of Edom might provide additional support for the link between Timna and Egypt, which I have mentioned previously, for we are told in the biblical account that during the fighting the Edomite crown prince Hadad, who was an infant at the time, was spirited out of the country and down to Egypt for his safety (1 Kings 11:14–22). When Hadad grew up, he married the sister of the Egyptian queen and had a son, Genubath, before returning to Edom after the death of King David and later rebelling against King Solomon.[50]

Although there is no independent corroboration to confirm this story either, Egyptologist Kenneth Kitchen suggests that it may have been Psusennes I who gave Hadad sanctuary in Egypt, as well as a "house, food allowance, and land" (1 Kings 11:18). Psusennes, whose long rule lasted until ca. 991 BC and whom we met above, would have overlapped with David for at least a decade if not more. However, it is also possible to suggest instead that the episode took place during the reign of Psusennes I's son, Amenemopet, who ruled for about ten years after his father's death and extended the Twenty-First Dynasty's rule over all of Egypt, both Upper and Lower, from his base in Tanis.[51]

The kingdom of Edom was first seriously explored in detail by the colorful American archaeologist Nelson Glueck in his surveys in Jordan in the 1930s. Glueck, an ordained rabbi and later president of Hebrew Union College in Cincinnati, remains one of the few archaeologists ever to appear on the cover of *Time* magazine, in 1963. (James Henry Breasted, the founder and director of the Oriental Institute at the University of Chicago, had previously been featured in 1931.) Heavily influenced by the Hebrew Bible, Glueck linked the copper mines at Wadi Faynan in the Arabah Valley to King Solomon's activities, calling him the world's first "copper magnate," though this designation is now considered unlikely.

More recently, two decades of research began in 1997, conducted by the Edom Lowlands Regional Archaeology Project of the University of California San Diego and the Jordanian Department of Antiquities. The project has now generated numerous publications by scholars such as Tom Levy, Mohammad Najjar, and Erez Ben-Yosef, as well as others. Their investigations of the copper mines at Wadi Faynan have shown that there was a sudden increase in the exploitation of these mines, as well as those at nearby Timna, beginning as early as the eleventh century BC, and then continuing into the tenth and ninth centuries. This new exploitation of copper ore in Wadi Faynan may have presented a challenge to Cyprus's previous domination of the copper export industry.[52]

The rise of Edom and the Edomites has now been suggested to be related to the exploitation of these copper resources, with Erez Ben-Yosef of Tel Aviv University suggesting that the management and operation was initially conducted by otherwise archaeologically invisible nomadic pastoralists who seized the opportunity to work the mines when the Egyptian authorities withdrew in the aftermath of the Collapse. According to his view, the nomadic miners eventually settled down and became the people whom the Bible calls Edomites. This latter suggestion in particular has engendered a lively ongoing debate. We may also note that if the area was mined before Solomon's time, then highlighting Solomon's presence in the Faynan as Glueck did is either irrelevant or not as significant as Glueck thought.[53]

Khirbet Qeiyafa and Tel Gezer

There are additional discoveries that may have bearing on the extent of David's territory, but they are not without their debates as well. A prime example is Khirbet Qeiyafa, located in the Valley of Elah to the southwest of Jerusalem, where the battle between David and Goliath reportedly took place. The site was excavated by Yossi Garfinkel of Hebrew University, beginning in 2007. He has dated it to the tenth century BC and discussed its relationship to King David and the extent of his territory during that time. The site is not far from both Tell es-Safi (biblical Gath) and Tell Miqne (biblical Ekron), which belonged to the Philistines, but Garfinkel thinks that his site is just on the other side of what is essentially an invisible border and is thus part of David's kingdom rather than being in Philistine territory. He has also tentatively identified Khirbet Qeiyafa as biblical Sha'arayim, mentioned in the biblical account of David and Goliath (1 Samuel 17: esp. 52), but such an identification has not been embraced by all other archaeologists.[54]

Among numerous other discoveries, the site has yielded two inscriptions so far. One is inscribed around the rim of a storage jar, in what appears to be Canaanite alphabetic script, and may include the personal name ʾIšbaʿal—perhaps the owner of the jar. The other inscription, found in 2008, caused much more discussion. It consists of five lines in black ink on a broken pottery sherd (such an inscribed sherd is known as an "ostracon" in archaeological terms). It is still not clear exactly what the lines say, but the various interpretations and translations have ranged from the mundane to the fantastic, in part because not everyone agrees on the language that is being used; most now lean toward a version of Old Hebrew script derived from Phoenician. One initial attempt at a translation included the lines "Judge the slave and the widow, judge the orphan and the stranger. Plead for the infant, plead for the poor and the widow," but this is still very much a matter of debate.[55]

There is also an unrelated inscription at the site of Gezer, located not far away, which similarly appears to date to the tenth century BC. The inscription is justifiably famous, although we can't assign it to any specific reign, whether that of David or any other ruler. This is the so-called Gezer calendar, an inscription written on stone in either paleo-Hebrew (the earliest known version of Hebrew) or possibly Phoenician. It was found long ago, in 1908, by R.A.S. Macalister (mentioned earlier), who was excavating on behalf of the Palestine Exploration Fund, which was based in London. It describes the principal agricultural activities conducted during the year and thus provides an insight into life in the region during this time. It reads: "Two months of ingathering, two months of sowing, two months of late sowing, one month of chopping flax, one month of barley harvest, one month of harvest and completion, two months of grape cutting, one month of summer fruits."[56]

Pharaoh Siamun and the Deir el-Bahri Cache

The site of Gezer is also featured prominently in a biblical passage stating that an Egyptian pharaoh captured the city and then gave it to Solomon as part of a dowry when the latter married the pharaoh's daughter (1 Kings 9:16–17). We are told that "Pharaoh King of Egypt had gone up

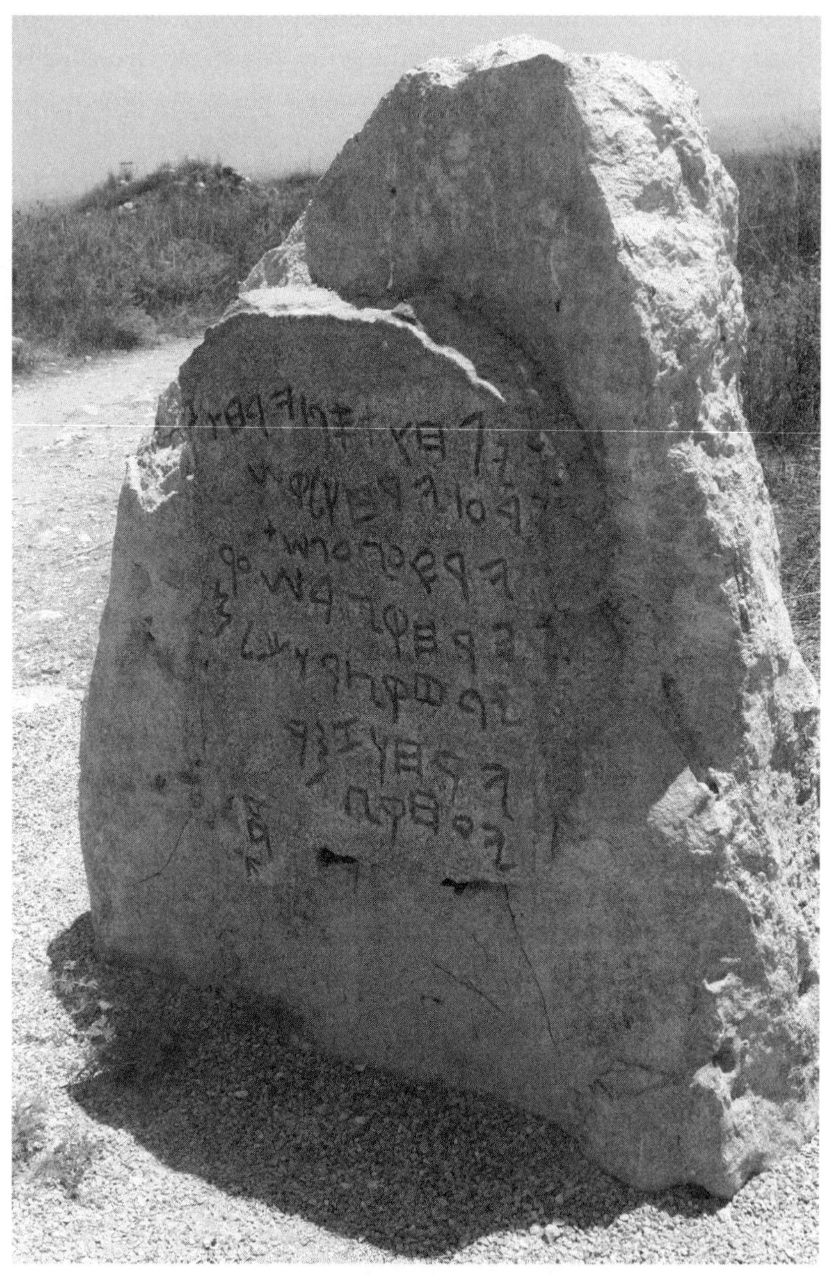

FIG. 3. Replica of Gezer calendar inscription. Photograph by E. H. Cline.

and captured Gezer and burned it down, had killed the Canaanites who lived in the city, and had given it as dowry to his daughter, Solomon's wife; so Solomon rebuilt Gezer."[57]

Note that the name of the pharaoh who did this to the city of Gezer is not given. However, a number of biblical historians and Egyptologists have suggested that Pharaoh Siamun of the Twenty-First Dynasty, who ruled for twenty years (ca. 979–958 BC), could be the Egyptian ruler in question. There is indeed evidence of a destruction level at Gezer that may date to this approximate period and that could conceivably be related to a campaign by Siamun, though there is nothing definitive tying him to it.[58]

If this account has any basis in reality, then there had clearly been a change in power dynamics after the Collapse, for never during the Bronze Age would an Egyptian pharaoh have given his daughter in marriage to a foreign king. However, we have already seen that things were now different in the Iron Age—remember that during David's reign, the Egyptian queen's sister had been given in marriage to the young Hadad, crown prince of Edom, according to the biblical account.[59] Now we hear of another such marriage, which would previously have been unthinkable. However, Solomon seems to have taken good care of the Egyptian princess, reportedly building a separate residence for her in Jerusalem: "But Pharaoh's daughter went up from the City of David to her own house that Solomon had built for her" (1 Kings 9:24).

It may be that such a royal marriage, which frequently accompanied some sort of alliance or mutual treaty, was part of an attempt by Siamun to shore up his reign in Egypt, for things may not have been going well for him. For instance, an additional shuffling of royal mummies may have reflected concerns for security at Thebes. Some were first moved into the tomb of Queen Inhapy in Siamun's Year 10. Sometime later (some would argue as late as Sheshonq I's Year 11, about 935 BC), they and others, now including Kings Ahmose I; Thutmose I, II, and III; Seti I; Ramses I, II, and III; and also members of the family of Panedjem II, ended up in a tomb near Deir el-Bahri. This seems to have been originally the tomb of the Eighteenth Dynasty queen Ahmes-Nefertiry and had recently been used for the family of Panedjem II.[60]

This hiding place, now usually called the Deir el-Bahri Cache (with the official number TT 320), was a good one, for it remained undiscovered for nearly three millennia. It was only about 150 years ago, sometime around 1870, according to the most prevalent version of the story now told, that it was found by a member of the Abd el-Rassul family, allegedly as he was searching for a goat that had fallen into the tomb shaft. Few believe this story, however, and there is much speculation that he was more likely searching specifically for tombs to rob, since the location was subsequently kept as a closely guarded family secret. The family treated the tomb as their own personal treasure vault, selling various objects one by one to well-to-do European and American tourists over a period of about ten years.

The scheme was finally uncovered in 1881 by Emil Brugsch, who had been sent by Gaston Maspero, the new director of the Egyptian Antiquities Service. Brugsch hired several hundred local villagers and removed all the reburied pharaohs, queens, and their goods from the tomb within a period of only about forty-eight hours, forsaking precise recording of the specific location of the contents in favor of a rapid removal. The story is now among the most repeated in histories of modern Egyptology, and the collection of royal mummies and burial objects has been among the most valuable treasures in the Cairo Museum for decades.[61] They now rest in a specially prepared crypt at the National Museum of Egyptian Civilization, in the Cairo suburb of Fustat. Unfortunately, the rapid removal meant that all information beyond the actual objects was lost or not recorded; had it been done in a slow and deliberate fashion, as should have been the case, much more data would have been gained—in comparison, the removal of objects from Tutankhamun's tomb by Howard Carter, which began in 1922, took ten years.

Solomon at Megiddo and Jerusalem

It was while Carter was carefully documenting and removing the objects in Tutankhamun's tomb that archaeologists from the Oriental Institute of the University of Chicago began excavating in 1925 at the site of Megiddo, in what is now northern Israel but which lay in British

Mandate Palestine at the time. Three years later, in 1928, they uncovered several large buildings that had internal aisles lined with standing stones and what appeared to be troughs. The field director, P.L.O. Guy, interpreted these as stables and sent a telegram to James Henry Breasted, the director of the Oriental Institute. It read in part "believe have found Solomon's Stables."

The news made headlines around the world, but debate still rages today, a century later. Most archaeologists accept that these are indeed stables, but the majority no longer think that they were built by Solomon. Based on radiocarbon dating, pottery styles, and other chronological indicators, it now seems more likely that they were built either in the ninth century BC, possibly by Omri or his son Ahab, or even in the eighth century BC, perhaps by Jeroboam II.[62]

Similarly, several decades later, the famous Israeli archaeologist Yigael Yadin and his team excavated at both Megiddo and Hazor and found that the large entrance gate at each looked identical—what is now known as a six-chambered gate. He also looked at the records from Macalister's earlier excavation at Gezer and recognized that the city gate was essentially identical there as well. He dated all three to the time of Solomon and declared that there was a "Solomonic blueprint" for entry gates that could be seen at such cities.[63]

However, just as with "Solomon's Stables," so too these city gates may date to the ninth century and the reign of Omri or Ahab, or even to the eighth century and the reign of Jeroboam II, rather than to the tenth century and the time of Solomon. The discussion has been ongoing for some time and is occasionally quite heated, since not all scholars agree, but it now looks as if this possible evidence for Solomon's building activities may have also disappeared.[64]

The textual evidence involved in this debate comes from a single biblical passage that mentions those specific cities as examples that Solomon supposedly fortified: "And this is the account of the forced labor which King Solomon levied to build the house of the lord and his own house and the Millo and the wall of Jerusalem and Hazor and Megiddo and Gezer" (1 Kings 9:15).

Note that the passage also gives credit to Solomon for building the original Temple in Jerusalem ("the house of the lord"). For this, according to the biblical account, Solomon turned to Hiram, the king of Tyre, located in what had been the central part of Canaan and is now the modern country of Lebanon, who reportedly supplied craftsmen and even the building plan for the Temple (1 Kings 5:1–7:51). Although archaeologists have not yet found anything that might directly confirm this biblical story (or even for the existence of Solomon, his rule, or the extent of his kingdom, for that matter), the biblical accounts about his reign are full of details of his relationship with Hiram and Tyre.[65]

In this case, we are further told specifically that "Hiram sent word to Solomon," saying as follows: "'I have heard the message that you have sent to me; I will fulfill all your needs in the matter of cedar and cypress timber. My servants shall bring it down to the sea from the Lebanon; I will make it into rafts to go by sea to the place you indicate. I will have them broken up there for you to take away. And you shall meet my needs by providing food for my household.' So Hiram supplied Solomon's every need for timber of cedar and cypress. Solomon in turn gave Hiram twenty thousand cors of wheat as food for his household, and twenty cors of fine oil. Solomon gave this to Hiram year by year" (1 Kings 5:8–11; see also 2 Chronicles 2:1–16).[66]

In this context, Hiram also spoke of dispatching skilled craftsmen to help Solomon, as follows: "I have dispatched Hiram-abi, a skilled artisan, endowed with understanding, the son of one of the Danite women, his father a Tyrian. He is trained to work in gold, silver, bronze, iron, stone, and wood, and in purple, blue, and crimson fabrics and fine linen, and to do all sorts of engraving and execute any design that may be assigned him" (2 Chronicles 2:13–14).

Since no part of Solomon's Temple is still standing, the biblical description is all we have to go on (1 Kings 6:14–22). As a result, as might be expected, there has been no end of scholarly discussion as to what it actually looked like, but it seems to fit the description of what is called by archaeologists a "long room" temple—that is, a long rectangular building that one would have entered on a short side and proceeded into a long main room, at the end of which is a much smaller room known as the "holy of holies" where one would keep something like the Ark of the Covenant.

However, the more usual temple form in the southern Levant at the time was a "broad room" temple, which was much more squat and where one entered through the middle of the long side. We can see an example of the latter in the tenth-century BC temple at the site of Arad, down by Beersheva in what is now southern Israel. The "long room" temple is more common farther to the north, for instance, at the site of Ain Dara in northern Syria where there is a temple that is thought to be the closest extant example of what Solomon's Temple might have looked like.[67] It may well be that Hiram's craftsmen brought the blueprint of the actual plan of the Temple with them, as well as the materials with which to build it.

We are also told that, in gratitude, Solomon gave Hiram twenty cities located in what is now northern Israel, but that Hiram refused to accept them (1 Kings 9:10–14). In addition, the two of them teamed up in sending an overseas expedition to Ophir (1 Kings 9:26; 2 Chronicles 8:17, 9:10), whose location has never been confirmed. Furthermore, we are told that Hiram sent expeditions to Tarshish (1 Kings 10:21–22; 2 Chronicles 9:21), which is frequently identified as Tartessos in Spain, although there is no firm foundation for such an identification.[68] It has recently been suggested that King Solomon may have also been involved in joining the Phoenician expeditions to Spain at this time, in particular to the region of Huelva, to acquire silver and other goods, though there is no proof of that at all and the hypothesis lacks any supporting physical evidence.[69]

Sheshonq/Shishak

At this point in our story, Egypt and the southern Levant became entwined once again, but this time it was because Egypt was, at long last, regaining strength, courtesy of Sheshonq I. He came to the throne of Egypt in the middle of the tenth century, ca. 945 BC, after Psusennes II, who ruled Egypt following the death of Siamun. Siamun and Psusennes II were the last two kings of the Twenty-First Dynasty; as I have mentioned above, they were both buried in the antechamber of Psusennes I's tomb. Sheshonq was to be the first king of a new dynasty, the Twenty-Second.[70]

Sheshonq was of Libyan origin, though his family had lived in Egypt for generations, and his uncle, Osorkon the Elder, had actually been king of Egypt directly before Siamun. Sheshonq maintained the capital at Tanis but brought Thebes under closer control by appointing his son Iuput as high priest of Amun. This replaced the previous hereditary line and for a few decades brought a degree of unity back to Egypt. He is also the first king to have left records of military operations in the Levant since the Late Bronze Age Collapse.[71]

This is where the Hebrew Bible may come into play again as well, for it just so happens that we are told an Egyptian pharaoh named Shishak besieged Jerusalem and carried away an untold amount of gold and other treasure from the city, palace, and Temple a few years after the death of King Solomon, that is, somewhere around 930–925 BC. "In the fifth year of King Rehoboam, King Shishak of Egypt came up against Jerusalem; he took away the treasures of the house of the Lord and the treasures of the king's house; he took everything. He also took away all the shields of gold which Solomon had made" (1 Kings 14:25–26).[72]

Although it is disputed by some, most biblical historians and Egyptologists are of the view that the Pharaoh Shishak mentioned in the Bible is to be equated with none other than Sheshonq I. This is based in part on an inscription that Sheshonq ordered to be carved onto what is known as the Bubastite Portal of the Temple at Karnak in Egypt, which formed part of the first major extension of the complex since the Twentieth Dynasty. Although it too is much debated, this lists a number of cities attacked by Sheshonq in the territory of what had been the United Monarchy of David and Solomon. Included among these is Megiddo, along with other cities in the Jezreel Valley, including Taanach and Shunem.[73]

Sheshonq's list of conquered cities has elicited a great deal of attention and some skepticism over the years, but confirmation of its accuracy may have come almost a century ago, in late 1925, when the University of Chicago archaeologists working during their first season at Megiddo recovered an inscribed fragment of stone on which was carved the cartouche of Sheshonq I. It had been excavated by the previous excavator of the site, Gottlieb Schumacher, when he was digging there from 1903 to 1905, but its importance was not recognized, and it was therefore thrown onto a backdirt pile next to an excavation trench, where the Chicago team found it twenty years later.

James Henry Breasted was able to translate the hieroglyphs on the recovered fragment when he visited his team in March 1926, and the news soon spread worldwide of the discovery that they had made, making a splash as great as the one that would follow two years later, with "Solomon's Stables." This fragment would seem to corroborate Sheshonq's claim, for it is thought to come from an inscribed monument originally standing perhaps ten feet tall that would have been set up in the city of Megiddo after its capture by Egyptian forces.[74] However, since Schumacher's men had not recorded the location of the fragment, we do not know in which of the levels at Megiddo it was found.

Nevertheless, at one point some scholars thought that they were able to identify the city at Megiddo that Sheshonq captured, which is the stratum known to excavators as Megiddo VIA. This level, which has been alternately described as the last Canaanite city or the first Israelite city built at the site, was burnt to the ground sometime during the tenth century BC. The Chicago excavators found unburied skeletons still lying in the ruined houses and the remains of wooden posts and trees still in situ. Others have suggested instead that the destruction might be attributable to King David's forces or even to the Philistines. However, the evidence—which includes cracked and leaning walls in addition to the skeletons and burnt trees and posts—strongly points instead to an earthquake, which may have also devastated nearby communities.[75]

What is especially interesting about Sheshonq's attack on Megiddo is that the city may have already been located within the northern kingdom of Israel by that time. This northern kingdom was established by Jeroboam at the same time that the southern kingdom of Judah was established by Rehoboam, after the United Monarchy had split into the Divided Kingdoms following the death of Solomon. Jeroboam and Shishak already had a relationship by that time, for the biblical account states that prior to Solomon's death Jeroboam had fled to Egypt and had been living there, sheltering under the protection of Sheshonq/Shishak: "Solomon sought therefore to kill Jeroboam; but Jeroboam promptly fled to Egypt, to King Shishak of Egypt, and remained in Egypt until the death of Solomon (1 Kings 11:40).[76]

This means that if Sheshonq did indeed campaign militarily against Megiddo and the other towns in the Jezreel Valley, as his inscription at Luxor and the stele fragment at Megiddo both imply, then—depending on the timing—either he would have been fighting against the forces of Jeroboam, the man whom he had until recently protected or, as has been tentatively suggested by Nadav Na'aman of Tel Aviv University, Sheshonq's campaign to the north may have been intended in part to place Jeroboam on the throne of the northern kingdom of Israel in the first place. Such an action is not mentioned in the biblical account, however, though it may have once been preserved in the now missing "Book of the Annals of the Kings of Israel" (see, e.g., 1 Kings 14:19).[77]

An interesting point is that the surviving list of cities attacked by Sheshonq I does *not* include Jerusalem, and the "itinerary" is not consistent with it being included in the campaign recorded on the Bubastite Portal. However, there are vast areas of the walls that Sheshonq added to the forecourt at Karnak, and it is likely that, had Sheshonq lived, additional tableaux and inscriptions would have been added, including one or more further campaigns that would have included the attack on Jerusalem.[78]

The Bee's Knees

Sheshonq also mentions the site of Rehov in his topographical list at Karnak. Rehov had been a major Canaanite city, located in the Beth Shean Valley, that somehow managed to make the transition to the Iron Age virtually unscathed. It is one of the largest archaeological tells in the southern Levant, consisting of a lower mound dominated by an upper mound at the southern end, covering between ten and eleven hectares (about twenty-five acres). It has been known since 1939, when a pottery sherd inscribed with a Proto-Canaanite inscription was found on the surface by two well-known archaeologists, Ruth Amiran, a pottery specialist, and Avraham Biran, the later excavator of Tel Dan, and was the focus of an intense and large-scale archaeological excavation directed by Amihai Mazar of Hebrew University from 1997 until 2012.[79]

The city seems to have escaped destruction by Sheshonq as well, only to be devastated by an earthquake that brought its Stratum VI to an end during the last third of the tenth century BC (perhaps the same one that devasted the similarly named Stratum VIA at Megiddo mentioned above). Rehov made headlines a few years ago when an apiary, or bee-keeping facility, was uncovered in the following phase, Stratum V, which lasted for the remaining years of the tenth century and into the first quarter of the ninth century BC. The city of this level appears to have been no stranger to foreign connections, for Phoenician, Cypriot, and even Greek pottery has been found at the site, as have Egyptian faience amulets and fishbones of Nile perch.[80]

The apiary was built in the heart of a dense urban area within the city, rather than on the outskirts as one might have thought.[81] The excavators found 30 beehives; they estimate that there may originally have been as many as 180, set up in three parallel rows. Each beehive consisted of a hollow cylinder made of unfired clay mixed with straw, which measured just under a meter (three feet) in length and with a volume of just over fifty liters. One end of the cylinder was sealed shut except for a small "flying hole" which allowed the bees to enter and leave as they wished. The other end had a removable clay lid that allowed the owners to open the hive and get access to the honey.

Within the hives were found the remains of honeycombs as well as the remains of actual bees—eyes, muscles, legs, and wings—which are the first to have ever been found in the ancient Near East. Intriguingly, it appears that these were Anatolian honeybees, rather than a more local variety, which means that they would have been deliberately imported over a distance of some five hundred kilometers. The excavators have suggested, in fact, that these bee swarms "were imported to the Beth-Shean Valley, directly or indirectly, from one of the Neo-Hittite/Luwian states in southern Turkey."[82]

It is estimated that each hive could yield up to five kilograms of honey annually, in addition to half a kilogram or more of beeswax, meaning that the 180 hives would have yielded nearly one thousand kilograms of honey and nearly one hundred kilograms of beeswax per year, perhaps part of the reason why ancient Israel is mentioned numerous times in the Hebrew Bible as "a land flowing with milk and honey" (e.g., Exodus 3:8; Numbers 14:8; Deuteronomy 31:20). All of that honey and beeswax is far more than could be consumed locally, so the archaeologists have suggested that perhaps the inhabitants were trading or selling both the honey and beeswax—the latter was in high demand for a variety of uses, including medicinal.[83]

A jar found in the vicinity of the apiary has an inscription written on it, "belonging to Nimshi," and so it has been suggested by the excavators that the apiary may have been owned by the Nimshi family, which eventually counted Jehu, king of Israel in the later ninth century BC, among its descendants. However, the apiary was subsequently destroyed in a violent event, probably another earthquake, which buried the hives under nearly a meter of fallen mudbricks and burnt wooden beams. This destructive event also brought Stratum V to a close in the late tenth or early ninth centuries BC, but we will meet up with the site again, as well as Jehu, in the pages below.[84]

Sheshonq's Successors

Sheshonq's campaign seems likely to have impacted the polities of Moab, Ammon, and Edom as well, perhaps stemming from Egypt's desire to retake the copper mines they had previously controlled. A few years ago, a scarab of Sheshonq was found lying on the ground during a surface survey in the area of the copper mines at Wadi Faynan, perhaps a remnant of his interest in this area.[85]

He also seems to have cultivated diplomatic, rather than military, relations with other powers of the time, including sending a statue of himself up to Byblos, where King Abibaal promptly put his own inscription on it, written in Phoenician, as we shall see in chapter 3. However, Sheshonq seems to have died about 924 BC, probably not long after his campaign against Israel and Judah. He may have been buried at Tanis, but his tomb has never been found.[86]

His son and successor, Osorkon I, sent a statue of himself to Byblos as well, and Elibaal, king of Byblos, promptly added his own inscription to it.[87] Osorkon thus seems to have kept up Egyptian diplomatic relations with Byblos, and perhaps other powers of the day as well. Osorkon I may have ruled for as many as thirty-five years, from 924 to 889 BC, into the ninth century BC. His tomb, like that of his father, has also not yet been located. He was followed on the throne of Egypt by a rather unremarkable pharaoh, Takelot I, of whom very little it is known. It might have been during his reign that Sheshonq IIa, whose coffin was found in the tomb of Psusennes I, may have ruled as a rival pharaoh. There are also two other sets of royal names belonging to Sheshonqs (today referred to as IIb and IIc), and opinion is split between whether they were real kings of this same obscure period, or respectively an early variant of the titles of Sheshonq I, and a spelling mistake by an ancient scribe.

However, the next pharaoh, Osorkon II, who is now thought to have ruled ca. 872–831 BC, most likely sent one thousand infantry to fight at the Battle of Qarqar, as part of a coalition amassed against Shalmaneser III of Assyria in 853 BC, which will be discussed in chapter 2 and to which Ahab also contributed chariots and troops. An alabaster vase inscribed with Osorkon II's cartouche has been found at Samaria, in the palace that has been attributed to Omri and Ahab, possibly reflecting some sort of further relationship between Ahab and Osorkon. At some point, Osorkon also sent a statue of himself to Byblos, but unlike those of his predecessors Sheshonq I and Osorkon I, whoever was ruling at Byblos at the time apparently did not inscribe the statue with his own name.[88]

Back at home, the end of Osorkon II's reign, as well as all of that of his successor Sheshonq III (831–791 BC), was beset by internal problems, including rebellions and civil war. By about 810 BC, Egypt was split four ways, with four pharaohs ruling at the same time.[89] Egypt was clearly at low ebb.

All too soon, this situation would lead to a gradual takeover of southern Egypt by Kushite kings from Nubia, who were overlords of the whole country (albeit with some local kings still surviving) as the Twenty-Fifth Dynasty from ca. 750 BC onward. The Kushite regime led a resurgence in Egypt's economy and power but in the end found itself dragged into the conflicts between the Levantine city-states and Assyria, with invasions of Egypt by the latter eventually driving the Nubian kings back into their heartlands in 664 BC.

Independence was regained by the Twenty-Sixth Dynasty, ruling from Sais in the Nile delta, whose members went from Assyrian vassals to Assyrian allies and then to masters of their own destiny. However, the Persian invasion of 525 marked the end of Egypt as power in its own right, and it subsequently passed during the fourth century BC into the hands of Alexander the Great and his Macedonian successors, the Ptolemies. Overall, while it survived the Bronze Age Collapse better than some other regions, Egypt never truly recovered its former glory.

Brief Summation

If we define "success" as a return to pre-Collapse levels of unification and involvement in international trade networks, then post-Collapse Egypt did not do very well. As we have seen in detail, it did continue, but only at a lower level of sociocultural existence, with the administration split into ruling factions and with a limited international role and relatively little power for most of the time. Overall, Egypt was never the same again, nor did it ever rise to the powerful position that it had once held during the New Kingdom period. Only occasionally was a ruler such as Sheshonq I able to attempt to return things to the way they had been in the Eighteenth or early Nineteenth Dynasties or acquire wealth such as displayed in the tomb of Psusennes I, but each time it was merely temporary.

As for the inhabitants of the southern Levant, they will be a flash point for further discussion, both in the final pages below and by other scholars in the future. Not only is there still an active discussion as to how and when the Israelites entered the land of Canaan, but it is also open to debate as to whether the southern Canaanites failed to navigate the change to the Iron Age and were assimilated into the new kingdoms in the region, including Israel, Judah, Edom, Ammon, and Moab, or whether they should be seen as having successfully transformed and actually formed a significant ethnically identifiable portion of the population within these newly established kingdoms.

By way of comparison, both Assyria and Babylonia fared much better than either Egypt or southern Canaan in the centuries after the Collapse. However, they too faced their fair share of challenges, as we shall see next.

CHAPTER TWO

Conquerer of All Lands, Avenger of Assyria

(Assyria and Babylonia)

"Slayer of the widespread hordes of the Ahlamu and scatterer of their forces . . . conqueror of all lands, avenger of Assyria!" That was how Aššur-reša-iši I, king of Assyria from 1133 to 1116 BC, proudly described himself on numerous clay cone fragments found at the site of Nineveh in ancient Mesopotamia.[1] It is because of him and his boasting that we possess the first written royal records in Assyria after the Bronze Age Collapse.

The "Ahlamu" to whom he refers are more commonly known today as the Aramaeans. They are probably best known for their mention in the Hebrew Bible, where Abraham famously declared, "My father was a wandering Aramaean" (Deuteronomy 26:5). Their language, Aramaic, eventually became the lingua franca, or common language, across the Near East, but that lay several centuries in the future.[2]

It is thought that these nomadic, or semi-nomadic, Aramaeans were greatly affected by new climatic and environmental conditions in the region—for example, a cessation of the rains in Mesopotamia as well as a change in the main channel of the Euphrates, which shifted to the west around this time. This resulted in a decrease of land available for irrigation and a related increase in salinization up in northern Mesopotamia.[3] As a result, they began raiding and attacking cities and towns in the Assyrian-controlled regions, which had also been affected by the same shift in arable conditions and were likewise more impoverished than previously.

Despite his boasting, Aššur-reša-iši's defeat of the Aramaeans was apparently not decisive, for his son, Tiglath-Pileser I, subsequently had to fight them as well. The Aramaeans remained a problem for the Assyrians from the twelfth century onward, and eventually, by the ninth century BC, they were able to establish "minor dynasties," as Nicholas Postgate of Cambridge University put it, all across the region.[4]

Aššur-reša-iši's reign began simply enough, with building activities at the sites of Aššur (just north of modern Tikrit) and Nineveh (now underneath modern Mosul, on the eastern bank of the Tigris). Here he constructed temples and palaces plus a possible armory.[5]

The armory may have been put into immediate use, for among his accomplishments he claims to have successfully resisted attacks made by a Babylonian king named Nebuchadnezzar I, who ruled 1125–1104 BC. Although Nebuchadnezzar initiated the hostilities, he lost to Aššur-reša-iši and the Assyrians on not one but two separate occasions. The first time, Nebuchadnezzar was forced to burn his siege engines while retreating, so that they wouldn't fall into Assyrian hands. The second time, Aššur-reša-iši "fought with Nebuchadnezzar, brought about his total defeat, slaughtered his troops and carried off his camp. Forty of his chariots with equipment were taken away and Karaštu (?), Nebuchadnezzar's field-marshal, was captured."[6]

We know this from what is called the "Synchronistic History," which is part of a series of texts known as the *Assyrian and Babylonian Chronicles* or simply the *Mesopotamian Chronicles*. These are records that list events which took place in both Assyria and Babylonia, with a date provided for each. They were written in the third person, that is, as impartial observations, and were part of an effort by contemporary, or relatively contemporary, chroniclers to synchronize the records of the two areas. Their efforts are much appreciated today by ancient historians studying the second and first millennia BC in this region.[7]

In addition, some of our most important information comes from accounts that describe the accomplishments of each king, often on a year-by-year basis. Now known as the *Assyrian Royal Annals,* these were written as if the king himself were the author (though in fact it was scribes who did the actual work), recording his campaigns and other accomplishments, building accounts, and so on. From these we can glean significant details, such as the number of troops involved in a battle and how many people were killed or captured, though they need to be taken with the proverbial grain of salt, since they are full of hyperbole, and the numbers may well be exaggerated. The specific details for each year can also vary depending on the inscription, for the copies were not always exact duplicates, but one thing is always constant and consistent—apparently the Assyrian kings were never defeated, which seems a bit hard to believe.[8] Clearly, the texts were as much propaganda as they were recordings of historical events.

Other royal records eventually include monumental reliefs that depicted battle scenes, hunting expeditions, and the king receiving tribute. These often were placed on the walls of their palaces but could also be inscribed on anything from throne bases and large standing stelae to natural cliff faces along various rivers. There were also administrative documents written on clay tablets, which included letters, diplomatic treaties, receipts, omen reports, and the like.[9]

Additional information can come from the various versions of what is known as the *Assyrian King List.* This latter list, which seems unbelievable in the sections on Assyria's early history but more credible in later parts, purports to name all of the Assyrian kings from the very first ones who "lived in tents" right up through the end of the reign of Shalmaneser V in 722 BC. In addition, there are also the so-called *Eponym Chronicles,* which are records that include brief mentions of events that happened in a particular calendar year (each year being associated with the name of a particular Assyrian official known as a *līmu,* so that everyone knew which year it was) and that may be more trustworthy than any of the above.[10]

Some of these types of records do not start until later, such as the monumental reliefs on the Assyrian palace walls, which only really begin to be seen regularly in the ninth century BC, but others begin earlier, including during the twelfth century BC. All of this provides us with a plethora of historical information, but again, we must be wary about accepting the details at face value. How much can we believe? How much is hyperbole on the part of the king and his scribes? How much is true and how much "true-but-exaggerated"?

These types of material evidence have been recovered for more than a century by now, ever since the early days of Mesopotamian archaeology conducted by pioneers such as Austen Henry Layard, Paul Émile Botta, and Hormudz Rassam. Their methods were not always to be condoned, from their excavation techniques to the colonialist attitudes of the non-local archaeologists, but they did unearth the buried cities of Assyria and Babylonia, known only from the Hebrew Bible at the time, and brought their stories to light.[11]

However, as always in dealing with such ancient eras, especially those recovered via archaeology and archaeologists, we have problems with differential sources. The nature of preservation means that we are often limited to state records, or archives kept by merchants or rulers at the highest levels of society, though sometimes we do get granular data, such as crop yields in a given year. Often if we have actual information on economic or social conditions, they are in the context of crises or triumphs addressed by the king. Still, that does provide us with some tidbits of information about everyday life at the time, but only upon occasion.[12]

Thus, we are usually only able to discuss such things at the state level, rather than at the lowest levels of society, for we simply don't have the written records for the latter, and even archaeological remains do not always provide clear data for the most impoverished peoples. But, except in unusual circumstances, we also usually don't have records showing how kings, mayors, or other rulers responded to calamity. Although we have evidence of a few specific instances where the Hittite or Ugaritic king asked for assistance during a famine or mentioned the sighting of enemy ships or troops, frequently we can only see the end result, which obviously came about because of how they responded (or not) and whether or not it was successful.

In any event, Nebuchadnezzar I may have learned something from his two initial defeats at the hands of Aššur-reša-iši and the Assyrians, for he subsequently undertook successful campaigns against the neighboring Elamites, who had attacked Babylon and stolen a copy of Hammurabi's Law Code and a statue of Marduk several decades earlier. Victory was not easy to come by, however. An initial campaign had to be aborted when an outbreak of plague ravaged the Babylonian troops while they were en route to Elam. A later poem tells the story from Nebuchadnezzar's point of view. "Erra, mightiest of the gods, decimated my warriors. The enfeebling bound my horse teams . . . a demon was killing my fine steeds. . . . I became afraid of death, did not advance to battle, but turned back," says Nebuchadnezzar.[13]

A second campaign was more successful. An inscription left on a *kudurru* stone, which is a well-known type of (symbolic) stone boundary marker often found in temple contexts, records a gift of land and various exemptions granted by Nebuchadnezzar I to someone named Shitti-Marduk, one of the officers involved in this second attempt against Elam. The inscription includes a detailed description of the march to Elam and then the battle in which Shitti-Marduk fought heroically from his chariot at the right side of the king.[14]

The surprise attack occurred in July, when the Elamites were least expecting it. And rightfully so, for the march to Elam was like a march to the gates of hell. The glare of the sun "scorched like fire," we are told; the paths along which the Babylonian troops were trudging "were burning like open flames!" There was no water in the wells and no other places where they could quench their thirst. "The finest of the great horses gave out, the legs of the strong man faltered," the inscription reads, but Nebuchadnezzar and his army continued on. "So hastened the mighty king, and reached the bank of the Ulaya river. Both kings met there and made battle. Between them a conflagration burst out, the face of the sun was darkened by their dust, whirlwinds were blowing, raging was the storm! In the storm of their battle the warrior in the chariot could not see the other at his side." In the end, the Elamite army was routed, their king "disappeared," and "Thus king Nebuchadnezzar triumphed, seized Elam, and plundered its possessions."[15]

Although he did not bring back Hammurabi's stele, Nebuchadnezzar I did return the statue of Marduk that had been stolen. For that act, he was remembered in the annals of the Babylonians for generations. In fact, Nebuchadnezzar dealt such a blow to the Elamites that there are virtually no written records and little archaeological evidence of the Elamites for the next several hundred years. They had showed resilience in the initial phases of the Late Bronze Collapse but then fell hard after this military defeat. They do not play a major role in international politics again until the late eighth century BC.[16]

Overall, the Assyrians and the Babylonians proved to be among the most resilient and successful of the affected societies to weather the aftermath of the Collapse. They were able to retain their knowledge of writing, undertake massive building projects, and keep their systems of government in place. However, even they did not escape unscathed. For instance, archaeological evidence obtained from surveys in the region of ancient Babylonia suggests that there may have been a decrease in population of up to 75 percent during the three hundred years between the Collapse at the end of the Bronze Age and the beginning of Babylonian resurgence after 900 BC.[17]

In addition, according to A. Kirk Grayson, a renowned scholar at the University of Toronto who was responsible for publishing all the known royal Assyrian inscriptions in a series of volumes that appeared from the late 1980s onward, there are almost no royal inscriptions that date to the seventy-five-year period from the end of the reign of Tukulti-Ninurta I in 1208 BC until the time of Aššur-reša-iši I. It is especially surprising that there are no such royal inscriptions left to us by a king named Aššur-dan I, who ruled for almost fifty years during this period, from 1179 to 1133 BC.[18]

It may be that we should see this lack of royal records during this period as a sign that the Assyrians were more affected by the Collapse at the end of the Bronze Age than we thought. However, we cannot know this for certain, especially since they could conceivably have been writing on perishable materials such as leather, wood, or lead strips, even if they had for some reason temporarily ceased to record royal inscriptions on stone. On the other hand, Eckart Frahm, an Assyriologist at Yale University, points out that royal inscriptions would usually have been written on stone or clay, so the gap may indeed be meaningful.[19]

Fortunately, as mentioned, the royal Assyrian records begin again with the reign of Aššur-reša-iši I, at a time when there may have been a fifty-year respite to the drought that had been impacting the entire Eastern Mediterranean and Aegean regions; I will discuss this further below.[20] If so, Aššur-reša-iši I will have benefited from this temporary climactic reprieve.

Tiglath-Pileser I

Aššur-reša-iši was eventually succeeded by his son, Tiglath-Pileser I, who came to the Assyrian throne in 1115 BC. His reign lasted nearly forty years, until 1076 BC. He made boasts similar to those of his father, stating at one point that he had crossed the Euphrates a total of twenty-eight times, twice a year for fourteen years, in pursuit of the Aramaeans. He also, like his father, withstood an attack or two by the Babylonians, including yet again by Nebuchadnezzar I.[21]

He is known to us in part because of the many inscriptions left behind by his scribes that describe his prowess, much of which is probably hyperbole:

> Tiglath-pileser, strong king, king of the universe, king of Assyria, king of all the four quarters, encircler of all criminals, valiant young man, merciless mighty man who acts with the support of the gods Aššur and Ninurta, the great gods, his lords, and (thereby) has felled his foes, attentive prince who, by the command of the god Shamash the warrior, has conquered by means of conflict and might from Babylon of the land Akkad to the Upper Sea of the land Amurru and the sea of the lands Nairi and become lord of all . . . storm-trooper whose

> fierce battles all princes of the four quarters dreaded so that they took to hiding places like bats and scurried off to inaccessible regions like jerboa [a small, hopping desert rodent].[22]

The scribes also recorded, on numerous clay octagonal prisms and in great and often gruesome detail, what Tiglath-Pileser I did to the unfortunate enemy soldiers who did not take to hiding places or scurry off to inaccessible regions after he defeated them in battle. For example, after having reportedly overwhelmed a coalition of five kings and their combined army of twenty thousand men in a battle fought during the first year of his reign, he proceeded to desecrate the corpses, loot their property, and take the rest prisoner: "Like a storm demon I piled up the corpses of their warriors on the battlefield and made their blood flow into the hollows and plains of the mountains. I cut off their heads and stacked them like grain piles around their cities. I brought out their booty, property, and possessions without number. I took the remaining 6,000 of their troops who had fled from my weapons and submitted to me and regarded them as people of my land."[23] The inscription then continues in a similar vein, describing victories over numerous other groups, listing each by name, ranging far and wide over parts of what is now Turkey, Iraq, and coastal areas of the Levant.[24]

In addition, the curses that Tiglath-Pileser I told the scribes to add at the end of this long inscription were enough to give anyone pause. He addressed these to whomever "breaks or erases my monumental or clay inscriptions, throws them into water, burns them, covers them with earth . . . who erases my inscribed name and writes his own name, or who conceives of anything injurious and puts it into effect to the disadvantage of my monumental inscriptions." Invoking the gods Anu and Adad to curse the potential offender, whom he assumed would be a future king or ruler, he then wrote: "May they overthrow his sovereignty. May they tear out the foundations of his royal throne. May they terminate his noble line. May they smash his weapons, bring about the defeat of his army, and make him sit in bonds before his enemies. May the god Adad strike his land with terrible lightning and inflict his land with distress, famine, want, and plague. May he command that he not live one day longer. May he

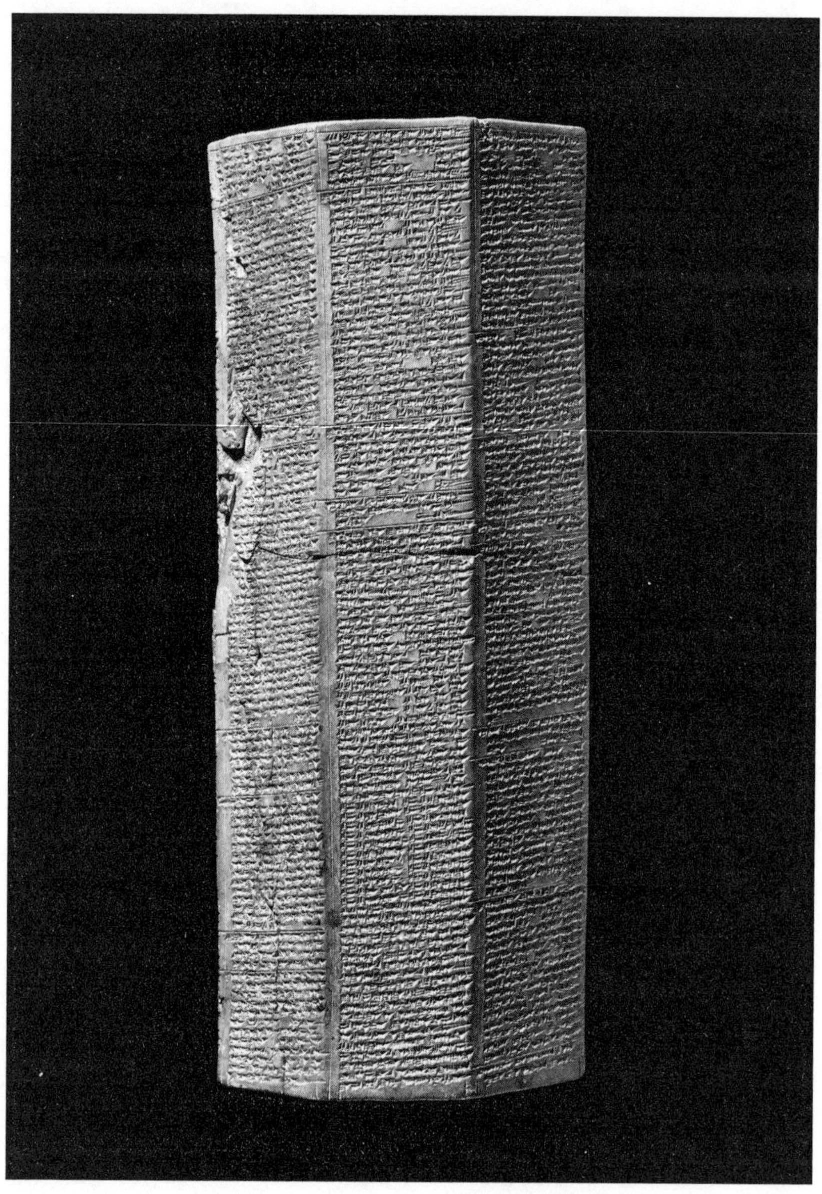

FIG. 4. Tiglath-Pileser I clay prism. British Museum no. 91033.
Photograph courtesy of the British Museum.

destroy his name and his seed from the land."[25] And, about the Aramaeans in particular, an early inscription notes that Tiglath-Pileser I conquered six of their cities, burning them to the ground and looting their possessions. He also massacred many of their troops, pursuing them across the Euphrates on rafts made from inflated goatskins.[26]

Although they were among the Assyrians' most dangerous opponents at this time and were frequently cast as the archenemy of the Assyrian king, especially during the early years of Tiglath-Pileser I, the Aramaeans were not his only opponents. Tiglath-Pileser claims in the same early inscription to have gained control over a variety of other lands, mountains, towns, and princes who were also hostile to him and to Aššur. "I vied with 60 crowned heads and achieved victory over them in battles, add[ing] territory to Assyria and people to its population," he boasted. "I extended the border of my land and ruled over all their lands."[27]

In other inscriptions, including a series of clay tablets as well as fragments of obelisks found by archaeologists at the site of Aššur, plus the so-called Broken Obelisk that was found at Nineveh and has now been redated to his reign, Tiglath-Pileser describes rebuilding and restoring various palaces and other buildings in Aššur and elsewhere, as well as digging out long-neglected moats and canals. He also documented yet more campaigns, including in what is now Syria and Lebanon to the west. He killed and/or captured wild bulls, elephants, and lions at the foot of Mount Lebanon and elsewhere, as well as panthers, tigers, bears, boars, and ostriches, cut down and carried off cedar beams to use in a temple back home, and then continued on to the land of Amurru (coastal North Syria) and conquered it.

He also received tribute from the coastal cities of Byblos, Sidon, and Arwad, where the Phoenicians were beginning to establish themselves, and lists gifts of exotic animals, which included a crocodile and a "large female monkey of the seacoast." He clarifies on the Broken Obelisk and elsewhere that these latter animals were given to him by an Egyptian pharaoh (probably Ramses XI, the last king of the Twentieth Dynasty), and that they also included a "river-man," which was previously identified as a water buffalo or perhaps a hippopotamus but has now been recently reidentified as more likely to be a Mediterranean monk seal.[28]

Tiglath-Pileser also says that he took a six-hour boat ride while at Arwad and that, while at sea, he killed "a *nahiru*, which is called a sea-horse." In a later inscription, he says specifically that he killed it with a harpoon of his own making. Although there has been a fair amount of discussion, scholars have still not decided what exactly is a *nahiru*; some have suggested that it was some kind of small whale, seal, or shark, but another text mentions ivory from a *nahiru*, so that would indicate teeth or a tusk of some sort and, in fact, current opinion may be leaning toward an identification as a hippopotamus.[29]

This is the first time that these Phoenician coastal cities have been mentioned in an inscription not of their own making since the Collapse of the Bronze Age. I will discuss them at greater length in the next chapter, but for now we can put them into context, for the new world of the late twelfth century BC was very different from the high point of the Late Bronze Age in the fourteenth century BC. Back then, the kings of Assyria were part of the Great Powers and exchanged huge royal gifts with other kings, from Egypt to Hattusa, while the smaller, petty kings of Byblos, Sidon, Tyre, and other nearby Canaanite cities practiced trade and diplomacy with both each other and the Great Powers. Now, with Tiglath-Pileser I at the helm, and especially later, from the ninth century onward, as will become apparent, the Assyrians simply took what they wanted from the Phoenicians and others, either by looting the smaller, defeated cities and seizing what they needed or by exacting tribute, or both.

No One Lives Here Anymore

In late October 2021, two journalists published an article in the *Washington Post* describing some of the problems currently facing southern Iraq. "No one lives here anymore," they wrote. "As climate change produces extreme warming and water grows scarcer around the Middle East, the land here is drying up. Across Iraq's south, there is a sense of an ending."[30]

They could just as easily have been describing the situation in ancient Assyria three thousand years ago, for things began to fall apart toward the end of Tiglath-Pileser I's reign, culminating in about 150 years of downturn before they began to recover once again.[31] Difficult times had finally come to the Assyrians, and to the neighboring Babylonians to the south as well. In fact, the respected Italian historian Mario Liverani has suggested that the crisis in Mesopotamia should have materialized much earlier but was delayed or postponed because of powerful leaders such as Tiglath-Pileser I in Assyria and Nebuchadnezzar I in Babylonia.[32] A large part of the successful resilience of these two societies in the immediate aftermath of the Collapse was indeed probably the result of having leaders such as these in place during their time of need.

We know that the two powers continued to fight against each other, even as both suffered from the elements. For instance, Tiglath-Pileser I campaigned against Babylonia twice in the eleventh century, conquering several cities and bringing booty back to Aššur. Specifically mentioned in the inscriptions are the cities of Babylon and Dur-Kurigalzu, which he describes as "the great towns of Karduniaš [Babylonia], together with their fortresses." His opponent was Marduk-nadin-ahhe, a king of Babylon who ruled ca. 1099–1082 BC and who had earlier raided the Assyrian city of Ekallate and stolen statues of two gods, Adad and Sala, an act that now required revenge.

Tiglath-Pileser claims to have defeated Marduk-nadin-ahhe both times, capturing and burning the palaces of Babylon that belonged to the king and retrieving the statues. However, there are now good indications that Tiglath-Pileser may have actually lost the first of these battles, during which two of his sons were killed, and that it was only during the second campaign that he actually defeated Marduk-nadin-ahhe.[33]

Tiglath-Pileser even gives the specific dates that these attacks occurred, but they are rendered in terms of eponym years. The first time was during the year named after an official called Aššur-šuma-eriš; the second was during the year named after an official called Ninu'ayu. We know now that these were probably 1092 BC and 1091 BC, respectively, which would have been Tiglath-Pileser's twenty-second and twenty-third years on the throne. There was probably also a revenge attack conducted by Marduk-nadin-ahhe several years later, in 1086 BC.[34]

Back home in Aššur, Tiglath-Pileser built an amazing palace, reportedly constructed entirely of cedar wood from Lebanon, that he called the "Palace of the King of All Lands." He also built a temple for An and Adad, two of the Assyrian gods, as well as a number of lesser buildings, including one constructed of boxwood just to store his weapons. He also ordered the creation of a statue of the *nahiru* that he had killed with a harpoon in Amurru; it was to be made of basalt and was presumably life-size or larger. And in the city of Nineveh, he ordered the construction of similar buildings and palaces, as well as a royal garden and a canal to irrigate it.[35]

—

The Assyrian texts from this period specifically mention additional attacks by the Aramaeans as well as a series of catastrophes, but we now also find indications of climatic problems in this region, essentially for the first time in these inscriptions. For example, in a text dating to 1082 BC, during the thirty-second year of Tiglath-Pileser I's reign, we are told that there was a famine so severe that the populace resorted to cannibalism—"[t]he people ate one another's flesh," reads the relevant entry in the *Assyrian Chronicles*. The same entry also states that Aramaeans had "plundered [the land], seized the roads, and conquered and took [many fortified cities] of Assyria" that year. The Assyrian citizens had to flee to the mountains northeast of Erbil to save their lives.[36]

And then, between two and six years later (1080–1076 BC), at the end of Tiglath-Pileser's long reign, there was a total crop failure. This was accompanied by another incursion by the Aramaeans, which is probably not surprising, since they would have been affected by the famine and crop failure as well. What is surprising is that they may have forced Tiglath-Pileser himself to flee. "All [of the] crops of Assyria were ruined," say the *Assyrian Chronicles*. "Aramaean 'houses' [i.e., invaders] penetrated the area around Nineveh and Kilizi; Tiglath-Pileser, king of Assyria, retreated to the land of Katmuhi." Katmuhi (or Katmuhu) is usually identified as a mountainous area near modern Midyat in what is now Turkish Kurdistan.[37]

The Assyrians survived the famine, drought, and attacks at the end of Tiglath-Pileser I's reign, but it was the beginning of their decline. The end came after the rule of a son of Tiglath-Pileser I named Aššur-bel-kala, who reigned ca. 1074–1057 BC. He has left us a number of inscriptions (though fewer than previously thought, since several have recently been reassigned to Tiglath-Pileser I). Just in case anyone was tempted to mess with his inscriptions in the future, on the back of one statue he had a curse inscribed: "As for the one who removes my inscriptions and my name: the divine Sebetti, the gods of the West, will afflict him with snake-bite."[38]

It is with the end of Aššur-bel-kala's reign ca. 1057 BC, with the Assyrians having staved off their own collapse for some 120 years after 1177 BC, that scholars bring to a close the so-called Middle Assyrian period. Drought had hit again during his reign, in the years between 1060 and 1050 BC, accompanied by rebellions and more invasions by the Aramaeans (sometimes called the Sutians in the Babylonian records of the period). Thereafter, drought is reported like clockwork every ten years, in 1040, 1030, 1020, and 1010 BC, according to reports by both the Assyrians and the Babylonians. There were also "troubles and disorder" that came with the drought in 1040 BC; plague that accompanied the drought in 1010 BC; and then more stress and famine along with a drought in 1007 BC.[39] The next phase stretches deep into the tenth century and once again features drought, famine, social disorder, and political fragmentation; I will elaborate on this in a moment.

All in all, the eleventh century BC was probably not a good time to be alive in either Assyria or Babylonia, whether one was an Assyrian, a Babylonian, or an Aramaean/Sutian. However, there was light at the end of the tunnel, albeit at a distance, for when the Assyrians reemerged in the latter part of the tenth century BC, under the guidance of their kings Aššur-dan II and Adad-nirari II, they began to establish the Neo-Assyrian Empire, which would then proceed to dominate the ancient Near East for nearly three hundred years.

Assyria and Babylonia in the Tenth Century BC

However, for the greater part of the tenth century BC, things were not much better in Assyria and Babylonia than they had been during the eleventh century. For example, beginning about 1007 BC, and continuing for the next twenty years, there seems to have been a grain shortage in Mesopotamia. An inscription written on a Babylonian *kudurru* boundary stone specifically mentions "distress and famine under king Kaššu-nadin-ahhe" (1007–1005 BC). We are told that "regular offerings [to the gods] were discontinued, and the drink-offering ceased." Things seem to have continued along this vein into the reign of the next king, for the same inscription records that a priest from the city of Sippar told him, "The temple-offerings to Shamash [the chief god] have ceased."[40]

Then, during a period of about thirty years, from about 970 BC onward, the Aramaeans began attacking again, at one point for nine straight years. We know that this took place during the reign of a Babylonian king named Nabu-mukin-apli (978–943 BC), for the *Babylonian Chronicles* record that "the Aramaeans were belligerent, so the king could not go to Babylon." There are also indications that there was a famine in 954 BC and then again about fifteen years later, when another famine and accompanying hunger are recorded in about 940 BC.[41]

The Assyrian recovery finally began again with the reign of king Aššur-dan II (934–912 BC). He started slowly, attacking the various small Aramaean kingdoms and retrieving Assyrian territory that had been lost during the previous century. In his annals, Aššur-dan II takes great pride in saying that he also brought back Assyrians who had fled from the area earlier. "I brought back the exhausted people of Assyria who had abandoned their cities and houses in the face of want, hunger, and famine, and had gone up to other lands," he wrote. "I settled them in cities and homes which were suitable and they dwelt in peace."[42]

The recovery continued under his successor Adad-nirari II (911–891 BC), who was so successful that he began to expand Assyrian holdings once again, which would eventually result in the behemoth we now call the Neo-Assyrian Empire. He campaigned virtually every year of the twenty-one that he spent on the throne, to the west against the Aramaeans, to the south and east against Babylonia, and to the north.[43]

He claims specifically to have defeated two kings of Babylonia in succession and to have invaded the land of Hanigalbat (known as the kingdom of Mitanni back in the Late Bronze Age) no fewer than seven different times. He seized booty that included a golden throne, polished gold dishes, and even "a gold tent befitting his sovereignty, the weight of which I did not determine." He also killed 360 lions from his chariot, 240 wild bulls, and 6 elephants during various hunts and restored temples that needed urgent care, according to his inscriptions.[44]

What is extremely interesting about this timing for the beginning of Neo-Assyrian resurgence under these two kings is that it apparently matches up extremely well with new evidence that the climate changed for the better at just about this time. A new study based on "a high-resolution and precisely dated speleothem record" from Kuna Ba Cave, located in the Kurdistan region of northeastern Iraq approximately three hundred kilometers southeast of Nineveh, reports that the period from ca. 925 BC to 725 BC was a much wetter era than any the Assyrians had seen since the end of the Late Bronze Age. As the investigators note, this period "is synchronous with the prominent phases of the Assyrian imperial expansion (c. 920–730 BCE)" and included a "peak wet period, termed here the Assyrian megapluvial" which lasted from 850 to 740 BC and was one of the "wettest periods of the past 4000 years" in that area.[45] We may also note that there are no more mentions in the Assyrian records of famine or drought during this period. If these new findings are any indication, it certainly seems as if the Neo-Assyrians wasted no time in taking full advantage of the change in climate.

Hormudz Rassam and the Balawat Gates

Information about the next major phase in the resurgence of the Neo-Assyrians came about in part because of an unusual gift that was sent in 1877 to Hormudz Rassam, an Iraqi archaeologist from Mosul who had been trained by the well-known British scholar Austen Henry Layard. Rassam was living in London at the time, in semi-retirement after a distinguished career. When he opened a package which had been sent by a friend in Iraq, he found that it contained brittle fragments of bronze, embossed with scenes of warriors and inscribed with brief texts. The friend said that the fragments had been found by a local villager digging a grave at the small site of Balawat, now identified as ancient Imgur-Enlil, located some seventeen miles (twenty-seven kilometers) southeast of Mosul.[46]

The following year, when the British Museum asked Rassam to come out of semi-retirement and return to Iraq to conduct excavations at Nineveh, he agreed to do so and took the opportunity to do some exploratory digging at Balawat as well. It turned out that the fragmentary pieces that had been sent to him were from the topmost of a series of bronze bands that had originally been attached as decoration to two large wooden doors, each twenty feet high and eight feet wide. The doors were part of a gate located at the entrance to a palace at the site, which had been built by Shalmaneser III, who ruled Assyria during the ninth century BC, from 858 to 824 BC.

There were eight pairs of bands in all, each about eight feet long and a foot high, affixed to the two doors. Digging down through the twenty feet of earth and fallen mudbrick that now surrounded and held them firmly, Rassam found most of them still in place, one pair above the other. At some point, the wood of the doors had been destroyed by fire or simply disintegrated over time, leaving only the bronze bands still "standing" in place, looking for all the world like a gigantic hat-rack, as he later wrote. The bands themselves, he said, were "embossed with a variety of subjects, such as battle-scenes, triumphal processions, and religious performances" and "divided into panels surrounded by a border of rosettes."[47]

In fact, the scenes and inscriptions turned out to record campaigns from the first dozen or more years of Shalmaneser's reign, beginning in 858 BC. We see enemy cities besieged; captured enemy combatants impaled; and various other depictions of either general or gruesome interest. Each scene is accompanied by an inscription identifying the specific event. Among the cities mentioned are Tyre, Sidon, and Carchemish, as well as others in Urartu (located to the north, in the eastern region of Anatolia, which I will discuss in chapter 4) and elsewhere in Mesopotamia. The bands are extremely important to our reconstruction of these areas and events during this period.

Rassam sent the bands that he had excavated back to the British Museum, where they are now on display along with other items that he said had been found at the site. However, his finds were almost immediately called into question by several of the curators, including the well-known Egyptologist E. A. Wallis Budge. In the definitive 1915 British Museum publication of these fragments, Budge publicly stated his doubts that they could have come from Balawat. "Having examined the mound," he wrote in the preface to the volume, "I found it impossible to believe that this insignificant site could have contained an Assyrian temple. . . . Therefore we must conclude . . . that the place where the bronze reliefs published herein were found has not yet been ascertained."

The author of the volume, L. W. King, who was an assistant keeper (curator) at the British Museum, agreed, writing, "We may conclude that the native finders of the gates took good care to conceal the actual site of their discovery." The two curators also insinuated that Rassam might have purchased all the bands, for they wrote in the volume that he "acquired" and "recovered" them, rather than having excavated them.[48] We must wonder why it was that Budge and King doubted Rassam, although it is likely to have been either inherent racism, colonialism, professional jealousy, or all of the above.

Interestingly, and perhaps because of these accusations, Rassam did not turn over to the British Museum the original fragments that had been sent to him as a gift from his friend in Iraq. Instead, they were kept by his family and were eventually acquired by the Walters Art Gallery in Baltimore, Maryland, where they remain to this day. Other fragments, all from the top two pairs of bands, which had been discovered by local villagers digging graves on top of the mound, made their way to other museums and private collections through various antiquities dealers.[49]

Matters came to a head when Rassam, supported by Layard, filed a lawsuit to clear his name, but it was not until 1955 that he was eventually vindicated, in an unexpected way. It began when the British Museum created the Department of Western Asiatic Antiquities that year and the storerooms were reorganized. To everyone's surprise, more bronze bands from yet another set of doors were found, in one or more boxes that had been languishing in the storerooms for decades at that point. They had been sent back by Rassam as well but had been forgotten. Many were found still wrapped in newspaper, from an edition of *The Times* with a date of 1880, presumably the time at which they had been unpacked from the crates or containers that Rassam had shipped to London. These all came from an earlier palace at the site, this one built by Aššurnasirpal II, Shalmaneser's father, who ruled earlier in the ninth century BC, from 883 to 859 BC. We can confidently state this because, even though the rest of the palace has not yet been located, seven of the bands are inscribed "Palace of Aššurnasirpal, king of the universe, king of Assyria, son of Tukulti-Ninurta, king of Assyria, son of Adad-nirari, also king of Assyria."[50]

Rassam had written about this second set of bands in his reports and final publication, describing them as coming from doors about half the height of Shalmaneser III's pair and located some sixty feet (twenty meters) away from the initial set of bands. However, in one letter sent to the British Museum in 1878, Rassam said, "Unfortunately, this second small monument is very much damaged . . . no sooner [was] it uncovered than it fell to pieces." He said something very similar in his book nearly two decades later, writing, "This was found very much injured, and as soon as it was exposed to the air, it crumbled to pieces." It is no wonder that this second set of bands had long been presumed to be lost; nobody expected that Rassam had collected the pieces and shipped them to London as well, but indeed he had done so.[51]

Once they had been recovered from the storerooms, examination of these additional bands revealed that the scenes on the bottom pair are almost identical, with both depicting prisoners "from Hatti" (i.e., North Syria) as well as Assyrians in procession. The other bands depict additional scenes, including Hatti several times more, as well as lion and bull hunts. In all, they, like the bands on the Shalmaneser III gate found earlier by Rassam, give us a decent visual picture of some of Aššurnasirpal's campaigns.[52]

These (re)discoveries in the British Museum storerooms led the trustees to sponsor another expedition to Balawat in 1956, this time led by British archaeologist Max Mallowan, who was married to the mystery writer Agatha Christie. The team immediately found more inscribed bronze bands. These came from yet another, smaller, double-leafed gate also dating to the time of Aššurnasirpal II. The gate was part of a temple to Mamu (possibly the Assyrian god of dreams) that Aššurnasirpal had built at the site at the same time as he had his palace constructed. Mallowan's discovery of the additional bands confirmed that Rassam had been telling the truth about his earlier finds at Balawat.[53] Moreover, Mallowan's team was able to ascertain that the gate they discovered had been burnt and collapsed when the town was destroyed centuries later, ca. 612 BC, at the same time that the Neo-Assyrian Empire came to an end. They were even able to determine that one door of the double gate was closed and the other was ajar at the time of destruction.[54]

Mallowan's bands were subsequently conserved and restored at the British Museum, where it turned out that the scenes pictured on them showed military campaigns and enemies bringing tribute to Aššurnasirpal. In particular, the inscriptions and iconography again identify cities in Phoenicia and Urartu, as well as Carchemish, and several Aramaean strongholds by the Euphrates.[55] The bands were subsequently returned to Iraq, where they were displayed in the Mosul Museum from 1974 onward. Unfortunately, the museum was looted in 2003 and then attacked again by ISIS in 2015. Many of the bands found by Mallowan were now missing, either stolen or destroyed, so it is lucky that they had already been fully studied and were published in a volume edited by British Museum curators John Curtis and Nigel Tallis that appeared in 2008.[56]

Resurgence of the Assyrians

The Balawat bands from the various doors describe for us what was happening across the ancient Near East during the ninth century BC. In fact, they form just one part of an abundance of material available to those who wish to attempt a reconstruction of this period, ranging from royal inscriptions found in Assyrian palaces, pictorial representations, additional remains retrieved by archaeologists, and details in the Hebrew Bible. As a result, we are able to get a pretty good picture of what was happening in the Eastern Mediterranean as the various societies and civilizations embarked on reestablishing and reconstituting the interconnected world that had been lost during the Late Bronze Age Collapse.

For example, this century sees the continued recovery and expansion of the Assyrian Empire, which Mario Liverani has described as a tenuous network of connected settlements and strongholds initially established in "alien lands," rather than as a solid "oil stain" stretching across the land.[57] In this resurgence of the Assyrians, we see the replacement of small, multi-state competitors and small city-states with the first large empire of the new millennium. The void created by the Collapse allowed for new political and economic structures (such as Phoenician Mediterranean trade) as the world recovered. Without any strong competitors, Assyria eventually filled the political void to become the most resilient large state recovering from the Late Bronze Age Collapse. In so doing, the Assyrians invented many of the elements that were adopted by later empires: standing armies, effective communication and transportation systems, and political propaganda (like the Balawat gate inscriptions).

Tukulti-Ninurta II (890–884 BC) started things off, campaigning in what are now parts of Syria and southeastern Turkey. This was eventually brought to fruition by his successor Aššurnasirpal II, who campaigned in the same area, including capturing and refounding the city of Tushan. This has now been identified as the current mound of Ziyaret Tepe, located on the upper Tigris River in southeastern Turkey, where an archaeological team headed by Tim Matney of the University of Akron may have found the royal palace that Aššurnasirpal said he built there.[58]

This latter king is seen by some scholars as the first to truly begin reestablishing Assyria's grip on territory across the ancient Near East. Grayson describes this king's reign as one of the most important eras in Mesopotamian history, pointing to the large number of detailed royal inscriptions, the tremendous number of building projects that he undertook, especially at the site of Kalhu but also elsewhere, and the number of military campaigns intended to expand the Assyrian Empire.[59]

Aššurnasirpal II's scribes went to great lengths to describe the barbaric treatment of those he captured during his campaigns. Such descriptions occur again and again within a single inscription, gruesomely itemizing what happened on each campaign. In one such inscription, for example, known as the Kurkh Monolith, he wrote of one ruler whom he defeated: "I flayed Bur-Rammanu, the criminal, and draped his skin over the wall of the city of Sinabu."[60]

This is one of two inscriptions discovered in 1861 by the British archaeologist John Taylor at the site of Kurkh (now known as the town of Üçtepe in modern Turkey, located not far from Ziyaret Tepe). The other inscription was set up later by Aššurnasirpal's son, Shalmaneser III, and includes a description of the events that took place during the Battle of Qarqar, which I will discuss in greater detail below. Taylor donated both inscriptions to the British Museum in 1863 and wrote about them in the *Journal of the Royal Geographic Society of London*, where he briefly described visiting the site and discovering them basically lying on the surface: "I had the good fortune to discover a stone slab bearing the effigy of an Assyrian king, and covered on both sides with long inscriptions in the cuneiform character. . . . Some little way below it, on the slope of the mound, and nearly entirely concealed by debris, I exhumed another perfect relic of the same description."[61] It seems a little hard to believe that they would have simply been lying on the surface rather than deep within the mound, but he does not mention doing any excavation, so we must take Taylor at his word.

Aššurnasirpal II's boasts are not unique to the Kurkh Monolith. In another instance, describing an attack on a city named Pitura, he wrote, "I conquered the city. I felled 800 of their combat troops with the sword and cut off their heads. I captured many soldiers alive. The rest of them I burnt. I carried off valuable tribute from them. I built a pile of live men and of heads before his gate. I impaled on stakes 700 soldiers before their gate. I razed, destroyed, and turned into ruin hills the city. I burnt their adolescent boys and girls."[62]

Aššurnasirpal II also fought against the Babylonian king Nabu-apla-iddina (who ruled ca. 887–855 BC), attacked the Aramaean kingdom of Bit-Adini, and mimicked the statement of Aššur-dan II from a number of decades earlier, claiming that he too had "brought back the enfeebled Assyrians who, because of hunger and famine, had gone up to other lands."[63]

Just a few years into his reign, Aššurnasirpal II moved his capital city from Aššur, where it had been located up to that point, to Kalhu (biblical

FIG. 5. Kurkh Monolith of Aššurnasirpal II. British Museum no. 118883. Photograph courtesy of the British Museum.

Calah), which was more centrally located within Assyrian territory. Kalhu then served as the Assyrian capital city for nearly two hundred years, from 879 BC until 706 BC. It later became known as Nimrud, by which name it gained fame during the excavations of Layard, which began in 1845.[64]

At the site, Aššurnasirpal II immediately built a palace, now called the "Northwest Palace." The initial remains of this tremendous structure came to light on the very first day that Layard started excavating, after having dreamt of finding underground palaces with "gigantic monsters," "sculptured figures," and "endless inscriptions" the night before. He found exactly that, for the palace walls were everywhere decorated with alabaster slabs covered with carvings and inscriptions depicting the king's achievements, his heroic conquests, the spoils and tribute he received, his description of building the palace (above), and so on.[65] Essentially, Aššurnasirpal had started a whole new genre of historical art by depicting his victories and other related activities in reliefs (rather than just inscriptions) on the walls in his palace (and on bronze gate bands such as at Balawat), a practice that was subsequently continued by later Assyrian kings in their palaces.

On hundreds of slabs lining the walls of the palace, Layard found what is now known as Aššurnasirpal's "Standard Inscription," which includes the following description of the building process:

> I cleared away the old ruin hill and dug down to water level. I sank the foundation pit down to a depth of 120 layers of brick. I founded therein a palace of cedar, cypress, daprānu-juniper, boxwood, meskannu-wood, terebinth, and tamarisk as my royal residence and for my lordly leisure for eternity. I made replicas of beasts of mountains and seas in white limestone and parūtu-alabaster and stationed them at its doors. I decorated it in a splendid fashion; I surrounded it with knobbed nails of bronze. I hung doors of cedar, cypress, daprānu-juniper, and meskannu-wood in its doorways. I took in great quantities and put therein silver, gold, tin, bronze, iron, booty from the lands over which I gained dominion.[66]

As the Austrian Assyriologist Karen Radner has described it, Aššurnasirpal's new palace was huge. It measured 200 meters by 130 meters (essentially two American football fields long by just over a football field wide), with colossal, human-headed, winged bulls or lions called *lamassu* guarding its entry gate, and featured courtyards, rooms, and private quarters for the royal family inside.[67]

And when it was finished, Aššurnasirpal II threw a tremendous celebration with a banquet that lasted for ten full days. According to an inscription that he ordered set up afterward, found during Mallowan's excavations at the site, nearly seventy thousand people were invited to the opening ceremonies. These included the entire population of the city as well as people from all around the empire, in addition to five thousand foreign diplomats, including representatives from the Phoenician cities of Tyre and Sidon. The menu included more than seventeen thousand sheep, lambs, calves, and oxen; ten thousand pigeons and ten thousand turtledoves, plus thousands of other birds; ten thousand each of fish, eggs, and bread; and huge quantities of vegetables, fruits, nuts, and spices, including pomegranates, grapes, pistachios (both shelled and unshelled), turnips, olives, onions, and garlic; all washed down with ten thousand jugs of beer, ten thousand skins of wine, and just one hundred containers of milk.[68]

To have generated this much excess and be able to devote it to a single feasting event, Aššurnasirpal II and the Assyrians must have been very successful with their expansive military campaigns and the booty and tribute that these produced. As Trevor Bryce, professor emeritus at the University of Queensland, has observed, such goods, which were taken from the defeated cities, and which were then frequently given as tribute on an annual basis thereafter, are undoubtedly the real reason for all of the Assyrian campaigns. They brought into the Neo-Assyrian coffers everything from timber to precious metals to luxury furniture to exotic items, all of which were needed and which contributed to the Assyrian economy.[69] However, the propaganda value of this particular feasting event and the political message that it also sent cannot be underestimated.

Aššurnasirpal also marched against the land of Amurru, located to the south of Carchemish, as well as Phoenicia, even further to the south. He collected tribute from Amurru as well as the Phoenician polities of Tyre, Sidon, Byblos, and Arwad (which he describes as located on an island). Impressively, he declared in his inscriptions, "I cleansed my weapons in the Great Sea" (i.e., the Mediterranean). Though we have seen such declarations before from the Assyrians, he was the first king to have done so in many generations. The tribute included objects of metal ("silver, gold, tin, bronze") as well as "linen garments with multicoloured trim, a large female monkey, a small female monkey, ebony, boxwood, [and] ivory of *nahirus*."[70]

We may be able to see some of this on the bronze bands found by Mallowan at Balawat, for it is thought that the middle bands on the doors from the Temple of Mamu, set up by Aššurnasirpal II, probably depict (or once depicted) Phoenician cities as well as Phoenician dignitaries bearing tribute. One scene from the left-hand door, which is now missing the depiction of the actual city, shows fourteen men with tribute, six of whom are traveling in boats of Phoenician type—"with prow and stern in the form of a duck's head." Its partner, on the right-hand door, shows the Assyrian king receiving the tribute from these men, including large, two-handled cauldrons, with two of the boats visible. This time the city is still present, depicted as a fortified town on what looks to be an island, so it is quite possibly Tyre (or perhaps Arwad). In all cases, the men are shown wearing soft caps "with bending tops" and boots "with upturned toes." One row further down, we see an almost identical scene on the left band, this time again with the city present and again shown surrounded by water, so perhaps on an island, with two more boats of the same Phoenician type depicted, and six men bringing tribute, in addition to the oarsmen.[71]

Shalmaneser III

When he became king, Shalmaneser III greatly increased the size of the Assyrian army and continued the relentless campaigning begun by his father. In his inscriptions, Shalmaneser described himself as "great king, strong king, king of the universe, unrivalled king, dragon, the weapon which destroys all quarters."[72] He was not exaggerating.

In order to extend his empire, Shalmaneser campaigned during all thirty-four years of his reign—each and every year—and attacked pretty much every area and major/minor king who lay within his orbit. At the end of one lengthy inscription, he gave a numerical summary of the number of men whom his army killed or captured, as well as animals taken as booty, over the course of the first twenty years of campaigning: "110,610 prisoners; 82,600 killed; 9,920 horses (and) mules; 35,565 oxen; 19,690 donkeys; (and) 184,755 sheep."[73] The numbers, if they can be believed, are astounding.

He did, though, also go to the aid of a newly installed king of Babylon named Marduk-zakir-sumi (ruled ca. 855–819 BC), whose own younger brother had rebelled against him. Shalmaneser defeated the brother and established good relations with the Babylonians. This aid was later repaid when the same Babylonian king helped Shalmaneser's son, Shamši-Adad V, put down a rebellion in Assyria some years afterward.[74]

During his numerous campaigns, including several against Urartu far to the north, Shalmaneser also battled in the Amanus Mountains, in what is now southeastern Turkey, and "cut down cedar timbers" (aka "cedars of Lebanon") and beams of juniper. He also went further west and south to the area that is today modern Lebanon, which are likely to have been the occasions when he collected some of the tribute depicted on the Balawat gates. One such occurrence is depicted on Band III of the gate that he erected at Balawat. Here the inscription for the upper register reads, "The tribute of the ships of the men of Tyre and Sidon I received." It is accompanied by a scene depicting boats being sailed from the island city of Tyre and goods being off-loaded to the mainland.[75]

Another fragmentary band, which is one of those originally sent to Rassam as a gift and is now in the Walters Art Gallery in Baltimore, shows a second instance of tribute that Shalmaneser received from the Phoenician cities. The accompanying inscription reads: "I received tribute from the cities of the people of Tyre and Sidon: silver, gold, tin, bronze, wool, lapis lazuli, (and) carnelian." These inscriptions and scenes corroborate the account on Shalmaneser's Monolith Inscription, where it states, "The tribute of the kings of the seacoast I received. On the coast of the broad sea I marched righteously and in triumph."[76] They also corroborate what we know about the tribute that Shalmaneser and other Neo-Assyrian kings demanded from Tyre, Sidon, and the other cities on the Phoenician coastline.

FIG. 6. Shalmaneser III at Tyre (note boats in the upper register), from Band III of the Balawat gates. British Museum no. 124661. Photograph courtesy of the British Museum.

Shalmaneser also fought numerous times against the Aramaeans, who by now had settled down in various small city-states, located primarily in what are now parts of Lebanon, Syria, and Iraq. Many of these little kingdoms had names that began with *Bit-* (meaning "House of . . . ," like *Beit* in Hebrew, reflecting the tribal origins in each case)—for example, Bit-Adini, Bit-Zamani, Bit-Aguši, and so on. Ironically, it was Shalmaneser and the Assyrians who helped the Aramaic language to flourish and spread during the ninth century onward—for as he conquered the Aramaeans, he began to employ scribes who could speak and write Aramaic as part of the administrative system designed to help govern the newly captured areas. Other Aramaeans began to function in additional roles within the Assyrian bureaucracy.[77]

Shalmaneser's empire was so far-flung that he also instituted a new mechanism for ensuring that communications could be made in a timely manner. This can best be described as a "Pony Express" system, such as was used in the United States in the 1800s, except that the Assyrians used mules instead of horses. This was an alternative to a single messenger carrying a letter or decree for an entire journey, as had been done previously. Now, the Assyrians set up a relay system along what was known as the "King's Road," in which a rider traveled a set distance and then handed the letter or communication to the next rider, who proceeded to the next point on the route and handed it to the next rider, and so on until it reached its destination. This was obviously much faster but not as secure as sending a single, private messenger. This method of speedy communication was used by the Assyrians during the next few centuries.[78]

The Battle of Qarqar

Shalmaneser III's most famous battle—or at least the one most frequently mentioned by historians—is the Battle of Qarqar, which took place in the sixth year of his reign (853 BC). The episode is recorded in the greatest detail on his Monolith Inscription, where it states that he fought against a coalition of twelve kings.

Grayson, the Assyriologist from the University of Toronto, has dubbed this the "Damascus Coalition," for among its number were Hadad-ezer (Adad-idri), the king of Aram-Damascus, who brought 1,200 chariots, 1,200 cavalry, and 20,000 troops to the battlefield. There was also Irhulenu, the king of Hamath, who brought 700 chariots, 700 cavalry, and 10,000 troops; and Ahab, the king of Israel, who brought 2,000 chariots and 10,000 troops (note that this is the first confirmation outside the biblical account for the existence of Ahab, whom we have already met above in the previous chapter). There were also 1,000 troops from Egypt, probably sent by Osorkon II as mentioned, and more who came from the Phoenician cities of Byblos, Arwad, and Tell Arqa (Irqata). All together, the members of the coalition were able to put into the field almost 4,000 chariots and 2,000 cavalry, more than 40,000 infantry, and 1,000 camels.[79]

However, Shalmaneser defeated the coalition of troops who had dared to face him. "I felled with the sword 14,000 troops, their fighting men, (and) rained down upon them destruction as the god Adad would," he says in one inscription. "I filled the plain with their spread-out corpses and <felled> their extensive troops with the sword. The plain was too small to lay the (incredible number of) their bodies flat; the extensive area was not sufficient to accommodate burying all of them. I dammed up the Orontes River with their bodies like a bridge."[80]

The episode is also mentioned in at least five other inscriptions as well. On these, the number of enemy troops that were killed is claimed to have been far more; on one set of clay tablets from the capital city of Aššur, which constituted a version of his annals, and on two monumental statues of bulls that Layard found at Nimrud/Kalhu, Shalmaneser III nearly doubled the number, claiming to have "put to the sword 25,000 of their fighting men (and) captured from them their chariotry, cavalry, (and) military equipment." He also added a new ending, claiming, "To save their lives, they ran away, boarded boats (and) went out upon the sea."[81]

The battle is also depicted on Band IX of the Balawat gates. Here we see the capture of several cities in the region of Hamath, including the city of Qarqar itself, which is on fire. Shalmaneser is seated in a tent, with captured prisoners and looted objects from the city being paraded in front of him.[82]

Some years later, Shalmaneser said that he again received tribute from the Phoenician cities Sidon and Tyre, during his eighteenth year on the throne. There are various versions of this inscription; in one version it specifically says that the tribute was from "Ba'ali-manzer of Tyre," who is mentioned immediately before "Jehu of the house of Omri" in the inscription. He can probably be identified with Baal-ma'zer [Baal-azor] II (855–830 BC) of Tyre, as named by Josephus, the later Roman historian.[83]

Shalmaneser also received tribute "from the land of Musri," that is, Egypt, which is still known as "Misraim" in modern Hebrew. The tribute from the latter included "two-humped camels, a water buffalo, a rhinoceros, an antelope, female elephants, (and) apes." It was originally thought that the pharaoh at the time would have been Takelot II, but since Osorkon II's reign has now been extended to 831 BC, it is more likely that he is the one who gave this tribute. Another Shalmaneser inscription says that he again received tribute from Tyre, Sidon, and Byblos three years later, in 838 BC.[84]

At about the same time, from ca. 839 BC onward, Shalmaneser also turned his attention toward southeastern Anatolia, to a region and kingdom known as Tabal, which had been established in the aftermath of the Hittite collapse in the region. He promptly defeated the Syro-Hittite kings there, as well as those ruling nearby in an area of Cilicia known at that time as Adanawa (alternatively called Que in Assyrian inscriptions and Hiyawa or Adana in various Luwian inscriptions). It is worth noting that, as Trevor Bryce has pointed out, the name "Hiyawa" comes from "Ahhiyawa"—the name by which the Hittites referred to the Mycenaeans, which may indicate that there had been a migration from mainland Greece to this area immediately following the Bronze Age Collapse.[85]

Hazael and Jehu

In the years following the battle fought at Qarqar by Shalmaneser III in 853 BC, he crossed the Euphrates numerous additional times and fought in Syria during several more campaigns, including against various additional permutations of the so-called Damascus Coalition, which I have noted was originally led by Hadad-ezer, the king of Damascus. These took place during his sixth, tenth, eleventh, fourteenth, eighteenth, twenty-first, and twenty-second years. During the last campaigns, the annals mention a new Aramaean king of Damascus, not Hadad-ezer, but Hazael, who is described as "son of a nobody"—meaning that he was a usurper.[86]

Thus far, I have not devoted nearly as much space to the Aramaeans in these pages as I should have. Overall, they never unified and seem to have primarily identified with their individual small kingdoms or city-states. However, this new ruler of Aram-Damascus, Hazael, appears to have had other things in mind. I have already mentioned him above, in connection with the Tel Dan Stele, which he probably set up after campaigning in the area late in the 840s BC. He is also now thought to have attacked a number of additional sites in the northern kingdom of Israel at about the same time, quite possibly including Megiddo and Hazor.[87]

Of particular interest is the fact that in addition to invoking the House of David, Hazael's inscription at Tel Dan mentions two specific kings, Joram of Israel and Ahaziah of Judah, who were ruling at the time of Hazael and who apparently fell victim to his campaigns, for he says that he killed them both. Intriguingly, this inscription parallels a discussion in the Hebrew Bible, where the same two kings (Joram and Ahaziahu) are killed, not by Hazael, but by a disloyal army officer named Jehu—the same Jehu whose name was mentioned previously in the discussion of the apiary at the site of Tel Rehov and whom I have just mentioned again above.

According to the biblical account, Jehu's assassinations took place in the aftermath of a battle fought at Ramoth-Gilead, following which he promptly usurped the throne in Israel, taking over as king immediately thereafter. Joram's mother, the infamous Jezebel, who was the widow of King Ahab and the daughter of Ethbaal, the Phoenician king of Tyre, was also murdered during this insurrection (see 2 Kings 9:14–16, 22–28, 32–37, 10: 1–17; 2 Chronicles 22:5–9).

It is unclear why the story of Jehu in the Hebrew Bible and the inscription at Tel Dan erected by Hazael have so many similar elements yet identify different assassins for the two kings. It has been suggested that perhaps Jehu was acting on behalf of Hazael, but this is still a matter of scholarly dispute, especially since the biblical account does not mention Hazael nor does Hazael's inscription mention Jehu.[88]

However, Shalmaneser III once again becomes relevant here, for he seems to have gotten the best of Hazael almost immediately afterward, in 841 BC. During the campaign of his eighteenth year, Shalmaneser says, "To save his life, he [Hazael] ran away (but) I pursued (him). I imprisoned him in Damascus, his royal city, (and) cut down his gardens." He also says that he killed 16,000 of Hazael's fighting men and captured 1,121 of his chariots and 470 of his cavalry that year, but then had to fight him again three years later, in 838 BC.[89]

It has now been suggested that Hazael rebounded from his defeat(s) at the hands of Shalmaneser III and may have wreaked havoc in the southern kingdom of Judah during the ensuing decades, including at the site of Tell es-Safi (biblical Gath), one of the five original Philistine cities, where a huge rock-cut siege ditch some two and a half kilometers in length has now been uncovered by archaeologists. The conquest of Gath by Hazael is attested in 2 Kings 12:17 ("At that time King Hazael of Aram went up, fought against Gath, and took it"), just before we are told that he also marched on Jerusalem, only withdrawing when he had been bribed by King Jehoash of Judah (2 Kings 12:18).[90]

A huge destruction has also been dated to this same time, which brought an end to Stratum IV at Tel Rehov, Jehu's probable hometown. It has been suggested that this too was at the hands of Hazael and his invading forces. The damage done was so great that the lower mound at the site was never occupied again; only the upper mound continued to be inhabited for another century, until it too was destroyed, this time by Tiglath-Pileser III and the Neo-Assyrians in 732 BC.[91]

It has also been suggested that Hazael's campaign(s) in the south may have been aimed at controlling the copper trade, in particular the sources in Edom. It is true that copper mining activities in the Arabah Valley and Wadi Faynan suddenly came to a halt at this time, though a resurgence of activity in the mines on Cyprus may have had an effect as well as Hazael's activities; it has also just been suggested that a lack of available fuel for the furnaces may have been the real reason that the mines were shut down at this time.[92]

At some point, Hazael also apparently campaigned either further to the north or to the east, after which he is thought to have inscribed and dedicated various items at the Temple of Hadad in Damascus. Several of these have now been recovered in archaeological contexts, but very far removed from Damascus. The first to be found, about a century ago, is a bronze horse blinker that came to light within the sanctuary of Apollo at Eretria on mainland Greece, of all places. Originally placed next to a horse's eye and used to focus its gaze straight ahead during battle, the piece had most likely been dedicated at the sanctuary by a worshipper at some point during the late eighth century BC. A different dedicant left a triangular piece of bronze known as a "frontlet," which protected the horse's forehead, at the Heraion (the sanctuary of Hera) on Samos, in a context dating to the early sixth century BC. The two pieces are most likely from the same set of horse trappings, for they are both identically inscribed in Aramaic: "That which Hadad gave our lord Hazael from 'Umqi [or 'Amqi] in the year that our lord crossed the river." It's not clear how either of these pieces reached the Aegean so long after their initial manufacture, but it has been suggested that they may have been looted from the Temple of Hadad when Tiglath-Pileser III conquered Damascus in 732 BC.[93]

Nota Kourou, of the University of Athens, also reports that there is "an unpublished bronze incense burner from the sanctuary of Apollo at Delphi" that may have a similar inscription. There is also a second bronze horse blinker, found by archaeologists in the same area at Eretria and in an eighth century BC context, though it is uninscribed and may be from a separate set, since both are reportedly for the right eye.[94]

However, there are also differences of opinion regarding how to interpret the inscription on some of these pieces: is it Hazael or the horse trappings that are from 'Umqi/'Amqi? If it is the objects that are from 'Umqi, then one may hypothesize a campaign by Hazael to northern Syria, for the area of Tell Tayinat was sometimes called Unqi/Umqi by the Neo-Assyrians at this point. However, 'Amqi is also a name used for the Beqa region in Lebanon during the Bronze Age, and so it is possible that this is simply a description of Hazael's origins—"Hazael from 'Amqi." That would mean that he simply conducted a generic campaign across the Euphrates River rather than going farther to the north.[95] At the moment, it is impossible to decide between these two possibilities.

Wrapping Things Up

Less than a year after Jehu took over the throne of Israel, which he ruled from 841 to 814 BC, he also had to face Shalmaneser III, just as Hazael did, and promptly surrendered. On a six-foot-tall stone monument known as the Black Obelisk, found at Nimrud/Kalhu by Layard and now in the British Museum, Jehu is shown kneeling in obeisance in front of Shalmaneser. In the accompanying caption, he is described as "of Bit-Humri" (i.e., the "House of Omri") and is listed as giving tribute, which included "silver, gold, a gold bowl, a gold tureen, gold vessels,

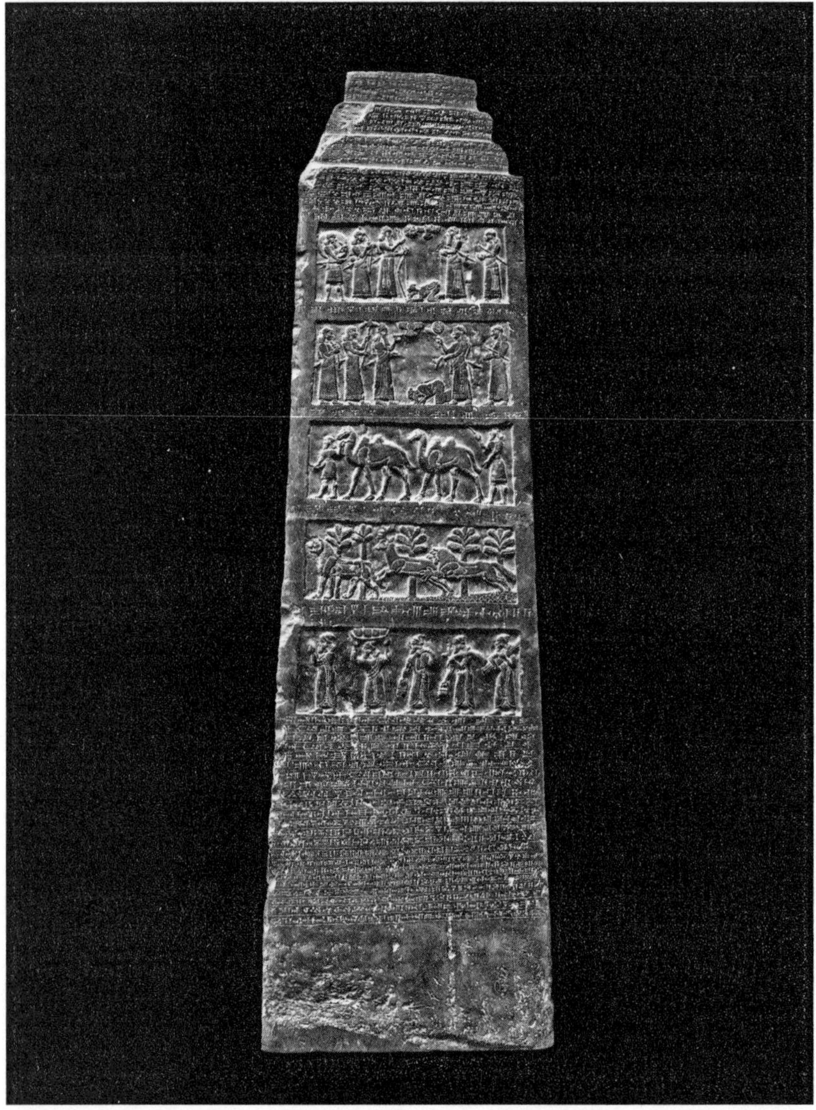

FIG. 7. Black Obelisk of Shalmaneser III, with the submission of Jehu. British Museum no. 118885. Photograph courtesy of the British Museum.

gold pails, tin, the staffs of the king's hand, (and) spears." Surprisingly, as Tammi Schneider of the Claremont Graduate School in California and others have pointed out, this episode of Jehu bowing in front of Shalmaneser and presenting tribute is not mentioned anywhere in the Hebrew Bible.[96]

A few decades later, Adad-nirari III came to the throne of Assyria, ruling from 810 to 783 BC. He claims to have registered important victories during his reign, including a number that took place in what is today modern-day Syria and Israel. In one text, known as the Tell er-Rimah stela, Adad-nirari describes subduing "the entire lands Amurru (and) Hatti"—that is to say, most of Syria. He specifically says that he received a huge tribute from the king of Damascus, which included 2,000 talents of silver, 1,000 talents of copper, 2,000 talents of iron, and "3,000 linen garments with multi-colored trim." In the very next sentence inscribed on the stela, he boasts that he also "received the tribute of Joash, the Samaritan" (i.e., Joash/Jehoash, the king of Israel, who ruled from ca. 804 to 789 BC), which is also not mentioned anywhere in the Bible, as well as from "the people of Tyre (and) Sidon," so it seems clear that his campaign extended far to the south.[97]

In a second text, known as the Calah inscription found at Nimrud, Adad-nirari claims to have received even larger amounts of tribute from the king of Damascus: "2,300 talents of silver, 20 talents of gold, 3,000 talents of bronze, 5,000 talents of ivory, linen garments with multi-colored trim, an ivory bed, (and) a couch with inlaid ivory." He also specifically says that all of the kings in Babylonia had become his vassals and that he conquered (or subdued) all of coastal Syria and all of the southern Levant, including "Tyre, Sidon, Humri [Samaria/Israel], Edom, (and) Palastu, as far as the great sea in the west (i.e., the Mediterranean)." As far as we know, this seems to be the first reference in an Assyrian inscription to "Palastu," that is, Philistia and the Philistines proper. We may note also that he specifically mentions Edom as well as the northern kingdom of Israel, in addition to Tyre and Sidon.[98]

This was just the beginning of Assyrian imperial expansion, however, which we know in great detail. Not more than a few decades after Adad-nirari's rule, Assyrian kings including Tiglath-Pileser III, Shalmaneser V, and Sargon II attacked and then finally destroyed the northern kingdom of Israel by 720 BC. Not long thereafter, Sennacherib battered the southern kingdom of Judah in 701 BC, during which time the city of

Lachish was destroyed and Jerusalem was besieged. These events are described in both the Hebrew Bible and Assyrian inscriptions, but they are outside the parameters of my discussions here and so I shall have to leave their story for another time.

Later Neo-Assyrian kings extended the rule of the empire as far as Egypt, Arabia, Iran, and Turkey, to put it in modern geographical and political terms, but eventually they fell to the resurgent Neo-Babylonian Empire at the end of the seventh century BC, just as the Neo-Babylonians would ultimately fall in turn to the Persians later in the sixth century BC. Those events also lie outside the story I am telling here, but we can already see that the numerous kingdoms and empires of the Late Bronze Age were eventually succeeded in the first millennium by even larger empires—Assyria, followed by Babylonia, Persia, Greece, and then Rome—whose territories stretched across the ancient Near East one after the other.

Brief Summation

So, in brief, what have we learned from this fast-paced and ultimately cursory examination of Mesopotamia in the centuries following the Late Bronze Age Collapse?

To put it concisely, it is clear that both the Assyrians and Babylonians initially succeeded in weathering the Collapse and the period of transformation from the Bronze Age to the Iron Age, but both civilizations were then belatedly impacted by drought, famine, and plague before coming to the fore again. It took the Assyrians two centuries to return, with a vengeance, in the late tenth and early ninth centuries BC, as the weather took a turn for the better, becoming wetter and thereby easing the drought conditions, though the Babylonians had to wait their turn until near the end of the seventh century BC.[99]

Elam initially survived virtually unscathed, only to be crushed and essentially eliminated as a power by the Babylonians by the end of the twelfth century; current sources indicate that they did not return until toward the end of the eighth century BC, as mentioned. We must also acknowledge the Arameans, who took advantage of the chaos following the Collapse to establish themselves as a presence across the ancient Near East during these centuries.

And, of course, during their empire building, the Assyrians impacted, influenced, and/or invaded virtually all of the other societies discussed in this book, including the Phoenicians and the Cypriots. We will consider them next.

CHAPTER THREE

The Mediterranean Became a Phoenician Lake

(Phoenicia and Cyprus)

Generations of schoolchildren, at least in the United States, have been taught that the Phoenicians are best known and remembered for their writing system. It was adopted (and adapted) in the Aegean and then later in Italy, forming the basis of what we now know as the Greek alphabet and the Latin alphabet (with the latter being used today to write English, French, German, Italian, Spanish, Czech, Turkish, and numerous other languages). It was also widely used in Iron Age Canaan, where modified versions soon developed and were used to write inscriptions in Old Hebrew, Aramaic, Moabite, Ammonite, and Edomite. Other modern languages that use writing systems considered to be derived directly or indirectly from Phoenician include Syriac, Arabic (through Nabataean Aramaic), and even Cyrillic (primarily by way of the Greek alphabet).[1]

The plaudits first began with the later Greeks. Herodotus, for example, said that the Phoenicians "came with Cadmus from Phoenicia to the land now called Boeotia," that is, settling in central Greece, and founding the city of Thebes. Moreover, he said, "These Phoenicians who came with Cadmus . . . brought with them to Hellas, among many other kinds of learning, the alphabet, which had been unknown before this, I think, to the Greeks." He continued, "As time went on, the sound and the form of the letters were changed. At this time the Greeks who were settled around them were for the most part Ionians, and after being taught the letters by the Phoenicians, they used them with a few changes of form. In so doing, they gave to these characters the name of Phoenician, as was quite fair seeing that the Phoenicians had brought them into Greece."[2]

Other ancient authors made similar statements, including Diodorus Siculus, a Greek historian who was born in Sicily and wrote during the first century BC. He says "when Cadmus brought from Phoenicia the letters, as they are called, Linus [a local scholar] was again the first to transfer them into the Greek language, to give a name to each character, and to fix its shape. Now the letters, as a group, are called 'Phoenician' because they were brought to the Greeks from the Phoenicians."[3]

However, he also says, "And in reply to those who say that the Syrians are the discoverers of the letters, the Phoenicians having learned them from the Syrians and then passed them on to the Greeks, and that these Phoenicians are those who sailed to Europe together with Cadmus and this is the reason why the Greeks call the letters 'Phoenician,' men tell us, on the other hand, that the Phoenicians were not the first to make this discovery, but that they did no more than to change the forms of the letters, whereupon the majority of mankind made use of the way of writing them as the Phoenicians devised it, and so the letters received the designation we have mentioned above."[4]

Most modern scholars agree with Diodorus Siculus. Rather than inventing the alphabet, the Phoenicians most likely simply standardized it. Moreover, some scholars would argue that it was not actually an alphabet, as we currently define it, but rather what's known as an "abjad"—which has only consonants and no vowels. It was the Greeks who modified the Phoenician script so that both long and short vowels were marked, and thus created what we now know as the Greek alphabet. What was important about the standardization and spread of the alphabet by the Phoenicians, and what made it so revolutionary, is that alphabetic writing is not as complicated as the non-alphabetic writing systems of ancient Mesopotamia and Egypt. This, in turn, meant that literacy rates could potentially rise, since anyone, from the lowest levels of society to the highest, could now learn how to read and write with greater ease. In short, literacy was no longer necessarily limited to a select few, as it had been during the Bronze Age.[5]

We also frequently credit the Phoenicians for manufacturing purple dye and for sailing the Mediterranean for centuries virtually untouched, establishing colonies and trading with people from Cyprus to North Africa to Spain. The most famous of the cities that they founded was Carthage, which would challenge Rome hundreds of years later, during the Punic Wars, while the dye that they made was prized over the centuries. Strabo, for example, says, "[T]he Phoenicians in general have been superior to all peoples of all times, and by means of their dye-houses for purple; for the Tyrian purple has proved itself by far the most beautiful of all; and the shell-fish are caught near the coast; and the other things requisite for dyeing are easily got; and although the great number of dye-works makes the city unpleasant to live in, yet it makes the city rich through the superior skill of its inhabitants."[6]

However, just as with the alphabet, the Phoenicians may have simply perfected the creation of purple dye, rather than "inventing" it. There is now evidence that such dye was already being created and used in the Bronze Age Aegean as well as on Cyprus centuries earlier, from the early second millennium on, and was then used both there and in the Near East throughout the Late Bronze Age.[7]

"Phoenicians" was not what they called themselves, of course, but that is what the later Greeks called them, including Homer in both the *Iliad* and the *Odyssey*. As Oxford historian Josephine Quinn has recently written, "'Phoenician' was a label [that] Greek writers used for Levantine mariners who spoke similar dialects of a language very different from their own. The term implied little about those people's cultural or ancestral ties, and it apparently meant nothing to the people themselves: no one from the coastal cities or their overseas colonies ever to our knowledge described themselves as 'Phoenician.'"[8]

Rather than calling themselves Phoenicians (as the Greeks did), these coastal denizens may have continued to call themselves

Canaanites (as did their Hebrew-speaking kin; see, e.g., Genesis 10:1–20), though this is a matter of scholarly debate. Even more likely is that they identified themselves as inhabitants of specific and separate city-states abutting the Mediterranean Sea—primarily Tyre, Sidon, Beirut, Byblos, and Arwad. Their combined territory lay principally in what is now modern Lebanon, but their control stretched further north into what we would today call Syria and all the way down to the south of Akko in what is now northern Israel.[9]

Whatever we call them, or they called themselves, it is clear that the Phoenicians were not newcomers to the area, as has been previously suggested in the past. Instead, it is now generally accepted that the majority, if not all, of the people in these cities were Canaanites who had survived the Collapse of the Bronze Age in this central coastal region of the Levant. Each of these cities had existed in Bronze Age Canaan and continued to thrive during the Iron Age. Although the evidence is still scanty from the larger sites, in part because of difficulties of access to remains buried under the modern cities, excavation data from smaller sites currently appears to indicate that the inhabitants of the region made the transition peacefully. They may actually have been among the most resilient of the peoples whom we are examining in this book, for they not only apparently carried on from the initial Canaanite city-states but even flourished in the vacuum created by the Collapse.[10]

In fact, it seems that the inhabitants of these cities either pivoted from, or perhaps simply expanded, the role that their predecessors in these same polities had played during the Late Bronze Age. They now assumed a new (or perhaps larger) role as independent traders and merchants, transporting many different sorts of goods across and around the Mediterranean and Aegean Seas. As Carol Bell, a British ancient historian and archaeologist, has described it, "Phoenicia's trading ventures shifted to the west and, from an economic point of view at least, the Mediterranean became a Phoenician lake."[11]

Christopher Monroe of Cornell University has elaborated on this, suggesting that the Phoenicians began sailing on "multiple preexisting routes via multiple ports known to sailors for a long time." He envisions these as essentially forming "a commercial information network produced by centuries of departures not only from Tyre but also Sidon, Arvad, Byblos, Ugarit, Kition, et cetera," and therefore credits the Phoenicians with eventually "creating the largest information network the world had ever seen by the tenth century BC."[12]

Thus, we may well suggest that the Canaanite survivors in these cities, now identified by specific city (e.g., Sidon) or simply rechristened as generic "Phoenicians" by the Greeks as early as the time of the Homeric epics, were more than simply resilient in the face of the Collapse. They might be better referred to as "anti-fragile," to borrow a term from Nassim Nicholas Taleb. He is the same man who popularized the phrase "black swan," used to describe an unexpected event, like the Collapse of the Bronze Age. According to Taleb, "anti-fragile" can be used to describe a situation in which an entity exhibits more than just resiliency or robustness, and actually "thrives under the right amount of stress"—taking advantage of the situation not only to survive but to flourish. Taleb describes it specifically as "things that gain from disorder."[13] In the case of the Phoenicians, they seem to have actively taken advantage of the chaos and, most important, of the destruction of Ugarit in northern Syria, to take over the maritime trade routes to the west, across the Aegean to Greece and thence further to Italy, Sicily, and Sardinia.

They may have also been trading to the east, for there is some indication that cinnamon may have been arriving from southeast Asia; traces have been found in some ten Phoenician flasks from this period, found at three different sites in what is now northern Israel, including at Tel Dor. It is now clear, in fact, from a variety of recent finds at sites such as Tel Dor, Tell Erani, and Tell es-Safi, that although there was much less trade going on in the Iron I southern Levant than in the Late Bronze Age, there was no cessation.[14]

Cyprus and the Change to Iron Technology

As for Cyprus, there is no doubt that the island and its inhabitants faced many of the same conditions during the twelfth century BC as elsewhere in the ancient Near East, in the immediate aftermath of the Collapse. However, although the situation is complex, the inhabitants of the island also appear to have been as resilient as the Phoenicians, not only coping and adapting but showing innovation and transforming to the new situation almost immediately. Their survival may well have been due in part to the wealth and prestige accumulated through the development of ironworking, which must be ranked with the alphabet as one of the great innovations of this age.

We can see this far away at the site of Perati, located on mainland Greece some twenty miles east of Athens on the other side of the Attica peninsula, near modern Porto Rafti. Here there is a large and very well-known cemetery that dates to the twelfth century BC. Among the grave goods left by grieving families in the burials of their loved ones are iron knives with bronze rivets. Similar ones have been found at the sites of Tylissos on Crete and Lefkandi on Euboea and on a few islands such as Naxos and Thasos. These bimetallic knives are some of the earliest examples of worked iron artifacts that have been found in the Aegean and Eastern Mediterranean. They all appear to have been made on Cyprus and were exported from there to various destinations, ranging from the Aegean to the southern Levant.[15]

These finds have led to a major change in our thinking, for it is now frequently suggested that it was most likely the innovative metalsmiths on Cyprus who were responsible for the shift from bronze to iron at this time, rather than the Dorians or the Sea Peoples as previous generations of scholars had suggested. Susan Sherratt, an archaeologist now at the University of Sheffield, has in fact called the Cypriots "nothing short of brilliant" for what she sees as their leading role in the dissemination not only of these objects but also the technology that was involved.[16]

It is true that later Greek authors, such as Strabo, Xenophon, and Apollonius of Rhodes, mention iron technology in connection with people whom they call variously the Chalybes, Chalybians, or Chaldoi, living and working in Anatolia, on the shores of the Pontus, aka the Black Sea, but that likely represents the situation centuries later, if it is even accurate.[17] In any event, it is probably not necessary to go that far afield, either chronologically or geographically.

We know, for example, that iron was already familiar to the powers-that-be during the Bronze Age, as shown by individual iron objects found in contexts dating to the centuries before the Collapse in Egypt, Anatolia, Greece, Mesopotamia, and elsewhere (although the Hittites did not have an initial monopoly on it, as used to be thought). However, many, and perhaps most, of these were made from iron found in meteorites, including a dagger with a gold hilt and an iron blade found in Tutankhamun's tomb, which may have originally been a wedding present from Tushratta, king of Mitanni, to Pharaoh Amenhotep III decades earlier.[18] Manufactured iron objects made from terrestrial ore deposits did not come into widespread everyday use until after the Collapse.

Since the metalsmiths on Cyprus and elsewhere apparently did not begin working extensively with iron until they absolutely had to, previous scholarly hypotheses for the increasing popularity of iron in the years after the Collapse favored the suggestion that there may have been a temporary lack of tin or even of copper, that is, the components of bronze, which necessitated a turn to local resources. This would have been especially true if any of the trade routes, such as those bringing tin from Afghanistan or elsewhere in Central Asia, were cut or affected by the collapse of the Late Bronze Age palatial economies.[19]

Thus, several decades ago, during the 1970s and 1980s, scholars were already stating that the change to iron was not really an advance but more like a reaction to "straitened circumstances" (i.e., lack of access to tin and/or copper). Such scholars also pointed out that the greatest initial impact of the new emphasis on iron was on crafts and farming, that is, ploughs, sickles, chisels, and saws, rather than on weapons and fighting.[20]

However, more recently, others have suggested that, even if there had been supply chain disruptions, there might not have been such a dire lack of bronze, copper, or tin, as had been previously supposed, and that copper was still being mined on Cyprus throughout the Iron Age, though the inhabitants may have been sending most of it west, for example, to Sardinia. Vasiliki Kassianidou, a specialist in archaeometallurgy and ancient technology at the University of Cyprus, has stated, for instance, "At the time of the 'Crisis Years' . . . Cyprus managed to ride the storm and survive. Cypriot merchants reached out to new markets which demanded large quantities of copper, such as Sardinia, and looked for new sources of tin and precious metals, the supply of which from the east had been disrupted."[21]

The change to iron may therefore have been the result of a simple economic decision, especially as iron began to increase in prestige. "In many regions, the adoption of iron did not represent an abandonment of bronze," Cranfield University archaeologist Nathaniel Erb-Satullo has argued. "In some areas, at least, early iron initially may have served more as an addition to an expanding metal economy, rather than as a replacement for bronze." Iron ore was readily available in many areas, including Italy and on the Greek mainland, which would have been useful as the technology spread.[22]

It also may not have been as difficult as some might suppose to turn to the production of iron, especially if the new technology came about as a by-product of mining and smelting copper ore that was rich in iron, as has been suggested. Kassianidou has said that "Cypriot metallurgists, supported by almost a thousand years of expertise with sulphide ore smelting, during which some iron may have been accidentally produced along with the copper, would have come across this new material and surely have experimented with it, employing the tools and skills of their trade." She notes, however, that once the iron is ready to be worked, it involves a very different process than working with copper, for "iron is based on mechanically forging a solid metal to shape and hardening by carburisation and quenching, copper on casting a liquid metal and hardening by cold-working."[23]

Nevertheless, working with iron seems to have caught on in Cyprus fairly quickly. It is, in fact, not out of the question that exporting iron objects, as well as disseminating knowledge of the technology required, may have been one of the factors that allowed the Cypriots to survive the Collapse and even flourish to a certain extent afterward, as Kassianidou has suggested. It has even been proposed that the Cypriots may have brought this knowledge all the way to Italy, Sicily, and Sardinia, for the trade routes between Cyprus and the Western Mediterranean were still operating at this time.[24]

However, these western regions, including possibly Sardinia, had also been affected by the Bronze Age Collapse. It now seems apparent, for example, that the Terramare culture in the Po Valley of northern Italy had also sustained a crisis and collapse at the end of the thirteenth and beginning of the twelfth century BC, and that there may have been a huge migration of people out of the southern part of this region, which was subsequently abandoned for several centuries, and a reorganization in the number and size of the settlements in the northern part of this area.[25]

So, while the reasons for the shift to iron remain a matter of debate, the possible motivations now suggested are generally more nuanced than previously. It is clear, however, that large-scale adoption of iron did not take place before the Collapse and seems to have been a response to events rather than a cause. It is also seen as having taken place at different times in different areas, though not earlier than the latter part of the twelfth century or into the first half of the eleventh century, as the technology was disseminated, and each region's metalsmiths mastered it in turn. Cyprus may have been first, or at least one of the first, but ironworking soon caught on in mainland Greece and elsewhere as well, undoubtedly ameliorated by the common availability of iron ore in virtually all the lands of the Mediterranean and Near East.

Thus, from what we can tell, and perhaps just like the Phoenicians, the Cypriots may have even flourished to a certain extent amid the chaos. As Carol Bell writes, "Cyprus and Phoenicia were able to seize the day when crisis struck the region. Unencumbered by imperial agendas, and already familiar with operating within a decentralised trading environment, traders and merchants from these two regions remained open for business, with their primary objective being to generate sufficient returns to continue to trade."[26]

We are, however, moving a bit more into the unknown here, since we have no lengthy inscriptions or other detailed written records from the island to give us concrete information as to the history of this period. We can only make educated guesses as to the actual political and economic circumstances on the island at this time, based on the archaeological evidence that has been found. However, there is, in fact, quite a bit of information that we can glean from these finds on Cyprus, including changes in burial customs and/or grave goods, new types of pottery, and the sudden abandonment or new establishment of various sites, though there is more for some periods than for others.

Overall, our understanding of Cyprus in the immediate aftershock of the Collapse, and in the centuries thereafter, has changed dramatically in just the past few decades. For example, despite the fact that Cyprus was clearly affected by the problems that were occurring elsewhere in the Mediterranean at that time, and despite the various destructions and evidence of disruptions at specific sites in the early twelfth century, including at Kition, Enkomi, Maa-Palaeokastro, Pyla-Kokkinokremmos, Kalavasos-Ayios Dhimitrios, Sinda, and Maroni, it is now generally agreed that there was not actually an overall islandwide collapse. Moreover, any population changes on Cyprus, previously viewed by earlier scholars as invasions and conquests, are now seen as more complex.[27]

Some scholars—like Maria Iacovou of the University of Cyprus—now argue that, despite the problems, what we see here on Cyprus is continuity from the Bronze Age to the Iron Age and that we should not suppose a huge break between the two periods on the island, but perhaps more of a reorientation. She argues that Cyprus was less affected by the Collapse than other areas in the Aegean and Eastern Mediterranean and that its people were able to adapt to the new reality rather quickly. Not everyone agrees entirely, and others have suggested that the island and its population may have been affected to a greater degree; the problem at the moment is that the archaeological evidence currently available is not specifically conclusive one way or the other.[28]

Regardless, all of this also represents a major shift in scholarly thinking. Back in the 1970s and then continuing through at least the early 1990s, the debates were still all about whether there were one or two waves of migrations to Cyprus from the Aegean at the end of the Bronze Age and the early decades of the Iron Age. It was thought that all advancements made during this period, including perhaps the development of iron technology, should be attributed to the arrival of displaced Mycenaeans arriving as refugees or the like. Now, the concept of such a migration is criticized and castigated as a colonialist attitude, perhaps rightly so.[29]

It has been replaced, or is in the process of being replaced, by suggestions that the population on Cyprus after the Collapse was of a hybrid nature, an agglomeration of different ethnicities and original nationalities as it were. It is, thus, a bit problematic to speak generically of "Cypriots" during these centuries, since there were undoubtedly people of numerous different ethnicities living on the island at this time, including Greeks and Phoenicians in addition to the local inhabitants.[30] So the use of the term "Cypriots" during this period should be understood to include not only the local survivors from the Late Bronze Age but also any newcomers who may have arrived in the aftermath.

———

Although Cyprus as a whole survived the Collapse, there is also archaeological evidence that toward the end of the twelfth century BC and into the early eleventh century, several Cypriot cities that had been important during the Bronze Age were abandoned, though usually for fairly prosaic and obvious reasons. It was at this time, for instance, that Hala Sultan Tekke, which had been a flourishing port throughout the Late Bronze Age with international connections both east and west, was abandoned when its harbor silted up. It is from the area around this site that Kaniewski and his team collected pollen data showing that the climate had changed to be more arid, and that the area was subjected to drought during the period from ca. 1200 to 850 BC. Whether it was the effects of climate change that caused the harbor to silt up is unknown, but regardless, the city's inhabitants are thought to have moved en masse to nearby Kition. The same goes for Enkomi, whose inhabitants relocated to a new city called Salamis just three kilometers away, after their own harbor also silted up at the beginning of the eleventh century BC.[31]

We see similar occurrences also at other major settlements such as Kalavasos-Ayios Dhimitrios and Maroni-Vournes, which had been happily flourishing until then. Given their location near the copper mines in these areas of Cyprus, some scholars have suggested that the abandonment of these cities may have come about because of a (possibly temporary) decreased demand for copper elsewhere in the Mediterranean (though we have just seen that others suggest that there was no decrease in the demand for copper).[32]

Other sites, however, such as Idalion, which would later go on to become of major importance, appear to have been founded at this same approximate time, perhaps to take advantage of the demise of the other cities. New port cities, such as Amathous, were also founded in the transition to the first millennium BC, and other cities, like Kition and Paphos, thrived as well, taking advantage of the massive changes occurring during the period.[33]

As a result of all this, most scholars also agree that political reorganizations almost certainly took place during this period, which would eventually lead to the establishment of the city-states that we can see on the island by the ninth and eighth centuries BC, if not before.

"Warrior Burials" and the Obelos of Opheltas

During previous decades, there has also been much discussion by archaeologists and ancient historians regarding possible migrations and/or colonization of the island by the Greeks in the aftermath of the Collapse. One item in particular, a bronze obelos (essentially a barbeque spit), has attracted a great deal of interest in this regard, for it is inscribed with the earliest known Greek name found on the island—"Opheltas." It is a man's name, written using five Cypro-Minoan syllabic signs, in the Arcado-Cypriot dialect of Greek, and in the genitive case (meaning "of" or "belonging to" Opheltas). It is therefore usually interpreted as the name of the owner of the spit.

It was found in Tomb 49 within the Skales cemetery at Palaepaphos ("Old Paphos"). This is a particularly rich tomb dating to the second half of the eleventh century BC. It was discovered by the well-known Cypriot archaeologist Vassos Karageorghis, who served for decades as director of antiquities on the island. Within the tomb, which contained two "almost intact human skeletons" lying on the floor, with fragments of a third skull found nearby, were three large amphorae, a large bronze strainer, a large bronze bowl, four smaller bronze bowls, a bronze tripod, a bronze spearhead, and three bronze obeloi, including the one inscribed for Opheltas.[34]

Although it might seem like a tangent, it is relevant to note at this point that several of the foundation myths for Iron Age cities on Cyprus, in particular Paphos and Salamis, involved some of the lesser-known heroes from the Trojan War, as well as Phoenicians. The foundation story for Paphos, for instance, gives credit to Agapenor, who had been the king of Tegea in Arcadia back on mainland Greece. While such foundation stories usually have no basis in reality—for instance, Paphos had already been in existence since well before this period—this is admittedly an interesting tidbit of information, given the use of the Arcado-Cypriot dialect to write Opheltas's name on the bronze spit found in the Palaepaphos-Skales cemetery (meaning that there had been some contact between Arcadia and Cyprus around this time, even if perhaps only indirectly).

Similarly, the city of Salamis on Cyprus was supposedly founded by Teukros (Teucer), who is described in Homer's *Iliad* as a legendary archer. He was not only the half-brother of Ajax but also the son of Telamon, who happens to have been the king of the island of Salamis back in Greece, which may explain the similarity of the names. We are also told, by Virgil in the *Aeneid* (1.619–26), that Teukros had help from a king of Sidon named Belos, that is, a Phoenician whose name is otherwise unknown to us.[35] Again, we cannot take these at face value, but it is interesting to see the reflection of Phoenicians, Greeks, and Cypriots in these stories.

However, the grave with Opheltas's bronze barbeque spit is also unusual in another respect, for it is counted among the so-called warrior burials that have been found on Cyprus, Crete, and mainland Greece at this time, dating from the mid-eleventh to the early tenth century BC. These graves almost always included expensive gifts buried with the dead man, who is frequently cremated. Among the grave goods in these burials are weapons, metal vessels, tripods, and spits, all made of bronze or iron. Often there is also a woman buried with the warrior, though in most cases she is not cremated and her relationship to the man is not always clear.[36]

On Cyprus, such graves have been found in cemeteries at Palaepaphos-Skales, Salamis, Lapithos-Kastros, Kourion-Kaloriziki, and Amathous. On Crete, they have been found in the North Cemetery at Knossos, as well as at Amari, where a bronze amphoroid crater held the ashes from a cremation. On mainland Greece, there may be one of these graves at Tiryns, in addition to a very well-known one at Lefkandi on Euboea. We shall return to these burials in the Aegean in chapter 5.[37]

Overall, Cyprus's role as a leader in international trade seems to have continued during this century. As Nota Kourou of the University of Athens, a specialist in Phoenician contacts with the Aegean whom I have previously mentioned, has stated, "the old maritime networks in the Mediterranean remained active in the hands of Cypriots, who even during the 11th century BCE continued their long-distance overseas travels, though at a much smaller scale than before."[38]

By this time, the Cypriots were seriously exporting iron objects, especially knives and swords. Though such iron weapons appear first on Cyprus in the twelfth century, as mentioned above, iron knives are now found in much larger quantities on Crete, the Greek mainland, Syria, and the southern Levant, in contexts dating to the eleventh century BC.[39]

In addition to the iron weapons and tools, finished Cypriot bronze objects such as vessels and stands have been found in eleventh-century BC contexts in the Aegean, especially on Crete. These include a bronze amphoroid crater and other Cypriot-derived items in a tomb at the site of Amari, mentioned above; a bronze stand in the North Cemetery at Knossos; and other items such as bronze bowls with lotus handles. Cypriot objects of this date have also been found as far away as Sardinia, Sicily, and the area of Huelva in Iberia.[40]

Along those lines, Jan Paul Crielaard, an archaeologist at the University of Amsterdam, had already suggested back in 1998 that "members of the Cypriot elite were in touch with high-status individuals in Sardinia and through them with distant areas elsewhere in the west" and that a Mediterranean-wide web of international trade was already beginning to take shape again, at least at an elite level, with the goal of acquiring "exotic goods with high intrinsic and symbolic value."[41]

But what about the non-elite Cypriots? What would it have been like for the ordinary inhabitants of Cyprus at this time, that is, the farmers, tradesmen, metalworkers, miners, and others who made up the middle and lower classes? It is, quite frankly, difficult to say anything about them during this period, for we simply don't have enough evidence at this time to comment one way or the other, but at the very least, it is certainly possible that the people living in smaller settlements, away from the town centers, may not have noticed much change, at least in terms of political structure, despite perhaps having to contend with more arid conditions.[42] For those in the urban areas, especially in the new centers that were founded at this time, and for the elite, it may actually have seemed that the island was continuing to show resilience and transforming in the face of the adverse conditions. Whatever one thinks of the "warrior burials" found on Cyprus and in the Aegean, the Cypriot goods exported both east and west at this time indicate that the Cypriots remained a potent force on the international trade routes and that they were continuing to flourish in the aftermath of the Collapse.

Enterprising Phoenicians in the Eleventh Century

The Phoenicians seem to have been in contact with these areas at this time as well. While we should consider whether Cypriots and Phoenicians were cooperating or competing for western markets at this time, Kourou dismisses this possibility. "The absence of Near Eastern objects during the same period in the Aegean," she says, "strengthens the scenario that the Cypriots were the only possible visitors to . . . Crete and the . . . Mainland."[43] This, though, would seem to be a topic ripe for further discussion.

We do know that the Phoenicians were in contact with Egypt at this point, which is not surprising. In particular, we have the details from a story known as the *Tale of Wenamun*, which was written on a papyrus scroll discovered in 1890 within the same jar at the site of el-Hibah in Egypt as the *Onomasticon of Amenemopet*.

Wenamun was an Egyptian priest who was sent from the Temple of Amon at Karnak to acquire cedars of Lebanon—timber—for a new boat that was to be built and dedicated to the god Amon-Re. His voyage took place probably around the year 1075 BC, during the opening decades of the eleventh century.[44] The story recorded on the scroll begins as follows:

> Year 5, fourth month of the third season, day 16, day on which Wenamun, the Elder of the Portal of the Temple of Amon, [Lord of the Thrones] of the Two Lands, departed to obtain lumber for the great and noble riverine barge of Amon-Re, King of the Gods. . . . On the day when I arrived at Tanis, at the place [where Smen]des and Tanetamon are, I gave them the rescripts from Amon-Re, King of the Gods, and they had them read out in their presence. . . . Smendes and Tanetamon sent me off with the ship captain Mengebet, and I went down to the great Syrian sea.[45]

Wenamun sailed first to the city of Dor, now located in northern Israel, which he described as a "Tjekker" town. "I reached Dor, a Tjekker town," he says, "and Beder, its prince, had fifty loaves, one amphora of wine, and one ox haunch brought to me." The Tjekker were one of the Sea Peoples mentioned in the attack on Egypt during the time of Ramses III and subsequently settled by him in "strongholds bound in my name." They were also one of the three groups mentioned on the *Onomasticon of Amenemopet*.

The site of Tel Dor, south of the modern city of Haifa, which has been under almost continuous excavation by archaeologists since 1990 and which I will mention again in the coming pages, has not yielded much evidence for being a stronghold of defeated Sea Peoples, though the Wenamun passage has been often discussed. Instead, it contains much Phoenician pottery in eleventh-century archaeological levels, which has added much to our knowledge of "southern Phoenicia." Recently, maritime archaeologists from the University of Haifa found evidence for the Iron Age harbor at Dor, which would have been in use during the eleventh and tenth centuries BC. Underwater excavations conducted in just the past few years have shown that what had been thought to be a natural reef is actually part of a well-constructed stone mole, used as a pier or breakwater.[46]

Unfortunately for Wenamun, while docked in the harbor at Dor, a sailor from his own ship stole the precious items designated as payment for the lumber. These items included a golden vessel, four silver jars, and a purse containing pieces of silver. After reporting the theft to the prince of Dor, from whom he received no sympathy and no satisfaction, Wenamun then proceeded farther north into Phoenician territory, to the city of Byblos. There he met the prince of the city—a man named Tjekkerbaal—who was actively hostile, possibly a reflection of Egypt's change in international status. Wenamun's mission had to wait until replacement items were sent from Egypt so the lumber could be paid for and the trees cut down. When the goods finally arrived, they included four gold bowls and another gold vessel; five bowls of silver; ten pieces of clothing; five hundred mats of smooth linen (or rolls of papyrus); five hundred ox hides; five hundred ropes; twenty sacks of lentils; and five baskets of fish.[47]

We are told specifically, "So the prince rejoiced, and he detailed three hundred men and three hundred oxen and assigned supervisors in charge of them to have them fell the timbers. They felled them, and they lay there throughout the winter. In the third month of the third season, they were hauled to the seashore." Wenamun tells us that the wood was loaded onto a ship, and the prince "sent me off from there at the harbor of the sea," heading back to Egypt.

That was not the end of Wenamun's trials and tribulations, however. The ship was blown off course almost immediately and eventually landed in Cyprus. Wenamun was almost killed by townspeople there and was rescued only when Hatiba, the princess of the unnamed town where he now found himself, came to his aid and had the townspeople arrested. The papyrus scroll, and the story, breaks off at this point. We don't know how it ended, though the existence of the tale suggests that Wenamun was ultimately able to get back to Egypt.

This *Tale of Wenamun* has been the subject of much scholarly discussion over the course of the past century. It is still not clear whether it is the official record of an actual historical voyage or a piece of narrative fiction. However, the details of the account ring so true and match so well with the tenor of the times, when Egypt's status on the international stage continued to wane and it faced political fragmentation, that it is usually regarded as reflective of the general era toward the end of the reign of Ramses XI, the last pharaoh of the Twentieth Dynasty (although it might have been written down a bit later, during either the Twenty-First or Twenty-Second Dynasty).[48]

Phoenician Territory and Overseas Contacts

The actual territory of the Phoenicians is a topic of growing interest to archaeologists and ancient historians these days. Part of the problem is that the larger ancient cities in Lebanon generally lie below their modern counterparts and are difficult to dig as a result. Periodic political unrest in the modern country has also slowed the pace of excavation of the key Phoenician cities. As a result, there has been little opportunity to retrieve material from this period in Lebanon at sites other than Tyre, Beirut, the island of Arwad, and Tell Arqa (ancient Irqata). There is also Sarepta, a site identified as biblical Zarephath, located on the coast between Sidon and Tyre, which was excavated by James Pritchard and the University of Pennsylvania in the 1970s. These various excavations have shed some light on Phoenician material culture, especially pottery, but not enough.[49]

However, we now know that Phoenician territory by that time also extended much further to the south, into what is now modern Israel. This is the area currently referred to as "southern Phoenicia" by some scholars, where sites such as Tel Dor have yielded evidence of Phoenician pottery and other remains in Iron Age levels, including silver hoards suggesting Phoenician contacts with Spain. At Dor, a hoard of eight and a half kilograms of hacksilver was found hidden in a ceramic jug covered by a bowl. It was reportedly found near a building that contained Greek pottery from Euboea, in a context that was initially dated to the late eleventh or early tenth centuries BC but is now thought to date to the second half of the tenth century.[50]

The silver in these hoards, at Dor and elsewhere, appears to be from a mixture of sources, among which Iberia (Spain) figures prominently.

Other pieces may come from Anatolia and Sardinia. This is of great interest, for many of the hoards in Israel dated to 1200–950 BC contain silver alloyed with copper. The authors of a study led by Tzilla Eshel at the University of Haifa interpret this dilution to mean that there may have been a shortage of silver following the Collapse at the end of the Late Bronze Age, and that this was why there was such an intensive search for new sources in Anatolia and the Western Mediterranean, which began to be imported by the mid-tenth century BC.[51]

The notion that the Phoenicians may have been importing silver from Spain as early as the eleventh century BC and certainly by the tenth century BC is not only based on analyses of the source of the silver found in Iron Age hoards in the Levant, such as the one at Dor, but also on Phoenician pottery actually found at the site of Huelva in Spain that some argue date as early as the eleventh century. The discovery and exploitation of a new source of silver in Spain would have been a major event of the time. As Mitchell Allen discussed in his 1977 UCLA dissertation, this allowed the Phoenicians great latitude, making them wealthy enough to eventually establish colonies throughout the Mediterranean and especially to help buffer them from takeover by the Assyrians by instead simply paying tribute whenever necessary.[52]

In addition, the nearby site of Tel Shiqmona, close by the modern city of Haifa, has now yielded good evidence for the production of purple dye from at least the tenth century BC and continuing down through the seventh century BC. The finds from the site, which was first excavated in the 1960s and 1970s, have been recently reexamined, especially the numerous pottery sherds, which are still stained purple and blue on the inside. Golan Shalvi and Ayelet Gilboa, both at the University of Haifa, suspect that the site was actively involved in the dye industry. Usually at such sites or nearby, we find only heaps of crushed shells from murex sea snails, which were an integral part of the manufacturing process, but here at Shiqmona there is additional evidence, such as these pottery sherds, which may help to shed additional light on the Phoenicians and the production of purple dye, including in this region of "southern Phoenicia."[53]

If they were traveling as far west as Spain, the Phoenicians would have had to make the journey in stages, including stopping at Cyprus and in the Aegean, perhaps docking at port sites on Crete and mainland Greece. Relevant in this regard are the Phoenician imports dating to this period that have been found on Cyprus, especially in tomb contexts on the west side of the island, such as Palaepaphos. Carol Bell has suggested specifically that the Phoenicians may have used western Cyprus as "a staging post for westward voyages." However, at the moment there are few material remains in the Aegean of Phoenician contacts during the eleventh century BC.[54] That doesn't mean that such contacts did not take place, especially if Phoenician ships were headed further west to Iberia, but we shall have to wait and see what future excavations unearth.

Phoenicians, Cypriots, and Greeks

Similarities between local Greek ceramics and pottery excavated at Tyre in the 1970s suggest that it was specifically the Tyrians who initiated maritime ventures to the Aegean and further west during the tenth century BC.[55] "A kind of small-scale pre-colonisation travelling of the Phoenicians in the beginning of the Early Iron Age is now considered very likely, possibly in the 10th century when the social and political organization of the Phoenicians changed radically," writes Kourou, the Phoenician contacts specialist who teaches at the University of Athens.

She continues, "The 10th century was a crucial period for Phoenicia as it was the time that the ruler of Tyre, Hiram I, succeeded in uniting the coastal cities under his leadership in a kind of commercial, although not yet political union. Hiram was the first to organize the commercial policy of the Phoenicians and to initiate their overseas commercial travels in the Mediterranean at about the end of the 10th century." Of particular interest is her declaration that "[i]t is actually now, i.e. in the second half of the 10th c., that both Phoenicians and Greeks try anew, after the end of the Bronze Age, to cross long distances for trade."[56]

Euboea, and specifically Lefkandi, as well as Knossos and Kommos on Crete, are the areas in the Aegean that have yielded the earliest Phoenician artifacts to date. It is at Kommos on the southern coast of Crete where some two hundred to more than three hundred sherds (according to various reports) of Phoenician pottery have been found in the Greek sanctuary at the site. The sanctuary is dated as early as the second half of the tenth century (though the sherds could come from as late as the ninth century, according to the most recent ceramic analyses).[57]

During the course of this century, Phoenician objects found on Crete and mainland Greece increase in number. It is by this time, some scholars have suggested, that this region was being used as a jumping off point for Phoenician ships heading much further west, toward Carthage or even Spain. Other scholars have even suggested that by this point there were Phoenician, North Syrian, or other Near Eastern emigrants living at sites like Knossos and Kommos on Crete or at Lefkandi or Athens on the Greek mainland.[58]

In return, there are a number of Greek sherds from this time period that have been found at various sites in the Levant, including at Byblos, Tyre, and Sarepta, as well as farther south in present-day Israel, including at Tel Dor. However, not least from the evidence at Lefkandi, it appears that Phoenicians may have now been joined by the Cypriots in sailing west and initiating sustained contacts with the Aegean and beyond. Cypriot and Near Eastern objects are almost always found together in Aegean contexts, such as the Cypriot bowl with a Phoenician inscription from the Tekke cemetery at Knossos and the sherds of Phoenician pottery found at Kommos. There are also other Cypriot items found on Crete at Fortetsa and in the North Cemetery of Knossos.[59]

The tenth century is usually seen as continuing the period of transition on Cyprus, but few studies discuss this period in any great detail, as there is little data specifically available at the present time. If it is mentioned at all, it is usually either in tandem with the developments during the eleventh century that we have seen above and setting the stage for the changes that were to come in the eighth century BC, or specifically in terms of the mortuary evidence from the various cemeteries.[60]

Kings of Byblos and Tyre

We do not know the names of any of the rulers on Cyprus during this period, apart from the literary mention of Queen (or Princess) Hatiba from the *Tale of Wenamun*, but we do have inscriptions providing the names of six kings of Byblos who ruled during the tenth and early ninth centuries BC: Ahiram, Ethbaal, Yehimilk, Abibaal, Elibaal, and Shipitbaal.[61] In fact, of all the Phoenician cities, we may know the most about Byblos with respect to its rulers during the tenth century BC.

Byblos had long been active on the international scene. Back in the early fourteenth century BC dozens of letters were sent by its king, Rib-Hadda, to the pharaohs Amenhotep III and his son Akhenaten, and were kept in their archives at Amarna in Egypt, where they were discovered in 1887.[62] It was also Byblos that was Wenamun's destination ca. 1075 BC, when it was ruled by Tjekkerbaal (aka Zakarbaal).

Now we have these six additional names, which come to us from inscriptions left by the various rulers of Byblos themselves. As a group, they have been known and debated by scholars for more than a century. In each case, we are told the name of the present king and then his ancestry going back one or more generations. For instance, we know of the king named Ahiram and his son Ethbaal from an inscription carved into the lid of a sarcophagus that Ethbaal had made for Ahiram when he died. That was discovered a hundred years ago, in 1922, when a landslide revealed the royal cemetery of Byblos. In addition to identifying the deceased king and giving credit to his son for having the sarcophagus made, there is a curse included in the inscription: "The sarcophagus that Ethbaal, son of Ahiram, king of Byblos, made for Ahiram, his father, when he placed him in his eternity. And if a king among kings, or a governor among governors, or a commander of an army should come to Byblos, and uncover this sarcophagus, may the scepter of his rule be ripped away, may the throne of his kingdom be overturned, and may rest flee from Byblos. And as for him, may his royal records be effaced from before Byblos."[63]

Unfortunately, there is no link specifically known between these two kings and the next four. However, on the basis of the style of the letters

FIG. 8. Sarcophagus of Ahiram with Phoenician inscription. Photograph courtesy of the Library of Congress, G. Eric and Edith Matson Photograph Collection, matpc.03491.

used in the various inscriptions, it is thought that these two are the earliest on our known list of kings, ruling ca. 1000 BC and 975 BC, respectively.[64]

Three of the other four kings are mentioned in an inscription that was "found near the wall associated with the acropolis of Byblos" and published in 1945. Known as the Shipitbaal Inscription, it reads: "The wall that Shipitbaal king of Byblos, son of Elibaal king of Byblos, son of Yehimilk king of Byblos built for Baalat of Byblos, his lord. May Baalat of Byblos lengthen the days of Shipitbaal and his years over Byblos." Thus, we have a three-generation sequence of rulers, beginning with Yehimilk, then his son Elibaal, followed by grandson Shipitbaal. It has been suggested that they ruled during the latter half of the tenth century BC.[65]

This order of kings is confirmed by another inscription found at Byblos, carved on the torso of a bust of the Egyptian pharaoh Osorkon I, mentioned in chapter 1 as ruling in Egypt ca. 924–889 BC. First published in 1925 and known as the Elibaal Inscription, it reads: "[The statue] that

FIG. 9. Pharaoh Osorkon I with Elibaal inscription, from Byblos. Photograph courtesy of Rama via Wikimedia Commons.

Elibaal king of Byblos, son of Yehi[milk king of Byblos] made for Baalat of Byblos his lord. May Baalat [of Byblos] lengthen [the days of] Elibaal and his years over [Byblos]." This not only gives us the two-generation sequence of Yehimilk followed by his son Elibaal, but it also tells us that the latter ruled at approximately the same time as Osorkon I, which gives us the approximate dates for Elibaal. We get the additional gift of learning the name of one of the deities of Byblos, Baalat, who is mentioned in both of these inscriptions.[66]

We also have an inscription left by Yehimilk, recording his construction of a temple in Byblos, which provides additional insight into the gods and goddesses of the day. The Yehimilk Inscription was first published in 1930 and says: "The temple [literally: "house"] that Yehimilk, king of Byblos, built. He restored all the fall[en] temples. May Baal-Shamen and Baalat Byblos and the Assembly of the Holy Gods of Byblos lengthen the days of Yehimilk and his years over Byblos because the righteous and just king before the Holy Gods of Byblos is he."[67]

Finally, we also have the Abibaal Inscription, which was found inscribed on a statue of Pharaoh Sheshonq I, Osorkon's father, who ruled in Egypt ca. 945–924 BC, also mentioned in chapter 1. If the restorations in the missing portions of this inscription are correct, it seems that Yehimilk also had another son, Abibaal, who also claimed to have succeeded him on the throne. First published in 1903, the inscription reads: "[The statue that] Abibaal king of [Byblos son of Yehimilk king] of Byblos brought from Egypt for Baalat [of Byblos, his lord. May Ba'alat of Byblos lengthen the days of Abibaal and his years] over Byblos." Just as with the Elibaal inscription on the statue of Osorkon I, so the Abibaal inscription of the statue of Sheshonq I likely gives us the approximate dates for the rule of Abibaal.[68]

At first glance, the inscriptions from these faceless rulers don't seem to indicate much beyond their genealogy, but it is actually extremely helpful to have this much information, particularly as it shows us that rule by a hereditary set of dynasts continued during the Iron Age in Byblos. Unfortunately, we do not have a list of contemporary rulers for Tyre available through archaeological finds (yet), but we do know of Hiram of Tyre, discussed in chapter 1 and mentioned again just a few pages ago, who probably ruled ca. 970–936 BC. There are also others who are mentioned by later Greek and Roman authors. According to the Roman historian Flavius Josephus, for instance, who wrote in the mid-first century AD, Hiram's successors who ruled Tyre were Baal-ma'zer [Baal-azor] and Abdi-Aštart [Abdastratus], both at the end of the tenth century, as mentioned above. They were followed by a usurper named Methusastratos and then by Iš-Aštart and Aštar(t)-imn at the start of the ninth century BC, if we can trust what Josephus says.[69]

The Bible may also tell us the name of another king who was ruling Tyre at approximately this time, for the biblical account speaks of a king of Tyre named Ethbaal who ruled in the early to mid-ninth century BC, after his predecessors Iš-Aštart and Aštar(t)-imn. Care should be taken not to confuse this king with the earlier king of Byblos of the same name, just mentioned, who ruled during the early tenth century immediately after his father Ahiram.[70]

According to the account in 1 Kings 16:29–32, Ethbaal of Tyre entered into an alliance with Omri, king of the Northern Kingdom of Israel (who ruled ca. 884–873 BC), and gave his daughter, the infamous Jezebel, in marriage to Omri's son Ahab (ruled ca. 871–852 BC). Their daughter, Athaliah, in turn married King Jehoram of Judah (2 Kings 8:16–18). That Jezebel was actively practicing the polytheistic religion of Tyre (and Byblos) in monotheistic Israel is famously confirmed by the biblical passages describing the battle between the priests of Baal and the Israelite priests on Mount Carmel (1 Kings 18–19, 21; 2 Kings 9).[71]

As for Omri, whom we met briefly toward the end of chapter 1, during his reign he established the capital of the northern Kingdom of Israel at the site of Samaria (later renamed Sebastia by Herod the Great), now located in the West Bank to the northwest of Nablus. Here he built a palace, later completed by his son Ahab, which stood for about a century and a half, until the final destruction of the city and the assimilation of the kingdom into the Neo-Assyrian Empire ca. 720 BC.

The site and its palace were first excavated by an American team of archaeologists led by George Reisner of Harvard University from 1908 to 1910. Subsequently, the so-called Joint Expedition led by British archaeologist John Crowfoot and involving archaeologists from the British School of Archaeology in Jerusalem, the Palestine Exploration Fund, and the Hebrew University of Jerusalem, dug at the site from 1931 to 1935. One of the members of this latter expedition was a very young Kathleen Kenyon, who would go on to fame in her own right as the excavator of Jericho and Jerusalem several decades later. In the ruins of the palace were found the alabaster vase inscribed with Osorkon II's cartouche, already mentioned above, as well as approximately one thousand ivory objects, usually now referred to as the Samaria ivories. These date to either the ninth or the eighth century BC and are now mostly on display at the Israel Museum in Jerusalem.[72]

———

Ethbaal of Tyre is also given credit by Josephus (who calls him Ithobaal) as being the first Phoenician king to establish colonies elsewhere in the Mediterranean, including at Kition in Cyprus. Indeed, as various scholars have pointed out, archaeology does seem to confirm that Kition is the earliest Phoenician colony on the island, though its inhabitants did not leave many remains behind.[73]

On the other hand, archaeological remains in both Sardinia and Spain, including at Huelva, have also now established that there seems to be a permanent Phoenician presence in those areas by the early ninth century BC (as opposed to the earlier and more ephemeral trading contacts in previous centuries mentioned above), perhaps in response to the continuing need for silver from those areas. There is also the well-known, and much debated, Phoenician inscription from the site of Nora on Sardinia, which was found long ago, in 1773. It probably commemorates the construction of a temple at that spot and may date to the end of the ninth century BC.[74]

Josephus also states that Ethbaal established a dynasty that ruled Tyre for the next century. Although we cannot be certain that the account is accurate and can be trusted, Josephus lists Ethbaal's successors as Baal-ma'zer [Baal-azor] II, Mattan I, and Pummayon [Pygmalion], ruling from the mid-ninth century to the early eighth century BC. An inscription from the Neo-Assyrian king Shalmaneser III, whom we met in chapter 2, states specifically that in his eighteenth regnal year (841 BC) he received tribute from "Ba'ali-manzer of Tyre." This should be the same king as Josephus's Baal-ma'zer and gives us more detail than simply the "Tyrians and Sidonians" who are more usually mentioned in the various versions of Shalmaneser's inscription. As Nadav Na'aman of Tel Aviv University has pointed out, this also gives us more confidence in the accuracy of Josephus's list, since Shalmaneser's list is both contemporaneous to the time period of this king of Tyre and (presumably) an independent source.[75]

As an interesting aside, according to much later Roman traditions, including Josephus as well as poets Ovid and Virgil (see his *Aeneid*), it was reportedly Pygmalion's sister Elissa (aka Dido) who fled from Tyre after Pygmalion killed her husband; she subsequently founded the city of Carthage in what is now North Africa ca. 814 BC. Although this may be no more than a foundation myth or legend, the archaeological remains at Carthage do suggest a founding date during the late ninth century (ca. 835–800 BC).[76]

This legend has also been linked to a recent discovery accidentally made by the US nuclear research submarine *NR-1* in 1997 while searching for the *Dakar*, an Israeli submarine that had been lost in the 1960s. Though the crew failed to find the *Dakar*, they did discover the remains of two Iron Age ships dating to the eighth century BC; both had sunk a little more than thirty miles off the coast of the Gaza Strip and now lay four hundred meters below the surface of the Mediterranean.[77]

It was in 1999 that Bob Ballard, who is perhaps better known as the discoverer of the *Titanic*, and Larry Stager, who was then a professor at Harvard and director of the excavations at the site of Ashkelon, returned to the area to further explore the two ships, nicknamed the *Tanit* and the *Elissa*, as part of the Ashkelon Deep-Sea Project. Using a remotely operated vehicle system known as *Medea/Jason*, they were able to scan and map both the *Tanit* and the *Elissa*, recording hundreds of amphorae on the seabed at both locations—385 amphorae were visible on or near the remains of the *Tanit* and 396 could be seen at the site of the *Elissa*. The *Tanit* was likely to have been about fourteen meters long by six and a half meters wide, while the *Elissa* was just a bit bigger, measuring about fourteen and a half meters long by about seven meters wide.

In order to sample and test some of the archaeological remains, the team brought up sixteen amphorae from the *Tanit* and eight from the *Elissa*, in addition to other types of pottery such as cooking pots and bowls. All of the amphorae could be readily identified as Phoenician, produced in "one or more of the Phoenician port cities," and dated on stylistic grounds to ca. 750 BC. In their subsequent article, published in the *American Journal of Archaeology* in 2002, Ballard and Stager invoked Elissa (Dido) and "Pumiyaton" (Pummayon [Pygmalion]) in their discussions, hypothesizing that the ships may have been sailing from Ashkelon to Egypt and thence to the newly founded Phoenician colony of Carthage.

Continuing Contacts in the Ninth and Eighth Centuries BC

As for Cyprus, its exports continued to reach the Aegean during the ninth century, ranging from iron knives to golden beads and a diadem, particularly at Cretan sites such as Knossos, Kommos, and Eleutherna. As Nota Kourou states, "by the mid 9th [century] regular communications in the Mediterranean had fully recovered and a number of Cypriot and Cypro-Levantine networks were already active in Crete."[78]

She also notes that, from the late ninth century onward, Cypriot visits to Crete become more regular and that the number of Cypriot imports grew. This, she says, also "coincides with the start of regular Phoenician travels in Central Mediterranean and the establishment of Carthage." This would explain the sudden increase in Phoenician imports on Crete at this time as well, since Crete would have been on this trade route, and there might have been "some common Cypro-Phoenician networks active in Geometric Crete at that time."[79]

At the same time, however, Cypriot objects decrease on mainland Greece, even while Near Eastern objects continue to appear at numerous Greek sites, including objects ranging from bronze bowls to faience objects to items made of gold and ivory. It may have been that the Phoenicians had taken over the routes to mainland Greece by this point and blocked trade by the Cypriots, as has been suggested, though this would seem a bit odd since concurrent trade to Crete was obviously not blocked. Be that as it may, Crielaard notes that it was only now, "in the ninth and especially eighth centuries B.C. that interregional exchange [once again] reached a level of complexity that could be compared to that of the Late Bronze Age."[80]

As we know, and as emphasized throughout the previous volume, *1177 B.C.*, drought likely played a significant role in the Late Bronze Age Collapse. However, the drought seems to have finally come to an end in all of these areas, in Cyprus and throughout the Eastern Mediterranean, during the mid-ninth century, and we might look to this as one possible reason for this period of renewed exchange. The arid conditions, which populations had been forced to adapt to over the past few centuries, were eventually replaced by warmer and wetter conditions that would last for the rest of the Iron Age and that may have helped the societies rejuvenate. Archaeological surveys have indicated, for instance, that from the late ninth century onward there is evidence for new settlements and resettlement of previously abandoned areas in Cyprus, no doubt reflecting new kinds of land use and engagement with the changing climate conditions.[81]

Significant copper production subsequently resumed on Cyprus during the eighth century BC. It is also by this period, if not perhaps even a little bit earlier, that most of the important cities on Cyprus had been either established, reestablished, or come to the forefront, perhaps as new sociopolitical formations, as some have suggested, and they would last through the fourth century BC or beyond. These include the seven Cypriot kingdoms whose kings are mentioned on a stele set up at Kition by the Neo-Assyrian king Sargon II in the later eighth century (ca. 709 BC) and the ten Cypriot kingdoms named on a clay prism by the Neo-Assyrian king Esarhaddon near the beginning of the seventh century (ca. 674 BC).[82]

It is at that later date that Cyprus was incorporated into the Neo-Assyrian Empire, even though there is no evidence that it had actually been physically conquered. The island would continue to flourish right up to and through the Roman period as a major supplier of copper, which remained in demand through the centuries.

Brief Summation

Both the Cypriots and the Phoenicians proved to be resilient as well as innovative during the centuries after the Late Bronze Age Collapse. The Phoenicians especially took advantage of the sack of Ugarit and other port cities to win control of the trade routes across the Mediterranean, spreading their version of the alphabet, and exchanging trade goods such as purple dye for silver and other metals coming from as far away as Sicily, Sardinia, and Iberia. The Cypriots did the same in terms of spreading iron goods and iron technology both east and west. Together, I would argue, they were the two societies that weathered the transformation to the new normal most successfully; both could even be labeled as anti-fragile, flourishing during the chaos that followed the Collapse. The same cannot be said for the Hittites in central Anatolia, however, as will become clear in the next chapter.

CHAPTER FOUR

King of the Land of Carchemish

(Anatolia and Northern Syria)

On the very first day of a new archaeological expedition to Carchemish in 2011, Nicolò Marchetti of the University of Bologna found an inscribed basalt stela. It had originally been set up at the site three thousand years earlier, in the tenth century BC, by a Neo-Hittite king who called himself Suhi, "Ruler, Country Lord of the City of Carchemish."

Marchetti was surveying the site by himself that day. Located on the modern border between Syria and Turkey, it was the first time that archaeologists had been allowed to officially work at the site since the final season by British archaeologists almost a century earlier, in 1920. Since then, the site had been split between the two countries following the Turkish War of Independence, with fifty-five hectares of the site in Turkey and thirty-five hectares in Syria.[1]

A Turkish army observation post had been established directly upon their portion of the site and, in 1956, when the region was rife with smugglers, anti-personnel and anti-tank mines had been planted along the border in a strip three hundred to five hundred meters wide (and stretching for five hundred kilometers). Thus, before the new archaeological investigations could begin, the area had to be de-mined. When Marchetti began his survey, he was told that the site was guaranteed to be 99.6 percent cleared of the mines. However, as he noted, that means "out of 1000 mines, there is a residual statistical risk of 4 of them having been overlooked." That is why, when the team finally began excavating, they employed professional de-miners to double-check the areas in which they were planning to dig.[2]

The inscribed stela that Marchetti found that day originally stood nearly two meters high. It had been commissioned by Suhi I to commemorate the resolution of a dispute between Ura-Tarhunta, the Great King of the land of Carchemish, and the "land Sura," which is usually taken to be a reference to Assyria, and which had apparently taken place sometime earlier.[3] The inscription reads: "The Great King Ura-Tarhunta, Great King, Hero, King of the land of Carchemish, son of Sapaziti, Great King, the Hero. For him a dispute arose with the land Sura, and he opposed the army. To King Ura-Tarhunta the mighty Storm-god and Kubaba [gave] a mighty protection, and they put the right arm on him, and he himself resolved the dispute. And Suhi, King Ura-Tarhunta's dear relative, the Ruler, the Country Lord of the city of Carchemish, put up this stela."[4]

This is now considered to be the earliest Iron Age inscription found at the site of Carchemish. Interestingly, it is an almost exact duplicate of another inscription that had been found much earlier by the British archaeologists at the site, but which had apparently been put up later by one of Suhi I's sons.[5] We can unpack this a bit more as well. We know of two earlier kings of Carchemish, namely, Kuzi-Tešub and Ini-Tešub, who ruled during the twelfth century. Now we have these two additional kings, Sapaziti and his son Ura-Tarhunta, who ruled the land of Carchemish in the late eleventh century BC. All of them bore the title "Great King." Unfortunately, because we are not certain of Ura-Tarhunta's exact dates, we also do not know which ruler of Assyria would have been in power at the time of the recorded dispute. Most likely it would have been Aššurnasirpal I, who ruled from 1049 to 1031 BC, or Shalmaneser II, who ruled from 1030 to 1019 BC, but that is just a guess.

However, the inscription also gives us the name of Suhi, who claims to have been a relative of Ura-Tarhunta. Suhi's rule seems to have begun in about 1000 BC—we know from both this and other inscriptions that he founded a dynasty of rulers who all called themselves not "Great King" but rather "Ruler, Country Lord of the City of Carchemish." They included his son Astuwalamanza, grandson Suhi II, great-grandson

Katuwa, and a great-great-grandson named Suhi III (who came to the throne about 900 BC).[6]

It is still an ongoing scholarly debate as to how the two different sets of rulers, the "Great Kings" and the "Country Lords," functioned. Since the full title used by Sapaziti and Ura-Tarhunta, as well as their successors, seems to have been "Great King, King of the Land of Carchemish," it may be that they ruled over the entire area controlled by Carchemish, whereas Suhi and his descendants were simply rulers of the city itself. That is the usual position taken by scholars, that is, that both dynasties were ruling at the same time for at least a brief period, since Suhi says that he is a "dear relative" of Ura-Tarhunta. However, Alessandra Gilibert, a professor at Ca' Foscari University in Venice, has suggested that Suhi I may actually have been a usurper who seized the throne of Carchemish, and that he and his successors then ruled the whole area, albeit with this different title. This may well be the case, for we do not see very much overlap, if any, in terms of regnal dates between the Great Kings and the Country Lords of Carchemish after the tenth century BC. But to complicate matters further, rulers of the nearby city of Malatya, who also claimed descent from Kuzi-Tešub, the "Great King of Carchemish" ca. 1200 BC, similarly called themselves "Country Lords" in their titles.[7] In short, the exact relationship of these groups of rulers to each other remains unclear.

Hittites and Neo-Hittites

We have jumped into this topic of Carchemish and Neo-Hittite rulers in the middle of things—*in medias res*, as it were—so let's backtrack for a minute and put everything into context.

As part of the Neo-Assyrian inscription(s) in which Tiglath-Pileser I mentions Byblos, Sidon, and Arwad, and gifts from the Egyptian pharaoh, discussed in chapter 2, he also says that he became "lord of the entire land [of] Hatti" and specifically says that he had received hostages, tax, tribute, and cedar beams from Ini-Tešub (or Ini-Teššub), "king of the land Hatti."[8] This is extremely useful for us, because we have just encountered Ini-Tešub, who is known from other textual records as a king ruling in the late twelfth century BC at Carchemish (as opposed to the earlier Hittite king of the same name who ruled in Anatolia during the Late Bronze Age). We can therefore correlate the reigns of these two Iron Age kings, Tiglath-Pileser I of Assyria and Ini-Tešub of Carchemish, and be fairly confident that this episode took place right at the very end of the twelfth century and the beginning of the eleventh century, ca. 1100 BC.[9] This is the first time that we have met the Anatolian and Syrian successor states to the Bronze Age Hittites in the texts of the time period and the first time that we see the heirs to the Bronze Age empires coming into contact and conflict.

Note that Tiglath-Pileser calls Ini-Tešub "king of the land Hatti," despite the fact that the actual Hittite Empire in Anatolia had collapsed and disappeared almost completely in the years after 1200 BC. The capital city of Hattusa was initially abandoned and then partially destroyed, with a small Iron Age village subsequently established on one small portion of the original city. The situation has been recently summed up by Lorenzo d'Alfonso of New York University and his colleagues as follows: "A deep transformation took place in the former core of the empire around the capital Hattusa, resulting in a drastic decrease in political complexity, a shift to a subsistence household economy and a lack of evidence for any public institutions." Furthermore, James Osborne, a professor at the University of Chicago, cites recent research stating that there may have been "a drastic settlement drop of about 90%" in south-central Anatolia at this time and says that "despite evidence for continuity in certain locations . . . the general picture is one of a marked decline in social complexity until the ninth century."[10]

Life did continue elsewhere in Anatolia, however, including in the hinterland where the farmers and villagers continued on much as before, though perhaps changing to raising more goats and cattle than sheep, as documented by Sarah Adcock in her University of Chicago dissertation, and as the climate change impacted the population throughout the area.[11] (As a side note, over on mainland Greece, recent research has shown that what was previously thought to be a similar shift to cattle at Nichoria in Messenia needs to be reconsidered, for the Early Iron Age remains in that region do not actually show that there were more cattle being raised at that time, as had been previously thought, and instead suggest that things remained essentially the same in this area in terms of raising animals during both the Late Bronze Age and the Early Iron Age.)[12]

In addition, at the central Anatolian site of Gordion we have new evidence, based on the redating of previously known remains, that there were people living at the site from the twelfth century BC onward and a reorganization of the local economy, even as Hittite influence over the area came to an end. This is of great interest, particularly since there is also now additional evidence, based on dendrochronology and isotope analyses of wood from juniper trees that were used at the site, that the area suffered from a series of dry spells at the end of the Late Bronze Age, including a three-year-long drought dated to 1198–96 BC.[13]

Later to become famous as the area where wealthy King Midas (of Greek mythology) ruled, and the location of the Gordion Knot that Alexander the Great cut in half, Gordion became known as the capital city of the Phrygians by the mid-ninth century BC. The Phrygians, whom many believe to have migrated into this region from elsewhere, were apparently known to the Assyrians as the kingdom of Mushki, though this is still a matter of debate among scholars. Tiglath-Pileser I claims to have fought and defeated them in at least one battle quite early on, but thereafter they did not seriously attract Assyrian attention until later in the eighth century BC.[14]

Attention has recently been drawn again to the area because of a discovery made in 2019 in the Konya area of modern Turkey, near the site of Türkmen-Karahöyük. Known informally as the Hartapu inscription, a local farmer brought it to the attention of a team of archaeologists who were conducting a survey in the region. Written in hieroglyphic Luwian inscribed on hard stone, it was set up by a local king named Hartapu, who claims to have conquered Phrygia in the eighth century BC. It begins: "When Great King Hartapu, Hero, son of Mursili, conquered the country of Mushka . . . the Storm God of Heaven (and) all the gods delivered (its) 13 kings (to) His Majesty, Great King Hartapu. In a single year he placed the 13 kings, the(ir) weapons [=troops?], and wild beasts under (the authority of) ten strong-walled fortresses."[15]

Even at Troy, on the western coast of Anatolia, where previous excavators had thought that there was a four-hundred-year hiatus of occupation following the Collapse, it is now apparent that there was some continuity of occupation, especially during the twelfth and into the eleventh century. In addition, there has always been much discussion regarding a possible migration into the area from Thrace or the Balkans immediately following the destruction of Troy VIIa. Regardless, the remains that were occupied are not nearly comparable to the wealthy city that had been there during the Bronze Age.[16]

Thus, despite the collapse of the Hittite Empire proper, we can see that there were survivors and that life did continue, especially in the hinterland, even if the centralized government and its attendant bureaucracy and administration had essentially vanished, leaving the various areas to their own devices. Among the impacted areas were those that are sometimes referred to as small "rump states," especially in what is now northern Syria. Here, for instance, branches of the royal family, descended from the Hittite king Suppiluliuma I, survived to rule at Carchemish and Aleppo during the twelfth century BC and beyond, as mentioned a moment ago. Archaeologists have labeled these polities the Neo-Hittite (or Syro-Hittite) states, for it is this area that Tiglath-Pileser and the Neo-Assyrians then referred to as the "land of Hatti," rather than the central plateau of Anatolia where the Hittite Empire had previously been based. And, of course, it is not only the Neo-Assyrians who referred to these small city-states and their culture in this manner, for they are also most likely the "Hittites" who are mentioned in the Hebrew Bible, since the original Hittites were long gone by the time the first versions of that religious text were being compiled.[17]

Altogether, these Neo-Hittites established (or continued to occupy) as many as fifteen small city-states in the region of what is now northern Syria and southeastern Turkey during the Iron Age, from the twelfth to the eighth centuries BC. This is the same general region that was hit by brutal earthquakes in February 2023, which killed nearly sixty thousand people and devastated the region. The city and territory of Carchemish that challenged Tiglath-Pileser I was among the most prominent in this area. The remnants of the site were first extensively investigated and excavated in the early twentieth century by several archaeologists, including T. E. Lawrence (who was later immortalized by Hollywood as

"Lawrence of Arabia"), and it is now once again being excavated (since 2011), this time by a joint team of Turkish and Italian archaeologists.

If we go back even a bit further in time, alert readers will remember that Carchemish had been specifically named by Ramses III in the inscription from his eighth year (1177 BC) as one of the areas that the Sea Peoples had overrun ("No land could stand before their arms, from Khatte, Qode, Carchemish, Arzawa, and Alashiya on . . ."). However, perhaps rather surprisingly, there is no archaeological evidence to indicate that the city suffered destruction at that time. It may be that Ramses was referring rather more generally to the region surrounding Carchemish, rather than specifically to the city itself, and indeed this remained a contested area right down to the latter part of the eighth century BC. In 1920, Sir Leonard Woolley wrote, ". . . climb the great mound of the acropolis, and you will understand at once why Carchemish was from immemorial time a fortress in a troubled land."[18]

We are learning more and more each year about these small Neo-Hittite (or Syro-Hittite and Syro-Anatolian) kingdoms. In large part this is due to finds made during renewed excavations at various sites, including the Turkish-Italian team at Carchemish and an American-German team at Zincirli (ancient Sam'al), but it is also because of advances in reading Hieroglyphic Luwian. Luwian as a language was one of several spoken in Anatolia during the Bronze Age and beyond, but it was also employed as a pictographic writing system by the Hittites for royal inscriptions carved on stone monuments. Later it was similarly used by the Neo-Hittites for their inscriptions carved in stone and erected in their cities. As a result, we are in the fortunate position of being able to trace the dynasties and lineages of the rulers in a number of these Iron Age cities and kingdoms.[19]

To give just one example, the early British excavators at Carchemish had by 1911 already described finding reliefs and inscriptions at the site. "Into the long lower wall seems to have been built a series of large reliefs, which faced outwards to the paved court," wrote D. G. Hogarth, the British field director at the time. "We found them fallen into the court to the number of thirteen in all. Six of these represent war chariots in action; two, warriors on foot; four, monstrous divine figures; and one, occurring about the middle of the series, bears a long inscription in relief characters, below which appear three bearded heads and sixteen cut-off hands. As these slabs originally faced outwards, they were the lining of a monumental approach to the stairway, and led up to a series which lined the north side of the latter."[20]

We know now that Suppiluliuma I had installed one of his own sons, Piyaššili (who assumed the name Sharri-Kušuh), as viceroy of the city back in about 1340 BC. The descendants of Piyaššili, including Kuzi-Tešub and Ini-Tešub, continued to rule the city and its adjacent land and surrounding villages (i.e., the city-state as a whole) for the next five generations or so, until its demise at the hands of the Neo-Assyrian Empire of Sargon II in 717 BC. Some successors even assumed the title "King of the Hittites" once the Hittite Empire itself had come crashing down and as portions of it split off and formed their own small Neo-Hittite kingdoms. We also know that Suppiluliuma I had installed another of his sons, named Telepinu, to rule over the city and kingdom of Aleppo, located not too far away, at approximately the same time (ca. 1340 BC). That dynasty also continued after the fall of the Hittite Empire proper.[21]

Tiglath-Pileser's actions foreshadow what occurs time and again in the coming centuries, especially the Assyrians attacking the small Iron Age city-states and kingdoms that replaced the Bronze Age empires across the ancient Near East. Some of these had been established as early as the later twelfth century BC, but others did not come into place until the eleventh, tenth, or ninth centuries BC. Among them were a whole host of political entities and various ethnicities, some of whom we have already met and others whom we will soon encounter: Syro-Anatolian or Syro-Hittite city-states such as Carchemish, Aleppo, Sam'al (modern Zincirli), and Til Barsip in what is now northern Syria and on the border with Turkey; as well as others, such as Que, that were located in the area of Cilicia (modern southeastern Turkey); Aramaean city-states such as Damascus and Hamath in what is now Syria proper; the Phoenician enclaves of Tyre, Byblos, Sidon, Arwad, and Beirut on what is now the coast of Lebanon; Philistine cities and the kingdoms of Israel and Judah in what is now modern Israel and the West Bank; and the other small kingdoms of the era such as Ammon, Edom, and Moab in what is now Jordan.[22] In all of these, of course, despite their assignation here to individual polities, we are likely to have found a mixture of various ethnicities among the populations, just as we would expect in modern cities across the region today.

This situation was not completely unlike what had been the case in the Levant during the Late Bronze Age, when each of the small Canaanite entities was ruled by a governor (or petty king) and owed allegiance to either the Egyptians or the Hittites. But now, with the collapse of the regional powers at the end of the Bronze Age, these city-states were able to exercise at least a bit more independence than they had previously enjoyed. The Assyrians would eventually take advantage of this power vacuum and create an empire of their own, but that would not take place until the ninth century BC, as we have seen.

Neo-Hittites at Tayinat and Carchemish

The surviving inhabitants in northern Syria demonstrated varying degrees of resilience during the later twelfth century and into the eleventh century. It was a time of transition for all of them, with some transforming and others adapting or simply coping. As Hélène Sader of the American University of Beirut has reported, "the transition from Late Bronze to Iron Age differed from site to site." At some places, there was a smooth transition without a break. At others, there was most definitely a rupture, such as at Ras Ibn Hani, the port city of Ugarit, which was reoccupied only after a violent destruction by invaders during the Collapse, not to mention Ugarit itself, of course. As Sader notes, though, "most sites were almost immediately reoccupied and resumed agricultural, industrial, and trade activity."[23]

Despite the fact that Carchemish was not destroyed, there are indications that it suffered some sort of contraction at this time and that a nearby kingdom, based at Tell Tayinat, took the opportunity to arise and flourish as well.[24] We know about this new Iron Age kingdom in part because of excavations at the site but also because of further interesting developments in terms of reading and understanding Hieroglyphic Luwian.

The advances in decipherment have resulted in an updated reading for the name of this new regional Iron Age kingdom, which was located in the Amuq Valley, also on the border between modern Turkey and Syria. Active especially from the eleventh century BC onward, and probably encompassing an area that included Aleppo and possibly as far south as Hamath, the kingdom was previously identified by scholars as "the Land of Padastin" (also appearing as "Padasatini," "Wadastin," and other variants). However, J. D. Hawkins of the School of Oriental and African Studies at the University of London and others have presented evidence that the proper spelling and reading is much more likely to be "Palistin" (appearing as "Walistin" in some inscriptions) and that the kingdom was probably known as the "Land of Palistin." The proposed new reading of the name of the city connotes, of course, both the Philistines of Sea Peoples' fame and the modern name of Palestine and has elicited all sorts of discussions among archaeologists in recent years, including some who are not entirely persuaded by the suggestion.[25]

Its capital was located at a city also known by a variety of spellings, including Kunulua, Kumulua, Kinalua, and Kinaliya, which is the site now known as Tell Tayinat. It was first excavated by the University of Chicago from 1935 to 1938 and more recently (since 2004) by the University of Toronto under the direction of Tim Harrison.

Tayinat itself, located just to the northeast of Ugarit and inland from the Syrian coast at a bend in the Orontes River, seems to have been a rather complex entity. Studies of its material culture have focused on the non-local (i.e., Aegean) nature of the pottery and other suggestions of foreigners having settled down at the time of the Bronze Age Collapse and immediately thereafter. Conversely, inscriptions found at the site "have highlighted the region's political continuity, from the period of Late Bronze Age Hittite imperial control to the Neo-Hittite rump states of the Iron Age." As the excavators themselves have recently stated, "there exists compelling evidence for both continuity and change" at the site, which is of unique interest to us.[26]

They also conclude that Tayinat was in contact, both economically and culturally, with societies and individuals located in a wide range of geographic locations during this time, including Anatolia, inland Syria, the Levant, and the Aegean. As a result, they do not see Tayinat as isolated, but rather "at the confluence of multiple cultural spheres." They suggest, in fact, that "the diverse spectrum of cultural links observed in Tayinat's Early Iron Age levels clearly reflect a considerably more complex and more ambiguous cultural reality than has previously been acknowledged."[27]

We now know from various inscriptions, uncovered at sites such as Aleppo, Arsuz, Ain Dara, and elsewhere, as well as at Tayinat itself, that one of the earliest kings of the "Land of Palistin" was a man named Taita I, who ruled in the eleventh century BC. Several of his inscriptions were found during the 2003–5 seasons of excavations within the Temple of the Storm God in Aleppo. The opening lines of one begin: "I (am) King Taita, the Hero, the King of [the Land] Palistin." A fragmentary second inscription contains his name along with mentions of both Carchemish and Egypt, but the context is broken off in both lines.

He was eventually followed by Taita II and his wife Kupapiya in the early tenth century, then Manana (recently redated from the ninth century) and then Suppiluliuma I (adopting the earlier Hittite king's name) later that same century. By the early and mid-ninth century BC the name of the kingdom had contracted slightly, to Patin(a) rather than Palistin, although it was also sometimes called Unqi by the Neo-Assyrians, as noted above, and was governed by kings such as Halparuntiya and Suppiluliuma II; the latter king is probably called Sapalulme by the Assyrian king Shalmaneser III in his inscriptions dating to 858 BC.[28]

Carchemish appears to have made a comeback during the tenth century BC, which was a period of resurgence for the city and its surrounding territory. Here, for instance, we now find what is called the "Water Gate" built on the side of the city facing the Euphrates River, which was decorated with sculpted orthostats (shaped stone slabs used to line walls or walkways) dating to the late eleventh or early tenth century BC. During his excavations at the site in 1920, Sir Leonard Woolley described it quite poetically, as follows:

> A sloping road broken by steps led from the quay between rows of sculpture. At the corner of the river-wall was a lion, then came bulls and lions again, and the group of guardian demons proper to a gateway—an architectural amulet, as it were, to keep evil spirits from the entrance; there is a scene of sacrifice, a bull and a goat led to the slaughter, and a seated priest or king who pours libations to the gods. The outer door-jambs were formed by huge basalt lions carved in the round, and measuring twelve feet from head to tail, with a long inscription carved upon their flanks. Today the gateway is a battered ruin, contrasting poorly indeed with the buildings inside the town; but apart from the picture which it enables us to draw of what it was in [b]almier days, it has a historical importance which the better-preserved ruins lack.[29]

Nearby is also the so-called Long Wall of Sculpture, dating most likely to the end of the tenth century BC, which has "an impressive sequence of large slabs with military scenes and a procession of gods," as Marchetti has described them. This was the "long lower wall" with "a series of large reliefs" that Hogarth wrote about in 1911, as quoted above.[30]

Thus, we now know that by this point in the tenth century BC, life in Carchemish had returned to the point where all of the trappings of a complex society were evident—monumental buildings and sculpture; inscriptions; rulers with titles; multiple levels of political hierarchy with lesser rulers holding lesser titles; specialized occupations such as that of priest; the worship of gods and goddesses within specific buildings and temples; and an area that was being governed and that presumably was producing agricultural goods and other produce to sustain the inhabitants of the region and the elite who ruled them. Although Carchemish was a much smaller political entity than the Hittite Empire, which one could say had given birth to it, clearly Carchemish was once again a player in the world of the ancient Near East. It would remain so until 717 BC when the city was destroyed by the Neo-Assyrians.

We also know that the region of Carchemish was among the areas that submitted and paid tribute to Aššurnasirpal II and the Neo-Assyrians in the ninth century BC, for a "Sangara, king of the land Hatti" is mentioned in connection with the land of Carchemish in an inscription dating to about 870 BC. Sangara, who is thought to have ruled ca. 875–848 BC, is also mentioned twice on the smaller set of bronze door bands from Aššurnasirpal II's palace at Balawat found by Rassam; one scene contains the caption "Plunder from Sangara, a man of Hatti" while the other, a scene showing a city being attacked, says, "The city Ulluba of Sa[n]gara, [king of] the land Hatti, I conquered." Another band, found by Mallowan, from the Temple to Mamu also built by Aššurnasirpal at Balawat, depicts tribute from the king of Carchemish, but unfortunately the name of the king is unreadable; presumably it is also Sangara.[31] The same king is mentioned later as well, by Shalmaneser III, as we shall see.

From Aššurnasirpal's precise wording in the inscription from 870 BC, and the amount of tribute listed, it is clear that Carchemish was not an impoverished backwater at the time.[32] It reads as follows:

> I crossed the Euphrates, which was in flood, in rafts (made of inflated) goatskins (and) approached the land Carchemish. I received tribute from Sangara, king of the land Hatti, 20 talents of silver, a gold ring, a gold bracelet, gold daggers, 100 talents of bronze, 250 talents of iron, bronze (tubs), bronze pails, bronze bath-tubs, a bronze oven, many ornaments from his palace the weight of which could not be determined, beds of boxwood, thrones of boxwood, dishes of boxwood decorated with ivory, 200 adolescent girls, linen garments with multi-coloured trim, purple wool, red-purple wool, *gišnugallu*-alabaster, elephants' tusks, a chariot of polished (gold), a gold couch with trimming—(objects) befitting his royalty. I took with me the chariots, cavalry, (and) infantry of the city Carchemish.[33]

The Land of Urartu

Aššurnasirpal II also says that he campaigned far to the north, where he conquered "the land Urartu." His army had ventured up into Anatolia where they encountered the forces of Urartian King Aramu, who had begun ruling near the end of Aššurnasirpal's reign.[34] It is possible that there may have already been interactions with this region back in the thirteenth century BC, according to Assyrian texts from the time of Shalmaneser I, for he claimed to have conquered a land called Uruatri, which may or may not be the same as Urartu.[35] But the Urartians whom Aššurnasirpal II encountered were essentially another new power on the scene, unique to the Iron Age.

The Urartians were the recipients of Assyrian animosity almost right away. Their cities were located directly to the north of Assyria in the same general region where the easternmost parts of the Hittite Empire had once been. From the area of Lake Van, the Urartians spread throughout what is now parts of eastern Turkey, Armenia, Azerbaijan, and northwestern Iran. Relations between the Assyrians and Urartians were hostile at almost all times; they seem to have been in a perpetual state of war since the moment they first met.

It was the Assyrians who called this kingdom "Urartu" (from which, by the way, the modern name for Mt. Ararat is derived). However, the Urartians themselves called their kingdom "Biainili." They later became famous for their metalwork. Scholars frequently attribute to them the creation of huge bronze cauldrons with bull, lion, or griffin heads (known as "protomes") attached to the rim, as well as incised and embossed bronze shields decorated with animal figures. These either made their way to, or were imitated, in northern Syria and may have reached as far west as Crete, mainland Greece, and even Italy, especially during the later eighth and seventh centuries BC.[36]

Earlier Assyrian kings, such as Tukulti-Ninurta I, Tiglath-Pileser I, and Aššur-bel-kala also reported campaigning in a region located by Lake Van that they called "Nairi." Although there is some dispute as to whether this region is the same as Urartu, the Urartians themselves sometimes referred to their kingdom by this name (Nairi) during the ninth century BC, and it certainly seems to have been assimilated by Urartu by the eighth century BC.[37]

Shalmaneser III continued the Assyrian assault on this northern kingdom when he came to the throne in 858 BCE. His inscriptions record as many as four campaigns against the Urartians and/or into Urartian territory. The initial one had already taken place during his first year on the throne, when he says that he approached Suguni, which was the name of "the fortified city of Aramu [or Arame] the Urartian." He besieged it, captured it, massacred many of its inhabitants, and then "erected a tower of heads in front of his city" before burning fourteen other cities in the area.[38]

This initial campaign is also recorded on both the lower and upper registers for Band I on the Balawat gates as well as in a longer inscription that is engraved twice elsewhere on the same gate, that is, on the bronze coverings that were attached to the edges of the two leaves (doors) of the gate itself where they met when the gate was closed. The inscription for the lower register on Band I says, "I captured Sugunia, the city of Arame of Urartu," while the shorter inscription for the upper register says, "I set up an image on the shore of the Sea of Nairi." Likewise, the longer inscription on the edges of the doors says, "Upon my passing by the sea I created a colossal image of my lordship (and) erected (it) where the image of Anum-hirbe (stands). . . . I created a colossal image of my lordship (and) wrote thereon the praises [of Assur, the great lord, my lord, and the mighty deeds which] I had been accomplishing [by] the sea. I erected (it) by the sea."[39]

This mirrors a similar statement that Shalmaneser made on his Monolith Inscription, which is the second of the two inscriptions discovered by British archaeologist John Taylor at Kurkh in 1861 and donated by him to the British Museum two years later, as mentioned in chapter 2. On that monument, Shalmaneser recorded the same details just mentioned, including the pile of heads and the destruction of the fourteen cities, and also noted that he marched to the Sea of Nairi. He added that the image he set up was made "in my own likeness," just in case that had not been previously made clear.[40]

The accompanying pictures on the upper register of Balawat Band I show that what Shalmaneser set up on the shores of the lake was not a stand-alone statue, as one might imagine, but was actually his image (shown in full profile from head to toe, facing to the right) carved into the living rock, just as the heads of four US presidents are carved into Mount Rushmore in South Dakota. The king is shown making a libation—pouring some sort of liquid onto the ground—and is accompanied by priests and musicians, along with a variety of animals about to be sacrificed. Also depicted are the troops who had escorted the king, including chariots, cavalry, and infantry.[41]

Shalmaneser apparently had a habit of ordering the creation of such memorials to himself while on the attack. During the same campaign, in fact, he says that he placed "a colossal royal statue of myself . . . before the source of the River Saluara, at the foot of the Amanus range." He also set up another "image of my lordship which establishes my fame for eternity," which he placed on the shore of the Mediterranean after defeating the "kings of the seashore" in the region of Amurru and the kingdom of Patin. There were also at least two other such images that he set up elsewhere as well, including one on Mount Eritia after he had captured yet another city belonging to Arame the Urartian as well as one by the Sea of Nairi.[42]

Six years later, during a campaign conducted during his seventh regnal year, Shalmaneser did it again. He says: "I marched to the source of the Tigris, the place where the water comes out. I washed the weapon of Aššur therein, made sacrifices to my gods, and put on a joyful banquet. I created my colossal royal statue and wrote thereon praises of Aššur, my lord, and all my heroic deeds which I had accomplished in the lands. I erected it therein." Eight years after that, he repeated the accomplishment, saying "In my fifteenth year I marched to the land of Nairi. I created at the source of the Tigris, where its water comes out, my royal statue."[43]

Rather unbelievably, both of these have been found and have been known for some time. Again, they are not actually freestanding statues, as these statements might lead us to believe, but rather more like carvings of the king and accompanying inscriptions incised into a rock face within the so-called Tigris Tunnel, located north of the modern city of Lice in Turkey and near a similar relief carved during an earlier campaign to the region by Tiglath-Pileser I. Taylor, the British archaeologist, was among the first Western explorers to visit the Tigris Tunnel. He did so in 1862, the year after he had found the two inscriptions at Kurkh, and published his description and discussion of the images carved on the rocks, as well as a preliminary translation by Sir Henry Rawlinson of one of the inscriptions, in the same edition of the *Journal of the Royal Geographic Society of London*.[44]

Just as Shalmaneser's likeness from his earlier campaign was shown on the upper register of Balawat Band I, so too one of these later reliefs belonging to Shalmaneser is also depicted on Balawat Band X (upper and lower registers). The Balawat bands contain depictions of other relevant scenes as well, for the lower register on Band I depicts an attack on the city of Sugunia on the left half and the aftermath of the battle on the right half, with a variety of prisoners shown yoked together. Together, these scenes on the upper and lower registers of Band I bring the events of his campaign in 858 BC to life. They are continued in a grim fashion on Band II, where the inscription simply reads "Smiting of . . . the land of Urartu" and which shows one or more additional Urartian cities being besieged, sacked, and burned—presumably from among the fourteen cities that were mentioned in the other inscriptions. We see prisoners and loot being carried off, their date plantations being chopped down, and some of the defenders impaled on tall wooden stakes on the walls while the heads of others are nailed to the towers.[45] Shalmaneser does not seem to have been merciful to the Urartians who resisted him during this first foray into their territory.

The same goes for his next campaign against them, which is depicted on Band VII of the Balawat gates. Here the inscription reads simply, "The city of Arame, the Urartian, I captured." This is a terse abbreviation for the much longer description on the Monolith Inscription, where he describes killing 3,400 Urartian soldiers, "raining destruction down upon them like the Storm-god," and dying the mountain like red wool with their blood, all while setting fire to various Urartian cities. All of this we see depicted in the upper register of Band VII, with Assyrian sappers tunneling under the walls of the city and setting fire to it while the Assyrian cavalry and infantry mow down the Urartian defenders without mercy.[46]

He also campaigned at greater length against a Urartian king named "Sarduri, son of Lutibri," who ruled ca. 834–828 BC and whom we now refer to as Sarduri I. It is during Sarduri's reign that we find the first inscriptions actually written in Urartian. Interestingly, they were inscribed using Neo-Assyrian language phrasing and cuneiform script, because they were apparently created by an Assyrian scribe who had been captured by the Urartians during the ninth century BC and brought back to their lands as a prisoner of war.[47]

In fact, for the very earliest inscription of Sarduri, the erstwhile scribe simply took a known Assyrian royal inscription of Aššurnasirpal II and carved it word for word onto the front-facing side of six huge blocks of stone, changing only the proper names so that it featured Sarduri instead of Aššurnasirpal—"Sarduri, son of Lutibri, great king, mighty king, king of the world, king of Nairi, king who has no equal, marvelous shepherd, fearless in battle, king who subdues those insubordinate to him."[48]

It was in 830 BC that Shalmaneser began fighting against Sarduri, who had taken over from the previous ruler (Aramu) in the interim. Sarduri founded a dynasty that would rule Urartu for the next two centuries, beginning with his son Ishpuini, followed by his grandson Menua, great-grandsons Inushpua and Argishti I, great-great grandson Sarduri II, and so on.[49]

Sarduri's main headquarters were located in the fortress of Tushpa (or Tushupa), located on a rocky outcrop by Lake Van, which is mentioned in a number of Assyrian annals. Many of the Urartian settlements were also fortresses similarly located in mountainous areas, making them difficult to attack. However, they were not impervious, and we have pictorial depictions such as those by Shalmaneser III on Band VII of the Balawat gates, showing Assyrian soldiers burning down Urartian fortresses built on mountain peaks.[50]

Thus, we may add Urartu to the list of new kingdoms that emerged during these centuries, filling the gaps left by the larger kingdoms and empires, such as the Hittites, which had not survived the Collapse of the Late Bronze Age. Overall, Urartu proved to be the most adept opponent of the Assyrians, putting up more fight than almost anyone else. It has been suggested that Shalmaneser's innovation of using cavalry in his army, which had not previously been much employed by the Assyrians, may have come from seeing the Urartian horseback riders among the forces whom they encountered. It has also been suggested that the later rise in the quantities of wine consumed by the Assyrians in the eighth century BC and thereafter was the result of interactions with (and importation from) Urartu, which was well-known as a wine-producing region back then, just as nearby Armenia still is today.[51]

Shalmaneser III and the Northern Levant

In 858 BC, during his first year on the throne, in addition to campaigning against Urartu, Shalmaneser describes fighting in the region of northern Syria against a number of Neo-Hittite kings, including Sangara of Carchemish and another whom he calls "Sapalulme, the Pantinean." Both of these kings have been mentioned just above; the latter is probably Suppiluliuma II, who ruled during the mid-ninth century BC in the Land of Palistin, shorted to Patin(a) by this time, after the better-known kings Taita I and II. Excavations in 2012 at the site of Tayinat, identified as his capital city of Kunulua by the University of Toronto team, uncovered the head and torso from a statue of this king, which may have originally stood as much as twelve feet tall (3.5–4.0 meters). On the large fragment is an incomplete inscription, which has not yet been published but reportedly includes the king's name.[52]

Shalmaneser also mentions his campaign against Sangara of Carchemish on Band VI of the Balawat gates. The inscription simply says, "The tribute of Sangara of Carchemish," which is then illustrated by the scenes in both the upper and lower registers. In the upper one, we see Shalmaneser standing in front of his tent (or royal pavilion), receiving an embassy sent by Sangara, complete with men carrying the tribute, which includes tusks of ivory and heavy bronze cauldrons. The actual city of Carchemish may also be depicted, off in the distance across the Euphrates. In the lower register, we see the fortified camp of the Assyrians on the riverbank and Sangara presenting his young daughter to Shalmaneser, with servants carrying her dowry; clearly she is part of the tribute offered by Sangara.[53] This apparently was not at all unusual, for on his Monolith Inscription, Shalmaneser mentions taking daughters and dowry from a number of other enemy kings during the course of his reign.

We know that one of the other Syro-Hittite kings who was allied with Sangara against Shalmaneser III in 858 was a man named Hayya, who ruled ca. 870/860–840 BC at Sam'al (modern Zincirli). Hayya is cited by name in Shalmaneser's annals for 858, 857, and 853 BC, where he is called "Hayyanu" (or "Haiianu") and specifically described as "the Sam'alite." After the conflict in 858, Shalmaneser says, "I took away from him many chariots and horses broken to the yoke. I erected pillars of skulls in front of his town, destroyed, demolished, and burnt down his towns." Following that defeat, Hayya submitted formally to Shalmaneser, reaffirming his loyalty over the next few years.[54]

His successors seem to have pledged allegiance to Assyria as well, including his son Sha'il (who seems to have served as co-ruler for a decade) and then another son named Kulamuwa (sometimes spelled Kilamuwa) who came to the throne ca. 840 BC and ruled for thirty years. Kulamuwa left us a basalt orthostat with a representation of himself carved into it, along with a sixteen-line inscription written in the Phoenician language but using an Aramaic script. Dating to ca. 825 BC, it was displayed in one of the buildings at Sam'al and was found long ago by German excavators. It has been the subject of discussions ever since. Here Kulamuwa records the names of both Hayya and Sha'il, while saying "My father's house was in the midst of mighty kings, and each stretched forth his hand to fight." He then indicates that he deliberately reached an agreement with an unnamed Assyrian king—probably Shalmaneser III, though it could possibly be Shamši-Adad V—and specifically worked with him to attack a mutual enemy: "The king of the Danunians was more powerful than me. But I engaged against him the king of Assyria."[55]

Shalmaneser III and the Country Lords of Carchemish

In his inscriptions, Shalmaneser III also lists a variety of other kings from whom he demanded tribute either just before or just after the Battle of Qarqar in 853 BC, in addition to the main combatants whom he defeated. Among them is "Sangara the Carchemishite," mentioned here numerous times and who also appears half a dozen times elsewhere in Shalmaneser's annals. In the final reference (Year 11), dated to 848 BC, Shalmaneser says that he captured ninety-seven of Sangara's cities, which is again an indication that Carchemish was by now a well-established kingdom with numerous cities answering to it. That is the last time Sangara is mentioned by Shalmaneser, which is why the dates of his rule are now typically given as 875–848 BC.[56]

This is not the last that we hear of Sangara, however, for he is mentioned again in another context, back home at Carchemish, almost sixty years later. This final inscription, dating to 790 BC, was ordered engraved by a descendant of Sangara named Kamani, when he became king at Carchemish. It was carved on a basalt stela more than two meters tall and dedicated to the goddess Kubaba, who is pictured on the uppermost part and called the "Queen of Carchemish." As part of the inscription, Kamani included his status and genealogy, listing the kings who had come before him, including his great-great-grandfather Sangara.[57]

The stela is now in six pieces, the first of which was found in 1876 and others of which were found by the British excavators in the years after 1911. Most recently, one of the fragments was located and retrieved in 2015, after having been stolen decades before and taken some 250 kilometers away. All told, the six pieces are now located in three different museums in three different countries: the British Museum, the Vatican Museum, and Gaziantep Museum in Turkey. They are all obviously from the same original monument and the detective work involved in tracking down the fragments is a story unto itself, which has been well told by others.[58]

Furthermore, with the help of another fragmentary inscription, we can flesh out the rest of the wording on this stela and reconstruct the genealogy of this dynasty of Country Lords who continued to rule Carchemish for more than a century, from 875 to 760 BC: "[I (am) Kamani, the Ruler,] the Country Lord of the cities Carchemish (and) Melid, son of Astiru(wa), the Country Lord, [grandson of Kuwalana-muwa, the Country Lord], great-grandson of Isarwila-muwa, the Country Lord, [great-great-grandson of] Sangara [. . .]."[59]

Thus, we now know that Sangara continued the line of Country Lords of Carchemish. We can also fill in, from other inscriptions, the names of still more Country Lords of Carchemish who ruled during the late ninth and into the eighth century BC as part of this dynastic line. All in all, we now know of approximately a dozen such rulers, from the time of Suhi I, ca. 1000 BC, right down to the last one, named Pisiri, who paid tribute to Tiglath-Pileser III in 738 BC but was then toppled from his throne by Sargon II in 717 BC when Carchemish was annexed and incorporated into the Assyrian Empire, finally ending four centuries of transformation and change after the Late Bronze Age Collapse.[60]

It would appear then that, from the early twelfth through the late eighth century BC, Carchemish continued to have a complex government hierarchy, rule over an outlying area with an unbroken string of kings, possess writing, and build monumental structures. Similar comments can be made, to varying degrees, regarding many of the other Neo-Hittite and Syro-Anatolian city-states across this region, and I think we can agree with Alessandra Gilibert that "the early Iron Age in Syro-Anatolia was not a period of deurbanization and stagnation but rather one of transition, marked by continuities as well as by changes in the sociopolitical structures."[61]

Brief Summation

It is clear that the Hittites failed to navigate the change to the Iron Age and yielded their territory to new kingdoms, including Urartu and the Phyrgians among others. An asterisk is required here, however, for credit must be given to the survivors who weathered the change successfully in southeastern Anatolia and the northern Levant, as represented, for example, by the territory governed by the sites of Carchemish and

Tell Tayinat, especially in the face of repeated aggression from the Assyrians over the centuries. A rather similar situation can be discovered in the Aegean, where the Mycenaeans also failed to properly adapt and the inhabitants of the Greek mainland had to essentially rebuild their society from scratch following the Collapse. We will turn to this next.

CHAPTER FIVE

In the Shadow of the Ruined Palaces

(Aegean Region)

In the 1870s, when the amateur archaeologist Heinrich Schliemann was excavating at the site of Mycenae on the Greek mainland, searching for the graves of Agamemnon and other heroes from the Trojan War, he found fragments of a large, smashed vase within a building on the acropolis. The vase was initially thought to date to the seventh century BC, but it was eventually realized that it comes from the twelfth century BC, that is, the time immediately after the destruction of the palace.[1]

On the sides of the vase can be seen two different groups of warriors, apparently marching to or from battle in full armor, complete with helmets on their heads, protective gear on their torsos, and greaves on their shins, plus shields and spears. It may well be that this can be seen as a dramatic representation of the period as a whole, with conflict and destruction a hallmark of these years. There are other fragmentary vases from this time period as well, from other mainland sites, depicting either warriors or ships or both, and indicating that this was a persistent theme during these years.[2]

Yet an unknown number of survivors or squatters occupied portions of Mycenae, even after the city had been destroyed. By the end of the century, though, even the citadel was abandoned by these few inhabitants. It then remained unoccupied until the eighth century BC, when a temple dedicated to either Hera or Athena was built at the very top, where the palace had once stood.

FIG. 10. Warrior vase from Mycenae. Photograph courtesy of Sharon Mollerus via Wikimedia Commons.

It is now clear that it took more than a century for the last vestiges of the Bronze Age Mycenaean palatial society to fade away and for the succeeding culture of the Iron Age to begin on mainland Greece. In some places, it is obvious that sites continued to be occupied in the twelfth century and even into the first decades of the eleventh, during what archaeologists call the post-palatial period.[3]

However, we have no written texts in Greece that date to the decades after the fall of the palaces or even just generally to the later twelfth century BC. Even the later accounts in Homer, Hesiod, Herodotus, and Thucydides discussing the time of the Trojan War and the period immediately thereafter cannot be taken at face value, because these are sources looking back at an era that no longer existed in their time.[4] Data gleaned from archaeology is our only hope.

Fortunately, just as is the case with Cyprus, there is a wealth of such data from both mainland Greece and Crete, including burials, pottery, and changes in settlement patterns. There are now literally hundreds of articles and numerous books that discuss topics either specifically about or relevant to the Iron Age in the Aegean region, emerging at an ever-faster pace as scholarly interest increases and new excavations and surveys take place.[5] All of this recent information has been subject to interpretation, reinterpretation, and, sometimes, decades of scholarly discussions and disputes, resulting in some new understandings about these centuries.

As a result, we now also have good evidence that some of the other inhabitants of the Greek mainland, not only at urban sites such as Mycenae but also out in the rural countryside, were able to hang on in the aftermath of the Collapse as well. For example, the tombs at Perati, mentioned in chapter 3, contain a myriad of imported small grave goods from Cyprus, Canaan, Anatolia, and Egypt, including items with pharaonic cartouches, indicating that the trade routes had not been completely cut.[6]

Not far from Mycenae, at Tiryns in the Argolid, the walls appear to have still been standing during much of the twelfth century, and extensive new building projects were undertaken, including the construction of Building T on top of the ruins of the Bronze Age palace in the Upper Citadel. In addition, the Lower City (the "Unterberg") continued to be occupied and used. Perhaps most surprisingly, there was even a new Lower Town built outside the city walls during this time. Only a small portion of this lower town has been excavated so far, but it appears to have been extensive, possibly built because of an influx of newcomers to the area. There is also evidence for various craftsmen still working at the site during this time, and imported goods still arrived, possibly along with some specific workers emigrating from the Near East. These immigrants may have brought with them a small ivory rod that was found at the site, bearing an inscription written in what appears to be Ugaritic. There is also a small clay ball inscribed with Cypro-Minoan markings that was found in these levels at the site. However, despite this evidence for cultural continuity, Tobias Mühlenbruch, who has published extensively on this period at Tiryns, calls it a time of "radical culture change." Eventually even this came to an end, though, as the site was finally abandoned by approximately 1100 BC.[7]

Down in the southern part of the mainland, the destruction at the Mycenaean palace at Pylos was also nearly complete, as discussed previously in *1177 B.C.* Yet here too there is evidence that some inhabitation and activity continued. New studies indicate that a few isolated rooms of the palace itself, including perhaps some pantries and the throne room, remained standing. They appear to have been in good enough shape to have been reused by survivors or squatters at some point between the time of the crisis and the early tenth century BC, though the date of occupation cannot be narrowed down more closely than that.[8]

Overall, in terms of overseas contact and trade, Sarah Murray, an archaeologist at the University of Toronto, has noted that imports from the Eastern Mediterranean also continued after the collapse of the palaces and that we should be talking about both quantitative and qualitive changes from the Bronze Age to the Iron Age. She has suggested that while there may have been a decrease in the intensity of such contacts, it is most likely attributable to the fact that there were simply fewer people living in Greece during this period. Ian Morris of Stanford University has also noted that "new settlements that grew up in the shadow of the ruined palaces in the twelfth century retained attenuated contacts with the Near East." However, he also notes that "trade declined sharply after a second wave of destruction circa 1100."[9]

Thus, in many ways, the Collapse did not constitute a completely clean break on the Greek mainland. There is unquestionably some degree of continuity during the twelfth century BC and into the eleventh, with obvious efforts at adaptation and transformation, even as the palaces fell one by one during the Collapse or in the decades thereafter. Agricultural practices, for example, seem to have continued despite the ongoing drought conditions. Even the pottery styles endure, such that we see modifications and variations on the standard Mycenaean forms and shapes—and hence the suboptimal, yet accurate archaeological name for this phase: Submycenaean. Continuity in religious beliefs is also in evidence, as the worship of Zeus, Hera, Poseidon, and others who are found in the Linear B texts of the Mycenaeans continues through the Iron Age and into the Classical Age.[10]

I wonder, though, what life would have been like in Greece for those living in the post-palatial period. Obviously, life in the urban centers had changed drastically; at virtually all of them, except perhaps at Tiryns, there seem to have been only squatters living amongst the ruins. Even at Tiryns it is not clear how much of the site was actually still occupied. As for the people out in the villages and towns of the hinterland, most scholars have concluded, on the basis of the meager evidence that we have, that many were now living in a less complex sociopolitical and economic environment than previously, quite possibly because of the loss of the palaces and the collapse of the administrative system that had been in place for centuries by that point.

In some cases, we can see the ripple effects that were felt as the palaces were replaced by smaller communities. For instance, it is clear from the eighth-century writings of Homer and Hesiod that the Linear B term *wanax* (wa-na-ka), which had previously been used to mean "king" during the Bronze Age, fell out of use during the early centuries of the Iron Age. In its place, *basileus* (qa-si-re-u), which had earlier referred to a lower-level "chieftain," was now used. And, instead of the previous palace administrators, there were now more local officials. In addition, writing itself was also temporarily lost as the palaces fell and the few literate scribes either died, moved, or simply lost their jobs since there was no longer any need for maintaining inventories and keeping accounts in the palaces, which had been the primary purpose for writing in Greece during the Mycenaean period.[11]

And yet, a number of scholars have suggested that not everyone in Greece would have mourned the collapse of the palaces, the passing of the palatial administrators, and the cessation of grand Mycenaean building and engineering projects, such as the Lion Gate and new fortification walls, the water tunnel, and the immense beehive tomb known as the Treasury of Atreus, all of which were constructed at Mycenae ca. 1250 BC. Such projects and the palatial economy may have impoverished the "regular" people toward the end of the Late Bronze Age. The demise of the palaces may have actually freed these people from a tremendous burden, such that some rural areas may have actually experienced a brief moment of prosperity in the decades immediately after the Collapse.[12]

Alex Knodell of Carleton College suggests, in fact, that we should see the palatial period in Late Bronze Age Greece as a failed experiment and that the Collapse allowed things to revert back to normalcy, as had been the case in Greece during the earlier part of the second millennium BC. "Rather than seeing the palaces as the culmination of an evolutionary trajectory of state formation followed by a collapse," he says, "we might see them as historical anomalies and societal experiments, which were ultimately unsuccessful."[13]

It is generally agreed, however, that the end of the Mycenaean period in Greece represents the end of an era. As Sigrid Deger-Jalkotzy, emeritus professor at the University of Vienna, has stated: "There is no doubt that the collapse of the advanced civilization of the Mycenaean palaces was a fundamental turning point in Greek history. The impressive palatial structures were not rebuilt, and very little of the representational arts and crafts of the palaces seems to have survived. The complex forms of political, social, and economic organization fell into oblivion. Palaces, kings, and royal families became matter for Greek myths. The art of writing was lost for centuries. In short, Greek civilization was reduced to the level of a prehistoric society."[14]

Meanwhile on Crete

By way of contrast, things on Crete seem to have gone even better in the immediate aftermath of the crisis, even if the specific trappings of Minoan society were no longer to be found. Recent research indicates that there were still signs of life at the capital city Knossos, for example. In addition, although it had been literally centuries since the Minoans were prominent enough in international trade to be mentioned by other societies, such as in the Mari tablets of the eighteenth century BC, or depicted in Egyptian tomb paintings during the fourteenth century BC, interactions with the Near East seem to have resumed, albeit at a lesser level than previously, just as Sarah Murray has documented for mainland Greece during this same period.

Saro Wallace, a senior research fellow at the Gerda Henkel Foundation in Germany, has noted recently that it was not that the inhabitants of Crete were less affected by the crisis of the Collapse than anyone else but rather that they seem to have better weathered the transition to the Iron Age via deliberate actions and widespread cultural readjustments that minimized the chaos. Their reaction, she says, stands out as a "strikingly early, coherent and creative" response to "conditions of increased insecurity and new opportunities," which resulted in what she calls a "positive collapse."[15] They seem to have adapted, and even perhaps transformed to a certain extent, rather than merely coping.

Along those lines, Polish archaeologist Krzysztof Nowicki's foot surveys on Crete, during which he daringly climbed many of the highest mountain peaks in order to search out archaeological remains, showed that there were numerous small settlements established in defensive positions high up in the mountains and away from the coast in the immediate aftermath of the Collapse, perhaps to avoid piracy.[16]

However, there is also evidence that life at several of the larger Cretan sites, such as Phaistos and Chania in addition to Knossos, continued without interruption even though the palaces were now in ruins. There was apparently much continuity in terms of urban settlement, economic stability, religious cults and sanctuaries, and burial practices, all of which formed the basis of the Cretans' successful strategy for survival, as documented by Wallace and others.[17]

In sum, the glory days of the Minoan civilization during the mid-second millennium BC may have disappeared forever, but Crete itself and its surviving inhabitants carried on during the Iron Age, adapting to the new normal. However, one could argue that it came at a cost, for they lost their cultural identity as "Minoans," that is, the "Keftiu" as they had been known to the Egyptians and "Caphtorians" as they were called by the merchants in Mari and Ugarit during the Late Bronze Age. However, to be perfectly transparent, they may have already been on the road to losing that collective identity when they were taken over by the Mycenaeans ca. 1350 BC; Metaxia Tsipopoulou, a specialist on the Bronze and Iron Ages in the Aegean and director of the Petras excavations on Crete, has suggested the term "Mycenoans" to describe the population living on Crete during the last phase of the Late Bronze Age, that is, from the late fourteenth century onward.[18]

The Arrival of the Alphabet

We have already explored in chapter 3 the general consensus that the alphabet was brought to the Aegean by the Phoenicians, at least according to the later Greeks. However, it is not at all clear when this took place. The first artifact with a Phoenician inscription found in the Aegean region is a bronze bowl likely to be of Cypriot manufacture that was found in Tomb J at the Tekke cemetery at Knossos on Crete. Incised on the rim of the bowl are four words that are difficult to read and even more difficult to translate. A variety of suggestions have been made thus far, with the most likely being "bowl of [or belonging to] x, son of y"). The tomb itself is now usually dated to the late tenth century, that is, 950–900 BC, but the bowl was probably already an heirloom at the time that it was buried, for it is thought to date a bit earlier, to about 1000 BC.[19]

The inscription on this bowl indicates that the alphabet may well have reached the Aegean long before ca. 800 BC, which is the usual date that most scholars have suggested in the past. Interestingly, although the oldest Greek inscriptions generally date to the second half of the eighth century, research has now shown that there may have been as many as thirty-three different variations of the alphabet in use within the Aegean area before a standard set of letters was accepted. Thus, some scholars are now cautiously suggesting that the initial arrival of the alphabet may have taken place as early as the eleventh century BC, and that inhabitants in the Aegean might have been writing on perishable materials such as leather, wood, or lead for some time.[20]

An attractive aspect of this suggestion is that an earlier date would match the timeline for the development and use of the alphabet in the Near East rather than having the Aegean lag three centuries behind their neighbors to the east. One of the earliest Phoenician inscriptions that we have in the Eastern Mediterranean is the Azarba'al Inscription, which was found at Byblos and dates to the late eleventh or early tenth century BC. The six lines of writing are incised into a bronze spatula, but unfortunately the text is broken and incomplete. Thus, we are not completely certain what it says, but it seems to involve both money and ancestral land. Another Phoenician text, dating from approximately the same time, is written on a bronze vessel that was found in a tomb at Kefar Veradim in Israel. It clearly identifies the owner: "The cup of Pesah, son of Shema."[21]

Willemijn Waal of Leiden University has observed that "Since the Greeks had contact with the Phoenicians (and other people) who made use of writing, it seems hardly credible that Greece, as the only region in the area, would have remained illiterate for over three centuries—especially since, as we now know, this period was not all bleak and regressive." It is clear that there was, in fact, a need for a new writing system in Greece at the time, since Linear B had promptly fallen out of use when the Mycenaean palatial system collapsed. If the Phoenicians brought the alphabet as early as the eleventh century BC, that would mean that there was only a brief period of time without writing on the Greek mainland, perhaps only about a century or so, rather than a gap lasting as long as four centuries.[22]

Regardless of when it arrived, the alphabetic system presented a breakthrough for the Greeks, for it enabled everybody and anybody to learn how to read and write, not simply palace scribes doing accounting for the administration. But how and why did the transfer of this new writing system take place? Did it initially happen in port cities, for instance, for use by private merchants importing goods? Did a Greek merchant or sailor learn it from a Phoenician trader? How did it then spread and why were there so many initial variants? Were there scribal schools that enrolled many young students learning a relatively simple system? Was it primarily used at first to inscribe one's name on an item, perhaps to mark one's property, as per the Tekke bowl and as Antonio Kotsonas has noted for the period when early Greek writing was for certain being used, namely, from the eighth century BC onward?[23]

Rudolf Wachter, of the University of Lausanne, has suggested that it would have only taken weeks, rather than months or years, for the alphabet to spread over much of the Aegean region once it had been adopted/invented. This seems perhaps a bit too rapid, but he envisions the original adoption to having probably taken place during "a rather casual meeting of some Greek and Phoenician traders in any Mediterranean harbour" and adds that it would have taken only "a small group of no more than one or two Greeks, preferably traders far from home, sitting together with a Phoenician who told them about the use of script for writing letters, order lists, short memoranda, and so forth, and then taught them the series of letter names and passed on to them an abecedarium. We might imagine such a meeting to have happened in a common settlement of Greeks and Phoenicians."[24]

However, the main problem with suggesting such an early date for the arrival of the alphabet is, quite simply, the apparent low level of complexity of Greek society in this period and the relative sparseness of the remains from eleventh century BC contexts on mainland Greece. This may be an accident of archaeological preservation, however, for as Ian Morris has noted, "Dark Age houses [were] flimsy, and . . . survive poorly." On the other hand, he also points out that "barely one-tenth as many sites are known from the eleventh century as from the thirteenth."[25]

There seems to have been a further downturn in Greece during the eleventh century. Styles of pottery change rather dramatically at this point and there was additional depopulation in the rural areas of Greece. Almost all remnants of Mycenaean "material culture" finally disappeared and it is fairly safe to say that we can point to the middle of this century, ca. 1050 BC, at the latest as the time when Mycenaean society as it had been known came to an end.[26]

And yet, not all was abysmal, for Morris suggests that there was also a "revolution" in Greece that began at approximately this same time, which included a shift from bronze to iron—seen predominantly in grave goods—and a new diversity in the types of burials, including possibly many that are now "invisible" to us, since they were of the lower classes and left few traces. He also sees this period, which lasted for the next century and a half until the beginning of the ninth century, that is, from 1050 to 900 BC, as an era of stability, since it ended the chaos left by the collapse of the Mycenaean palaces.[27]

Sites began to grow larger again, especially over the course of the tenth century. For instance, Athens may have been made up of a group of villages by this time (much as Sparta would be later), though this is still a disputed point, and there may have been as many as three thousand to five thousand people living in this one city by the end of the tenth century BC. Morris also stated, in publications from 1995 and the early 2000s, that he thought there were also other sites with relatively large populations, including 600–1,200 people living at Argos in the Peloponnese and perhaps 1,250–2,500 living at Knossos on Crete.[28]

However, it seems now that even Morris may have underestimated the situation, at least at some of the sites. On Crete, for example, there is now new evidence that Knossos may have been larger than previously expected at this time. Some had already suspected as much, with Nicholas Coldstream—one of the most revered British scholars ever to study the Iron Age Aegean and Cyprus—remarking on the fact that numerous cemeteries at Knossos date to this time period, covering an area of five kilometers from north to south. Assuming that the cemeteries were on the outskirts of the city, which seems most likely, Coldstream noted in 2006, "If the size of a community were measured by its cemeteries, then Early Greek Knossos would be by far the largest city of its time in the Aegean world."[29]

Surveys conducted since the early 2000s by the Knossos Urban Landscape Project (KULP) now indicate that during the eleventh century BC this might actually be correct. If their findings are accurate, it appears that Knossos was three to four times larger than we thought, covering an area up to fifty to sixty hectares (almost 150 acres)—enough to house a population of at least three thousand to four thousand people. While that is a smaller area than Knossos covered during the Bronze Age, it is extremely large for a Greek Iron Age city and is more than even Ian Morris had suggested twenty years ago.

As a result of the new surveys, Kotsonas of New York University has recently declared that it appears "Knossos recovered quickly from the upheavals of the late 2nd millennium, grew rapidly in size, and flourished as a cosmopolitan hub of the Aegean and the Mediterranean in a way that revolutionizes our understanding of the Greek Early Iron Age."[30]

Still, it can no longer be called a Minoan city, for Minoan society had vanished along with that of the Mycenaeans by this time, and Crete was beginning the transition to a new phase in its history. Nevertheless, the islanders did not forget their Bronze Age antecedents, as we shall see in a moment.

"Warrior Burials" Again

Already back in the 1990s, Hector Catling, a former director of the British School of Archaeology at Athens known for his work with ancient bronze vessels, suggested that the so-called warrior burials that have been found on Cyprus and in various parts of the Aegean in eleventh- and tenth-century BC contexts (mentioned in chapter 3), should be "associated with the return of 'Homeric' heroes from Troy," in part to explain the Cypriot objects found on Crete in these contexts. For example, a man buried in Tomb 186 within the North Cemetery at Knossos has been identified as "a man-at-arms, equipped with bronze spear and iron dirk, iron knife, and two stones for honing his blades." Catling pointed especially to the iron dirk and knife, as well as the two honing stones, as being most likely from Cyprus, citing parallels from the tombs at Palaepaphos-Skales.[31]

In another burial (Tomb 201) within the same cemetery at Knossos were found the cremated remains of two adults (one male, one female) and possibly a child as well. The grave goods included fragments from a bronze tripod stand identified as coming from Cyprus, and a number of weapons, in addition to other items. Catling identified the male burial as that of a warrior who "was fully armed with sword, spear, and massive arrowheads." In addition to the sword and spear, there was also evidence that he was buried with a shield and a boar's-tusk helmet; the arrowheads would have come from now-disintegrated arrows that were probably in a quiver, of which a few fragments were also found.[32]

Catling was especially taken with the presence of the boar's-tusk helmet, which must have been an heirloom at that point, for such helmets had gone out of use, and fashion, long before. He concluded, "Our warrior was a flamboyant figure, in the light of his possessions—at least, in terms of the Greek Dark Ages. I believe he is a figure for whom analogies can be found in Homer, and for whom there are parallels in other archaeological discoveries."[33]

Catling then went on to make a rather daring suggestion, namely, that the evidence from this cemetery at Knossos suggests that some of the inhabitants in these eleventh-century BC burials "may have been survivors and descendants of the old Minoan stock, but it is likely that there were new elements among them, people from outside Crete, or returned to Crete following a prolonged absence, perhaps spent in the E[astern] Mediterranean. Newcomers may have forced their leadership on the native population; it may have been their choice to open new burial grounds, the N[orth] Cemetery among them. I suggest the warriors whose ashes were buried in [Tombs] 186 and 201 may have been such newcomers, set apart from the autochthonous population by their funerary customs, particularly the rite of cremation."[34]

In addition, in relation to the various grave goods in these burials, Catling cited Homer's *Odyssey*, which described the various heroes' journeys back to Greece after the Trojan War had ended (known in general as the *Nostoi*, i.e., the "Returns") and the goods they brought back with them. In one instance, when Menelaos, Helen's husband, talks about his wanderings around the Eastern Mediterranean, he says, "My travels took me to Cyprus, to Phoenicia, and to Egypt. Ethiopians, Sidonians, Erembi, I visited them all; and I saw Libya" (*Od.* 4.83–85). Later, Menelaos describes a bowl that he is about to give to Telemachos, which also has a storied biography: "I'll give you a mixing bowl of wrought metal. It is solid silver with a rim of gold round the top, and was made by Hephaestus himself. I had it from my royal friend the King of Sidon, when I put up under his roof on my journey home" (*Od.* 4.615–19).[35]

This is why Catling links these "warrior burials" seen on Cyprus, Crete, and mainland Greece to Odysseus, Menelaus, and other Homeric "heroes" who wandered around the Eastern Mediterranean while en route home from the Trojan War. He suggested "that some Cretans spent extended periods in Cyprus in the first half of the eleventh century B.C." and that "the grandees/heroes of North Cemetery Tombs 186 and 201 could have spent part of their lives in Cyprus, where they might have been children of ethnic Cretans, born and bred in Cyprus, or they might have started their lives in Crete and returned there after a prolonged absence, of which part at least was spent in Cyprus."[36]

While not all scholars accept Catling's suggestions, these burials might indeed represent the emergence of a new group of local elites in both Cyprus and Greece. James Muhly, emeritus professor at the University of Pennsylvania, for instance, sees them as "ruthless warlords, warrior princes determined to create something new out of the wreckage of the old: warriors with the drive, energy, and ambition to seize everything they could and fashion some sort of power base for themselves." Others have suggested that, in Cyprus at least, they might be "glimpses of evidence for the presence and activity of armed men who may have been involved in a power struggle over the island's new territorial definition."[37]

More recently, Kotsonas reexamined Catling's "warrior" in Knossos Tomb 201 and linked it specifically with the figure of Meriones, a young and lesser-known Achaean hero of the *Iliad,* famous for his prowess as an archer, who came to Troy under the leadership of Idomeneus, king of Knossos. Kotsonas notes that the entire assemblage of weapons and other related grave goods is unique to this particular burial, out of all of the graves that have been excavated in the Iron Age Aegean, and that the assemblage as a whole is comparable to the equipment that Meriones gives to Odysseus in book 10 of the *Iliad,* which includes a bow, a quiver, a boar's tusk helmet, and a sword (*Il.* 10.260–65). As Kotsonas remarks, "These weapons are very uncommon in the epic, as much so as in the archaeological record." He further points out that Meriones possesses the only boar's-tusk helmet mentioned by Homer in the *Iliad* and that he "is exceptional among the Greeks in using the bow," noting that Meriones wins the archery contest at the funeral games for Patroclus (*Il.* 23.859–95).[38]

This is not, of course, Meriones himself who is buried in this grave at Knossos, since Meriones is thought by scholars to be a very early Greek hero, much like Ajax and a few other Mycenaean warriors from the Trojan War whose preexisting stories were incorporated into the *Iliad* during the development of the epic over time. However, Kotsonas advances the intriguing suggestion that what we are seeing here is the burial of a prominent inhabitant of Iron Age Knossos whose family "staged his funeral as a performance that promoted the connection of the deceased with Meriones," the hero from Crete.[39]

How Kotsonas's suggestion may or may not fit with Catling's earlier musings on Homeric "heroes" wandering around the Eastern Mediterranean or Iron Age Cretans spending time on Cyprus has yet to be determined, but it is certainly food for thought, especially since this tomb also contained a bronze tripod stand identified as coming from Cyprus. It also fits well with Renfrew's definition of a system collapse, in which the survivors look back to the previous age with envy and concoct romantic tales about it, as perhaps the man buried in this Iron Age tomb, or his family, looked back to the Bronze Age figure of Meriones.

The Hero of Lefkandi

Of all the so-called warrior burials, the one known as the "Hero of Lefkandi" may be considered among the most important, although it dates slightly later, to ca. 950 BC. The story of its discovery begins back in 1981, when the owner of a plot of land located at Lefkandi on Euboea began bulldozing a large earthen mound on the property, in an illegal attempt to build a summer home. Fortunately, he was stopped by the authorities who then authorized archaeologists to begin salvage excavations. They soon uncovered an apsidal building made of mudbrick. It measures forty-five to fifty meters (150 feet) long and is the largest known built structure from this period. After it went out of use, it was deliberately covered over with a huge mound of earth, which is what the modern landowner was trying to remove with his bulldozer.[40]

Underneath the floor of the apsidal building, the archaeologists uncovered an unusual double burial, which contained the remains of a man who had been cremated and a younger woman who had been buried but not cremated. A second grave nearby contained the remains of four horses, two of them with iron bits in their mouths. They had presumably been sacrificed at the time of burial.[41]

The ashes of the cremated man had been wrapped in a textile and placed in a bronze amphora of Cypriot manufacture decorated with bulls, lions, and human archers around the rim and on the handle. His female companion was buried near him along with grave goods that included an iron knife with an ivory handle perhaps imported from the Levant, which lay near her head. Some have suggested that the woman was sacrificed at the man's death, based on the location of the knife and indications that her hands may have been bound, but there is no proof either way at this point. She was also wearing a necklace with an impressive golden pendant imported from the Near East. This is clearly an heirloom, since it dates to the Bronze Age. There were also gold and iron dress-pins as well as sheet-gold ornaments that may have once been attached to her dress or tunic.[42]

Scholars are divided on whether the huge apsidal house was already in use and the graves were dug beneath its floors, much as infants were often buried beneath the floor of a house, or whether the house was built after the graves had been dug in order to mark their position. Regardless, the inhabitants of the area subsequently buried the apsidal building under a mound of earth (the same mound that so disturbed the modern farmer who owned the land), and it stood as a giant tumulus—archaeological jargon for a mound of earth raised over a grave—for thousands of years. Many scholars refer to this whole arrangement as a *heroön*, or "hero's grave," which is usually associated with a cult of hero worship. These are known especially from the Iron Age in Greece, which fits this instance well.[43]

Personally, I suspect that the building was most likely in existence prior to the deaths of the man and woman buried beneath it, though I would say that it is not clear whether it served as a private home or more of an administrative building. Either way, Irene Lemos, of the University of Oxford, who has been directing excavations at Lefkandi since 2003, says, ". . . there is no doubt that the man buried at Toumba was the leader of Lefkandi in the early 10th century. The male burial in the Toumba building was given the most amazing funeral so far evinced in EIA Greece."[44]

So, was he really the leader of Lefkandi during this period, as Lemos thinks? Why was he cremated rather than simply buried? And how exactly was he cremated—should we imagine it to be like the scene of

Patroclus's funeral pyre in book 23 of the *Iliad*? Furthermore, who was the woman buried with him? Was she his wife? A consort? Or simply a random sacrifice? All have been suggested. Why wasn't she also cremated? Was the knife near her neck involved in her death? There are no answers yet, but the existence of such an elaborate, rich burial within such a large structure and with imported objects shows the resurgence of Greek society, the increase in social inequality, and, once again, close links to the Eastern Mediterranean.

There are also additional tombs from elsewhere in the so-called Toumba cemetery located near the Lefkandi *heroön* that date to the tenth century BC as well. Some scholars have suggested that the cemetery grew up around the hero's tumulus. These tombs also contain imported objects such as a Phoenician jug and a Cypriot wheeled stand made of bronze. It is unclear how these imported objects reached Lefkandi or who brought them; it has been variously suggested that they could have been carried by Phoenicians or Cypriots, or even by local Euboeans who were returning from the Eastern Mediterranean.[45]

Overall, the evidence from mainland Greece makes it clear that contact with the Near East had been reestablished by ca. 925 BC and perhaps much earlier, if indeed it had ever been lost. Morris notes that "bronze, gold, ivory and other Near Eastern imports return to central Greek graves, and more Greek pottery is found overseas." He says, in particular, "by 925, Phoenicians were once again voyaging to the central and West Mediterranean, sometimes calling into the Aegean along the way."[46]

Of particular interest is a recent study that presents evidence for copper from the Wadi Faynan region of Jordan, which reached southwestern Greece by ca. 950 BC. I mentioned these copper mines in chapter 1, but this is the first indication that any copper from the region was reaching Greece. Interestingly, it was used to produce bronze cauldrons at the site of Olympia, where the Olympic Games would be launched some two centuries later.[47] The use of copper from Faynan rather than from Cyprus is surprising, but perhaps it is yet another indication that the Cypriots had turned primarily to working in iron by this point.

The Rich Athenian Lady and Other Burials

We should also keep in mind something that Anthony Snodgrass said in 1971, when he suggested that the second half of the tenth century in Greece was in some ways "a false dawn," stating that the "slow progress of Greek culture in the ninth and early eighth centuries comes as a disappointment after this."[48] I believe that we may be more optimistic now and would suggest instead that Greece might have begun the road to recovery by this point, though it would be a long and hard haul.

In this context, we can point especially to a discovery that was made in Athens, in an area on the North Slope of the Areopagus near the Acropolis and the Classical Agora. Here, in June 1967, American archaeologists uncovered the grave of what was soon dubbed the "Rich Athenian Lady." Dating to the mid-ninth century (ca. 850 BC), it portrayed a picture of more affluence during that period than had previously been expected. When Evelyn Smithson, a professor at the University at Buffalo (State University of New York), first published the tomb the following year, she described it as "the richest of post-Mycenaean times in the Agora area and perhaps the richest of its period in Athens."[49]

The lady in this grave had been cremated, with her burned remains gathered up and placed in a very large urn decorated with geometric designs. The mouth of the urn had been tightly closed by inserting an intact cup at the time of burial, which prevented any earth from getting into the vessel. Included among the grave goods were pieces of gold jewelry, including gold rings and a pair of earrings; faience and glass beads thought to have come from a necklace; two stamp seals made of ivory; a pair of bronze fibulae; and three or four straight pins (one of iron, the rest of bronze). There were also numerous ceramic vases and bowls, plus what is now an extremely well-known small ceramic chest with five model granaries on it.[50]

Smithson thought that the woman buried in the grave might have been either the daughter or the wife of a high-ranking member of the aristocracy. She also suspected that the Rich Athenian Lady was not alone in her grave but could not prove that, even though the remains were examined by J. Lawrence Angel, one of the most celebrated and respected biological anthropologists working in Greece at the time, who had been tasked with studying many of the human remains from the Late Bronze Age and Early Iron Age tombs in this area.[51]

However, it was not until 2004, nearly forty years after the initial publication, that Maria Liston of the University of Waterloo and John Papadopoulos of UCLA announced that Smithson's intuition had been correct. The lady had, in fact, been pregnant at the time of her death, and the bones of the fetus have now been conclusively identified, mixed in with hers. Since the woman seems to have been thirty to thirty-five years old and otherwise in good health, Liston and Papadopoulos suggest that there is a good chance she died in childbirth.[52]

Other ninth-century graves in addition to that of the Rich Athenian Lady have also been excavated in Athens, both near the Classical Agora and in the Kerameikos cemetery, including numerous burials that have recently been published and/or restudied. For instance, in the same general area as the Rich Athenian Lady is Tomb 13, known as the "Warrior Grave." First published by Carl Blegen in 1952, this cremation burial dates to the Early Geometric I period, ca. 900–875 BC. Because of the numerous weapons and tools found within it, all made of iron, Blegen thought that it was the burial "of a warrior-craftsman," who appeared to have been about thirty-four years old when he died. More recent discussions have simply called him a "warrior," and his age at death is now thought to have been closer to forty years old.[53]

The burned bones of this warrior had been placed into a large amphora that stood approximately half a meter high. The mouth of the jar was covered with a large field stone, though dirt had gotten in over the centuries. There were a number of ceramic vessels in the tomb, not unexpectedly, but what was unusual were the weapons and tools that had apparently been gathered up from the funeral pyre, wrapped in cloth, and placed in the tomb—Blegen noted that "clear traces of the warp and the woof of the fabric were visible on some of the pieces of iron."[54]

Along with two spearheads, two knives, a chisel, and an ax, all of iron, there was also a long, iron sword that had been ritually "killed" before burial, by being bent into an almost complete loop before being dropped over the top of the amphora, so that it lay as a band around the neck and handles, resting on the shoulders of the jar.[55] The dead man must clearly have been someone of importance, for it is unusual to have sent him into the afterlife with all of these fine iron objects rather than reusing them.

As for burials elsewhere, Nicholas Coldstream has pointed out that there is an almost universal change to cremations for the burials at this time, possibly to help conserve space in already-crowded family tombs. He also notes that the number of new interments in the North Cemetery at Knossos on Crete indicates "a rapid growth of population" at this time. Supporting evidence comes from new settlements that were established in this period, some of which would become the nucleus of the various city-states that flourished in Archaic Crete.[56]

There is also an interesting burial in the Tekke cemetery at Knossos—the same cemetery that held the grave containing the Cypriot bowl with the Phoenician inscription. This burial is in what appears to have originally been a Minoan tholos tomb, which was subsequently reused for generations from the late ninth century to the early seventh century BC. Among the numerous objects and burial urns in the tomb, there are items of jewelry, including a beautiful gold necklace with crystal and amber inlays, and raw materials that were buried together in two jars hidden beneath the floor of the tomb just inside the entrance.

These items were initially hypothesized to be the property of a jeweler or goldsmith, thought to be from northern Syria, who had emigrated to Crete and settled at Knossos with his family. This fanciful suggestion, made long ago by Sir John Boardman, has been used and debated ever since to discuss whether there were Near Eastern immigrants, particularly craftsmen, who settled on Crete during this century. However, restudy of these items and their context within the tomb has cast doubt on the hypothesized owner of this particular set of objects, with suggestions that the family might have been local elites rather than immigrants. Even without the evidence of this tomb, it is still accepted that there were probably Near Eastern craftsmen living on Crete at this time.[57]

Eventual Resilience and Adaptation

Ian Morris sees the links between Greece and the Near East dwindling again between 825 and 800 BC, so that "by the early eighth century graves are generally poorer and simpler than at any time since the tenth century." In fact, he has suggested that the whole system on mainland Greece "ran into trouble by 900, and collapsed around 750, with the rise of the *polis*." Since there were still contacts with the Eastern Mediterranean at this time, Morris thinks that it means that "by 800 BC, Greeks had negotiated among themselves a new relationship to the Near East."[58]

But such a second collapse isn't at all clear, for we have evidence of continued contacts between the Near East and the Aegean throughout this time. Phoenician pottery has been found at Knossos on Crete in contexts dated to ca. 800 BC. Additional objects, though primarily from later eighth-century BC contexts, have been found at the site of Eleutherna in western Crete. Both may indicate the continuous presence of resident Near Eastern craftsmen in Crete. Vice versa, it has also long been argued that Aegean personnel may have been in residence at the port site of Al Mina, located in what is now the region of coastal southeastern Turkey and northern Syria.[59]

Eventually, by the middle of the eighth century BC, ca. 750 BC at the earliest, we can talk about Greek culture resuming on a path that led to more than simply basic subsistence and eking out a living. James Whitley, the author of a volume on Iron Age Greece, says that "the Aegean is a region where state formation . . . happened twice: the first took place in the Bronze Age, and led to the Palace civilisations of Minoan Crete and Mycenaean Greece; the second took place in the Early Iron Age, and led to the civilisation of Archaic and Classical Greece."[60]

We must therefore, give the Greeks credit for resiliency in some form, for despite the instability and insecurity that was present during these centuries in Greece, overall they did eventually rebuild rather than being completely replaced by new people. Here in the Aegean, despite the false tradition of the Dorian invasion, the ethnicity and identity of the people themselves may not have changed too terribly much—that is to say, there weren't necessarily huge migrations and new peoples coming into the area in the aftermath of the Collapse—but rather it was the sociocultural and political circumstances that changed for the most part—an adaptation of the remaining population to the new harsh realities of an environment beset by drought and where famine and political instability were a matter of course.

Now, however, in the eighth century BC, the Greeks were positioned once again to take a full-fledged part in an international network of contacts and interconnections from the Western Mediterranean to the Eastern Mediterranean. It had been a hard trek through the centuries—harder than it had been for most of the other civilizations and societies that we have considered here—but on the horizon during the rest of the eighth century would be the lasting tales of poets Homer and Hesiod; the occasion of the first Olympics, traditionally dated to 776 BC;[61] the rise of the *polis* and the Greek colonization movement; new forms of pottery; and many of the other societal trappings and complexities that had been temporarily lost with the collapse of the Mycenaean palaces some four hundred years earlier.

Brief Summation

In brief, the Mycenaeans and Minoans of mainland Greece and Crete failed to navigate the change to the Iron Age with their societies intact. Although there is continuity between Bronze Age Greece and Iron Age Greece, and the same for Crete, the societies that we identify as Mycenaean and Minoan came to an end certainly by the close of the eleventh century BC at the latest. The survivors had to rebuild, essentially from scratch, and, despite occasional instances to the contrary, when not all was bleak and regressive, it is not until the eighth century BC at the earliest that we can talk about Greek culture resuming on a path that led to more than simply basic subsistence and scratching out a living.

At this point, since we have now completed our brief examination of all the societies that were directly affected by the Late Bronze Age Collapse and how they fared in the centuries immediately after, we can begin analyzing what we have learned. We will do this in the next, and final, chapter.

CHAPTER SIX

From Collapse to Resilience

For some, the end was sudden—invaders sacked their city or an earthquake brought down the walls of a house upon its occupants. For others, it was a catastrophe in slow motion, with drought impacting the crops and famine decimating the population. Nobody in the Aegean or Eastern Mediterranean regions escaped the effects of the Late Bronze Age Collapse. Virtually everyone was affected in some way, shape, or form: rich and poor, aristocrat and peasant, victims and survivors, those whose lives changed drastically or just a little. Life as they knew it, and as they had known it for centuries before, changed irrevocably. Those who survived the calamities of that age had to adapt, carry on, find some way to persist—even as the drought continued, the trade routes disappeared or became prey to bandits and raiders, and basic resources became scarce.[1]

Whether one sees this as a collapse, a transformation, or both, it is clear that the interconnected world as its inhabitants had known it during the Late Bronze Age ceased to exist.[2] Many of the large empires and kingdoms that had flourished during the second millennium BC fell like dominoes. As we have now seen during the course of the previous chapters, this resulted in a reconfiguration of the regions, as some were replaced by smaller entities, including those known from the Hebrew Bible as the Israelites, Judahites, Phoenicians, Moabites, Ammonites, and Edomites, as well as others including the Arameans and Neo-Hittites. That much is clear and unarguable.

Archaeologists Patricia McAnany and Norman Yoffee have said that studying any societal collapse is like viewing a low-resolution digital photograph: "it's fine when small, compact, and viewed at a distance but dissolves into disconnected parts when examined up close."[3] That is certainly correct, but I think that the Collapse and its aftermath can also be even more reasonably compared to an Impressionist painting. When viewed from a distance, the picture of what happened is clear: the globalized Mediterranean network collapsed, and there was a dramatic change or transition from the Bronze Age to the succeeding Iron Age. But when we get right up close, as we have done in the chapters above, things become more granular; the individual dabs of paint (i.e., societies) become more discrete to the eye; outliers and exceptions begin to surface; and the overall picture becomes less unified, with the viewer potentially losing the forest for the trees. What appears as a collapse to someone looking from a distance becomes merely societal transformations to another viewer perched just inches from the scene. And yet, both are correct in their own way.

A Sense of Endings and Beginnings

Painting with broad brush strokes, what we see in general from the twelfth century BC onward is a fragmentation and decline in security and material standards of living in the years immediately after the Collapse, continuing down through the tenth century or thereabouts, as the Bronze Age kingdoms fell apart. In the areas that were affected to the greatest extent, including mainland Greece, Crete, Anatolia, and the southern Levant especially, there was a collapse of the local palaces, states, or kingdoms (including government, centralized economy, and so on) even if segments of the population managed to survive.

However, reintegration then begins during the ninth century and continues through the eighth century as the Assyrians conquer most of the area, Mediterranean trade booms in the hands of Phoenicians and Cypriots, and potential rivals like the United Monarchy, Damascus, and Egypt eventually fall by the wayside, to be followed later by Assyria and then Babylonia in the late seventh and sixth centuries, respectively.

To put it another way, and to emphasize the material side of things, in general the period from the twelfth through the tenth centuries BC saw population crashes, abandonment of cities, violence, probable migrations, the collapse of trade routes, disease, earlier ages at death, falling economic output, lower standards of living, and the loss or decline of advanced skills, though the extent varies depending on where one looks in the region. In contrast, the period from the beginning of the ninth century BC onward saw many of those trends reversed. By the time we reach the second half of the eighth century BC, we see new life and new innovations in many of the areas, and a fully interconnected world begins to take shape once again for the first time in several centuries.[4]

Many things remain unclear, however, including the extent to which migration played a role across the entire region and whether the fluctuations in population seen in some areas during these centuries, such as on mainland Greece, could have had as much to do with migration as it did with the actual demise of people. Investigation of such possible migrations during and immediately after the LBA Collapse is ongoing today, and we might do well to remember that at the beginning of this book we discussed the Dorian invasion as likely to have been more of a migration than an actual invasion. We have also noted in passing the hypothesis that the Ammonites may have migrated down from Anatolia in the aftermath of the LBA Collapse. Other possibilities have been suggested as well, including conjectured migrations of Luwian speakers into northern Canaan and of Phrygians into central Anatolia. Even Herodotus was convinced that there had been a migration from Lydia (in modern Turkey) to Italy because of a drought ca. 1200 BC, which explained the origins of the Etruscans for him.[5]

Speaking of the drought, I also cannot help but wonder just how much role climate change played in the recovery, for we can see several breaks in the weather that may be directly or indirectly related to developments in the various areas. For example, we have noted (a) slightly wetter climate conditions in the southern Levant during the period from ca. 1150 BC to 950 BC, which in turn permitted "intense olive and cereal cultivation" and may have given the Israelites and others a chance to establish their kingdoms;[6] (b) a change to a much wetter era in Mesopotamia from ca. 925 BC onward, which may have allowed the Neo-Assyrians to regroup and begin conquering the surrounding territories; and (c) a general change from arid conditions to warmer and wetter conditions in the entire region, including Cyprus and perhaps Greece as well, from ca. 850 BC onward, which may have helped all of the areas and societies to begin (or continue) climbing back to full recovery.

The Adaptive Cycle and the IPCC Reports

It is at this point that we may find some modern studies to be of additional use, in terms of comparison and analysis, including those of other societies in different times and different places. For instance, some scholars argue that collapse is simply part of the natural rhythm of things that every empire or society experiences—that is, it is part of an infinite cycle of rise and fall, collapse, restructuring, rebirth, and rebuilding. One could think of it in terms of another line from *Hamilton,* "oceans rise; empires fall," but this rise and fall is known officially in resilience literature as the "adaptive cycle" and is drawn as a figure eight on its side, with four phases.[7]

Two parts of this concept, the alpha and omega phases, may be especially important to help explain what we see during the Collapse and in its immediate aftermath. The omega (Ω) phase is defined as the "chaotic collapse and release" part of the adaptive cycle, whereas the alpha (α) phase is seen as the "phase of reorganization." This latter reorganization phase can take place either quickly or slowly, but most important, it is also the phase "during which innovation and new opportunities are possible." The other two phases, namely, the "growth and exploitation phase (r)" and the "conservation phase (K)," are what we would see once the reorganization is complete, but that will only last until the next "collapse and release" phase comes about and the cycle starts all over again.[8]

To my mind, the internationalized system that was in place during the Late Bronze Age in the Aegean and Eastern Mediterranean fits into an adaptive cycle. One could readily argue that the years of interconnection and prosperity in the Aegean and Eastern Mediterranean that lasted from ca. 1700 to 1200 BC could be seen as the growth and exploitation phase (r) plus the conservation phase (K). The Collapse itself could be considered as the subsequent omega (Ω) or release phase,

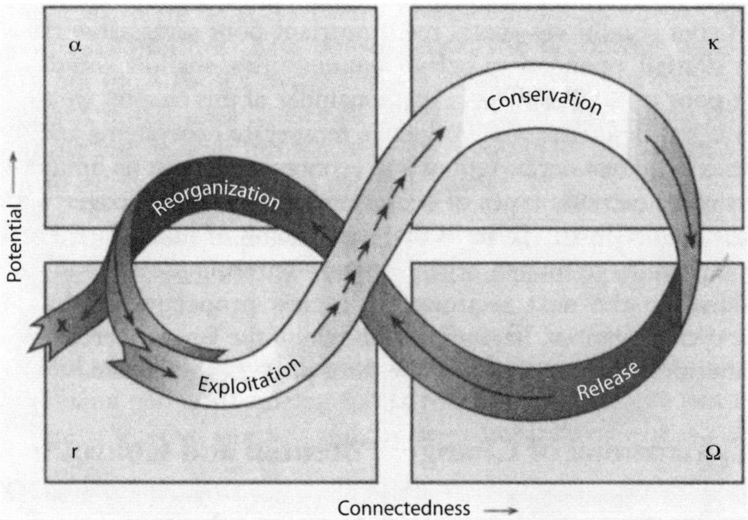

FIG. 11. Visualization of the adaptive cycle, from Holling and Gunderson 2002: fig. 2-1; image from *Panarchy: Understanding Transformations in Human and Natural Systems*, edited by Lance H. Gunderson and C. S. Holling; copyright 2002 Island Press; reproduced by permission of Island Press, Washington, DC.

while the aftermath during the centuries of the Iron Age, which we are considering here, is the alpha (α) or reorganization phase that immediately followed.[9]

This concise description of system change also allows us to compare the Late Bronze Age Collapse directly to other instances elsewhere in time and place, such as the collapse of the Roman Empire or the collapse of the Maya. But we also need to ask whether the individual societies within the broader system followed such a cycle as well. That is to say, did any of the Late Bronze Age societies or regions that experienced the Collapse also follow their own individual adaptive cycle during the Bronze Age and after?[10]

The answer, I believe, is yes. Ian Morris has, in fact, claimed that "Greece between 1500 and 500 BC is one of the best-known cases of the collapse and regeneration of complex society." Citing Anthony Snodgrass, he essentially lays out an adaptive cycle for Greece: "a period of

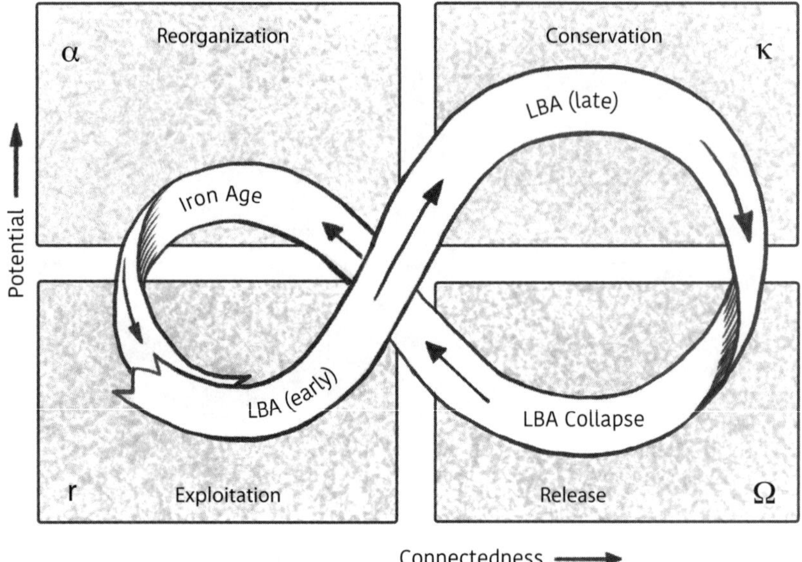

FIG. 12. Reconceptualization of the adaptive cycle, with the phases labeled in terms of the Late Bronze Age, LBA Collapse, and Iron Age. Drawing by Glynnis Fawkes; adapted from Redman and Kinzig 2003: fig. 3.

sophisticated palaces (ca. 2000–1200 BC) gave way to a depressed Dark Age (ca. 1200–750), only to be replaced by new and brilliant Archaic (ca. 750–480) and Classical (ca. 480–323) civilizations."[11] A graphic representation of this process makes it easy to envision.

Morris also believes that Greece was an example of "genuine" regeneration—that it was a case of the entire system transforming.[12] However, I prefer to see it more as a rebuilding. Unlike other societies, such as the Phoenicians and the Cypriots who transformed themselves, the Greeks had to remake their society almost entirely from the bottom up during the Iron Age (aka Morris's Dark Age). However, even though our terminologies differ, Morris and I are largely describing the same process.

If each of the areas or societies was undergoing its own adaptive cycle, this means that we need to bring in the related concept of "panarchy." This notion recognizes that the individual components within an overall complex system that is going through an adaptive cycle are also each on their own adaptive cycles in addition to being part of the larger

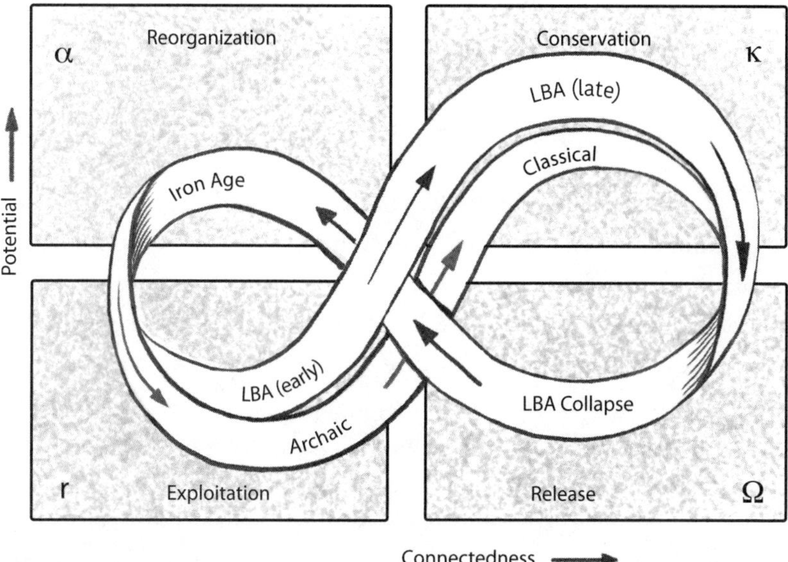

FIG. 13. Reconceptualization of the adaptive cycle specifically for Greece, from the Late Bronze and Iron Ages through the Archaic and Classical periods. Drawing by Glynnis Fawkes; adapted from Redman and Kinzig 2003: fig. 3.

overall progression, and that each one releases and then reorganizes (omega and alpha phases) at different rates and in different ways. Some are slower, others are faster, but each one affects both the others and the overall system, especially if there are simultaneous problems with the different components.[13]

To put it a different way, if we were to envision an intricate system of cogs and gears, all enmeshed and working together to create a working machine, like a pocket watch for instance, but with each rotating at its own speed, that might be a correct visual aid for a panarchy. In our case, the overall system would be the Bronze Age in this region as a whole, while the individual cogs or gears would be the Mycenaeans, Minoans, Hittites, Egyptians, and other component societies. Upon occasion, if something goes wrong with one or more of the cogs/gears (i.e., the various societies), the whole machine can begin to sputter and stall, or even come to a sudden screeching halt, and will need to be jump-started again.[14] This, I would suggest, is precisely what happened at the end of the Late Bronze Age in the Aegean and Eastern Mediterranean.

I would also suggest that we look to the various publications concerned with modern resilience and mitigation in the aftermath of more recent disasters, such as Hurricane Katrina in New Orleans, for they too contain relevant concepts that might be applied to what we have seen in the aftermath of the Bronze Age Collapse. Particularly germane, in my opinion, are the various reports compiled by the United Nations' Intergovernmental Panel on Climate Change (IPCC), which was established in 1988 and won the Nobel Peace Prize in 2007.[15]

Even though the IPCC reports rarely incorporate examples from the past in their compilations or take the opinions of archaeologists into consideration during their reviews,[16] they include detailed looks at recent disasters, such as droughts, floods, and earthquakes, in order to determine how the affected societies were able to deal with them successfully or not, just as we would like to do for the societies in the aftermath of the Bronze Age Collapse. Using these reports may help us to gather our thoughts in a productive way, though we need to beware of creating anachronisms and unlikely rationalizations when transporting our twenty-first-century ideas, definitions, and explanations back to a time some three thousand years ago, which may or may not be a valid exercise.

Most useful, I believe, is a 594-page report that was released by the IPCC in 2012, titled *Managing the Risks of Extreme Events and Disasters to Advance Climate Change Adaptation*. The acronym for the report is *SREX*, which stands for the shorthand title, *Special Report on Extreme Events*. This was the first IPCC report to explicitly consider both climate change and disaster risk management in the same document and to provide initial definitions for the concepts being discussed, including a number of the terms that I have invoked at various points in the previous chapters, such as "coping," "adapting," and "transforming." The assorted concepts have been further developed, with some tweaking and

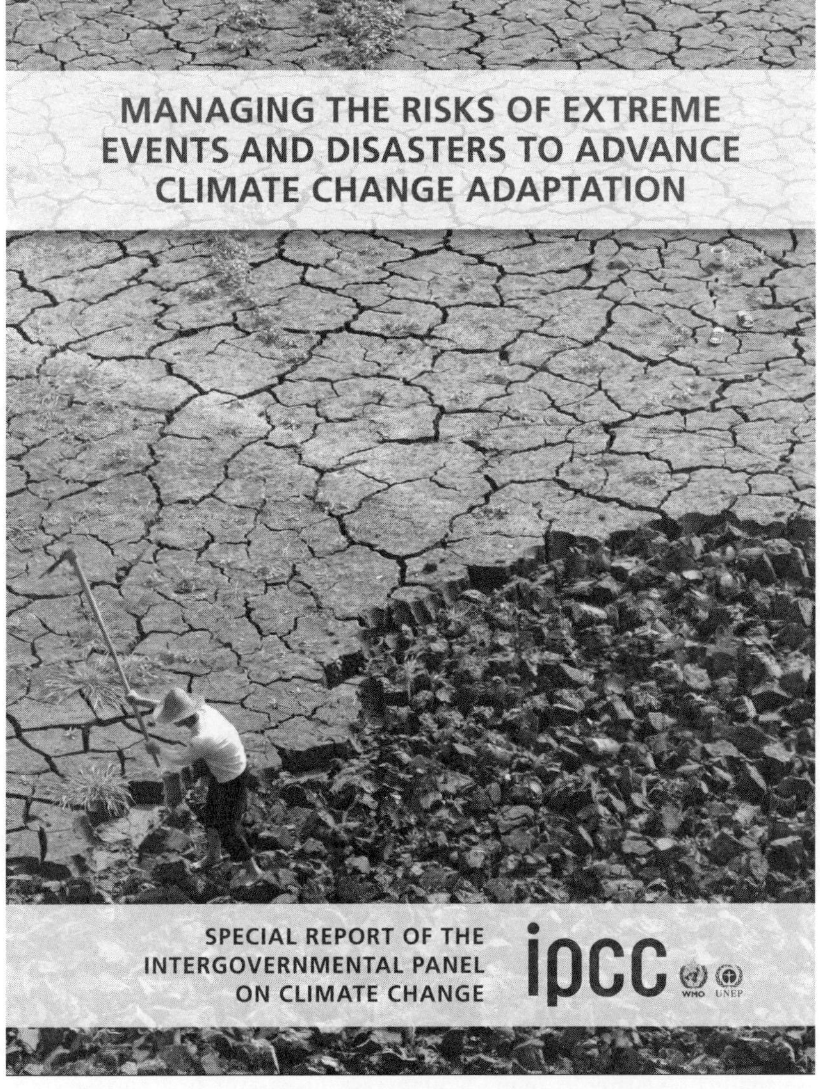

FIG. 14. United Nations Intergovernmental Panel on Climate Change, *SREX* cover, 2012. Image courtesy of the IPCC.

updating of the definitions, in subsequent IPCC reports, including the more recent Fifth and Sixth Assessment reports (2014 and 2021/22, respectively), and I have noted those where appropriate below, but the 2012 report is still the most useful for our purposes.[17]

First and foremost, even though they are concerned with the modern world and do not include examples from the ancient world in their report, it is clear from their definitions that the authors would undoubtedly consider the Late Bronze Age Collapse to be what they call "an extreme impact" event, as it resulted in "highly significant and typically long-lasting consequences to society, the natural physical environment, or ecosystems." As they note, such "extreme impacts" can result from a variety of causes, among which are "a single extreme event, successive extreme or non-extreme events, including non-climatic events (e.g., wildfire, followed by heavy rain leading to landslides and soil erosion), or simply the persistence of conditions, such as those that lead to drought."[18]

As such, they would undoubtedly further agree that the Collapse could be considered a "disaster" in a modern technical sense, since they define disasters as "extreme impacts suffered by society, which may also be associated with extreme impacts on the physical environment and on ecosystems." They note in particular that "a disaster results when the impact is such that local capacity to cope is exceeded or such that it severely disrupts normal activities." Today, just as in antiquity, such disasters "occur first at the local level and affect local people," following which "these localized impacts can then cascade to have national and international ramifications."[19]

Following upon the above, in their 2012 IPCC report, the authors also consider "disaster mitigation," which refers to "actions that attempt to limit further adverse conditions once disaster has materialized." These revolve around attempts to avoid a "second disaster," as they call it. This frequently occurs close on the heels of the initial catastrophe and is usually due either to an inadequate response to the first disaster or to some additional unforeseen circumstances. They note that the outcomes of either the first or the secondary disasters frequently include migration, economic vulnerability (in both the public and private sectors), increased violence, and impacts on work and livelihoods at both the individual and community levels.[20] We can see all of this during and after the Bronze Age Collapse, for in our particular case the "first disaster" might be any of the stressors that were considered in *1177 B.C.*, such as climate change, drought, famine, disease, or earthquakes, while the "second (or secondary) disaster" might be the ensuing collapse of one or more of the societies or of the interconnected network itself, resulting in exactly the observable outcomes that they note.

Especially important in the 2012 report are the general comments about a society's capacity to respond to a disaster as well as its capacity to recover and change, both of which depend on the extent to which the society was affected by the disaster. It is in conjunction with the recovery from extreme disasters, and specifically the idea that resources might be reorganized by the survivors into a new system to take advantage of opportunities created by the disaster, that the concept of "resilience theory" (or "resilience thinking") is now frequently used, including by some archaeologists.[21]

We must clearly understand, however, that the concept of resilience has a variety of distinct meanings, depending on the discipline invoking it. The 2011 National Research Council has defined resilience as the ability to "continue to operate under stress, adapt to adversity, and recover functionality after a crisis," while another set of scholars has recently defined it as "the capability of a community to face a threat, survive and bounce back or, perhaps more accurately, bounce forward into a [new] normalcy." Both definitions work well for those studying antiquity as well as those researching and working on more recent disasters.[22]

The IPCC authors note in particular that not all societies have the capacity to adapt or transform during or after a disaster. Some can only just barely cope, if even that. Therefore, they emphasize the difference between *coping*, which reflects the ability to deal with something that has just happened (i.e., focusing on the moment and simply surviving), as opposed to *adapting*, which reflects the ability to deal with something that might happen in the future and "where learning and reinvention are key features and short-term survival is less in question."[23]

As they point out, a society that is simply coping with a disaster is usually just trying to absorb the blows and maintain the status quo, while a society that is actively trying to adapt will be implementing changes and even adjusting things and reorganizing to a certain degree, so that they are better prepared for the next time that something similar happens.[24] This is where I think it gets particularly interesting for us, since we can now see there were clearly a variety of responses on the part of the societies that were impacted by the Bronze Age Collapse, including those that we could characterize as either successfully coping or even more successfully adapting.

All of this, however, is still one step less than actually *transforming*. As the IPCC authors note, the most resilient societies are those that are able to learn and adjust on the fly, including reorganizing after a disruption, all while continuing to maintain their basic structures and functionality even during the event (or disaster) in question. The adjustments that are made are referred to as "transformational changes" and can either be incremental (i.e., small steps) or much more radical.[25] We have seen this in at least one instance, if not two, in chapter 3—namely, the Phoenicians as well as the Cypriots.

The IPCC writers also invoke the concept of "vulnerability" as potentially being useful when considering why some societies succeed but others fail to recover in the aftermath of a disaster or extreme impact. They see vulnerability as being "situation-specific," which I would suggest was exactly the case at the end of the Late Bronze Age, and they point especially to a lack of either coping or adaptive capacities in such situations. I will consider this further in a moment, but the report's authors also note that there may be "windows of vulnerability," that is, periods when external (or even internal) hazards pose a greater threat than usual.[26] Again, I would suggest that was certainly the case ca. 1200 BC, when I believe the "perfect storm" of calamities occurred.

I would also note that the concept of fragility, also explored in this same 2012 report, may come into play here as well, for scholars are now beginning to suggest that societal fragility ("weakened, disintegrating, or collapsing state apparatuses") can be related, or even a precursor, to vulnerability. In this regard, it has been suggested that cities or societies can sometimes be more fragile and vulnerable than they appear, in part because their apparent success up to that point covers and masks the instability (usually this only becomes clear in hindsight). Although there may be an appearance that all is well, the foundations or perhaps the appendages are actually rotted and weak, so that the smallest gust

TABLE 4. Terms and definitions related to resiliency

Term	Brief definition
Adapting, aka adaptive capacity	The ability to deal with something that might happen in the future; learning and reinvention are key, whereas short-term survival is less in question
Anti-fragile	The condition of a society that exhibits more than just resiliency or robustness and actually thrives under the right amount of stress, taking advantage of the situation not only to survive but to flourish
Coping, aka coping capacity	The ability to deal with something that has just happened (i.e., focusing on the moment and simply surviving)
Fragility, aka societal fragility	Weakened, disintegrating, or collapsing state apparatuses
Resiliency	The ability to continue to operate under stress, adapt to adversity, and recover functionality after a crisis
Transformational adaptation	Includes actions that change the fundamental attributes of a system in response to actual or expected impacts of climate change
Transforming	The ability to reorganize after disruption and retain fundamental structure and function in the face of system stress; characterized by the capacity to learn and adjust
Vulnerability	The likelihood of a society suffering adversely when impacted by extreme events
Windows of vulnerability	Periods in which hazards are greater because of the combination of circumstances

Sources: National Research Council 2011; 2012 IPCC *SREX* Report; 2014 IPCC Fifth Assessment Report; Taleb 2014.

of wind or stress is enough to begin the process of collapse. I strongly suspect that this may have been the case for both the Mycenaeans and the Hittites.[27]

However, the opposite may have been true of the Phoenicians, for they appear to have been "anti-fragile," as discussed in chapter 3. It certainly appears that the Phoenicians took advantage not only of Ugarit's destruction but also the cessation of both Egyptian and Hittite influence in their area and the general chaos of the times to take over the trade routes leading to the south and the west, that is, to Egypt, Cyprus,

Greece, Crete, Sicily, Sardinia, Italy, and Iberia, just after 1200 BC.[28] They then enriched themselves through their control of these trade routes for centuries afterward.

Another possible way to describe the Phoenicians' role after the Late Bronze Age Collapse is to invoke *both* resilience theory *and* the adaptive cycle, for—as mentioned—the "alpha" or reorganization phase within the cycle has been described as a time "in which resources are reorganized into a new system to take advantage of opportunities."[29] Thus, I view the Phoenicians both as anti-fragile and as a prime example of the innovation that can take place during the alpha phase of an adaptive cycle.

I think that such resilience terminology can be extremely useful in helping to explain why the various societies each went down at slightly different times during the Collapse and why each one recovered at different rates (and in different ways) during the ensuing decades and centuries. However, the elephant in the room is the question of whether it is legitimate to attempt to explain these ancient events using modern terms and ideas—resilience, transformation, coping, and adaptation. Are we introducing anachronistic concepts into the debate that don't apply to the world of three thousand years ago?

Perhaps we are, but despite the possibility of such errors, it seems to me worthwhile to attempt to address all the questions that we have posed above by looking at the success or failure of the various societies through the lens of resilience and resilience theory. As Erika Weiberg of Uppsala University has noted, resilience theory may help us to further achieve a more nuanced view of this period, allowing us to better decide "what exactly [the] 'collapse' entailed and for whom."[30]

Categories and Rankings

I believe that we can successfully apply some of the definitions and discussions from the 2012 IPCC report on *Managing the Risks of Extreme Events and Disasters* to the historical and archaeological details that we have contemplated from the centuries following the Bronze Age Collapse. Although it will necessarily be subjective, one could make the case, for instance, that the Assyrians, Babylonians, and Egyptians had a "capacity to absorb," to use the language of the IPCC authors, for they were able to *cope* with the situation and carry on, although the Egyptians were not quite as successful as the other two. The Phoenicians and the Cypriots, on the other hand, apparently were not only able to go one step further and *adapt* to the situation but actually go two steps further and *transform*—for they seem to have had the "capacity to change and adjust" (again using IPCC language) and were able to reorganize in new ways after the disruption.

Furthermore, in terms of both the Cypriots and the Phoenicians, we should note that the 2012 IPCC authors observe that adaptive capacity and thus transformation can also be described as the ability to be innovative and to anticipate future situations. Such innovations, they say, can be both social and technological, and either incremental or radical, as mentioned.[31] I would point to the adoption and spread of both iron and the alphabet as just two of the more obvious such innovations during these centuries.

We can also try to summarize our observations from a different angle, namely, by separating into categories and ranking the various societies that suffered through the Collapse, based on the concepts of resiliency, vulnerability, and fragility, and the additional definitions of coping, adapting, and transforming, to see if that exercise yields anything useful.

I would stress at the outset, however, that I am not privileging states (or kingdoms or empires) as the desired unit of sociopolitical organization but am simply working from the observation that the kingdoms and empires that formed the Late Bronze Age globalized network each subsequently transformed into or were succeeded by smaller Iron Age kingdoms and city-states located in the same areas. Our goal is to explain how we got from one situation to the other during the centuries after the LBA Collapse, which I think we can do based on the material that has been laid out in the pages above.

I would also stress that my suggestions are, of course, tentative, in part because of the fragmentary and incomplete nature of our evidence

TABLE 5. Broad categories of resilience for the various areas/societies in the centuries following the Collapse

Category	Rationale	Area/society
1	More than simply resilient, perhaps even anti-fragile	Central Canaanites (Phoenicians); Cyprus
2	Very resilient (to varying degrees); adapting and perhaps even transforming	Assyria; Babylonia; Neo-Hittites; northern Canaanites
3	Resilient, but just barely; coping but not necessarily adapting	Egypt
4	Not resilient as a society but with some continuity to their successors, who eventually rebounded	Mainland Greece (Mycenaeans); Crete (Minoans)
5	Not resilient; either vanished or were assimilated	Hittites; southern Canaanites

and in part because some involve a judgment call or putting a label on something that may actually be difficult to categorize properly. I also note that a number of the societies or areas fluctuated in their degree(s) of resilience over the centuries, which means that we need to keep in mind the nuances as well as the broad overall picture. Thus, while knowing that some may prefer to place certain societies into different categories than I have done here, I would tentatively suggest the following summary statements and observations, listed according to order of resilience.

1. More Than Simply Resilient—Perhaps Even Anti-fragile

There are two principal examples here; as I see it. One would be the Canaanite societies of the central Levant who evolved or transformed so much that we now call them "Phoenician" to mark this shift. The other would be the inhabitants of Cyprus. These both transformed and flourished amid the chaos, in some cases taking over roles previously played by others and demonstrating innovations such as standardizing the alphabet, producing purple dye, and working with iron to create weapons and tools. As Carol Bell has said, "Cypriot merchants and their

Phoenician counterparts were . . . well positioned to capitalize on the opportunities that arose from the catastrophic events at the end of the Bronze Age."[32]

Although the central Canaanites now have a new name, that is, the Phoenicians, the cultural continuities are evident. They were not only resilient and innovative while morphing from the Canaanite city-states of the Late Bronze Age and transforming to the new normal but were actually anti-fragile and flourished in the chaos that followed the Collapse, taking particular advantage of the sack of Ugarit and other port cities to seize control of the trade routes across the Mediterranean in order to exchange goods such as purple dye for silver and other metals coming from Sicily, Sardinia, and Iberia—and thereby to spread their standardized version of the alphabet.

The inhabitants of Cyprus similarly displayed an admirable resilience, including possibly transforming their political system and with individual populations moving to new areas on the island and creating new municipalities as needed, especially as harbors silted up. They were also at the forefront of the new iron industry, if our current understanding is correct that the metalworkers there were the leaders in this transition to iron as the predominant metal of the age. The craftsmen and metalworkers not only kept their usual bronzeworking going but were also innovative in adapting and spreading this new metalworking technology. And they too were able to maintain a presence on the international trade routes, which were still in existence even if initially perhaps at a lower level than during the Late Bronze Age.

2. *Very Resilient*

Prime examples of societies that proved to be very resilient would be the Assyrians and the Babylonians. Both coped and adapted as necessary, adjusting to the new situation(s) in which they found themselves. This included dealing with either old enemies (e.g., the Elamites in the case of the Babylonians) or new adversaries (such as the Aramaeans and the Urartians in the case of the Assyrians), as well as simply taking what they needed from others.[33]

I see the Assyrians and Babylonians as fitting into this category because they both initially succeeded in weathering the Collapse and adapting during the transformation from the Bronze Age to the Iron Age, with almost no changes to be seen in their basic societal structure, from government administration to religion (including deities worshipped). However, both societies were then belatedly impacted by drought, famine, and plague. Even though they were able to continue to cope at that point, it took the Assyrians two centuries to regroup and return, with a vengeance, in the ninth century BC, and the Babylonians even longer than that, at the end of the seventh century BC.

Into this category I would also place the Neo-Hittites who lived in northern Syria and southeastern Anatolia, as well as the northern Canaanites and others who may have lived alongside them in those regions. They all successfully weathered the initial change and lived in the various territories governed by Carchemish, Tell Tayinat, and other small Syro-Hittite and Syro-Anatolian kingdoms or city-states in this region during the Iron Age. They also persisted in the face of repeated aggression from the Assyrians, though it would seem likely that the Canaanites who lived in the inland areas as far south as Damascus were eventually assimilated into the many smaller Aramaean kingdoms that were established in this region during the ninth century BC. Placing the Neo-Hittites in this category means, however, separating them from the main body of Hittites in central Anatolia, who were not as resilient; others may argue that we should keep the two groups together, though I think that it is valid to divide them, given the great disparity in resilience.

3. *Resilient but Just Barely*

Within this category, I would include the groups that were able to cope and continue to exist but failed to really make the transition properly, such that their societies declined to a certain extent and lost any larger international role that they may have held previously. The prime example here, I suggest, would be the Egyptians during the centuries following the Collapse, for although Egypt survived, it was never the same again, nor did it ever rise to the powerful position that it had once held during the New Kingdom period. While there were no substantial changes in terms of rule by the king and the administration, or even in their religion, the standard of living most likely decreased for the average person. There was also an uptick in anarchy, mutiny, simultaneous claims by rival pharaohs, and civil war, to the extent that Egypt was sometimes ruled by multiple kings at the same time and certainly played a much lesser role in international trade during the centuries after the Collapse than it had done previously.

However, when we first began discussing Egypt above, we noted that much of this period, beginning with the death of Ramses XI in 1070 BC, which marked the end of the Twentieth Dynasty and the New Kingdom, is known to Egyptologists as the Third Intermediate Period, with rival and multiple claimants to the title of pharaoh at times. Similar eras, known as the First and Second Intermediate Period, respectively, had followed the earlier Old Kingdom and Middle Kingdom eras. So, in many ways what happened in Egypt in the aftermath of the Collapse was not new but rather a cycle that had played out there before—its own version of the adaptive cycle.

4. Not Resilient as a Society but with Some Cultural Continuity

Here I would list the entities that failed to really cope, adapt, or transform from the societies that they had once been, but nevertheless their cultural continuities did not disappear altogether. I see this as potentially one of the most contentious categories and very much open to debate.

The primary example here, to my mind, would be the Mycenaeans of mainland Greece, who appear to have been more vulnerable and fragile than anticipated.[34] Although they vanished as a society, there is enough continuity with their successors, and an eventual reemergence of the latter by the eighth century BC, that I would place them into this category rather than the very lowest. My reasoning is as follows:

There is little question that Mycenaean society came to an end by ca. 1050 BC at the absolute latest. Given the lowered standard of living in Greece after the Collapse, we can presume that they were not particularly resilient, at least at first, and that life as they knew it during the

Bronze Age had effectively come to an end. We should note, though, that even if we say that that the Bronze Age society in Greece absolutely collapsed, life did continue for a large number of people, especially at the lower levels of society, and that there is certainly continuity between the Bronze Age and the Iron Age on mainland Greece.[35]

However, we can also say that the Greeks who survived eventually transformed and remade their culture and society from the ground up. This was neither easy nor rapid, but we can see an evolution in pottery styles, burial customs, and house types, for instance, as well as some continuity, including in the titles of some of the administrators (such as *basileus*) and the names of many of the gods and goddesses, from Zeus and Hera on down. However, as mentioned at the beginning of this book, it is unlikely that anyone would have still considered themselves to be Mycenaeans after ca. 1050 BC (if indeed, they had ever self-identified as such, rather than as the inhabitants of a particular kingdom, such as Mycenae or Pylos).

Because the survivors eventually were able to rebuild and start again on the road that would lead to Archaic and then Classical Greece, I would suggest that perhaps already by the later ninth and early eighth century BC they had eventually rebounded enough that they could be moved at that point into the next-higher category (no. 3). On the average over time, however, they remain in this category (no. 4).

In this category also, after much internal debate, I would include the inhabitants of Crete, for while they were more successful than the Mycenaeans at adapting, they nevertheless also lost their previous identity, that is, what we would recognize as "Minoans." As noted in chapter 5, Minoans, and Minoan society as it had been known, including to their previous trading partners overseas (i.e., "Keftiu" to the Egyptians and "Caphtor/Caphtorians" to the Canaanites and Babylonians), essentially ceased to exist as an identifier, possibly even as early as the Mycenaean takeover of the island in the mid-fourteenth century BC, even though many of the inhabitants continued to navigate the transition to the Iron Age and eventually flourished again as Archaic Crete.

However, I will be the first to note that this is a subjective call to make, for the inhabitants of Crete were certainly able to make cultural adjustments. While they did not return to the heights of earlier Minoan participation in international trade during these centuries, they were able to ensure some degree of continuity, leading eventually to the growth of the Archaic city-states on the island, and could also be considered to have rebounded enough to eventually be moved to the next-higher category (though again the average over the centuries keeps them in this current category). As Saro Wallace has labeled it, one might consider this a "positive collapse," though again I would note that it came at the cost of losing their identity as "Minoans" (either at the hands of the Mycenaeans or as a result of the Collapse).[36]

5. Not Resilient—Essentially Vanished

Within this final category, I would place the societies that were not resilient and essentially vanished entirely, although some small pockets might remain in outlying areas. Here we find the Hittites and their empire, who essentially failed to navigate the change to the Iron Age and yielded their territory to new kingdoms, including the Urartians in eastern Anatolia and eventually the Phrygians in central/western Anatolia, as noted in chapter 4. Even here I must be nuanced, though, because I have already placed and discussed above the small successor groups that survived as Neo-Hittite city-states in Syro-Anatolia and the northern Levant, continuing Hittite traditions in writing, architecture, and administrative systems while creating their own independent systems. In addition, although the Hittites may have ruled over most of Anatolia, their societal collapse did not necessarily mean the automatic death of everyone living in the entire region, especially in the hinterland at sites such as Çadir.[37]

Furthermore, while fully realizing that this will be an issue for continued discussion, I have also placed the Canaanites who lived in the southern Levant into this category, for I see them overall as having been either overcome by or assimilated into the new kingdoms that emerged in the region, including Israel and Judah, as well as Philistia, Edom, Ammon, and Moab. However, this exemplifies some of the problems involved in trying to assign labels to fluid situations, for in his recent book on southwestern Canaan in the Bronze and Iron Ages, Ido Koch of Tel Aviv University has argued that "the regenerated society in Iron Age I southwest Canaan exhibits both continuity and transformation." At the same time, though, he admits that "the social structure that emerged in post-collapse southwest Canaan during the Iron Age I was different from its predecessor"; that "[n]ew centers . . . replaced the traditional ones"; and that "a different settlement pattern developed."[38]

In brief, as I interpret the situation as we currently understand it, while individual ethnic Canaanites (and even small communities) may have been resilient to a certain extent, Canaanite society, and individual Canaanite city-states, ceased to be uniquely identifiable as the transition to the Iron Age continued in the southern Levant, even as they undoubtedly influenced the new kingdoms that arose in the region. This could be interpreted as either transformation and high resiliency on the one hand or as assimilation into the new kingdoms and low resiliency on the other. However, just as we no longer see identifiable Mycenaeans or Minoans in the later Iron Age Aegean, so too we no longer generally talk about Canaanites in the later Iron Age Levant, but rather Israelites, Judahites, Ammonites, Edomites, Moabites, and so on. I have therefore chosen to interpret this situation as assimilation, albeit with some cultural survivals and influences, and have placed these southern Canaanites into this category. Others may prefer to see this as a successful transformation and put them in a higher category.[39]

Other Categories?

There are other groups that may or may not fit into any of the above categories, depending on how one interprets the available data. For instance, if the monotheistic Israelites had indeed been in the region of the southern Levant for some time by that point and simply came down from the highlands where they had been living previously (i.e., the "invisible Israelites," as per Finkelstein), then we could potentially separate them out as another Bronze Age culture in the area that proved to be resilient and innovative while morphing eventually into the United Monarchy and then the separate kingdoms of Israel and Judah, all while transforming to the new normal. If, however, they had recently migrated into the region by whatever means, such as the Exodus for instance, then they would be viewed as newcomers taking advantage of the chaos that followed the Collapse, which would be a different story altogether.

Similarly, if Ben-Yosef is correct that the Edomites had previously been nomadic but inhabiting the region of Wadi Faynan, and then settled down to create the kingdom of Edom, as discussed in chapter 1, do we consider that to be a transformation in reaction to the Egyptian withdrawal from the area and the other related events during the period of the Late Bronze Age Collapse? Or do we envision the kingdom as having developed in some other way, as other scholars have argued, and thus simply consider it as a new entity entirely, which grew in the power vacuum after the tumultuous events of the late thirteenth and early twelfth centuries BC?

A similar situation pertains to the other peoples in the area. For instance, the jury is still out on whether the Ammonites migrated into the area during the Late Bronze Age Collapse, perhaps from as far away as Anatolia; or migrated from elsewhere in Canaan at that time; or were essentially indigenous and survived the Collapse right where the Iron Age kingdom of Ammon was located.[40] All have been suggested. If the final possibility is correct, then they could be placed in category 2; if either of the other two possibilities is correct, then we have to consider where we would place them or if they are even to be considered part of the equation here.

The same goes for Moab and the Moabites, who may have first established their kingdom ca. 1300 BC, if not earlier, but who also may not have entered the region much before 1200 BC or even established their kingdom before the eleventh century BC. Again, all of these suggestions have been made, and again, how we are to rank them, or even if we should rank them, for the moment remains open to discussion.[41]

I would stress again that my assignation of the various societies to the individual categories and to viewing their ups and downs over the centuries is preliminary, tentative, and completely dependent on our current knowledge and my own assumptions and intuitive feelings (however unscientific that might be). More archaeological work might eventually suggest a different trajectory for some of them, but currently the categorizations presented here reflect my own inclinations after reviewing the available evidence.

I also think that it is useful to remember that the situation for each changed over time, which I have tried to show in table 6, where I indicate my opinion about the status of each society century by century. This may be especially helpful given that we have proceeded geographically in the above chapters rather than chronologically.

Needless to say, other scholars will undoubtedly hold different opinions, perhaps wishing to place Egypt in a different category—for instance, either further up with the Assyrians and Babylonians or further down with the Mycenaeans and Minoans, depending on how one views factors such as political instability. In short, I see my suggestions here as beginning the discussion, not ending it.

What is very evident from all of the above, beginning with the material in chapters 1–5 and continuing through the analyses just presented, is that each case was unique. Of the societies that had been active during the Late Bronze Age in the Aegean or Eastern Mediterranean, some were more successful at weathering the storm than others. Questions about how and/or why each of them was or was not vulnerable in the first place and how and/or why each of them did or did not successfully transform to the new situation are not easy to answer. Indeed, in some cases we might not be able to answer such questions at all because of the fragmentary nature of our data—we are often heavily dependent on the finds of burials and pottery, perceived changes in settlement patterns, and so on, as pointed out several times above. We are like forensic detectives trying to reconstruct multiple ancient crime scenes, all grown cold long, long ago—CSI, NCIS, Columbo, and Kojak come to mind, but even those television investigators wouldn't be able to solve any of these cases with much chance of persuading a jury to reach a unanimous verdict; even Hercule Poirot or Sherlock Holmes would be hard-pressed to do so.

TABLE 6. Resilience, or lack thereof, by area/society and century BC, also indicating adaptive cycle phases

Area/society	12th	11th	10th	9th/8th
Assyria	Very resilient; constant Aramaean raids and occasional conflicts with the Babylonians, but essentially unaffected. Adaptive cycle phase: omega	Coping, but downturn begins with onset of drought, famine, and plague, which lasts through the next century. Adaptive cycle phase: omega	Downturn continues; coping and perhaps adapting, but simply surviving until final third of the century. Adaptive cycle phase: omega	Transformation into the Neo-Assyrian Empire; conquest of Near East begins. Adaptive cycle phase: alpha
Babylonia	Very resilient; constant Aramaean raids and occasional conflicts with the Assyrians, but essentially unaffected. Adaptive cycle phase: omega	Problems similar to those of the Assyrians; coping with onset of drought, famine, and plague. Adaptive cycle phase: omega	Similar to the Assyrians; still coping and merely surviving. Adaptive cycle phase: omega	Still coping and surviving. Adaptive cycle phase: omega
Canaan (northern)	Transition varied by site; some (e.g., Ugarit) were abandoned, but others were very resilient and had continuity. Adaptive cycle phase: omega	Resilient and adapting/coping; likely some assimilation into Neo-Hittite polities in the region. Adaptive cycle phase: omega	Resilient and adapting/coping as in the previous century. Adaptive cycle phase: omega	Resilient and adapting/coping as in the previous century; likely assimilation into Aramaean kingdoms in northern Syria at this time. Adaptive cycle phase: omega
Canaan (central): Tyre, Sidon, Byblos, Arwad, etc.	Anti-fragile; transformation into Phoenicians, who begin to take over maritime trade routes. Adaptive cycle phase: initially omega but transitioning almost immediately to alpha	Anti-fragile; maritime ventures continue. Adaptive cycle phase: alpha	Anti-fragile; maritime ventures continue; rulers at Byblos leave inscriptions. Adaptive cycle phase: alpha	Anti-fragile; maritime ventures continue. Adaptive cycle phase: alpha

(continued)

TABLE 6. (*continued*)

Area/society	12th	11th	10th	9th/8th
Canaan (southern)	Initially resilient and able to adapt; possibly transformed to a certain extent, but not initially anti-fragile	Possibly resilient, but probably beginning to be assimilated by the Philistines and others.	Could be construed as adaptation on the part of the original inhabitants, but most likely assimilated into the new kingdoms established in area, including Israel, Judah, Edom, and Ammon.	Various new kingdoms, including Israel and Judah, thriving.
	Adaptive cycle phase: omega, but transitioning almost immediately to alpha	Adaptive cycle phase: alpha	Adaptive cycle phase: alpha	Adaptive cycle phase: alpha
Crete (Minoans)	Continuity and cultural readjustments; transformative adaptation to weather the transition.	Minoan society per se now gone, but Cretans have recovered and adjusted to the new realities.	Cretan society continues; renewed contacts with the Near East.	Cretans thriving.
	Adaptive cycle phase: initially omega, transitioning to alpha	Adaptive cycle phase: alpha	Adaptive cycle phase: alpha	Adaptive cycle phase: alpha
Cyprus	Able to adapt and possibly even transform; perhaps anti-fragile; innovation in working iron.	Resilient and thriving; new cities appear and old ones continue, though with some changes; actively engaged in international trade, especially with items of iron.	Continuing resilience, setting the stage for the eventual transformation to the Archaic period.	Cypriots thriving.
	Adaptive cycle phase: initially omega, but almost immediately transitioning to alpha	Adaptive cycle phase: alpha	Adaptive cycle phase: alpha	Adaptive cycle phase: alpha

Egypt	Coping, but not particularly successfully; impacted by drought, famine, looting, and societal and political problems. Adaptive cycle phase: omega	Problems with resilience continue, especially with political fragmentation, but possibly beginning to adapt and to resume some trade toward the end of the century. Adaptive cycle phase: omega	More resilience shown and improvements made in international relations; a return to military might and diplomacy in the time of Sheshonq. Adaptive cycle phase: initially omega, but transitioning to alpha in Sheshonq's time	Downturn again, with political problems and rival pharaohs; eventually taken over and ruled by Kushite kings from Nubia from mid-eighth century. Adaptive cycle phase: returns to omega
Hittites	Hittite society ends for all intents and purposes in central Anatolia. Adaptive cycle phase: omega	Hittites gone.	Hittites gone.	Hittites gone.
Neo-Hittites	Continuation of Neo-Hittite kingdoms in north Syria (northern Canaan) and southeastern Anatolia. Adaptive cycle phase: omega	Varying degrees of transforming, adapting, and coping among the various Neo-Hittite cities and territories. Adaptive cycle phase: alpha	A time of resurgence; Neo-Hittite rulers leave inscriptions. Adaptive cycle phase: alpha	Carchemish and other Neo-Hittite cities thriving. Adaptive cycle phase: alpha
Mainland Greece (Mycenaeans/Greeks)	Some degree of continuity, although already at a lower sociopolitical level. Adaptive cycle phase: omega	Mycenaean society per se gone by 1070–1050 BC; inhabitants on mainland Greece continue at lower sociopolitical level. Adaptive cycle phase: omega	Greek society begins to rebuild from the ground up, starting process of transformation and recovery. Adaptive cycle phase: initially omega, transitioning to alpha	Greeks rebounding. Adaptive cycle phase: alpha

Again, remember that we are hampered in particular by the fact that not one of these societies left any records that mention specifically that there had been a change in their world system. Nothing about "in my father's (or grandfather's) day, we were in touch with the Hittites (or Egyptians or . . .), but they are not seen here any longer," for example. The reason for this may be as simple as the fact that we have very few written records dating from immediately after the Collapse—remember that there was a period in Assyria of some seventy-five years, from 1208 BC onward, from which we have few records for the first twenty-five years and then no royal records at all for nearly fifty years (1179–1133 BC). We do not have anything specifically relevant from the other societies during that time either; not even the Egyptians mention anything particularly untoward after Ramses III's triumphal claims of his victory over the Sea Peoples in 1177 BC, except for some internal problems such as a workers' strike and then eventually his assassination. Of course, most of the centers that would have kept such records, including Ugarit, Hattusa, and Mycenae, had all just been dramatically impacted, invaded, or abandoned at the time, so perhaps this lack of written references should not be surprising.

Vulnerability, Fragility, and Resilience Theory

Finally, I think that we can also further explore and apply the additional concepts of vulnerability and fragility from resilience theory, which I introduced a few pages ago, in looking again at the material presented in the above chapters. For example, in hindsight it seems pretty clear that Mycenaean society was vulnerable. The kingdoms that we know from Homer and other authors, as well as from archaeology—Athens, Mycenae, Pylos, Thebes—all collapsed, and life became more local than global. However, the survivors eventually reemerged to play a larger role on the international scene beginning in the eighth century BC, en route to new life as the Classical Greeks.[42]

The obvious question to ask at this point, therefore, is why were the Mycenaeans so vulnerable or fragile? And, were they more so than other societies? Moreover, did everyone within their society suffer to the same extent? Did the Collapse affect the lower class or peasants out in rural Messenia the same way that it affected the elites in palatial Mycenae? Were those peasants simply able to shrug their shoulders and carry on with subsistence-level farming while the royal family and elite administrators either succumbed or fled in the face of Bronze Age supply chain issues?[43] All of these are matters of scholarly debate, with no clear resolution in sight.

However, as noted in chapter 5, a few scholars have suggested that the palatial economy of the Mycenaeans was no longer suited for the lower levels of society and that the various large-scale projects, whether architectural or geographical, such as the draining of the Kopais Basin, may have essentially bankrupted the system and caused great hardship for those who were not among the elite living in the palatial centers. Erika Weiberg and Martin Finné, for instance, have suggested that for the non-elites on mainland Greece the Collapse may actually have provided "the window of opportunity needed to 'escape' from an unsustainable socio-political structure."[44]

Joseph Maran, who has directed the excavations at Tiryns for several decades, agrees with this suggestion and adds that there may also have been other, longer-term and systemic problems as well, including conflicts among the elites at the various capital centers, which undermined the Mycenaeans as a whole, and by "internal contradictions that had long built up in the palatial polities." He also suggests the possibility of internal rebellions that were "supported and organized by disenfranchised members of the second or third tier of the elite, which could have recourse to parts of the military infrastructure of the palaces and turn it against the rulers."[45]

Thus, the Mycenaeans may have been ripe for a fall no matter what, and the various problems that came about during the "perfect storm" of the Collapse, and perhaps even before to a certain extent, may have created a societal tipping point from which it proved impossible for the Mycenaeans to recover.[46] This would mean that neither their collapse nor their inability to recover was the result of random chance but rather is documentable and quite possibly predictable in hindsight.

The same questions may be asked of the Hittites in Anatolia, who dueled with Egypt for control of the Eastern Mediterranean region during the Late Bronze Age. Their society also essentially disappeared, except for the small city-states and kingdoms that survived in southeastern Anatolia and northern Syria. Did the people out in the rural countryside simply carry on or were their lives disrupted as much as those who had lived in the capital city of Hattusa? The debate continues here too, though the recent dissertation by Sarah Adcock at the University of Chicago investigated exactly such questions: "In the Hittite case, for example," she asked, "what did it mean for the people of rural Çadir [a town in the hinterland] when the empire lost its coherence? Were their lifeways disrupted, and if so, how did they react?" As Miguel Centeno and his colleagues at the Global Systemic Risk project at Princeton University's Institute for International and Regional Studies have recently noted, "one person's collapse may be another's opportunity."[47]

One can certainly argue that the Hittites were on the verge of collapse anyway. There are indications of infighting within the royal family, including challenges to the throne, and that they had abandoned their former capital city again (after having done so previously for a short period during the thirteenth century BC) and were now based somewhere in Tarhuntassa rather than at Hattusa. All of that would have also contributed to their fragility, vulnerability, lack of resiliency, and subsequent inability to rebound from the Collapse.[48]

In contrast, the Assyrians in northern Mesopotamia do not appear to have been nearly as vulnerable or fragile as either the Mycenaeans or the Hittites and managed to survive the Collapse more or less intact. Why was that? What was different about them? Cambridge University scholar Nicholas Postgate referred to the entire period from 1200 to 900 BC as merely a "recession" for the Assyrians.[49] This is perhaps too positive a spin, as some have said, but it is true that they were nothing if not resilient in the years immediately after the Collapse. They were able to survive despite the fact that climate clearly continued to play a role in the region into the eleventh century and beyond, with extended periods of little rain and a change in the course of the Euphrates itself, all of which contributed to drought, crop failures, grain shortages, and famine. There were plagues as well, affecting not only the Assyrians in the north but also the Babylonians in southern Mesopotamia.[50] And yet they persevered.

Regardless of the challenges facing them, the Assyrians do not ever appear to have entirely lost the trappings of their society, nor did they have to completely rebuild or even transform their society to any great extent. Although the period after the Collapse cannot have been enjoyable for the Assyrians, perhaps reflected in the lack of royal inscriptions for much of the twelfth century BC, they emerged intact in the ninth century BC ready to reestablish their new dominance across the Near East for another three centuries, until 612 BC.

Their world had changed, of course. Gone were most of the other Great Kings and the international relations of the Bronze Age. Royal inscriptions, when we have them, were now concerned almost solely with military campaigns, not international trade. However, many of the hallmarks usually cited as characteristic of a dark age—including the losses of centralized administration and economy as well as the disappearance of traditional elites and of writing—were not manifested in Iron Age Assyria (or Babylonia, for that matter).

Their cuneiform writing system continued in use, for instance. Monumental inscriptions were still engraved on stone and posted in palaces and various cities, as they had been during the previous centuries of the Bronze Age; letters and documents were still recorded on clay tablets; individual identities were still recorded on cylinder seals. Moreover, the upper elite, that is, the king and his family, along with their retainers and servants, continued as they had before 1177 BC, without significant interruption. So too did the government officials and administrators, the different societal classes, and the centralized economy.[51] Despite significant fluctuations in climate and external attacks, the Assyrians managed to make their way through the centuries essentially unchanged in terms of societal structures and norms.

Again, why was this the case? Why them more than others? Was it their location at the confluence of the Tigris and Euphrates Rivers, so they were not as immediately affected by drought or the famines that contributed to the fall of their trading partners and enemies alike? Were they far enough from the Mediterranean coast to avoid being attacked by the Sea Peoples who ravaged coastal kingdoms? Perhaps it was the good fortune of having the right leader(s) in place during their time of need; or enough redundancies in their state administration and policies; or an army capable of fighting off invaders and/or conquering others to take the resources they needed with the collapse of international trade—or all of the above? Perhaps they just got lucky?

However, the fact that they were able to continue and to prove resilient seems to have had little to do with chance and perhaps even little to do with being better prepared than some of the others.[52] Instead, they may have proved to be resilient because of four things that they were able to retain for whatever reason: their centralized government, still led by the king; their basic economy; their writing system; and their army.

I also see each of the responses and resiliencies involved as being dependent on exactly what collapsed in each case. For instance, one could argue that the Mycenaean and Hittite societies went down the hardest because they each lost their centralized administration and centralized economy—this is certainly the case for the Hittites, who lost their empire, and probably also for the Mycenaeans, where the small kingdoms each had their own centralized administration and economy, for example, at Mycenae, Thebes, and Pylos. But one could also argue that the Mycenaean centers were not self-sufficient enough and too heavily dependent on imports of raw materials like copper, tin, and gold. The same might be said of others as well, including the Hittites.

In contrast, the Assyrians, Babylonians, and Egyptians did not lose their royal dynasties at the time of the Collapse, nor their centralized administrations, nor their economies; they just experienced disruptions that could be overcome through resilience. They didn't need to rebuild as the Greeks were forced to do. In the case of the Assyrians, they were also able to grab, by conquest or tribute, the raw materials that they needed.

The authors of the 2012 IPCC report also point out, "Extreme events will have greater impacts on sectors with closer links to climate, such as water, agriculture and food security. . . . For example . . . there is high confidence that changes in climate have the potential to seriously affect water management systems."[53] As such, it may be worth noting that, of the four societies that I would consider to have had the highest impact ranking among the Late Bronze Age "Great Powers"—namely, the Egyptians, Assyrians, Babylonians, and Hittites, based in part on their status as depicted in the fourteenth-century BC Amarna Letters—three

TABLE 7. Sequels of civilizations/societies in the centuries following the Collapse

	Transformed into	**Assimilated into or replaced by**
Assyrians	Neo-Assyrians	—
Babylonians	Neo-Babylonians	—
Central Canaanites	Phoenicians	—
Southern Canaanites	—	Israel, Judah, Edom, Moab, Ammon, Philistia
Cypriots	Archaic Cypriots	—
Egyptians	Egyptians	—
Hittites (and northern Canaanites)	Neo-Hittites (in northern Canaan and southeastern Anatolia)	Urartu (in eastern Anatolia); Phrygians (in central/western Anatolia)
Mycenaeans and Minoans	Archaic Greeks and Cretans	—

were located on river systems; the Egyptians had the Nile, while both the Assyrians and the Babylonians had the Tigris and Euphrates. The Hittites, on the other hand, did not have such a large and dependable river system in their vicinity—they had only the Kızılırmak (Halys) River as a similar resource—and they are the only one of the four who completely collapsed.

In addition, I would suggest, as others have done previously, that the rise of small Iron Age micropolities ranging from the Aramaean kingdoms to Israel and Judah is perhaps simply a matter of their kingdoms coming out from under the shadow of what had been the mighty empires like the Hittites, Egyptians, Assyrians, and Babylonians, as Renfrew says happens after a system collapse, and of small, private mercantile enterprises taking over from the state-run endeavors of the Bronze Age. But it could also be more like a return to the way things had been earlier in the second millennium BC in both Canaan and Greece, during the Middle Bronze Age.[54] These are also matters for future consideration and further debate.

It might also be of interest to further consider the alternative outcomes that might have taken place, had things gone otherwise for some of the societies, and to wonder if any of them could have avoided their fate. There are lots of "would've, could've, should've"s here, but certainly if the Hittite royal family had not had internal problems and if they had not moved their capital elsewhere, they might not have collapsed so rapidly and thoroughly. Similarly, if the Mycenaeans had been more self-sufficient, and not as dependent on others for raw materials, and if they had eased up on the exploitative construction and engineering products that impacted the lower classes, they might have survived better also.

Furthermore, what if one or more had not collapsed? Could the whole system have survived if only the Hittites had succumbed? Or only the Mycenaeans? What would have happened if Ugarit had not been destroyed or if the Egyptians had not withdrawn from the area of southern Canaan?

All of this is difficult to model or predict, even in hindsight, because of the variety of factors involved, both known and unknown. We are hampered by the fact that we still do not know exactly what brought each of the societies down, including whether it really was a combination of factors, as I have suggested previously. For example, were the Mycenaeans overrun by the Sea Peoples, or were they overcome by internal uprisings at the various palaces? Or did the drought bring them down? Or was it all of the above or something else entirely?

Depending on which factor(s), stressor(s), or combination it was, perhaps one could suggest different possible solutions that they might have employed in an attempt to avoid their societal collapse, but this is fodder for speculation. It is also the core of probabilistic thinking and the stuff from which alternative histories are written.[55] Regardless, we can imagine scenarios to our heart's content but, to quote Omar Khayyam, "the moving finger writes; and, having writ, moves on: nor all thy piety nor wit shall lure it back to cancel half a line, nor all thy tears wash out a word of it."

Collapse *and* Transformation

Some thirty years ago, the respected sociologist Shmuel Eisenstadt said bluntly that "ancient states and civilizations do not collapse at all, if by *collapse* is meant the complete end of those political systems and their accompanying civilizational frameworks."[56] I would take issue with his declaration, for in fact that is exactly what happened to both the

Mycenaeans and the Hittites. Even if vestiges did remain, as in the case of the Neo-Hittites, and even if there is still some continuity into the next period, as was the case in Greece with the names of the gods, for instance, the Bronze Age Collapse certainly did see the complete end of the political systems and accompanying civilizational framework for both the Hittites and the Mycenaeans.

However, Eisenstadt then went on to say, "Collapse, far from being an anomaly . . . presents in dramatic form not the end of social institutions, but almost always the beginning of new ones."[57] This sentiment I am more inclined to agree with, though I would rephrase it as "Collapse can involve both the end of old social institutions and the beginning of new ones."

While it is clear by now that the Bronze Age Collapse was complicated, it is just as obvious that the rebirth was even more complicated; blanket, sweeping statements simply don't work. And to claim, as some have done, that there was no collapse, but only transformation or transition, is not only insufficient but may even be harmful to a degree, as using only the latter bland and desensitized terms runs the risk of whitewashing or minimizing the human element in all of this, especially in terms of the suffering and misery that may have impacted many during that time.[58]

In the chapters above, we have looked at eight different examples—with each having a separate road back to success (or not). There is no doubt that the way of life as it existed from the fifteenth through the thirteenth centuries came to an end shortly after 1200 BC. There is no arguing against that, as a whole. But each area was affected differently; each fell at a slightly different time, albeit still during the same general period; and each took a different trajectory toward recovery.[59] As we have seen, there was resilience on the part of some, like the Assyrians. There was transformation on the part of others, like the Cypriots. There was also complete collapse, like the Hittites. I would therefore suggest, as others have previously, that the transition between the Bronze Age and the Iron Age in the Aegean and Eastern Mediterranean was both a time of collapse *and* a time of adaptation and/or transformation, depending on where one looks in the region. It was both alpha and omega (or rather, omega followed by alpha), to put it in terms of the adaptive cycle.

How can we sum all of this up in a single sentence? Clearly, everybody in this region was trying to recover from the same Collapse, but then each society followed its own individual route to recovery, or not. Perhaps it would help if we envisioned the break as a wall or a barrier between the Bronze Age and the Iron Age, but that wall or barrier was porous and allowed certain strands of continuity to get through, rather than completely blocking everything. Alternatively, we could envision all of this as a competitive footrace, such as those found in the Olympics, both in antiquity and today. All of the participants will have begun at the same time and from the same starting line, in terms of having to simultaneously recover from the Collapse, but they ended up at the finish line staggered, as each crossed the endpoint at a different time—and some did not finish at all.

Mycenaeans or Phoenicians?

By way of conclusion, we should ask one final set of questions as well: does this story of the events that took place three thousand years ago hold any additional lessons for us today? Is there anything to be learned from the overall dramatic story of resurgence and revival of the globalized Mediterranean network just four centuries after the Bronze Age Collapse? And is there an easy answer for what to do if our own society/civilization collapses?

About a decade ago, the 2012 IPCC report that I have cited so often above concluded, "The potential for concatenated global impacts of extreme events continues to grow as the world's economy becomes more interconnected."[60] It seems appropriate to quote that here, in the final paragraphs of this book, for I submit again that our societal vulnerabilities and fragilities were suddenly exposed when COVID-19 first exploded worldwide in 2020 and then again when problems involving the global supply chain subsequently developed during the later part of 2021. I am not exaggerating when I say that it has really felt to me on occasion as if we are on the brink of societal collapse ourselves, "coming soon to an area near you," as they say in the movies. When will it happen? What will be our tipping point? I cannot say for certain, obviously, but I strongly suspect that it is a matter of sooner rather than later—a question of when, not if—and that we will need to utilize for ourselves the lessons learned from those who survived a societal collapse more than three thousand years ago, including how to transform rather than simply cope or adapt and to embrace new innovations and inventions as needed.

There are certainly lessons to be learned, but unfortunately there is no easy answer for what to do, for this also ultimately depends on the stressors or drivers that might be involved. Regardless, logic dictates that one should have multiple contingency plans in place, so that if the primary systems of administration, trade, agricultural production, or banking fail, there is a secondary, or even a tertiary, system that could be implemented without undue delay in each case. In short, we need to have enough redundant systems to fall back on if the primary ones fail. We also need to be resilient enough to withstand whatever blows may come; self-sufficient enough to remain standing even if/when our trading partners fall; innovative enough to adapt or transform as necessary; and strong enough to withstand any enemy invasions or attacks even while we are already reeling. But all of those are common-sense recommendations that others would probably suggest even without having studied what happened in the aftermath of the Late Bronze Age Collapse.

The main takeaway from all of this is that clearly such a collapse is survivable, provided that we are resilient enough and able to cope, adapt, or transform as necessary. Societal collapse doesn't always take everyone with it, and often cultures continue, even if at a simpler level or perhaps in a new iteration.[61] And even for those who are hit hardest, there is often a period of regeneration after the worst of times that leads to the resumption of life, prosperity, and happiness (as the ancient Egyptians would say).

Thus, if our own globalized civilization comes to an end, how we deal with it will depend on how total the collapse is and how well we have prepared for it in advance. Let us hope that it does not come to that, but instead remember the words of John Wooden, the longtime coach of the UCLA Bruins basketball team (and possibly Benjamin Franklin before him): "By failing to prepare, you are preparing to fail."[62]

For those who are looking despairingly into the current abyss of global warming, endless violence, resource shortages, drought, and pollution, there may be some reassurance in knowing that if we develop the right resilience strategies, we may be able to minimize the damage as well as

TABLE 8. Societal lessons learned from the LBA Collapse and aftermath

1. Have multiple contingency plans in place and redundant systems to fall back on if your primary ones fail.
2. Be resilient enough to withstand whatever blows may come and strong enough to withstand any enemy invasions or attacks.
3. Be as self-sufficient as possible, but do call on friends for assistance when needed.
4. Be innovative and inventive, ready to turn nimbly and adapt or transform, rather than simply cope.
5. Prepare for extreme weather conditions: if they come, you will be ready; if they don't, it won't matter.
6. Be sure to have dependable water resources.
7. Keep the working class happy.

speed up the recovery following a societal collapse. At the very least, we can hope that there will be someone left to pick up the pieces and carry on.

I also think here of a professor of management and marketing at Louisiana State University named Leon Megginson who in 1963 paraphrased Charles Darwin's *Origin of Species* along the following lines: "It is not the most intellectual of the species that survives; it is not the strongest that survives; but the species that survives is the one that is able best to adapt and adjust to the changing environment in which it finds itself."[63] That surely seems applicable to what we have seen during the centuries of the Iron Age in the Aegean and Eastern Mediterranean, and it would be good to keep it in mind for the future as well.

So, are we Mycenaeans or are we Phoenicians? Are we more vulnerable and fragile today than we might care to admit? If we see problems continue to affect us, will we transform? Will we be innovative and inventive? Will we flourish amid chaos? Or will we simply exhibit a capacity to adapt or to cope, and merely try to adjust to the situation? Or, worse still, will we choose to do nothing and risk a cascading failure and systemic collapse, repeating what happened more than three thousand years ago?[64]

We shall have to leave it to the academicians of the next century or beyond for a detailed report and an analysis on how we responded . . . and whether we were successful or not.

EPILOGUE

End of a Dark Age

We can now come full circle and ask again the question posed at the beginning of this book: was this period—the centuries following the Bronze Age Collapse—truly a dark age or not? Although the designation of a period as a dark age is really only meant by scholars to imply a lack of written records and a simplification of society in general, it is more often employed by those outside academia to imply total collapse and degeneration, with wild dogs howling and barbarians prowling in the darkness just outside the sight of frightened survivors squatting in the ruins of their once-proud cities.[1]

As we have seen, however, neither scenario is entirely accurate for the centuries following the Collapse. While as a whole this era does meet many of the criteria for a dark age laid out in this book's prologue, including the loss of writing, the cessation of constructing large buildings, and the collapse of centralized economies and administrations, we see this only in some of the societies that we have been discussing, but not in all the regions. And even in the areas that suffered the most, we still see evidence of invention and innovation.

In fact, few, if any, of my colleagues still refer to this period as a dark age; it is now usually simply called the Iron Age by archaeologists, ancient historians, biblical scholars, and other academicians. However, the general public doesn't seem to have gotten the message yet—just look again at the definition for "dark age" in *Merriam-Webster's* dictionary (as well as for "Greek Dark Age" in the *World History Encyclopedia)*, which

I mentioned at this beginning of this book. This needs to change, as can easily be made clear.

Ian Morris has noted that it was only in the 1890s that the concept of the Dark Age in the history of ancient Greece was born, after historians and archaeologists realized that at least four centuries separated Homer (who lived during the late eighth century BC) from the Trojan War (which most likely took place in the early twelfth century BC).[2] To give one classic example, in 1962, Sir Denys Page, an eminent British historian of the Homeric period, described this era as follows: "Sometime soon after 1200 B.C., the Mycenaean civilization was wiped off the face of the earth. . . . For the next three or four hundred years, Greece was isolated, impoverished, parochial. The art of writing was lost; contact with the outside world was reduced to little or nothing; the arts and crafts of Mycenaean Greece were disused or greatly debased. The contrast is about as extreme as it could be."[3]

Chester Starr, who was a revered professor of ancient history at the University of Michigan, had said essentially the same thing one year earlier, but a bit more poetically, in his inimitable style: "As the last embers flickered out at the destroyed Mycenaean palaces, darkness settled over Greece. Men continued to live in most parts of the Aegean, to beget families, and to die; but their dull routine of daily life and final burial deposited only the scantiest of physical remains. Not until the eighth century B.C. does this obscurity slowly begin to lift."[4]

As Morris notes, this model of the Greek Dark Ages held sway for nearly a century, until the 1980s, albeit with much discussion and debate swirling around the topic. By that time, it had become dogma to many in the field, especially after seminal publications in the 1970s by three prominent British archaeologists—Anthony Snodgrass of Cambridge (*The Dark Age of Greece*, in 1971); Vincent Desborough of Oxford (*The Greek Dark Ages*, in 1972); and Nicholas Coldstream (*Geometric Greece*, in 1977).[5]

However, there has been much new material coming out of Iron Age archaeological excavations in Greece in recent decades that undercuts this model, as we have seen in chapter 5. Even Chester Starr eventually acknowledged in the early 1990s, "Our knowledge . . . of no other period of ancient history has changed and expanded in recent generations so much on the factual level as has our picture of early Greece."[6]

Partly as a result, a number of scholarly "gradualists," as Ian Morris calls them, now argue that there was not such an abrupt break following the Late Bronze Age Collapse as we had previously thought; that the changes are likely to have been more measured; and that, overall, the Dark Age was not quite as bleak as had been previously painted and therefore should not even be labeled as such. Indeed, Sarah Morris of UCLA has stated emphatically, "Recent archaeology has dispelled Greece's 'Dark Age.'" She adds that it "has been illuminated too brightly by recent discoveries to retain its name or reality."[7]

I think that our explorations in the chapters above have shown that this holds true not only for the Aegean but also for the Eastern Mediterranean as well. Joshua Jeffers, in his 2013 University of Pennsylvania dissertation, observed that for ancient Near Eastern historians, the term "dark age" is often used simply to "describe a period for which there is a relative lack of documentation to illuminate and reconstruct that period's history." As he notes, "thus, the application of this phrase to the Near East has no value judgment, but rather only describes the difficulty of the task that faces the modern historian."[8]

As for the Levant, Benjamin Porter of UC Berkeley says, "[T]he Iron Age I was hardly a dark age lacking historical development as earlier scholars had assumed. Groups adapted to new political and economic circumstances." And Susan Sherratt, even two decades ago, said, "Few probably would nowadays subscribe to quite such a dramatic, millennial vision of the onset of a dark age. . . . Each region of increasingly specialized archaeological endeavor now has its own version of what happened in this period, some distinctly less 'dark' than others."[9]

Thus, despite the views of historians and archaeologists of previous generations, I would agree with the scholars who now argue that the initial centuries of the early first millennium BC in the Aegean and Eastern Mediterranean regions were not quite so dark as we used to think. As early as 1991, for instance, James Whitley stated bluntly, "The Dark Age of Greece is our [own] conception."[10]

Furthermore, if we recall that the alpha (α) phase of the adaptive cycle is seen as the "phase of reorganization" and a time "during which innovation and new opportunities are possible," it is relevant to note that John Papadopoulos of UCLA has specifically pointed out that there are "a remarkable number of 'firsts'" during this period in Greece—too many, in fact, to call it the Dark Age. Among these he would include concepts and innovations that were created during those centuries as well as those that would come to fruition later but that must have begun to develop during this period. These include mass literacy ("for the first time in world history, writing . . . became a tool that anyone could use"), which came with the introduction of the Phoenician alphabet; the invention of coinage, which began in Lydia in the seventh century BC; the creation of the Greek city-states, that is, the *polis* (pl. *poleis*); and, of course, the use of iron tools and weapons.[11] Papadopoulos also says specifically that "the fact that an era designated as a 'Dark Age' is ushered in by a technological innovation as evidently singular as the widespread use of iron in the Greek mainland is, in itself, important." Not least, he notes that "the Greeks themselves knew of no Dark Age," and asks, "Why not trust their better judgment?"[12]

Indeed, why not trust their better judgment? I think that it is time for everyone, not just academics but the general public as well, to refer to the twelfth through eighth centuries BC in the Aegean and Eastern Mediterranean as the Iron Age rather than the Dark Age, just as the other "Dark Age" to which *Merriam-Webster's* dictionary refers—that is, the centuries after the fall of Rome—is now more commonly referred to by scholars either as "Late Antiquity" or the "Early Middle Ages." The period after the Late Bronze Age Collapse was not entirely bereft of innovation and invention, as we have seen for ourselves and as Papadopoulos and others have pointed out. Although there is an obvious break overall with the previous period, it is clearly also a time of transition and adjustment, involving transformation as often as regeneration. In

Canaan, Syro-Anatolia, Cyprus, and elsewhere, for instance, there were new kingdoms, including Israel and Judah, Edom, Moab, and Urartu; there were new elites in place, new centralized economies, and new administrations; and, in some cases, there was now a new writing system to be used during the long climb back to an internationalized world system in this region. In short, it was overall more a period of rebirth and renewal than it was of darkness and despair.

Therefore, calling this period simply the Iron Age, as archaeologists and other academics do, makes the most sense. It is a label that casts no aspersions, has no obvious sociopolitical or economic associations, and is a simple statement of fact that many tools and weapons during this period were now made of iron rather than bronze.[13] As the alpha phase of the adaptive cycle in this area, rather than a dark age, this period was the start of something new, a set of ideas and cultures that ultimately resulted in the world to which we now belong.

AUTHOR'S NOTE AND ACKNOWLEDGMENTS

For a variety of reasons, very few scholars have previously discussed in detail the transition from the Bronze Age to the Iron Age across the entire area stretching from the Aegean to the Eastern Mediterranean and beyond to Mesopotamia. This is in part because, as several of my colleagues, especially John Papadopoulos of UCLA and Maria Iacovou of the University of Cyprus, have pointed out, there is a real divide between the archaeologists and ancient historians who study the Bronze Age (the period before the Collapse) and those who study the Iron Age (the period after the Collapse) in the Aegean and Eastern Mediterranean—Papadopoulos has called it "the 'iron curtain' between Aegean prehistory and Classical archaeology." There is an even more obvious divide between the scholars who study the ancient Aegean and those who study the ancient Near East; only a handful of scholars do both. That is why I am hoping that this book will help, to some small extent, to bridge these divides and span the gaps, thereby creating some sort of continuity of study so that we may not only "see history as a [chronological] continuum," as Papadopoulos has eloquently requested, but also as a geographical continuum.[1]

However, I am fully aware of the difficulties involved in writing a book that touches on so many topics while keeping within the allotted word limits (or close to them). Some may complain that there are far too many details and too many caveats, not to mention too many unfamiliar names. However, this is meant to be a summation and overview of the current state of our knowledge, presenting facts and hypotheses concerning what we know about the four hundred years after the Late Bronze Age Collapse in the Aegean and Eastern Mediterranean regions. It is essentially a history book with some archaeology tossed in, followed by a lengthy analysis and musings on the relevance of this topic to us today; the names of people and places may be new and unfamiliar to many, but they allow us to visualize the world of the Iron Age and bring to life some of the inhabitants of these regions. I have tried to present the myriad details in an interesting narrative, but only time will tell if I have succeeded.

On the other hand, since the professional archaeologists, ancient historians, art historians, biblical scholars, and other specialists in each area, not to mention the academic reviewers, will almost certainly grouse, either publicly or privately, that I have not provided nearly enough detail or explored the various nuances about their favorite time period or region, let me be the first to say that each of the above chapters could have been a full book (or two) unto itself and that there is much more that I would have liked to cover. However, I have had to be necessarily selective because of length constraints and hence have not been able to include everything that I might have wished. As I have said elsewhere—albeit when writing about a different topic, but which is just as relevant here and now—"a truly comprehensive discussion of every topic in this book would take many years, dozens of volumes, and numerous scholars working together—and would probably end up being something that only a handful of people would read," which means that the whole point of writing this as a single volume with a single voice would be lost.[2]

Let me also state here for the record that I welcome critical comments, suggestions, and feedback from all readers, perhaps to be incorporated down the line in a revised edition or debated in other contexts and locales. However, I am reminded again of the metaphor invoked at the beginning of chapter 6: if we regard the Iron Age as an Impressionist painting but insist on standing just inches away, we may lose the forest for the trees. While the more intimate and detailed observations presented in this book will be subject to debate and discussion, as of course they should be, I hope that the overall picture presented here, if viewed from further away so that the individual brushstrokes blend together into a recognizable scene, will hold up to scrutiny and provide us with the larger perspective of what happened overall in the centuries after the Late Bronze Age Collapse, when the globalized Mediterranean network broke down and the individual societies were forced to grapple with the aftermath, with varying degrees of success.

Finally, I am acutely aware that the later eighth century is replete with other significant historical events, including large tectonic calamities like the destruction of the northern kingdom of Israel in 720 BC. Nor have I even broached the topic of Homer, Hesiod, and the advent of literature in Greece. One could, and perhaps should (some would say), go on and on, down to the sixth, fifth, or fourth century BC and beyond, if there were no restraints on the size of this volume, but as it is, such further discussions will have to be left for another book.

As for acknowledgments, they are many and varied; such is the nature of writing a synthesis like this. I must first acknowledge my indebtedness to all the archaeologists, historians, and scientists who have gone before me—not only those who excavated, translated, analyzed, and published decades ago, but also those who have done so more recently, including in just the past few years. Without all their efforts and their publications, I simply would not have been able to write the current book, full stop. They are too numerous to name individually here, but readers will get an idea of those on whom I have leaned most strongly by simply leafing through the endnotes and then perusing the bibliography. We would not be where we are today if it were not for both the earlier and the more recent efforts. The study of our past—informed by archaeology and epigraphy in particular—is, quite simply, a communal project, with advances in our knowledge coming as the result of individual efforts by a multitude of scholars over many years; it really does take a village.

That being said, I would also like to once again thank my intrepid editor, Rob Tempio, this time for persuading me to write this sequel to *1177 B.C.: The Year Civilization Collapsed* and for his support, especially down the stretch. I would also especially like to thank my family, as always, for putting up with me during the research and the writing of this book, and especially my wife, Diane Harris Cline, whose Fulbright grant at the University of Crete during the spring 2019 semester led to our presence in Rethymnon, where I first began writing significant portions of the initial draft, and who provided much food for thought and valuable suggestions along the way. A plethora of thanks go also to University of Crete faculty members Katerina Panagopoulou and Kostas Vlassopoulos for their incredible hospitality and to Elias Kolovos for renting us his lovely apartment during our three months in Rethymnon.

Thanks go also to the understanding administrators at George Washington University, and especially to Associate Dean Youngwu Rong for initially awarding me a Dean's Research Chair Fellowship, which allowed me to rearrange my teaching schedule so that I could have the spring 2019 semester off to work on various book projects, including starting the current manuscript. Subsequently, Dean Paul Wahlbeck and Associate Deans John Philbeck, Kim Gross, and Evie Downie allowed me to have the fall 2021 semester off as well, when I was the beneficiary of a Getty Scholar Grant, courtesy of the Getty Foundation, and was part of the wonderful cohort of scholars within the "Phoenicians, Philistines, and Canaanites: The Levant and the Classical World" Scholars Program.

I was thus able to write much of the final portions of the manuscript at the incomparable Getty Villa in California, in the company of very talented colleagues who provided welcome feedback to earlier drafts and to a lecture based on the manuscript that I gave while it was in its early stages. I am very grateful to Tim Potts, Jeffrey Spier, Claire Lyons, Ken Lapatin, Alexa Sekyra, Rose Campbell, Kylie Morgan, and others at the Getty Villa and the Getty Research Institute, as well as to my fellow "Phoenicians" (Melissa Cradic, Brien Garnand, and Jessica Nitschke) and those in the cohorts before and after us, in addition to the other scholars who called the Pink Palace in Brentwood "home" during the fall of 2021. I am especially grateful to Robert J. Lempert of the Rand Corporation and Nancy Perloff of the Getty Research Institute for meeting with me and discussing relevant topics during my time at the Getty, which led me directly to the 2012 IPCC report that plays such an important role in the final portion of the book.

I am also indebted to Miguel Centeno and the other organizers and participants in the Historical Systemic Collapse workshop, held at Princeton University on April 26–27, 2019, as well as the subsequent weekly seminar on historical societal resilience organized by John Haldon, also of Princeton University, during the fall of 2020 and conducted via Zoom during the pandemic. The presentations, readings, and conversations about collapse, resiliency, and transformation with the various participants at the workshop, during the seminar, and in the months afterward, especially with John Haldon, Luke Kemp, and Jim Newhard, sparked many thoughts that have made their way into this book.

In addition to my presentations at the Princeton conferences and workshops in April 2019 and the fall of 2020, and at the Getty in November 2021, some of this material was also presented in other venues, either virtually or in person, including at New York University in October 2020, the annual meetings of the American Society of Overseas Research in November 2020, the Biblical Archaeology Society's Spring Bible and Archaeology Fest in April 2022, the annual meetings of the Mediterranean Archaeology Australasian Research Community in February 2023, and at Yale University in April 2023. I am grateful to all of the participants and audience members for their feedback during and after those events.

I would also, belatedly, like to thank my professors in graduate school who tried so long ago to introduce me to the basic facts, as well as the nuances and details, about the Iron Age in both the Aegean and the Eastern Mediterranean, including Keith DeVries, John Graham, James Sauer, Irene Winter, and especially James D. Muhly. Little did I know at the time that more than three decades later I would attempt to write a book on the same topics; I hope that it comes close to doing justice to their impassioned and learned teaching.

In addition, and with many apologies in advance to anyone whom I neglect to mention, I would like to thank numerous friends and colleagues for sending relevant publications my way and/or bringing various topics to my attention, including W. Sheppard Baird, J. A. Brinkman, Trevor Bryce, Guy Bunnens, Hanan Charaf, Violetta Cordani, Aidan Dodson, Anne Duray, Meir Edrey, Carl S. Ehrlich, Eckart Frahm, Norma Franklin, Gil Gambash, Brien Garnand, Ayelet Gilboa, John Haldon, Rachel Hallote, Louise Hitchcock, Christopher W. Jones, Katie Kearns, Luke Kemp, Gunnar Lehmann, Megan Lewis, Susan Lupack, James Osborne, Beatrice Pestarino, Benjamin Porter, Federico Rocchi, Karen Rubinson, Golan Shalvi, Trevor Van Damme, Marcus Wallas, Mark Weeden, and Assaf Yasur-Landau.

For answering my questions about various topics and suggesting possible solutions, I am grateful as well to Carol Bell, Shirly Ben-Dor Evian, Erez Ben-Yosef, Nathaniel Erb-Satullo, Eckart Frahm, Tamar Hodos, Nota Kourou, Robert Lempert, Tom Levy, Barry Molloy, James D. Muhly, Vana Orfanou, Christopher Rollston, Jane Waldbaum, Jonathan Wood, Naama Yahalom-Mack, and Paul Zimansky.

Above all, I am extremely grateful to a number of colleagues who read portions, or the entirety, of this manuscript as it was in various stages of research and writing, and suggested changes, edits, deletions, and other emendations. These include Hanan Charaf, Bill Dardis, Aidan Dodson, Eckart Frahm, Norma Franklin, Brien Garnand, John Haldon, Rachel Hallote, Randy Helm, Katie Kearns, Luke Kemp, Robert Lempert, Aren Maeir, Jim Newhard, Jessica Nitschke, James Osborne, John Papadopoulos, Chris Rollston, Assaf Yasur-Landau, and most especially Mitchell Allen of Scholarly Roadside Service (who helped curb my tendency towards verbosity and condemned my love of commas).

I am also indebted to the anonymous peer reviewers who read and commented on the entire manuscript, which resulted in some major changes, improving the final product, I hope. I am especially grateful to the George Washington University students in my "Collapse and Resilience in the Ancient World" seminar during spring 2023, who valiantly debated the semantics of "societal collapse" and other terms throughout the semester; investigated the applicability of using such concepts when studying the end of the Harappa, Maya, and Roman societies, among others; and provided much useful feedback on the penultimate version of this manuscript. And, last but by no means least, I am indebted to Michele Angel for creating the wonderful maps and to Glynnis Fawkes for drawing several of the figures.

As always, I have tried to the best of my abilities to give proper attribution to other scholars' ideas and publications. If I have failed to give proper credit anywhere, it is most assuredly unintentional, and I will make every effort to remedy the situation in future printings and editions. Responsibility for any remaining errors in this manuscript, or for misinterpretation of their work, is mine alone.

DRAMATIS PERSONAE

(in alphabetical order)

The following list includes most of the major rulers and related personnel mentioned in the text.

Abdi-Aštart (Abdastratus): King of Tyre; ruled late tenth century BC
Abibaal: King of Byblos; ruled mid–late tenth century BC
Adad-apla-iddina: Babylonian king; ruled 1067–1046 BC
Adad-nirari II: Neo-Assyrian king; ruled 911–891 BC
Adad-nirari III: Neo-Assyrian king; ruled 810–783 BC
Ahab: King of Israel; ruled ca. 871–852 BC
Ahaziah: King of Judah; ruled ca. 842–841 BC
Ahiram: King of Byblos; ruled early tenth century BC
Amenemopet: Pharaoh of Egypt, Twenty-First Dynasty; ruled 991–982 BC
Aramu: King of Urartu; ruled ca. 859–844 BC
Argishti I: King of Urartu; ruled ca. 786–764 BC
Aššur-bel-kala: Middle Assyrian king; ruled 1074–1057 BC
Aššur-dan I: Middle Assyrian king; ruled 1179–1133 BC
Aššur-dan II: Neo-Assyrian king; ruled 934–912 BC
Aššurnasirpal I: Neo-Assyrian king; ruled 1049–1031 BC
Aššurnasirpal II: Neo-Assyrian king; ruled 883–859 BC
Aššur-reša-iši I: Middle Assyrian king; ruled 1133–1116 BC
Aštar(t-)imn: King of Tyre; ruled early ninth century BC
Astiru(wa) I: Country Lord of Carchemish; ruled ca. 810 BC
Astuwalamanza(s) (alt. Astuwatamanza): Country Lord of Carchemish; ruled tenth century BC

Baal-ma'zer (Baal-azor) I: King of Tyre; ruled late tenth century BC
Baal-ma'zer (Baal-azor) II: King of Tyre; ruled mid-ninth century BC
Baba-aha-iddina: Babylonian king; ruled ca. 812 BC
David: King of United Monarchy; ruled ca. 1000–970 BC
Elibaal: King of Byblos; ruled mid–late tenth century BC
Enlil-nadin-ahi: Babylonian king; ruled ca. 1157–1155 BC
Ethbaal: King of Byblos; ruled early tenth century BC
Ethbaal: King of Tyre; ruled early–mid-ninth century BC
Hadad: Crown-prince and then king of Edom; ruled early tenth century BC
Hadad-ezer: King of Aram-Damascus; ruled ca. 858 BC
Halparuntiya: King of Patin(a); ruled early ninth century BC
Hatiba: Princess of an unnamed town in Cyprus who interacted with Wenamun; ca. 1075 BC
Hayya: King of Sam'al (Zincirli); ruled ca. 870/860–840 BC)
Hazael: King of Aram-Damascus; ruled ca. 842–796 BC
Herihor: High priest of Amun, later ruled as pharaoh, 1080–1074 BC
Hiram: King of Tyre; ruled ca. 970–936 BC
Ini-Tešub: Great King of Carchemish; ruled late twelfth century BC
Inushpua: King of Urartu; ruled (with Menua) ca. 810–786 BC
Isarwila-muwa: Country Lord of Carchemish; ruled second half of ninth century BC
Iš-Aštart: King of Tyre; ruled early ninth century BC
Ishpuini: King of Urartu; ruled ca. 828–810 BC
Jehoram: King of Judah; ruled ca. 849–842 BC
Jehu: King of Israel; ruled ca. 841–814 BC
Joash/Jehoash: King of Israel; ruled ca. 804–789 BC
Joram: King of Israel; ruled ca. 850–840 BC
Kamani: Country Lord of Carchemish; ruled ca. 790 BC
Kaššu-nadin-ahhe: Babylonian king; ruled ca. 1007–1005 BC
Katuwa(s): Country Lord of Carchemish; ruled late tenth century BC
Kulamuwa: King of Sam'al (Zincirli); ruled ca. 840–810 BC
Kupapiya: Wife of Taita II, king of the "Land of Palistin"; early tenth century BC

Kuwalana-muwa: Country Lord of Carchemish; ruled second half of ninth century BC
Kuzi-Tešub: Great King of Carchemish; ruled ca. 1200–1180 BC
Lubarna I(?): King of Patin(a); ruled early ninth century BC
Lubarna II: King of Patin(a); ruled late ninth century BC
Manana: King of the "Land of Palistin"; ruled mid-tenth century BC
Marduk-balatsu-iqbi: Babylonian king; ruled 819–813 BC
Marduk-nadin-ahhe: Babylonian king; ruled ca. 1099–1082 BC
Marduk-sapik-zeri: Babylonian king; ruled 1082–1069 BC
Marduk-zakir-sumi: Babylonian king; ruled ca. 855–819 BC
Mattan I: King of Tyre; ruled late ninth century BC
Menua: King of Urartu; ruled (with Inushpua) ca. 810–786 BC
Mesha: King of Moab; ruled mid-ninth century BC
Methusastratos (usurper): King of Tyre; ruled late tenth century BC
Mutnedjmet: Wife of Pharaoh Psusennes I, Twenty-First Dynasty (ruled 1039–991 BC)
Nabu-apla-iddina: Babylonian king; ruled ca. 887–855 BC
Nabu-mukin-apli: Babylonian king; ruled ca. 978–943 BC
Nebuchadnezzar I: Babylonian king; ruled 1125–1104 BC
Omri: King of Israel; ruled ca. 884–873 BC
Osorkon I: Pharaoh of Egypt, Twenty-Second Dynasty; ruled ca. 924–889 BC
Osorkon II: Pharaoh of Egypt, Twenty-Second Dynasty; ruled 872–831 BC
Panamuwa I: King of Sam'al (Zincirli); ruled ca. 790–745 BC
Panedjem I: Pharaoh of Egypt; ruled 1074–1036 BC
Pilles: King of Tyre; ruled early ninth century BC
Psusennes I: Pharaoh of Egypt, Twenty-First Dynasty; ruled 1039–991 BC
Psusennes II: Pharaoh of Egypt, Twenty-First Dynasty; ruled 958–945 BC
Pummayon (Pygmalion): King of Tyre; ruled late ninth–early eighth century BC
Qalparunda II: King of Patin(a); ruled mid-ninth century BC
Qurila: King of Sam'al (Zincirli); ruled ca. 810–790 BC

Ramses III: Pharaoh of Egypt, Nineteenth Dynasty; ruled 1186–1155 BC

Ramses IV–X: Pharaohs of Egypt, Twentieth Dynasty; ruled 1155–1098 BC

Ramses XI: Pharaoh of Egypt, Twentieth Dynasty; ruled 1098–1070 BC, overlapping with Smendes and Herihor

Sangara: Country Lord of Carchemish; ruled ca. 875–848 BC

Sapaziti: Great King of Carchemish; ruled late eleventh century BC

Sarduri I: King of Urartu; ruled ca. 834–828 BC

Sha'il: King of Sam'al (Zincirli); ruled ca. 850–840 BC

Shalmaneser II: Neo-Assyrian king; ruled 1030–1019 BC

Shalmaneser III: Neo-Assyrian king; ruled 858–824 BC

Shamaš-mudammiq: Babylonian king; ruled ca. 900 BC

Shamši-Adad V: Neo-Assyrian king; ruled 823–811 BC

Sheshonq I: Pharaoh of Egypt, founder of Twenty-Second Dynasty; ruled ca. 945–924 BC

Sheshonq IIa: Pharaoh of Egypt, Twenty-Second Dynasty; ruled ca. 890 BC

Sheshonq III: Pharaoh of Egypt, Twenty-Second Dynasty; ruled 831–791 BC

Shipitbaal: King of Byblos; ruled late tenth century BC

Siamun: Pharaoh of Egypt, Twenty-First Dynasty; ruled 979–958 BC

Smendes: Administrator in the Nile delta region of Egypt, later ruled as pharaoh and founder of the Twenty-First Dynasty, 1077/1069–1043 BC

Solomon: King of United Monarchy; ruled ca. 970–930 BC

Suhi I: Country Lord of Carchemish; ruled ca. 1000 BC

Suhi II: Country Lord of Carchemish; ruled tenth century BC

Suhi III: Country Lord of Carchemish; ruled ca. 900 BC

Suppiluliuma I: King of the "Land of Palistin"; ruled late tenth century BC

Suppiluliuma II/Sapalulme: King of Patin(a); ruled mid-ninth century BC

Taita I: King of the "Land of Palistin"; ruled eleventh century BC

Taita II: King of the "Land of Palistin"; ruled early tenth century BC

Takelot I: Pharaoh of Egypt, Twenty-Second Dynasty; ruled 889–872 BC
Takelot II: Pharaoh of Egypt, Twenty-Third Dynasty; ruled 834–810 BC
Tanetamon: Daughter of Ramses XI; wife of Smendes; ca. 1050 BC
Tiglath-Pileser I: Middle Assyrian king; ruled 1115–1076 BC
Tjekkerbaal/Zakarbaal: King of Byblos; ruled ca. 1075 BC
Tukulti-Ninurta I: Middle Assyrian king; ruled 1244–1208 BC
Tukulti-Ninurta II: Neo-Assyrian king; ruled 890–884 BC
Tuthaliya II: Great King of Carchemish; ruled late eleventh century BC
Ura-Tarhunta: Great King of Carchemish; ruled late eleventh century BC
Yariri: Regent (ruling as Country Lord) of Carchemish; ruled ca. 800 BC
Yehimilk: King of Byblos; ruled mid-tenth century BC

NOTES

Preface. It's the End of the World as We Know It (. . . and I Don't Feel Fine)

1. The study was published by the Institute for Public Policy Research; see "Climate and Economic Risks 'Threaten 2008-Style Systemic Collapse,'" *Guardian*, February 12, 2019, https://www.theguardian.com/environment/2019/feb/12/climate-and-economic-risks-threaten-2008-style-systemic-collapse; BBC News, "Environment in Multiple Crises—Report," February 12, 2019, https://www.bbc.com/news/science-environment-47203344; and Laurie Laybourn, Lesley Rankin, and Darren Baxter, "This Is a Crisis: Facing Up to the Age of Environmental Breakdown," Institute for Public Policy Research, December 2, 2019, https://www.ippr.org/research/publications/age-of-environmental-breakdown. Note that this was an entirely different study from the one released a year later, in early 2020, which I quoted at the beginning of the revised version of *1177 B.C.* (Cline 2021: xv).

2. Cline 2014, 2021.

3. Quotation is from the revised and updated version (Cline 2021: 165–66). In my opinion, the Late Bronze Age Collapse should be considered as a prime example within the category of scholarship now designated as "the History of Climate and Society" (HCS), which involves studying "climate-society interactions" and emphasizes "the mechanics by which climate change has influenced human history" (Degroot et al. 2021: 539).

4. See Haldon, Chase, et al. 2020: 5, 12; also Haldon, Binois-Roman, et al. 2021: 261–62; and previously Haldon, Eisenberg et al. 2020. See also Kuecker and Hall 2011: 26; Johnson 2017: 1.

5. For recent volumes on collapse and "after collapse," see, e.g., Tainter 1988; Diamond 2005; Middleton 2017c; and the edited volumes by Yoffee and Cowgill 1988; Schwartz and Nichols 2006; McAnany and Yoffee 2010; Faulseit 2016; Middleton 2020a. See also, e.g., specific papers such as Kuecker and Hall 2011; Storey and Storey 2016.

6. Quotations from Cumming and Peterson 2017: 696; Haldon, Eisenberg, et al. 2020. See now also Haldon, Binois-Roman, et al. 2021: 262.

7. Colby Bermel, "Dixie Fire Becomes Largest Single Wildfire in California History," *Politico*, August 6, 2021, https://www.politico.com/states/california/story/2021/08/06/dixie-fire-becomes-largest-single-wildfire-in-california-history-1389651; "Greece Wildfires: Evia Island Residents Forced to Evacuate," BBC News, August 9, 2021, https://www.bbc.com/news/world-europe-58141336; Matthew S. Schwartz, "Wildfires Rage through Greece as Thousands Are Evacuated," NPR, August 8, 2021, https://www.npr.org/2021/08/08/1025947847/wildfires-rage-through-greece-as-thousands-are-evacuated; Associated Press, "Grim View of Global

Future Offered in U.S. Intelligence Report," NBC News, April 8, 2021, https://www.nbcnews.com/politics/politics-news/grim-view-global-future-offered-u-s-intelligence-report-n1263549; Brad Plumer and Henry Fountain, "A Hotter Future Is Certain, Climate Panel Warns: But How Hot Is Up to Us," *New York Times*, August 9, 2021, https://www.nytimes.com/2021/08/09/climate/climate-change-report-ipcc-un.html; Jake Spring, "Once-in-50-Year Heat Waves Now Happening Every Decade—U.N. Climate Report," Reuters, August 9, 2021, https://www.reuters.com/business/environment/once-in-50-year-heat-waves-now-happening-every-decade-un-climate-report-2021-08-09.

8. See now, e.g., Ehrenreich 2020.

9. Cowgill 1988: 246. He said further that we need to make a distinction between the "decline or deterioration of something and its actual termination" (255), for "the complete termination or even the rapid drastic transformation of a civilization has been a rare event, at least so far. Political fragmentation is more common" (256). See now Haldon, Chase, et al. 2020 for an extremely important, and nuanced, recent discussion of what "collapse" involves; also Johnson 2017: 7; Middleton 2017b, 2020b; Kemp 2019; Nicoll and Zerboni 2019; Haldon, Binois-Roman, et al. 2021: 238.

10. See Frahm 2023: 24–25 for similar comments regarding Assyrian records in particular.

Prologue. Welcome to the Iron Age

1. See Thucydides (Thuc. 1.12.1–3; also Thuc. 1.2.2); also Herodotus (Hdt. 8.73; also Hdt. 1.56.2–3) and Pausanias (Paus. 4.3.3; also Paus. 2.12.3).

2. See the debates and discussions in English, frequently citing earlier studies in German and French, found in Casson 1921; Heurtley 1926/27; Hammond 1931–32; Daniel, Broneer, and Wade-Gery 1948; Starr 1961: 72–74; Cook 1962; Desborough 1964: 246–48; Snodgrass 1971: 300–312; also more recent discussions reviewing the previous situations, e.g., Muhly 1992: 12; J. M. Hall 1997: 3–4, 12, 41, 56–65; 2002: 32–35, 73–82; 2003; 2006: 240–42; 2007: 43–51.

3. See "Mycenaean Civilization," *Columbia Electronic Encyclopedia*, 6th ed., March 2021, http://search.ebscohost.com.proxygw.wrlc.org/login.aspx?direct=true&db=a9h&AN=134483212&site=ehost-live (accessed September 30, 2022).

4. Carpenter 1966: 40; Snodgrass 1971: 312; Hooker 1979: 359; Tainter 1988: 63–64 (who also quotes Carpenter); J. M. Hall 2002: 79 (who quotes Hooker); Papadopoulos 2014: 185; Nagy 2019b (citing Palaima 2002), 2019b. See also, e.g., Schnapp-Gourbeillon 1979: 1–11, 2002: 131–82; S. P. Morris 1989: 48–49; Coulson 1990: 14–17; Muhly 1992: 11; R. Osborne 1996: 33–37; Lemos 2002: 191–93; Papadopoulos and Smithson 2017: 24, 980; Wallace 2018: 311–15; Kotsonas and Mokrišová 2020: 221–22; Knodell 2021: 187–88. For the Dorians on Crete, see now, e.g., Hatzaki and Kotsonas 2020: 1036–37, citing Wallace 2010: 365–73 and others.

5. See, e.g., J. M. Hall 1997: 111–31, 2002: 78–82; Tainter 1988: 63–64; I. Morris 2000: 198–218; Voutsaki 2000: 232–33; Montiglio 2006: 161; Wallace 2010: 371–73; Bryce 2020: 114; Ruppenstein 2020b; Knodell 2021: 132; Osborne and Hall 2022: 9; Maran 2023: 240.

6. Nagy 2019b, citing Palaima 2002; also Nagy 2019a; Ruppenstein 2020b.

7. See most recently Murray 2017: 7, 211, 231–32, 234–39, also 2020: 202; previously Snodgrass 1971: 364–67; Desborough 1972: 18; I. Morris 1987: 146, 2006: 80, 2007: 218; Chew 2007: 95. See also discussions in Tainter 1988: 10–11, 1999: 1010; Dickinson 2006a: 93–98, 2006b: 117–18; Eder 2006: 550; J. M. Hall 2007: 59–61; Deger-Jalkotzy 2008: 393–94; Wallace 2010: 88; Eder and

Lemos 2020: 140; Nakassis 2020: 277; Knodell 2021: 119–29, 144, 153, 240. See also some of the other discussions, by specific areas, in both Middleton 2020a and Lemos and Kotsonas 2020.

8. See again, e.g., J. M. Hall 1997: 111–31, 2002: 78–82; Tainter 1988: 63–64; I. Morris 2000: 198–218; Voutsaki 2000: 232–33; Montiglio 2006: 161; Wallace 2010: 371–73; Bryce 2020: 114; Ruppenstein 2020b; Knodell 2021: 132.

9. S. P. Morris 1989: 48–49. On the other hand, in their textbook *A Brief History of Ancient Greece*, Pomeroy et al. (2020: 39–40) give an accurate summation of the problem and of our current thinking about the Dorian Invasion, or lack thereof, concluding by saying: "no material trace of such invaders can be seen in the archaeological record." But see also Elayi 2018: 90, who refers to "the Doric invasions in Mycenaean Greece, which would have driven the ancient Aegean populations before them."

10. See, e.g., J. M. Hall 1997: 153–67. See now Bryce 2020: 113–14, citing Finkelberg 2011: 217–18 on "miscellaneous population movements" at the end of the Bronze Age on mainland Greece; also Ruppenstein 2020b; J. Osborne and Hall 2022: 10–11; Van Damme 2023: 179.

11. Migrations can also be "a series of time-lapse events involving individuals or family groups, rather than waves of people or 'cultures' covering whole landscapes in single events" (see Georgiadis 2009: 97, citing Anthony 1997: 23). On the example of the Pueblo Societies, see most recently Scheffer et al. 2021, with details and further references. On migrations at the end of the Late Bronze Age, see now Knapp 2021; also Middleton 2018a, 2018b.

12. Coulson 1990: 7, 9–10; Coldstream 1998, also 1992–93: 8, cited by Muhly 2003: 23; see now also J. Scott 2017: 216–17.

13. *Merriam-Webster's* online entry: https://www.merriam-webster.com/dictionary/dark%20age; see also the *World History Encyclopedia*: https://www.worldhistory.org/Greek_Dark_Age (both last accessed December 9, 2022).

14. I discussed this at length in *1177 B.C.*; see Cline 2021: 167, citing esp. Renfrew 1978, 1979: 482–87; see also now Faulseit 2016 (in his own edited volume): 5. Muhly (2011: 48) notes, "The loss of the art of writing is the defining characteristic of a Dark Age, but it remains a symptom, not the cause of such a period." See also Snodgrass 1971: 2 and now Sherratt 2020: 196–97 on the characteristics of a Dark Age. See also previously Chew 2001: 9–10, 60–62; 2005: 52–58, 67–70; 2007: xvi, 6–10, 13–14, 16–17 (nn. 9–10), 79–83, 94–99; 2008: 92–93, 120–21, 130–31 for his definitions and characteristics, as well as specifically on what he sees as the Dark Ages in Greece following the Collapse; relevant to this are T. D. Hall's (2014: 82–84) comments on the first edition of *1177 B.C.*

15. Tainter 1988: 4, 19–20, 193, 197; 1999: 989–91, 1030; see also now Middleton 2017a, 2017c: 46.

16. Hesiod, *Works and Days* 174–79.

17. J. Scott 2017: 213, see also 214–18. See also Murray 2018c: 19, 22; previously the discussion in Dickinson 2006a: 3–9 and now the useful online summation by M. Lloyd (2017).

Chapter One. The Year of the Hyenas, When Men Starved

1. On the following, see previous discussion in Cline 2021: 131–32, with further references, esp. Redford 2002; also de Buck 1937; Clayton 1994: 164–65; Peden 1994: 195–210; Kitchen 2012: 7–11; Snape 2012: 412–13; Dodson 2019: 2.

2. The acquisition history of the papyrus follows Redford 2002: 5.

3. See Hawass et al. 2012, with further media reports in the *Los Angeles Times*, *USA Today*, and elsewhere, available, e.g., at http://articles.latimes.com/2012/dec/18/science/la-sci-sn-egypt-mummy-pharoah-ramses-murder-throat-slit-20121218 and http://www.usatoday.com/story/tech/sciencefair/2012/12/17/ramses-ramesses-murdered-bmj/1775159.

4. See again the references just cited.

5. See Cline 2021: 158, 160–61, with references; also Kaniewski, Guiot, and Van Campo 2015. See also Butzer 2012: 3634–35; Mushett Cole 2017: 5; Creasman 2020: 17–19, 29. On the food crisis, nonpayment of wages, and general strike, see Butzer 2012: 3634–35; Eyre 2012: 119–21, 124, 139; Goelet 2016: 456; Mushett Cole 2016: 47, 2017: 5–7; Dodson 2019: 2.

6. See Butzer 2012: 3634–35; Mushett Cole 2016: 47–48; Dodson 2019: 2. On Ramses IV in general, see Clayton 1994: 166–67; Eyre 2012: 121–23; Snape 2012: 413; Mushett Cole 2016: 48–49.

7. See Cline 2021: 150–51, with full references.

8. On Ramses V in general, see Grimal 1988: 287–88; Clayton 1994: 167; Snape 2012: 413, 423; Mushett Cole 2016: 50; also previously Cline 2021: 150–51. On the mines in the Sinai and Egyptian control, see Grimal 1988: 288; Clayton 1994: 168; Snape 2012: 414–15; Weinstein 2012: 173; Mushett Cole 2016: 49–52. On the Egyptian withdrawal see, in addition, e.g., Bunimovitz and Lederman 2014: 252–53.

9. See now further discussion, with earlier references, in Cline 2020: 185–86, 200 and fig. 31; also Snape 2012: 415; Mushett Cole 2016: 51.

10. See Grimal 1988: 288–89; Clayton 1994: 168–69; Chew 2007: 90; Snape 2012: 414; Mushett Cole 2016: 52–53.

11. See Grimal 1988: 289–90; Clayton 1994: 169–70; Eyre 2012: 134, 137, 139; Snape 2012: 415; Mushett Cole 2016: 53–55; Dodson 2019: 4–7. On the possible loss of Nubia at this time, see Mushett Cole 2016: 63; see now also Muhs 2022: 204.

12. Grimal 1988: 289–90; Peden 1994: 225–58; Reeves and Wilkinson 1996: 191; Eyre 2012: 134; Snape 2012: 415; Goelet 2016: 458–60; Mushett Cole 2016: 54–55; Dodson 2019: 4–6.

13. Peden 1994: 259–66; Reeves and Wilkinson 1996: 192; Goelet 2016: 460–61.

14. Clayton 1994: 168.

15. Grimal 1988: 291; Clayton 1994: 170; Mushett Cole 2016: 56.

16. Eyre 2012: 139. Mushett Cole 2017: 7–8 presents a slightly alternate translation: "year of hyenas when there was a famine." See also Grimal 1988: 291; Snape 2012: 426; Koch 2021: 71–72.

17. Kitchen 1973: 248; Grimal 1988: 292; Clayton 1994: 171, 175; Snape 2012: 427; Mushett Cole 2016: 63; Dodson 2019: 16, 18–19, 21–24.

18. Kitchen 1973: 250; Grimal 1988: 291–92, 314; Clayton 1994: 171; Snape 2012: 427; Mushett Cole 2016: 64–65; Dodson 2019: 17–18, 24–29; Koch 2021: 72.

19. See now Reeves 1990: 186, 191–92, with further references; Reeves and Wilkinson 1996: 188–207; Aston 2020: 31–68; also Grimal 1988: 290; Snape 2012: 428; Dodson 2019: 42.

20. Kitchen 1973: 249–50, 254, 256–59; Grimal 1988: 292, 311; Clayton 1994: 178–79; Hallo and Simpson 1998: 283–84; Mushett Cole 2016: 64–66.

21. Kitchen 1973: 248–50, 257–59, 262; Grimal 1988: 292; Clayton 1994: 172, 176; Snape 2012: 428; Mushett Cole 2016: 64–66; Dodson 2019: 24–32, 39.

22. Grimal 1988: 290; Clayton 1994: 177–78; Reeves and Wilkinson 1996: 68–69, 101–3, 198–99; Snape 1996: 190; Reeves 2000: 101–4. Other royal bodies that apparently received Panedjem's attention, in terms of being repaired though not necessarily moved, included Thutmose II, Amenhotep I, and Ramses III; see Dodson 2019: 42.

23. See, e.g., Kitchen 1973: 261, 271, 274–75; Grimal 1988: 314–15, 317–19; Clayton 1994: 179–81; Hallo and Simpson 1998: 284; Mushett Cole 2016: 66–67, 2017: 8; now Muhs 2022: 195, 204.

24. For the following, I am indebted to the original publication by Montet 1951: see esp. 19–21; Dodson 2019: 42, 66–67, 95–96, 101–2, figs. 24, 47, and 79; and the recent discussion in Brier 2023: 282–83. See also Kitchen 1973: 271; Grimal 1988: 317–18; Clayton 1994: 180–81; and the recounting of the discovery by McDowall 2014 and the PBS documentary *Secrets of the Dead: The Silver Pharaoh* (broadcast November 2, 2010).

25. Montet 1951: 19–21; Brier 2023: 282–83. See also Dodson 2019: 42, 95–96, 101–2, fig. 79.

26. Montet 1951: 21; translated from the French by E. H. Cline.

27. Montet 1951: 21–22; translated from the French by E. H. Cline.

28. Montet 1951: 21–22; translated from the French by E. H. Cline. On the translation and identification with Merneptah, see Montet 1951: 111–12.

29. Montet 1951: 22, also plate 95; translated from the French by E. H. Cline. Regarding the inscription on the black sarcophagus, see Montet 1951: 126–30; for the inscription on the silver coffin, see Montet 1951: 130–32. See also the discussion in Dodson 2019: 66–67, fig. 47.

30. Montet 1951: 22; Dodson 2019: 66–67, fig. 24.

31. Montet 1951: 22. Note again, for all of this, the further discussions in Brier 2023 and Dodson 2019. For the photographs and drawings of the three nested coffins and the gold mask, see Montet 1951: esp. plates 75–82, 95–105.

32. Ben-Dor Evian et al. 2021: 3; see also David 2021b for the reporting of this story in the popular media.

33. Ben-Dor Evian et al. 2021; cf. also previously Kassianidou 2014: 263–67; Yahalom-Mack et al. 2014: 174; Ben-Dor Evian 2017: 36. The area of the Timna mines was also the focus of media stories earlier in 2021, not for copper or turquoise, but because analysis of a piece of cloth dating back to the late eleventh or early tenth century BC was shown to have been dyed with the royal purple color perfected by the Phoenicians; see Sukenik et al. 2021 and media reports such as Borschel-Dan 2021; David 2021a; and Tercatin 2021.

34. See, e.g., with further references, Dothan 1982: 3–4; Cline and O'Connor 2003: 114–15; Killebrew 2005: 204–5; Yasur-Landau 2010: 2–3; now also, e.g., Schipper 2019: 15–18, 22; Yasur-Landau 2019: 416; Koch 2021: 76–80; Master 2021; Maeir 2022d. The literature on the Philistines and their initial settlement in this region is immense; in addition to the above references, see also, e.g., Howard 1994; Finkelstein 1995; Ehrlich 1996; Barako 2013; Ben-Shlomo 2014; Faust 2019; Maeir 2019, 2020; Koch 2020.

35. Macalister 1914; see also mentions, e.g., in Dothan 1982: 24; Yasur-Landau 2010: 2. On the recent excavations, see most recently the contributions in Maeir 2012; Maeir and Uziel 2020.

36. Ehrlich 1996: 56.

37. See, with previous references, Cline 2000: 44–59, 2004: 19, 2007: 119, 2009; also Broodbank 2013: 452; most recently Maeir 2022a; also relevant is Ben-Yosef and Thomas 2023.

38. See esp. the various recent publications by Avraham Faust of Bar Ilan University; e.g., Faust 2007, 2012, 2016, 2019.

39. The literature here too is vast. See, as just one example, Finkelstein 1988; also Cline 2004: 17, 2007: 114–18, 2009: 77, all with further references; Killebrew 2005: 152–54, 181–85.

40. Cline 2007: 118–19, 2021: 91. The literature on the boom in Israelite settlements during the Iron I period, and their characteristics, is again immense; see most recently, e.g., Killebrew 2005: 155–59, 173–81; Finkelstein 2013: 22, 27–28, 32–33; now also Ilan 2019; Schipper 2019: 15–18; and Ben-Yosef and Thomas 2023, who (if I understand their proposal correctly) suggest that there was still a nomadic segment of society that continued down into the United Monarchy in the tenth century BC.

41. Cline 2007: 119.

42. Langgut, Neumann, et al. 2014: 294–98 and table 3; also Langgut, Finkelstein, et al. 2015: 217, 229–31; Finkelstein 2016: 116; Finkelstein and Langgut 2018. Note again, as stated above, that Kanieweski and his colleagues modified their original conclusions regarding climate change in the Eastern Mediterranean to also include this temporary uptick in moisture and better climactic conditions; see again Kaniewski et al. 2019a, esp. 6–9 and figs. 4–6, 2019b, 2020; also Finné et al. 2019: 859 (also 855 and fig. 2) and previous discussion in Cline 2021: 157–58.

43. Langgut, Neumann, et al. 2014: 298. On Moab, see Mattingly 1994; Finkelstein and Lipschits 2011; Finkelstein 2014; Steiner 2014. On Ammon, see Younker 1994, 2014. On Edom, see references given further below. On all of the above, i.e., "ancient Israel's neighbors," see now the very useful book by Doak 2020.

44. Cf. most recently Palmisano, Woodbridge, et al. 2019; Palmisano, Lawrence, et al. 2021: 7, 22–23, 106739; also now, including introducing the United Monarchy into these discussions, Ben-Yosef and Thomas 2023; Thomas and Ben-Yosef 2023. See also brief discussions below, with further references.

45. See full discussion, with references, in Cline 2000: 65–74, 2004: 20; also mentions in Dothan 1982: 16; Finkelstein 2013: 35–36.

46. See most recently Rollston 2019: 379. For the initial publication of the fragments, see Biran and Naveh 1993, 1995.

47. Translation following Schniedewind 1996: 77–78.

48. The inscription has been the subject of much debate over the years; for my previous discussions of this find, with references, see Cline 2000: 83–87, 2009: 59–63, with references.

49. On the proposed reading, see, e.g., Lemaire 1994. For contrasting views, see, e.g., Finkelstein, Na'aman, and Römer 2019; Na'aman 2019a. See also previous discussion in Cline 2009: 16–18, with earlier references; also Horn 1986. For additional publications regarding the story of the discovery of the Mesha Stele and its interpretation, see now also Richelle 2018: 28–30; Porter 2019: 324–25 and fig. 17.1; Schipper 2019: 38. On Mesha and the Moabites, see, e.g., Na'aman 1997.

50. Kitchen 1973: 273–75, 280; Grimal 1988: 318–19; see again Crowell 2021: 25, 196–201, 364–66, 382; also Na'aman 2021: 24–26.

51. Kitchen 1973: 271–72; Grimal 1988: 317–18; Clayton 1994: 181; Mushett Cole 2016: 68. See, most recently, the discussion in Crowell 2021: 25, 196–201, 364–66, 382; also Finkelstein 2020: 24, who doubts its contemporaneity to the actual events.

52. The literature is already substantial; see esp. Levy et al. 2008; Ben-Yosef, Levy, et al. 2010; Ben-Yosef, Liss, et al. 2019; Liss et al. 2020, with references to earlier publications, including Hoglund 1994, plus the many contributions in the two volumes published as Levy, Najjr, and Ben-Yosef 2014. Regarding the challenge to the industry on Cyprus, see, e.g., discussions in Crielaard 1998: 194–95; Muhly and Kassianidou 2012: 125, 134, with previous references; Finkelstein 2013: 127, 2020: 18–19; Kassianidou 2014: 263–64; Yahalom-Mack et al. 2014: 174; Erb-Satullo 2019: 589; Knapp and Meyer 2020: 232–43. On Wadi Faynan, see discussion below and, e.g., Ben-Yosef, Levy, et al. 2010; Ben-Yosef, Liss, et al. 2019, with previous references; also Schipper 2019: 28.

53. See, e.g., Ben-Yosef 2019b, 2019c, 2020, 2021a, 2021b; Ben-Yosef, Liss, et al. 2019; Ben-Yosef and Thomas 2023, all with many earlier references. See also subsequent discussions by, e.g., Crowell 2021: 36–37, 41–42; Maeir 2021; and a rebuttal by Finkelstein 2020; now also Na'aman 2021; Bienkowski 2022. See now the overview in Crowell 2021: 8–16, with references to Glueck's relevant publications.

54. The literature on this topic is already immense. See, e.g., as just a few examples, Garfinkel and Ganor 2008, 2010; Finkelstein and Fantalkin 2012; Finkelstein 2013: 54–59; Garfinkel 2017, 2021; Na'aman 2017; Schipper 2019: 23; and now Ussishkin 2022.

55. Regarding the multi-line inscription, see, e.g., Misgav, Garfinkel, and Ganor 2009; Galil 2010; Rollston 2011; now also Donnelly-Lewis 2022. Regarding the more recent inscription, see, e.g., Garfinkel et al. 2015.

56. See previously Cline 2009: 25–27, fig. 4, with references; Rollston 2019: 376–77.

57. Kitchen 1973: 280–82; Grimal 1988: 319; Mushett Cole 2016: 69–70; Schipper 2019: 27–28.

58. Mushett Cole 2016: 69–70, citing Dever 1993: 37.

59. Kitchen 1973: 282; Grimal 1988: 318–19; Clayton 1994: 181; but note also again the discussions in Crowell 2021 cited above.

60. See now Reeves 1990: 186, 191–92, with further references; Reeves and Wilkinson 1996: 188–207; Aston 2020: 31–68, with references. See also summaries in Grimal 1988: 318; Clayton 1994: 181; Snape 1996: 188; Mushett Cole 2016: 68, 70.

61. A. B. Edwards 1882a: 185–97, 1882b: 113, 116; Wilson 1887: 1–10; Gardner 1923: 30–52; Kitchen 1973: 277–78; Grimal 1988: 290–91; Reeves 1990: 186, 191–92; Clayton 1994: 177–78; Reeves and Wilkinson 1996: 194–97, 204, 207; Snape 1996: 188–90; Fagan 2004: 194–98; Bickerstaffe 2010: 13–36; Graefe and Belova 2010; Hawass 2010: 1; J. Thompson 2015: 8–10; Dodson 2019: 76–77; Aston 2020: 31–68.

62. See now discussion in Cline 2020: 1–2, 85–91, with references; previously Yadin 1976; also now Cantrell 2006; Cantrell and Finkelstein 2006; Franklin 2017.

63. See discussion in Cline 2009: 43–46, 64–66, 2020: 234–35, both with references; previously Yadin 1970.

64. See, e.g., Finkelstein 1996, 1999, 2013; see again now brief discussion in Cline 2009: 43–46, 64–66, with previous references. See now, e.g., Ortiz and Wolff 2021, who disagree with Finkelstein and argue that the remains from their Stratum 8 at Gezer "must date . . . more or less to Solomon's reign" (238); see also the recent discussions by Richelle 2018: 82–83, 85–89; Garfinkel 2021; Garfinkel and Pietsch 2021.

65. See now Rollston 2016: 296–97; Bourogiannis 2018a: 73–74; Elayi 2018: 117–22; Bunnens 2019b: 65; Doak 2019: 660–61; Edrey 2019: 40; Na'aman 2019b; Hodos 2020: 40–41; López-Ruiz 2021: 288–89; previously Markoe 2000: 33–35; Aubet 2001: 44–45; Abulafia 2011: 66–67. See also previous discussions in Yadin 1970, 1976; Finkelstein 1996, 1999, 2013; Cantrell 2006; Cantrell and Finkelstein 2006; Cline 2009: 43–46, 64–66, 2020: 1–2, 85–91, 234–35, both with references; and now Franklin 2017; Richelle 2018: 82–83, 85–89; Garfinkel 2021; Garfinkel and Pietsch 2021; Ortiz and Wolff 2021.

66. All translations from the Hebrew Bible follow the NRSV version.

67. On Ain Dara, see, e.g., Sader 2014: 615–16, with references; also now J. F. Osborne 2021: 115–17, 200. The temple at the site was severely damaged in January 2018, reportedly by Turkish aircraft, according to media reports; see, e.g., Claire Voon, "Iron Age Temple in Syria Devastated by Turkish Air Raids," Hyperallergic, Janaury 9, 2018, https://hyperallergic.com/423867/ain-dara-temple-destroyed; Erika Engelhaupt, "Iconic Ancient Temple Is Latest Victim in Civil War," *National Geographic*, January 30, 2018, https://www.nationalgeographic.com/history/article/syria-temple-ain-dara-destroyed-archaeology; Sarah Cascone, "Turkish Forces Nearly Destroy the Ancient Syrian Temple of Ain Dara," Artnet News, January 30, 2018, https://news.artnet.com/art-world/destruction-ain-dara-1210982.

68. See, e.g., Markoe 2000: 33–34; Aubet 2001: 204–5; Lipiński 2006: 181–82; recently Elayi 2018: 121–23; Bunnens 2019b: 60–61, with previous references; also Edrey 2019: 40; Roller 2019: 645–46; Sader 2019b: 127–28; Hodos 2020: 57–58, 104, 143–44.

69. See Kingsley 2021 and various media reports, including Jarus 2021.

70. Kitchen 1973: 283; Grimal 1988: 319; Clayton 1994: 181, 184–85; Chapman 2009, 2015; Sagrillo 2015; Mushett Cole 2016: 70, 72–74; Dodson 2019: 77–81, 87–89, 95, 101–2, fig. 79; Höflmayer and Gundacker 2021.

71. Kitchen 1973: 286–87; Grimal 1988: 319–22; Clayton 1994: 183–84; Kuhrt 1995: 626–28; Snape 2012: 431; Mushett Cole 2016: 75–76; Dodson 2019: 92–93.

72. See also 2 Chronicles 12:2–9; discussion includes, e.g., Kitchen 1973: 295–96; Clayton 1994: 184–85; Cline 2004: 38–41; Mushett Cole 2016: 76–77, among many others.

73. See, e.g., Kitchen 1973: 296–300; Clayton 1994: 184–85; Ehrlich 1996: 63–65; Finkelstein 2002, 2013: 41–44, 76–77; Mushett Cole 2016: 76–77; Dodson 2019: 93, 95, figs. 66, 68, 70; Schipper 2019: 30–31, 36–37. See now also the numerous conference papers in James and van der Veen 2015.

74. See now the full discussion of the discovery in Cline 2020 and of the inscription itself previously in Cline 2000: 75–82, with earlier references found in both.

75. See Cline 2011 and now the relevant pages in Cline 2020.

76. See, e.g., Kitchen 1973: 294–95; Grimal 1988: 322–23.

77. Na'aman 2021: 24–26.

78. See now Dodson 2023: 297–307.

79. The results of the excavation have recently been published in a five-volume set (Mazar and Panitz-Cohen 2020), but briefer accessible articles have recently been published in *Near Eastern Archaeology* magazine in 2022; these will be cited below. On the mention by Sheshonq I, see Mazar 2022b: 122–23.

80. Mazar 2022b: 110–11, 114–15, 122.

81. All of the following information is based on the extremely useful article by Mazar, Panitz-Cohen, and Bloch 2022: 126–28, with references to the more comprehensive discussions published by those authors elsewhere.

82. See Mazar, Panitz-Cohen, and Bloch 2022: 128–29.

83. See again Mazar, Panitz-Cohen, and Bloch 2022: 126–27.

84. Mazar 2022b: 116; Mazar, Panitz-Cohen, and Bloch 2022: 127.

85. On the scarab, see the brief article in *Antiquity* by Levy, Münger, and Najjar 2014; on the campaign to this area, see also, e.g., Finkelstein 2016: 118, 2020: 20; Crowell 2021: 364; Na'aman 2021: 21–24. On related matters, see now also Ben-Dor Evian 2017: 36, 2021: 11; Maeir 2022a.

86. Kitchen 1973: 292; Grimal 1988: 322–23; Mushett Cole 2016: 75–77; Dodson 2019: 95; contra, Clayton 1994: 186.

87. See, e.g., Kitchen 1973: 308–9; Mushett Cole 2016: 78 (citing Louvre AO.9502); Dodson 2019: 99.

88. Kitchen 1973: 309–10, 324–25; Grimal 1988: 324–26; Clayton 1994: 186–87; Kuhrt 1995: 628; Ben-Dor Evian 2011: 98, 2017: 36; Mushett Cole 2016: 79, 81, 83; Dodson 2019: 104, 109, 192; Muhs 2022: 196–97, 199. Note that the lack of an inscription on the statue may simply be accidental; like the others, only a fragment of the statue is left to us, and it is possible that any Phoenician inscription that might have been carved into it is now not preserved. Muhs 2022: 200–201 notes a number of Egyptian stone vessels with inscriptions related to Osorkon II, Takeloth II, and Sheshonq III that have been found in Phoenician cemeteries in southern Spain, which he suggests were "presumably brought from Egypt by Phoenician merchants and colonists."

89. Cf. Kitchen 1973: 331, 335; Grimal 1988: 328–30; Clayton 1994: 188–89; Kuhrt 1995: 625, 628; Mushett Cole 2016: 85–87, 89; Dodson 2019: 114–15, 119–21, 124–25, 127, 192.

Chapter Two. Conqueror of All Lands, Avenger of Assyria

1. Grayson 1987: 309–11 (A.0.86.1); Neumann and Parpola 1987: 178, app. A, no. 1 (citing Borger 1964: 103, no. 6); Kuhrt 1995: 358. Note that Grayson prefers to translate it as "the extensive army of the Ahlamu" rather than "the widespread hordes" as per Borger; regardless, the general idea is the same; also I have followed Eckart Frahm (pers. comm.) in translating the first word as "slayer" rather than "murderer" as per Grayson. Note also that "š" is to be pronounced as a "sh" sound in the pages below, but that I have also been deliberately inconsistent and when "Š" begins a word, I have rendered it as "Sh" (as in Shalmaneser III), for ease of reading and pronunciation in English.

2. Oates 1979: 106; Postgate 1992: 249; Kirleis and Herles 2007: 7–10; Younger 2016: 100, 2017: 198; J. F. Osborne 2021: 36–40.

3. See again the references given above. On the shift in the Euphrates, see, e.g., Reculeau 2011: 2, with earlier references; Bryce 2016a: 66.

4. Neumann and Parpola 1987: 161; Postgate 1992: 247, 249; Kirleis and Herles 2007: 7–9; Bryce 2012: 163–64, 2014: 105–6; now Younger 2016: passim; Bunnens 2019a: 351, 362.

5. Grayson 1987: 309–22 (A.0.86.1–14); Jeffers 2013: 10–11; Radner 2018: 2.

6. See Grayson [1975] 2000: 164 (no. 21 ii, lines 6–7 and 8–13, respectively, for the first and second engagements); see also Brinkman 1968: 110; Frame 1995: 11; Glassner 2004: 186–88, with previous citations; Jeffers 2013: 213; Younger 2017: 199–200, 212 and n. 90.

7. Brinkman 1968: 3–4, 17; Kuhrt 1995: 477; Grayson [1975] 2000; Schneider 2014: 99, citing Glassner 2004; Frahm 2017: 163.

8. Schneider 2014: 99; see also Kuhrt 1995: 473–77; Grayson 2005; Frahm 2017: 163; Frahm 2019.

9. Schneider 2014: 98–99; see also Kuhrt 1995: 473–77.

10. Jeffers 2013: 75–76, with earlier references and documentation.

11. See, e.g., the discussions in Cline 2017: 52–65 (chap. 4), with full references; now also Frahm 2023: 4–14.

12. See now Frahm 2023: 24–25 for similar comments; also Reculeau 2011 for an example of grain yields recorded in Assyrian texts, albeit from the thirteenth century BC.

13. Translations by Foster 2005: 382. See Brinkman 1968: 88–89, 104–106; Frame 1995: 11; Potts 1999: 252–53; Foster 2005: 376; Jeffers 2013: 24–25; Liverani 2014: 458; Bryce 2016a: 65–66; see also Cline 2014, 2021. The dates for Nebuchadnezzar I can vary by a year or two, depending on the scholar (e.g., 1126–1105 BC).

14. Brinkman 1968: 106–8, 112–13; Oates 1979: 105; Frame 1995: 11, 33–35; Kuhrt 1995: 375–76; Potts 1999: 253; Foster 2005: 383. According to Frame, the *kudurru* stone was found "in room 50 of the temple of the god Shamash at Sippar by Abd-al-Ahad Thoma in 1882 and is now in the British Museum (BM 90858; 82-5-22,1800)."

15. Translation by Foster 2005: 383. See also previously Brinkman 1968: 106–8; Oates 1979: 105; Frame 1995: 33–35; Kuhrt 1995: 375–76.

16. Potts 1999: 233, 236–38, 240–41, 247, 252–63; Foster 2005: 376–80, 385–87; see also now Álvarez-Mon 2013: 457, 471; Waters 2013: 478–79; also previously Kuhrt 1995: 372–73.

17. Brinkman 1984: 172–75.

18. See Grayson 1987: 305–8 for the few inscriptions that might be tentatively dated to Aššur-dan I's reign, none of which can be considered to be a record of deeds or events occurring during his reign. See also Jeffers 2013: 3, 10–11; also Postgate 1992: 248 for the regnal dates.

19. Frahm (pers. com., February 24, 2023). However, he also notes that "it is clear from administrative texts that Assyria's provincial system was still largely intact under Tiglath-pileser I, (which is) an argument against Assyria having experienced a dramatic decline during the previous decades." Regarding writing on materials such as lead or wood, Bryce (2012: 57, 60) and Fuchs (2017: 254) both suggest this as a possibility for the Neo-Hittites as well, since there are a few examples of Luwian found written on lead strips in slightly later contexts at sites like Zincirli and Kululu (see now also J. F. Osborne 2021: 20–21, 45, 51); it is also a possibility for the earliest Greek inscriptions.

20. Finné et al. 2019: 859 (see also 855 and fig. 2); Kaniewski et al. 2019a, esp. 6–9 and figs. 4–6, 2019b, 2020.

21. Brinkman 1968: 92; Neumann and Parpola 1987: 178, app. A, no. 2; Grayson 1991: 43 (A.0.87.4) and see also 37 (A.0.87.3), on which the number is unclear; Kuhrt 1995: 358–61; Grayson 2005; Fales 2011: 11; Bryce 2012: 197–201; Jeffers 2013: 10–11; Liverani 2014: 463–66; Younger 2016: 36, 85, 168–69, 171, 2017: 200–201, 206–7; Radner 2018: 9; Düring 2020: 136; J. F. Osborne 2021: 39–40. Note the new redating of the Broken Obelisk to his reign instead of his son

Aššur-bel-kala (Mahieu 2018: 79–86; Shibata 2022; Frahm 2023: 444n3), and see also Grayson 1991: 87, 99–105 (A.0.89.7); Neumann and Parpola 1987: 176, table 2, and 179, app. A, no. 8; Frame 1995: 50; Kirleis and Herles 2007: 9–10; Fales 2011: 18, 31; Liverani 2014: 443; Radner 2015: 69; Younger 2016: 37, 85, 181; Frahm 2023: 86–87.

22. Grayson 1991: 41 (A.0.87.4) and 52 (A.0.87.10).

23. Grayson 1991: 14 (A.0.87.1).

24. Grayson 1991: 14–25 (A.0.87.1), with quote taken from p. 14.

25. Grayson 1991: 30–31 (A.0.87.1).

26. Grayson 1991: 23 (A.0.87.1); see also an abbreviated version in a second inscription: Grayson 1991: 34 (A.0.87.2). See now also Younger 2016: 167, 2017: 202–3.

27. Grayson 1991: 13 (A.0.87.1). On the Aramaeans as archenemies, see, e.g., Grayson 1991: 5; Jeffers 2013: 10–12; Younger 2017: 208; Düring 2020: 136.

28. Grayson 1991: 37 (A.0.87.3), 42 (A.0.87.4), 53 (A.0.87.10), 98 (A.0.89.6), 103–5 (A.0.89.7), and 108 (A.0.89.10); Frame 1995: 50; Kuhrt 1995: 361; Sherratt 2003: 52; Bryce 2014: 114, 116; Rollston 2016: 295; Fales 2017: 218; Younger 2017: 205; Elayi 2018: 107–8; Monroe 2018: 237, 255–56; Sader 2019b: 34–35; Hodos 2020: 143; Regev 2021: 68; also in particular Frahm 2009: 11, 28–32, 2011: 61–62, 2023: 86–87, 444 n. 3, as well as again Mahieu 2018 and Shibata 2022 for discussions of redating the Broken Obelisk to this period and related matters. On the identification of the pharaoh as Ramses XI, which is dependent on the dates for that ruler, see, e.g., Kitchen 1973: 252; Frahm 2009: 31; Koch 2021: 72; Shibata 2022: 121. On the identification of the "river-man" as a monk seal, see now Nahm 2022: 236–37; I am indebted to Christopher W. Jones for bringing this to my attention.

29. Grayson 1991: 37 (A.0.87.3), 44 (A.0.87.4), and 57 (A.0.87.11); see, e.g., K. Yamada 2005, for a brief consideration of what a *nahiru* might have been; see also now Bryce 2012: 200–201, 2014: 116; Broodbank 2013: 459 (who suggests that it is a "sperm whale"); Younger 2016: 172, 2017: 205; Elayi 2018: 104–6 (who suggests that it was a hippopotamus); Monroe 2018: 217; also now DeGrado 2019: 109 and n. 14, who agrees and provides discussion that it is a hippopotamus. Note that Fales (2017: 218–20, with references), covers all of the possibilities: "The identification of the nāḫiru is still at present the subject of controversy, with a vast gamut of suggested solutions (hippopotamus, dolphin, shark, seal, walrus, monk seal, sperm whale, orca (killer whale), humpback whale, toothed whale, cetacean)."

30. Louisa Loveluck and Mustafa Salim, "From Cradle to Grave: Where Civilization Emerged between the Tigris and Euphrates Climate Change Is Poisoning the Land and Emptying the Villages," *Washington Post*, October 21, 2021.

31. Younger 2016: 158, 165, 2017: 196; Frahm 2017: 165–67.

32. Fales 2011: 14, citing Liverani 1988a: 657; see now also Liverani 2014: 467.

33. Brinkman 1968: 124–30; Oates 1979: 106; Grayson [1975] 2000: 164–65 (no. 21 ii, lines 14–24); Grayson 1991: 43–44 (A.0.87.4) and 53 (A.0.87.10); Frame 1995: 38; Jeffers 2013: 10–11, 214–24, 233–44, 252–54; Younger 2016: 173, 2017: 210, 212–17, 221–22.

34. See Grayson 1991: 43–44, 2005; Millard 1994; Kuhrt 1995: 477; Younger 2016: 173–74, 2017: 210, 221–22; Frahm 2017: 162–63. Younger gives these absolute dates, citing Jeffers 2013: 120–28, 185–210, who goes into a detailed discussion as to why these eponym dates should be considered correct.

35. Grayson 1991: 44–45 (A.0.87.4), 54–55 (A.0.87.10), and see also fragmentary inscriptions (e.g., A.0.87.5, 8, and 11); Jeffers 2013: 45; Elayi 2018: 106–7.

36. Brinkman 1968: 387–88; Grayson [1975] 2000: 189, 1991: 5; Neumann and Parpola 1987: 176, table 2, and 178, app. A, no. 4; Glassner 2004: 188–91; Radner 2015: 68; Younger 2016: 174, 2017: 218–20; Frahm 2023: 87.

37. Brinkman 1968: 387–88; Grayson [1975] 2000: 189; Neumann and Parpola 1987: 176, table 2, and 178–79, app. A, no. 5; Kuhrt 1995: 361; Jeffers 2013: 254; Younger 2016: 174–76, 2017: 200, 220; Frahm 2023: 87. Both this crop failure and the previous famine were possibly caused by climate change, according to some scholars (see esp. Kirleis and Herles 2007: 12–13, cited by Younger), which seems very likely to be correct, in light of data that has since emerged elsewhere (see, e.g., summary in Cline 2014, 2021).

38. Grayson 1991: 86, 92 (A.0.89.2), 96 (A.0.89.4), 108 (A.0.89.10); Frame 1995: 50; Kuhrt 1995: 361; Elayi 2018: 107–8; Monroe 2018: 256. See again Mahieu 2018 and Shibata 2022 for discussions of redating the Broken Stele and other inscriptions to the time of Tiglath-Pileser I.

39. Brinkman 1968: 189, 387–89; Neumann and Parpola 1987: 176, table 2, and 179–80, app. A, nos. 9–12, with earlier references; Kuhrt 1995: 362.

40. Brinkman 1968: 189, 388; Neumann and Parpola 1987: 176, table 2, and 180, app. A, no. 12.

41. Oates 1979: 108; Neumann and Parpola 1987: 176, table 2, and 180–81, app. A, nos. 13–15.

42. Neumann and Parpola 1987: 176, table 2, and 181, app. A, no. 15; Grayson 1991: 131, 134–35 (A.0.98.1); Postgate 1992: 248–50 and table 1; Kuhrt 1995: 479–81; Kirleis and Herles 2007: 13; Liverani 2014: 475; Radner 2015: 69; Younger 2016: 221–24; Frahm 2017: 167–68, 2023: 88–92; Radner 2018: 11; Düring 2020: 144.

43. Grayson 1991: 142, 145; Kuhrt 1995: 482; Liverani 2014: 475–76; Frahm 2017: 168, 2023: 93; Elayi 2018: 108–9. Note that his name is sometimes rendered as Adad-nerari II; e.g., by Younger 2016: 221, 234–35.

44. Brinkman 1968: 169–70, 180–82; Grayson [1975] 2000: 166 (no. 21 iii, lines 1–11), 1991: 148–55 (A.0.99.2), 156 (A.0.99.4); Bryce 2016a: 67; Radner 2018: 11.

45. Sinha et al. 2019: 1–4 and fig. 3. I am grateful to Eckart Frahm for bringing this study to my attention.

46. Rassam 1897: 200–201; see Curtis and Tallis 2008: 2, 7, 9–10. On Rassam, Layard, and Nineveh, see Cline 2017: 58–63. On the identification of Balawat as Imgur-Enlil, see Tucker 1994.

47. Rassam 1897: 207–8, 210–12; quoted also by S. Lloyd 1980: 151; Curtis and Tallis 2008: 10–12. See King 1915: 10–13 for the additional quotations and other statements of interest. See also Curtis and Tallis 2008: 84–87 for copies of Rassam's correspondence to the British Museum during 1878. See also discussion in Harmansah 2007: 193–95, with references.

48. King 1915: 5, 9–12. See also Curtis and Tallis 2008: 2–3, 9–10, 12–13, 17–18.

49. Curtis and Tallis 2008: 10–12.

50. Curtis and Tallis 2008: 2–3, 8, 15, 23, 85. See Grayson 1991: 321–23, 345–51 (A.0.101.51 and A.0.101.80–97).

51. Rassam 1897: 214–15; S. Lloyd 1980: 152; Curtis and Tallis 2008: 85–86.

52. See now, updating Grayson 1991, Curtis and Tallis 2008: 26, 32, 35, 37, 45, figs. 11–12, 17–18, 21–22, 37–38.

53. Curtis and Tallis 2008: 2–3, 17–18, 47. On Mamu, originally a Sumerian deity, see, in passing, Tucker 1994: 107.

54. Curtis and Tallis 2008: 19, 48–49.

55. Curtis and Tallis 2008: 19.

56. Curtis and Tallis 2008: 3, 19–20.

57. Liverani 1988b: 85–86, 91; Postgate 1992: 255–56; Schneider 2014: 99–100; Düring 2020: 144–45, 152; Frahm 2023: 90–93.

58. On the various campaigns, see Liverani 2014: 476; Frahm 2023: 93–94; also Oates 1979: 108; Neumann and Parpola 1987: 176, table 2; Grayson 1991: 163–64, 169–70; Postgate 1992: 248 and table 1; Kuhrt 1995: 482–83; Bryce 2012: 210–17; Schneider 2014: 100; Frahm 2017: 168–69. On Ziyaret Tepe, see MacGinnis and Matney 2009; Matney et al. 2017.

59. Grayson 1991: 189–90; Kuhrt 1995: 483–84; Liverani 2014: 476; Schneider 2014: 100; Frahm 2017: 169, 2023: 83–84, 95–96.

60. For the translation, see Grayson 1991: 256–62 (A.0.101.19); Younger 2016: 183.

61. See Taylor 1865: 21–56; the quotation is found on pp. 22–23.

62. Grayson 1991: 210 (A.0.101.1) and also repeated nearly verbatim again on the Kurkh Monolith (A.0.101.19), see Grayson 1991: 260. There are numerous other instances that could also be quoted; see, e.g., Grayson 1991: 237–54 (A.0.101.17) for another inscription with detailed descriptions of what was done in the aftermath of a battle; also Frahm 2017: 169.

63. Neumann and Parpola 1987: 181, app. A, no. 16; Grayson 1991: 213–16 (A.0.101.1), 243 (A.0.101.17); Kuhrt 1995: 484; Grayson 2005; Kirleis and Herles 2007: 13n27; Schneider 2014: 100; Radner 2015: 69; Bryce 2016a: 68.

64. Grayson 1991: 189; Bryce 2012: 215; Liverani 2014: 480; Radner 2014b: 107, 2015: 27–28, 32, 2016: 44, 2017: 213, 2018: 11–12; Cline 2017: 58; Frahm 2017: 169–70, 2023: 95–97.

65. Grayson 1991: 192; Fagan 2007: 115; Radner 2015: 29–30, 35; Cline 2017: 57–58, with further references; Larson 2017: 586–88; Frahm 2023: 97–99; see also Layard 1849.

66. Grayson 1991: 268–76 (A.0.101.23), esp. 276; see also, e.g., 227–28 (A.0.101.2); Kuhrt 1995: 485–86.

67. Radner 2015: 35–37, 2016: 45; see also Kuhrt 1995: 486–87.

68. Grayson 1991: 3, 288–93 (A.0.101.30), esp. 292–93; Kuhrt 1995: 486–87; Aubet 2008: 183–84; Bryce 2012: 217; Podany 2014: 100–101; Radner 2015: 35–37, 2016: 44; Fales 2017: 224; Frahm 2017: 170, 2023: 95–96; Monroe 2018: 258–59; Bunnens 2019b: 59, 63–64.

69. Bryce 2012: 217–18.

70. Grayson 1991: 218–19 (A.0.101.1), 226 (A.0.101.2); see also Kuhrt 1995: 485; Aubet 2001: 55, 2008: 183–84; Schneider 2014: 100; Rollston 2016: 298; Fales 2017: 221–24; Elayi 2018: 129–31; Monroe 2018: 256, 258–59; Bunnens 2019b: 62, 66; DeGrado 2019: 109 and n. 14; Sader 2019b: 56; Hodos 2020: 143; Frahm 2023: 104–5.

71. Curtis and Tallis 2008: 52, 57–58, 65, figs. 63–66, 79–80.

72. Grayson 1996: 98 (A.0.102.25); Radner 2014b: 106; Frahm 2017: 170–71. See also King 1915: 17–20 and Grayson 1996: 27–32 (A.0.102.5) for the long inscription accompanying the reliefs on the Balawat gates.

73. See again, e.g., Kuhrt 1995: 488–89. On the summation, with the numerical figures given, see Grayson 1996: 55 (A.0.102.10).

74. Brinkman 1968: 191–200; 204–5; Grayson [1975] 2000: 167 (no. 21 iii, lines 22–34), 2005; Oates 1979: 109–10; Bryce 2012: 218–44; see also Kuhrt 1995: 487–89, 577; Frahm 2017: 171, 2023: 110–11.

75. Rassam 1897: 214; Kuhrt 1995: 487; Grayson 2005. Regarding Band III, in the British Museum, see King 1915: 23, pls. 13–18; Grayson 1996: 141 (A.0.102.66). On the scene of Tyre and the mention of both Tyre and Sidon, see also Aubet 2001: 51, 55, 2008: 183–84; Abulafia 2011: 69; Fales 2017: 226; Elayi 2018: 134–35; Bunnens 2019b: 59, 62, 66; Garnand 2020: 146. Note that some (e.g., Aubet 2001: 51; Abulafia 2011: 69) state specifically that King Ethobaal (or Ithobaal) of Tyre is pictured, but that is wishful thinking; he is not mentioned in the inscription, and it is not clear who the specific figures are.

76. On the fragment in the Walters Art Gallery, see Grayson 1996: 147 (A.0.102.84). On the Monolith Inscription, see Grayson 1996: 17 (A.0.102.2). See also the references just mentioned in the previous note, e.g., Rassam 1897: 214; Aubet 2001: 55, 2008: 183–84; Fales 2017: 226; Bunnens 2019b: 59, 62, 66; Garnand 2020: 146.

77. See, e.g., Fales 2011: 12 and Bryce 2012: 163–65 on some of these settlements. Also Grayson 2005; Radner 2014a: 84. See, e.g., Grayson 1996: 11–24 (A.0.102.2) for mentions of the various Aramaean city-states against whom he campaigned. See now also Younger 2016; Düring 2020: 148.

78. Radner 2014a: 71, 74; see also p. 6 in the same volume.

79. See Kuhrt 1995: 487–88; Grayson 1996: 11–24 (A.0.102.2), esp. 23–24, 2005; J. Miller and Hayes 2006: 247, 292, 294 (text no. 3); Bryce 2012: 175–77, 226–30; Schneider 2014: 100–101; Frahm 2017: 171, 2023: 109–10; Elayi 2018: 134–35; Schipper 2019: 40–41.

80. See Grayson 1996: 11–24 (A.0.102.2), esp. 23–24, 2005; quoted by Bryce 2012: 226–30, 2014: 124–25; also Frahm 2023: 110. See also Fales 2017: 226–28; Monroe 2018: 259; Bunnens 2019b: 66; Sader 2019b: 82; Garnand 2020: 146. On the gifts from the Egyptian pharaoh Osorkon II to Byblos and Samaria, as well as the Egyptian participation at Qarqar, see, e.g., Kitchen 1973: 324–25, with references; also Muhs 2022: 196–97, 199.

81. See, e.g., Grayson 1996: 32–41 (A.0.102.6), esp. 36, and 42–48 (A.0.102.8), esp. 45; also a large stone tablet in the wall at Aššur, recorded by Grayson 1996: 50–56 (A.0.102.10), esp. 52; and other instances listed by Grayson (passim). However, on the Black Obelisk, he says that the number killed were "20,500" and elsewhere the figure is given as "29,000"; see, e.g., Grayson 1996: 65 (A.0.102.14) and 75 (A.0.102.16). See also full discussion in S. Yamada 2000; Grayson 2005.

82. King 1915: 29–30, pls. 48–53; Grayson 1996: 144–45 (A.0.102.76).

83. Grayson 1996: 48, 54, 60 (compare A.0.102.8 and A.0.102.12 with A.0.102.10); Lipiński 2006: 180.

84. On all of this, see variously Kitchen 1973: 327; Grayson 1996: 151 (A.0.102.89); Aubet 2001: 55; Miller and Hayes 2006: 307 (text no. 5); Fales 2017: 228; Dodson 2019: 109, 192; Sader 2019b: 129.

85. Bryce 2012: 39, 153–54, 239–41, 2016b: 67–69, 74; J. F. Osborne 2021: 65–66.

86. These various campaigns are listed in a large number of Shalmaneser III's inscriptions; one is depicted on Band XIII of the Balawat gates, with graphic scenes of the capturing of cities. See, e.g., Grayson 1996: 5–6 and passim, esp. 48–49 (A.0.102.9), 50–56 (A.0.102.10), esp. 54, as well as 58–61 (A.0.102.12), esp. 60, and 62–71 (A.0.102.14 = the Black Obelisk), esp. 67. See also

King 1915: 34, pls. 72–77; Na'aman 1995; Grayson 2005; Miller and Hayes 2006: 292; Bryce 2012: 175–77, 237–38, 2014: 126–27, 236–37; Schneider 2014: 101; Frahm 2023: 110.

87. See my previous discussion of this matter, and the biblical parallels, in Cline 2000: 82–88. See also Biran and Naveh 1993, 1995; Schniedewind 1996; Na'aman 2000, 2006; Sergi 2017; Richelle 2018: 31–32; Schipper 2019: 42; Younger 2020. Note that Arie (2008: 34–38) suggests that Hazael set up the inscription when he (re)built the city, rather than simply conquering it; this suggestion has been contested by Thareani (2016b, 2019a, 2019b). On Hazael and the Aramaeans in the southern Levant in general, see now Finkelstein 1999, 2013: 119–26; Kleiman 2016; Sergi 2017; Sergi and Kleiman 2018; Younger 2020.

88. See, e.g., discussions in Schniedewind 1996; Na'aman 2006, with references; Finkelstein 2013: 85. See also 1 Kings 19:17, for which I thank Chris Rollston.

89. On imprisoning Hazael, killing his men, and capturing chariots and cavalry, see Grayson 1996: 58–61 (A.0.102.12), esp. 60; see also, on simply the killing and capturing, but without the imprisoning, 62–71 (A.0.102.14 = the Black Obelisk), esp. 67; also Frahm 2017: 171.

90. On the siege trench and Hazael's destruction at Gath, see now Maeir and Gur-Arieh 2011, with many previous references; Kleiman 2016: 63, 67–69; Maeir 2017a, 2017b, 2022d: 230–31; Ben-Yosef and Sergi 2018; Gur-Arieh and Maeir 2020; Chadwick 2022. On his destruction at Gath in general, as reported by the biblical account, see, e.g., Ehrlich 1996: 72–74; Levin 2017.

91. Mazar 2022a: 86, 2022b: 110–11, 122–23; Mazar and Mullins 2022: 146; Panitz-Cohen and Mazar 2022: 144–45.

92. On Hazael and the ending of copper production in Wadi Faynan and the Arabah Valley, see, e.g., Fantalkin and Finkelstein 2006: 30–32; Finkelstein 2013: 126, 2020: 21–22; Ben-Yosef and Sergi 2018; Crowell 2021: 42; Maeir 2021. These activities, and the cessation of the copper route from Faynan, may have affected sites as far away as Tel Dor, on the coast; see Arkin Shalev et al. 2021: 146. On the possibility of a sudden lack of available fuel for the furnaces, see now Cavanagh, Ben-Yosef, and Langgut 2022.

93. On the translation(s), see Bron and Lemaire 1989; Eph'al and Naveh 1989; Na'aman 1995, all with earlier references. On the topic as a whole, see most recently Bourogiannis 2018a: 57–58, 2020: 171–72, 2021: 103, with earlier references; López-Ruiz 2021: 185–86; J. F. Osborne and Hall 2022: 6–7. See also previously S. P. Morris 1992a: 147; Kourou 2004: 17–18, 2008b: 367.

94. See again Kourou 2004: 17–18, 2008b: 367 and the other references cited above.

95. On the interpretation, see again Bron and Lemaire 1989; Eph'al and Naveh 1989; Na'aman 1995.

96. Schneider 2014: 101. Re the Black Obelisk, see Grayson 1996: 62–71 (A.0.102.14); for the depiction and inscription regarding Jehu in particular, see Grayson 1996: 149 (A.0.102.88); Postgate 1992: 253, fig. 3, and 255; originally Layard 1849: pl. 53. See also Kuhrt 1995: 488; Grayson 2005; Miller and Hayes 2006: 236, 247, 307 (text no. 5); Fagan 2007: 122–23; Younger 2016: 613–18; Cline 2017: 57–58, with further references; Frahm 2017: 171, 2023: 110; Schipper 2019: 41–42.

97. See Grayson 1996: 209–12 (A.0.104.7), esp. 211; Miller and Hayes 2006: 238, 247; Bryce 2012: 50–52, 245; Schneider 2014: 101; Fales 2017: 228–29; Frahm 2017: 174–75; Elayi 2018: 136–37; Bunnens 2019b: 67; Sader 2019b: 66. On the dates of Joash/Jehoash, king of Israel (not to be confused with the slightly earlier king of Judah who had the same name), see Miller and Hayes 2006: 222.

98. Ehrlich 1996: 81–85, 168–71; Grayson 1996: 212–13 (A.0.104.8), esp. 213; Bryce 2012: 50–51; Ben-Shlomo 2014: 717; Schneider 2014: 101; Fales 2017: 228–30; Bunnens 2019b: 67; Na'aman 2021: 19–20.

99. Sinha et al. 2019.

Chapter Three. The Mediterranean Became a Phoenician Lake

1. I am indebted to Brien Garnand and Chris Rollston for these points (pers. comm., July 10 and 12, 2022); see now also López-Ruiz 2022: 37.

2. Hdt. 2.49, 5.57–58; translation following A. D. Godley, 1920. See also Flavius Josephus, *Against Apion* 1.6; Tacitus, *The Annals*, XI.14. See, e.g., Bourogiannis 2018b: 236; Elayi 2018: 96; most recently Rollston 2019: 384–85; Bendall and West 2020: 67–68. See also Quinn 2018a: xv; López-Ruiz 2021: 234–36.

3. Diodorus Siculus, *Bib. hist.* 3.67.1; translation following Oldfather 1933. See again Bourogiannis 2018b: 236; Rollston 2019: 384–85; Sader 2019b: 151–55, 268–69.

4. Diodorus Siculus, *Bib. hist.* 5.74.1; translation following C. H. Oldfather. See again Bourogiannis 2018b: 236; Rollston 2019: 384–85.

5. I am indebted to Chris Rollston for his thoughts on these points (pers. comm., July 12, 2022); he notes that Hebrew and Aramaic (and related languages) did have a fledgling system of marking long vowels, but not short ones. On the Phoenicians standardizing the alphabet prior to spreading it across the Mediterranean, and its relative ease of use, see now Rollston 2016: 276, 278, 2019: 374–78, 384–85, 2020: 76; also Liverani 2014: 390–91; Bourogiannis 2018b: 236, 238, 241, 2021: 100; Elayi 2018: 96; Sader 2019b: 151–55, 315; Steele 2020: 260, 263–65; López-Ruiz 2021: 228–29. The Phoenician alphabet was deciphered as early as 1758; see Quinn 2018a: 17.

6. Strabo XVI.2.23; translation following H. L. Jones, 1932. For comprehensive overviews and/or discussions of the Phoenicians in recent decades, see Aubet 1993 (rev. 2001); Markoe 2000; Niemeyer 2006; and more recently, Elayi 2018; Monroe 2018; Quinn 2018a, 2018b, 2019; Edrey 2019; Killebrew 2019; Sader 2019a, 2019b: 1, 251, 296–97, 315–16; López-Ruiz 2021; Regev 2021; see also previously Katzenstein 1973. See also briefer mentions in Aubet 2008: 182; Broodbank 2013: 449; Liverani 2014: 420–21, 423; Bell 2016: 91–92, 101; Rollston 2016: 267; Bourogiannis 2018a: 43–44; Knodell 2021: 181–83; previously Kuhrt 1995: 402–3.

7. On the Phoenicians and purple dye in general, as well as earlier use in both the Aegean and the Near East, see, e.g., Sader 2019b: 296–300, 315–16, with earlier references, including Reese 1987, 2010; see also Stieglitz 1994. See now also Veropoulidou, Andreou, and Kotsakis 2008; Veropoulidou 2014; Apostolakou et al. 2016; López-Ruiz 2021: 291–92; Gambash, Pestarino, and Friesem 2022.

8. Monroe 2018: 234; Quinn 2018b, also 2018a: xv, xviii, xxii–xxiv, 25–26, and passim, 2019: 672; Edrey 2019: 4, 205; Sader 2019b: 1–3; Hodos 2020: 60–61; Regev 2021: 5–6, 8–9, 14; Gilboa 2022: 32–33; J. F. Osborne and Hall 2022: 15; López-Ruiz 2022: 28; previously, e.g., Sherratt 1994: 82; Aubet 2001: 6–13. For examples of Homer and the Phoenicians, see, e.g., Sherratt 1994: 82n34, 2010; Quinn 2018a: 48–49; Bendall and West 2020: 68; Sherratt 2020: 198; Regev 2021: 13; previously Kuhrt 1995: 403; Winter 1995. See also, e.g., Bourogiannis 2018a: 46–47 (with earlier references), who cites a variety of passages from the *Iliad* and the *Odyssey*, including *Il.* 6.289–92, 23.741–45; *Od.* 4.83–84, 4.615–19, 13.272–86, 14.285–301, 15.415–25, 15.446, 15.450–56, and 15.461–83.

9. Markoe 2000: 14–15; Aubet 2001: 16, 25, 2008: 182; Bell 2006: 113, 2016: 92 (citing Lehmann 2008); Sherratt 2010: 122–26, 2019: 129; Abulafia 2011: 64; Broodbank 2013: 449; Liverani 2014: 420; Quinn et al. 2014; Rollston 2016: 267; Fales 2017: 208; Bourogiannis 2018a: 44–47; Monroe 2018: 263; Quinn 2018a: 16, 2018b; Edrey 2019: 5, 14–15, 20, 205–6, 222; Bunnens 2019b: 58, 60; Ilieva 2019: 66–67; Killebrew 2019; Lehmann 2019: 466, 2021: 272–73; Sader 2019a: 125, 2019b: xii–xiv, 1–3, 6, 8–11, 313–14; Garnand 2020: 140, 144; Manolova 2020: 1198–200; López-Ruiz 2021: 9–11, 15–17, 2022: 31; Regev 2021: 5–7; Gilboa 2022: 31–32; S. P. Morris 2022: 100. See also Charaf 2020–21 on the excavations at Tell Arqa in Lebanon and the brief discussions encompassing the entire Levant during the Iron Age I in Welton and Charaf 2019–20, 2020–21.

10. E.g., Bell 2006: 92, 99, 113; Abulafia 2011: 65–66; Liverani 2014: 420; Edrey 2019: 218–20, 223; Ilieva 2019: 66; Sader 2019b: 4; López-Ruiz 2021: 17, 80, 283–84; Gilboa 2022: 36; see also previously, e.g., Aubet 2001: 25.

11. Bell 2006: 113. See also, e.g., Sherratt and Sherratt 1993: 364–65; Bikai 1994: 34; Bell 2006: 94; Fletcher 2012: 212–13, with previous references; Bourogiannis 2013: 141–42, 2018a: 47; Bunnens 2019b: 60, 70; Edrey 2019: 207; Manolova 2020: 1200.

12. Monroe 2018: 260.

13. See Taleb 2007, 2014: 3, 5, 17, 31–32. It seems especially fitting to invoke this term "antifragile" here, as Taleb—who was born in Lebanon—refers to "the Phoenician trader in me (or, more exactly, the Canaanite)"; see Taleb 2014: 17. See discussion about Taleb and "black swans" previously in Cline 2021.

14. On the cinnamon, see Namdar et al. 2013; Finkelstein, Weiner, and Boaretto 2015: 200; Gilboa and Namdar 2015; Finkelstein 2016: 119–20 and fig. 3; Regev 2021: 49, 133. Such contacts may have involved the Philistines as well, as evidence for the importation of bananas has now been found at Tell Erani; see A. Scott et al. 2020. On the finds at Safi, see now Maeir 2022b, c. For a very important overview of such trade, see Maeir forthcoming.

15. See, e.g., the catalog in Sherratt 1994: 86–88, updating the original catalogs in Waldbaum 1978, 1982 and Desborough 1972: 119. See now also Muhly and Kassianidou 2012: 125–26, 134–35; Kassianidou 2014: 264–65; Georgiou and Iacovou 2020: 1145; also previously Crielaard 1998: 191.

16. See Karageorghis 1994: 4–5; Sherratt 1994: 60–61, 65–66, 83–85, 2003: 43–44, 47–48, 2015: 77; also Snodgrass 1983: 285–94, 1994: 167–68; R. Osborne 1996: 25–27; Crielaard 1998: 191; Iacovou 2008: 641–42, 2012: 211–12, 2014c: 799, 801; Kassianidou 2012: 237–39, 2014: 264–67; Muhly and Kassianidou 2012: 124, 134–35, with previous references; Broodbank 2013: 451; Georgiou and Iacovou 2020: 1144–45; also Papadopoulos and Smithson 2017: 976–78. See, however, Schachner 2020b: 1121, for a brief discussion of an alternative suggestion that the technology might have been developed in the region near Lake Van during the eleventh and tenth centuries BC. Some scholars have suggested that the Phoenicians may have also facilitated the spread of iron technology as well, perhaps as additional agents bringing such objects to the Aegean; see Bell 2016: 101; Fales 2017: 249–50, 260; Erb-Satullo 2019: 567, with previous references; also briefly Johnston and Kaufman 2019: 408.

17. E.g., Strabo, *Geography* XII.3.19; Xenophon, *Anabasis* V.v.1; Apollonius, *Argonautica* II, 1002–8. See also discussions in, e.g., Waldbaum 1978; Bryer 1982; Muhly et al. 1985: 74; Kostoglou 2010; Bebermeier et al. 2016; Erb-Satullo, Gilmour, and Khakhutaishvili 2020.

18. See discussions, all with references, in, e.g., Snodgrass 1967: 36; Muhly et al. 1985: 70–71; Sherratt 1994: 64–65; Cordani 2016; Hodos 2020: 37. On the dagger with the iron blade in Tutankhamun's tomb, see now Comelli et al. 2016; Matsui et al. 2022.

19. See, e.g., Snodgrass 1971: 237–39; I. Morris 1989: 503; Bell 2006: 110; Chew 2007: 103–4; Kassianidou 2014: 262; now Papadopoulos and Smithson 2017: 976, reiterating the arguments in brief. New studies now show that about one-third of the tin found on the Uluburun shipwreck, which went down ca. 1300 BC, came from sources in Uzbekistan and Tajikistan, and the rest came from sources in Anatolia; see Powell, Johnson, et al. 2021; Powell, Frachetti, et al. 2022.

20. See Oates 1979: 104, citing an unpublished paper by Snodgrass; also Snodgrass 1971: 237–39, 1980: 348–49, 368–69, 1994: 167–68; Muhly 1980: 47, 53; Waldbaum 1980: 82–83, 90–91; Wertime 1980: 1; Karageorghis 1994: 4; Chew 2007: 103–4. See also the reviews by Waldbaum 1999; Kostoglou 2010; Enverova 2012: 25–27; and Erb-Satullo 2019: esp. 580–81.

21. Kassianidou 2014: 265–67. See also Muhly and Kassianidou 2012: 134; Erb-Satullo 2019: 558, 566–68, 572–74, 580–83, 593; also Papadopoulos and Smithson 2017: 976–78. See previously, i.e., I. Morris 1989; Muhly 1992: 17–18; Sherratt 2000: 82–83; Dickinson 2006a: 144–45; Eliyahu-Behar et al. 2012: 55, 2013: 4319; Enverova 2012: 25; Kassianidou 2013: 69, 71; Yahalom-Mack and Eliyahu-Behar 2015; Murray 2017: 174–75, 261–63; Eliyahu-Behar and Yahalom-Mack 2018: 447; Knodell 2021: 171–72.

22. Erb-Satullo 2019: 557–58, 574, 582–83, with references; previously, e.g., Snodgrass 1980: 336–37; I. Morris 1989: 502–6; Karageorghis 1994: 5; Sherratt 1994: 59, 2000: 82–83; Chew 2007: 101; Muhly and Kassianidou 2012: 124, 135; see now also Johnston and Kaufman 2019: 408, on the Phoenicians, Cyprus, and the spread of iron technology.

23. Muhly and Kassianidou 2012: 124, 135, with previous references; see also Kassianidou 2012: 231, 239–40, 2013: 52; Knodell 2021: 171–72; previously, e.g., Snodgrass 1971: 214–15, 1994: 168; Karageorghis 1994: 4–5; Sherratt 1994: 62, 66, 2015: 77; Enverova 2012: 73–74; Broodbank 2013: 451.

24. Snodgrass 1971: 217–19, 229, 1994: 167–68; Karageorghis 1994: 4–5; Sherratt 1994: 60–62, 68–75, and app. 1, 2016: 295–97; Dickinson 2006a: 146–47; Iacovou 2008: 641–42, 2012: 211–12, 2014b: 670, 2014c: 799, 801–2; Enverova 2012: 75–78, 81, 89–90; Kassianidou 2012: 237–39; Muhly and Kassianidou 2012: 125–26, 134–35, with previous references; Broodbank 2013: 450–51; Kearns 2015: 37–38; Wallace 2018: 393; Georgiou and Iacovou 2020: 1145; Knodell 2021: 172–73. On possible trade routes between Cyprus and Sardinia, see, e.g., Blake 2014: 104; Saltini Semerari 2017: 553–54; Sabatini and Lo Schiavo 2020.

25. On the problems affecting the Terramare culture, see previously Cline 2021: 153, citing Kristiansen 2018: 100–103. See now also Cardarelli 2009; Palmisano, Bevan, and Shennan 2017; Dalla Longa 2019; Cupitò, Dalla Longa, and Balista 2020; Palmisano, Bevan, et al. 2021; Parkinson et al. 2021; Molloy 2022: 36–37, 45, 47 (online version). On Sardinia and the end of the *nuraghe* building structures (which some see as continuing until ca. 900 BC), see, e.g., Tronchetti 2014; Gonzalez 2018: 54–55; Bernardini 2020.

26. Bell 2006: 113; see also Bell 2009: 38; Bourogiannis 2018a: 50–51.

27. See, e.g., Muhly 1992: 11–12, 14, 19; Sherratt 1992: 327–28; H. W. Catling 1994: 133–36; Deger-Jalkotzy 1994: 16, 20; Iacovou 2002: 84–85, 2006a: 325–27, 2006b: 34–35, 2007: 465–66, 2014c: 661; Janes 2010: 127–28; Georgiou 2011: 109–10, 118–22, 125, 2015: 133–35, 138, 2017: 207, 210–11, 217, 219; Cline 2021: 127–30, with relevant references; Knapp and Meyer 2020: 237–38.

28. See Iacovou 2006a: 326–27, 2007: 461–62; also Georgiou 2011: 125; but see contra Rupp 1987, 1988, 1989, who tended to view the situation a bit differently (at least back during the 1980s). For recent takes on the debates around continuity, see, e.g., Knapp and Meyer 2020;

Kearns 2022: 113–19, 130–50. I am indebted to the latter for her thoughts on the matter (pers. comm., March 2, 2023).

29. See, e.g., Muhly 1992: 14, with earlier references; Coldstream 1994: 144–46, but subsequently the discussions in Iacovou 2005a: 128–29, 2012: 207–12, 217, 2013: 17, 2014a: 103–4, 107, 2014c: 798; Karageorghis 1994: 1–2, 6; also Voskos and Knapp 2008: 659–65, 673, 676–79; Janes 2010: 128–32, 2014: 571; Georgiou 2011: 123–24; Counts and Iacovou 2013: 10–11; Knapp 2014: 39–43; Sherratt 2015: 72–75.

30. I am grateful to Brien Garnand for reminding me of this (pers. comm., July 10, 2022).

31. See Kaniewski, Van Campo, et al. 2013; Cline 2021: 159; previously Sherratt 2003: 51–52. On Enkomi and Salamis, see, e.g., Iacovou 2005b: 25–27; Kourou 2019.

32. On the abandonment of Kalavasos-Ayios Dhimitrios, Maroni-Vournes, and other places, see Iacovou 2007: 465–66, 2008: 631, 2012: 216, 2013: 25–26, 2014b: 662–63. See also Georgiou 2011: 116–17, 2015: 131, 2017: 210; Kassianidou 2014: 264; Georgiou and Iacovou 2020: 1142–43; Knapp and Meyer 2020: 238.

33. Re Idalion, see, e.g., Georgiou 2011: 117–18, 2015: 132–33, 2017: 209–10; Iacovou 2005b: 31. Re Amathus, Kition, Paphos, and other cities, see, e.g., Iacovou 1994: 155–56, 2005b: 28–29, 31–34, 2008: 638, 2013: 26; Satraki 2012: 267–73; Janes 2013: 154, 158; Georgiou 2017: 210. On the abandonment of Hala Sultan Tekke and Enkomi as well as the continuations at Kition and Paphos, see Iacovou 1994: 153–54, 2005a: 130, 2006a: 325–26, 2006b: 35–36, 2007: 466–67, 2008: 635, 637, 2012: 217–18, 2013: 25–26, 28, 2014b: 664–65, 667; also Sherratt 1992: 328–29; Smith 2008: 274–75; Georgiou 2011: 116–17, 2015: 131–34, 2017: 209, 222; Satraki 2012: 264, 270; Janes 2013: 155, 2014: 572, 574, 579; Kassianidou 2014: 265; Georgiou and Iacovou 2020: 1142–43; Hodos 2020: 41; Knapp and Meyer 2020: 238. See now also Petit 2019.

34. Karageorghis 1983: 59–76, see also app. 4. For subsequent discussions, see, e.g., Sherratt 1992: 329; Deger-Jalkotzy 1994: 11; Iacovou 2006b: 38, 2008: 633; Voskos and Knapp 2008: 674–75; Satraki 2012: 268; Janes 2013: 146–47; Knapp 2014: 41; Kearns 2015: 29, fig. 1.4; Georgiou and Iacovou 2020: 1147; Steele 2020: 256–57 and fig. 2.6.2; López-Ruiz 2021: 252–53, 270–71.

35. On these foundation myths, see esp. Iacovou 2006a: 328, 2006b: 44–46, 2007: 467; also Kearns 2015: 29, with references.

36. H. W. Catling 1993: 91–92; Crielaard 1998: 187–91, 198–99; Kourou 2008a: 364; Iacovou 2012: 214; Muhly and Kassianidou 2012: 124–25; Georgiou and Iacovou 2020: 1145–46.

37. Popham, Touloupa, and Sackett 1982; H. W. Catling 1993, 1995, 1996; I. Morris 1996: 3; Crielaard 1998: 187–90, 198; Kourou 2008a: 363–65, 2016: 54–55; Iacovou 2012: 214; Muhly and Kassianidou 2012: 124–25; Georgiou and Iacovou 2020: 1145–46; S. P. Morris 2022: 104. Note that Kourou 2008a: 363–64 says "the Amari tomb suggests that apparently some kind of direct contact existed in the 11th century BCE between Crete and Cyprus."

38. Kourou 2008a: 364.

39. Muhly and Kassianidou 2012: 125–26, 134–35; see also Iacovou 2014c: 799, 801. See Sherratt 1994: 73–75, as well as the additional entries in the catalog compiled on 88–92, updating the original catalogs in Waldbaum 1978, 1982.

40. Crielaard 1998: 187, 192–93, 196; Iacovou 2008: 641–42; Kourou 2008a: 363–64, 2012: 38, 2016: 53–55, 2019: 77–78; Satraki 2012: 265–66; Arruda 2015: 273–74; Pappa 2020; S. P. Morris 2022: 104.

41. Crielaard 1998: 193–94, 197–98.

42. Kearns (pers. comm., March 2, 2023); see now Kearns 2022: 130–54 for a current overview.

43. Kourou 2019: 78. Note that in 2016, Kourou had earlier written: "From the 11th c. onwards a new pattern of travel and trading networks, in which eventually Phoenicians become involved, starts gradually to develop. The phenomenon can best be followed in Crete, where a large number of Cypriot and Phoenician objects have been found in Early Iron Age (EIA) contexts, while Cretan art frequently betrays Cypriot or Levantine influence" (Kourou 2016: 51).

44. The date has been the subject of much discussion; see, e.g., Wente 2003: 116 and Jeffers 2013: 22–23. See further details below.

45. Translation follows Wente 2003: 116–24; several other translations of the tale have recently been republished as Pritchard [1958] 2011: 14–21; and Lichtheim 2019: 561–68. See also detailed discussions, with further references, in Kitchen 1973: 251–52; Dothan 1982: 4–5; Clayton 1994: 170–71; Hallo and Simpson 1998: 284–85; Aubet 2001: 356–62; Sherratt 2003: 52; Eyre 2012: 133; Broodbank 2013: 445–48; Jeffers 2013: 22–23; Ben-Dor Evian 2017: 34–35; Elayi 2018: 100–104; Dodson 2019: 16–19; Yasur-Landau 2019: 417–20; López-Ruiz 2021: 284–85.

46. See, e.g., Gilboa 2005, 2006–7, 2015; Gilboa, Sharon, and Boaretto 2008; Sharon and Gilboa 2013; Stern 2013; Yasur-Landau 2019; Arie 2020: 6. On the new discovery of remains from the Iron Age harbor at Dor, see now Arkin Shalev, Gilboa, and Yasur-Landau 2019; Arkin Shalev, Galili, et al. 2021.

47. Note that there are some differences in the various translations; for instance, Pritchard translated the name of the prince of Byblos as Zakar-Baal, rather than Tjekkerbaal (though this might just be a difference in pronunciation), and there is a difference between "smooth linen" and "rolls of papyrus." See also Kuhrt 1995: 408 on the items (re)sent to Wenamun and again Yasur-Landau 2019 on the treatment of Wenamun at Byblos.

48. See, e.g., Wente 2003: 116; Ben-Dor Evian 2011: 97; Jeffers 2013: 22–23. See also now esp. Yasur-Landau 2019. On the discussions as to whether it is the official record of an actual historical voyage or a piece of narrative fiction, see, e.g., Markoe 2000: 27–28; Aubet 2001: 30–31, 114–17; Wente 2003: 116; Edrey 2019: 36; Sader 2019b: 35, 81, 272; on the eleventh century BC date, see also Fales 2017: 218–19; Sass 2002 suggests that it might be of tenth century BC date.

49. See, e.g., Pritchard 1978; Bikai 1978; Markoe 2000: 24; Aubet 2001: 66–69; Bell 2006: 113. See now the very useful concise overview by Aubet 2014; also Sader 2014, 2019a: 127–28, 2019b: 17–20, 38–41; Killebrew 2019; Charaf 2020–21.

50. Other nearby sites with Phoenician remains in Iron Age levels include Tell Abu Hawam, Akko, Achziv, Atlit, and Tel Keisan; see, e.g., Fales 2017: 204; Killebrew 2019; Sader 2019a: 127–28, 2019b: 31, 41–42; Hodos 2020: 153–54; previously Aubet 2001: 66–69. On Dor, see, e.g., Gilboa 2005; Bell 2006: 99; Gilboa, Sharon, and Boaretto 2008; Gilboa and Sharon 2008; Sharon and Gilboa 2013; Bell 2016: 95–96; Gilboa, Waiman-Barak, and Jones 2015; Fales 2017: 203; Sader 2019b: 20–21, 42–44; Arie 2020: 1, 3; Hodos 2020: 97, 150–51; Gilboa 2022: 40. On using the term "southern Phoenicia," see Lehmann 2019, 2021; Arie 2020: 7–9. Regarding Dor and the silver hoard in particular, see, e.g., Aubet 2008: 183 and see again the sources cited re the silver hoards, esp. C. Thompson and Skaggs 2013; Eshel, Yahalom-Mack, et al. 2018: 4, Ben-Yosef 2019a; Eshel, Erel, et al. 2019; Sader 2019b: 256, 315; Hodos 2020: 144, 150–51; Wood, Bell, and Montero-Ruiz

2020: 4, with earlier references; López-Ruiz 2021: 99; Gilboa 2022: 43. On the original discovery, see Stern 1998, 2001.

51. Eshel, Gilboa, et al. 2021; see also Ben-Yosef 2019a.

52. Allen 1977: 157–62. Note that this reverses the original model for Phoenician expansion, such as proposed by Frankenstein in 1979; see the discussion in Monroe 2018: 232–33, 247, 257–60, who describes the previous view (i.e., that the Phoenicians were essentially at the beck-and-call of the Neo-Assyrians, fetching raw materials for them, including metals, and thus moved out into the Mediterranean because of these demands placed on them), as the Assyrian Pressure Paradigm (APP); also (briefly) J. F. Osborne 2021: 73–74; Regev 2021: 2. Compare also Faust 2011 to Thareani 2016a and see discussions by Aubet 2001: 88–91 with citations of previous scholarship, 281–83, 2008: 183, 2016; I. Morris 2006: 83; Fletcher 2012: 211 (with earlier references), 216–18; Broodbank 2013: 482–84, 488–89, 491; Fales 2017: 271; Edrey 2019: 206–8; Hodos 2020: 77–78, 143–44. See also the discussions in, e.g., C. Thompson and Skaggs 2013; Arruda 2015: 275; Bell 2016: 98–100; Eshel, Yahalom-Mack, et al. 2018; Gonzalez 2018: 39, 175–76; Monroe 2018: 240–41; Wood 2018; Aubet Semmler 2019: 75–78; Eshel, Erel, et al. 2019; Sader 2019b: 256, 275; Wood, Montero-Ruiz, and Martinón-Torres 2019; Sherratt 2020: 200–201; Wood, Bell, and Montero-Ruiz 2020; Knodell 2021: 183; López-Ruiz 2021: 27–28, 97–98, 100; Regev 2021: 120–21; Gilboa 2022: 35n9, 43.

53. Shalvi 2018, 2020; Stub 2020; Regev 2021: 80–81. Note that other sites in the region also have stained pottery sherds and/or crushed murex shells in contexts ranging from the thirteenth to the seventh century BC, including Akko, Dor, Abu, Hawam, and Tel Kabri, as mentioned with earlier references by Shalvi; see now also Gilboa 2022: 37, 44; Shalvi and Gilboa 2023.

54. See Bell 2006: 104, 113, 2009: 36–37, 2016: 97, 100–102, with references; also Gilboa 2005: 62–63; Sherratt 2010: 130, 2019: 132, 134–35; Kourou 2012: 37; Bourogiannis 2018a: 49–51, 53, 61, 73; Sader 2019b: 267–68.

55. Published by Dr. Patricia Bikai; see Bikai 1978.

56. Kourou 2012: 39, citing in particular Aubet 1993: 167, 2008: 250; see also now Kourou 2016: 57–58, 2019: 79–80.

57. See Kourou 2008a: 366; Gilboa, Waiman-Barak, and Sharon 2015; Bell 2016: 97; Bourogiannis 2018a: 73–74; Monroe 2018: 245–46; Sader 2019b: 269; Hodos 2020: 107; S. P. Morris 2022: 106; for the initial publication, see Bikai 2000; see also previously, e.g., Aubet 2001: 54.

58. See, e.g., Kourou 2012: 40. On the various Phoenician and other Near Eastern items on Crete and mainland Greece in these contexts, see, e.g., Sherratt and Sherratt 1993: 365; Hoffman 1997; Kourou 2000: 1067–70; Stampolidis and Kotsonas 2006: 341–43, 346, 351, 355; Fletcher 2012: 214–15; Broodbank 2013: 451; Bourogiannis 2018a: 54–66; Sogas 2019: 408–14.

59. See, e.g., the summation in Sader 2019b: 270, with references to earlier publications. See previously Waldbaum 1994; Crielaard 1998: 198; Fantalkin 2001; Coldstream and Mazar 2003; Satraki 2012: 266; Iacovou 2014c: 802; Fantalkin et al. 2015, 2020; Gilboa, Waiman-Barak, and Jones 2015; Mazar and Kourou 2019; Hodos 2020: 5, 98; also comments by Kourou 2008a: 364–66, 2016: 57–58, 2019: 79–80.

60. See, e.g., Janes 2013: 147, 2014: 571; also Satraki 2012: 263–64; previously Iacovou 2005b: 24. See now, however, the dissertation by Kearns (2015) and her recent book (Kearns 2022).

61. Fales 2017: 190–91; Bunnens 2019b: 58; Rollston 2019: 375–77; Sader 2019b: 81–82, 86, table 3.2. It should be noted, however, that Benjamin Sass has suggested that some or all of these

should be redated to the ninth century (Sass 2005, 2021), but his suggestion in turn has been disputed by Rollston (2008: 57–61, 2010: 24–27). For now, I have followed the traditional tenth century BC dating for these kings.

62. See Rollston 2016: 268. On the Amarna letters from Byblos, see Moran 1992; also recently, e.g., on Byblos in the Late Bronze Age, Kilani 2020.

63. Translation following Rollston 2016: 286, 2019: 376, 2020: 76; see also Rollston 2008: 58, 2010: 20–21, fig. 2.2. References to earlier publications regarding the discovery and subsequent discussions may be found in Rollston's publications, but see also Kuhrt 1995: 404, with references; Elayi 2018: 110–12; Doumet-Serhal 2019: 718.

64. See Rollston 2008: 59–60, with references.

65. Translation following Rollston 2016: 289; see also Rollston 2008: 59, 2010: 23, fig. 2.4, all with earlier references; Elayi 2018: 115. See though again Sass (2005, 2021), who would redate these all to the ninth century, which is a suggestion that has been disputed by Rollston (2008: 57–61, 2010: 24–27).

66. Translation following Rollston 2016: 288; see also Rollston 2008: 58–59, 2010: 21–22, all with earlier references; previously, e.g., Kitchen 1973: 308–9. See also Elayi 2018: 114–15; Bunnens 2019b: 69; Muhs 2022: 196–97.

67. Translation following Rollston 2016: 287, 2019: 376, 2020: 77; see also Rollston 2008: 59, 2010: 21–22, fig. 2.3, all with earlier references; also Elayi 2018: 112–13; Richey 2019: 223, fig. 16.1.

68. Translation following Rollston 2016: 288; see also Rollston 2008: 58, 2010: 21, all with earlier references; previously, e.g., Kitchen 1973: 292. See also Elayi 2018: 113–14; Bunnens 2019b: 69; Dodson 2019: 95; Muhs 2022: 196–97.

69. See, e.g., Lipiński 2006: 174, 176, 180; Aubet 2008: 182–83; Bourogiannis 2018a: 49–50; Elayi 2018: 122, 296 (table 2); Bunnens 2019b: 58–59; Na'aman 2019b: 76, 82.

70. Lipiński 2006: 174, 176–77; Aubet 2008: 183; Bourogiannis 2018a: 49–50; Elayi 2018: 131–33; Edrey 2019: 41–43; Lehmann 2019: 470; Na'aman 2019b: 82; López-Ruiz 2021: 288.

71. As noted by Rollston 2016: 298; see now also Elayi 2018: 132; Bunnens 2019b: 65; Doak 2019: 663–64; Sader 2019b: 128–29, 263; López-Ruiz 2021: 306; previously Markoe 2000: 37–39; Aubet 2001: 46–47.

72. I have previously discussed this briefly; see Cline 2007, 2009, 2020, with earlier references; see also, e.g., Schipper 2019: 38–40. For the original publications by the two teams, see Reisner, Fisher, and Lyon 1924; Crowfoot and Crowfoot 1938; Crowfoot, Kenyon, and Sukenik 1942; Crowfoot, Crowfoot, and Kenyon 1957. See also Tappy 1992, 2001, in addition to numerous additional smaller publications or mentions by other scholars (e.g., Killbrew 2014: 738 on the ivories).

73. Aubet 1993: 42, 2001: 51–52, 2008: 183; Bikai 1994; Iacovou 2005a: 131–32, with references, 2006b: 41; Bell 2006: 113, 2009: 37; Janes 2010: 129; Satraki 2012: 269; Fourrier 2013: 113–14; Bourogiannis 2018a: 50–51, 74–75; Bunnens 2019b: 63; Sader 2019b: 266–67; Sherratt 2019: 134–35.

74. Aubet 2008: 179, 2016; Fletcher 2012: 214; Arruda 2015: 273; Bell 2016: 98–100; Eshel, Erel, et al. 2019: 1, 5, 8–11; Sherratt 2019: 134–35; Garnand 2020: 147; Muhs 2022: 203. On the Nora Stone inscription, which has a long history of scholarship, see, e.g., Aubet 2001: 206–9, fig. 45; Monroe 2018: 246; Rollston 2019: 376–77, with earlier references; also Hodos 2020: 185–86.

75. See, e.g., Lipiński 2006: 174, 180, 183; Na'aman 2019b: 82–83; Sader 2019b: 128–29, 138, table 3.4; previously, e.g., Aubet 2001: 51. See also Grayson 1996: 48, 54, 60 (compare A.0.102.8 and A.0.102.12 with A.0.102.10).

76. Aubet 2001: 163, 214–18, 2008: 179, 185, 2016: 258; Docter et al. 2005; Lipiński 2006: 183–84; Abulafia 2011: 74; Broodbank 2013: 490; Bourogiannis 2018a: 52, 74–75; Elayi 2018: 138–41; Quinn 2018a: xv, 2019: 679; Bunnens 2019b: 59, 61; Roller 2019: 648; see now Aubet Semmler 2019: 78; Garnand 2020: 147.

77. On all of the following, see Ballard et al. 2002.

78. Kourou 2016: 59, 60–61.

79. Kourou 2016: 60–61.

80. Crielaard 1998: 187; Kourou 2008a: 366–68, 2019: 81, 89–90; Satraki 2012: 266; Janes 2013: 152.

81. Kearns 2015: 17–18, 138–39, 2019: 272–73, 276–78, 280, 2022: 130–54; see also previous studies by Kaniewski and his team, including at Hala Sultan Tekke (Kaniewski, Van Campo, et al. 2013), which indicated the end of the megadrought in this region at approximately this time.

82. Kassianidou 2014: 267; Knapp and Meyer 2020: 239–41, 243. See also, e.g., previously Iacovou 2002: 85; Satraki 2012: 263–64, 266–67; Finkelstein 2013: 127; Janes 2013: 147; Hodos 2020: 61.

Chapter Four. King of the Land of Carchemish

1. Marchetti 2012: 132–34, 2014: 36; Aro 2013: 234n5; Dinçol et al. 2014b: 143–44; Younger 2016: 118–19; J. F. Osborne 2021: 153–54.

2. See again Marchetti 2012: 132–34, 2014: 36; Dinçol et al. 2014b: 143–44; Younger 2016: 118–19.

3. Dinçol, Dinçol, Hawkins, and Peker 2012: 145; Marchetti 2012: 144–46; Weeden 2013: 10; Dinçol et al. 2014a: 128; Hawkins and Peker 2014: 107; Hawkins and Weeden 2016: 11–12; Younger 2016: 119. See also Simon 2012, for a divergent opinion regarding the identification of Sura, with plentiful previous references.

4. Translation following Peker 2016: 16; see previously Dinçol, Dinçol, Hawkins, and Peker 2012: 145; Dinçol et al. 2014b: 148. See also Marchetti 2012: 144–46; Weeden 2013: 8–10; Dinçol et al. 2014b: 147, 2014b: 128–30; Younger 2016: 119.

5. Hawkins 2000: 80–82 (Karkamiš A4*b*); Marchetti 2012: 144–46; Dinçol, Dinçol, Hawkins, and Peker 2012: 145; Dinçol et al. 2014b: 143–44, 151, 2014b: 128; Hawkins and Weeden 2016: 11; Younger 2016: 119.

6. See, e.g., Hawkins 2000: 76–77; Gilibert 2011: 12; Bryce 2012: 89–91, 202; Aro 2013; Marchetti and Peker 2018: 98; Bryce 2020: 108; J.F. Osborne 2021: 100; and all of the additional references cited in the next note.

7. Hawkins 1995, 2000: 76–77; Gilibert 2011: 12; Marchetti 2012: 144–46 and table 2; Dinçol et al. 2014a: 130, 2014b: 150; Hawkins and Peker 2014: 107–8; Brown and Smith 2016: 23–25; Marchetti and Peker 2018: 98; J. F. Osborne 2021: 195; see also various tables in other relevant articles, as cited previously.

8. Grayson 1991: 37 (A.0.87.3), 42 (A.0.87.4), and 53 (A.0.87.10); Hawkins 2000: 73–74; Frahm 2009: 28–32; Bryce 2012: 200; Younger 2016: 118, 172, 2017: 205–6.

9. See, e.g., Hawkins 2000: 73–74; Gilibert 2011: 12; Bryce 2012: 4, 84, 87, 99, 200–201; Weeden 2013: 8; Brown and Smith 2016: 23; Hawkins and Weeden 2016: 11; Younger 2016: 117–18, 121 (fig. 3.3), 172, 2017: 206.

10. For quotes, see J. F. Osborne 2021: 55; d'Alfonso et al. 2022: 38. See also Schachner 2020a, 2020b: 1109–12; also Summers 2000: 55, 58; Seeher 2010; Genz 2013; Kuzucuoğlu 2015: 32–38; Bryce 2016b, 2019; Middleton 2017c: 165, 172, 175–76; de Martino 2018; Alaura 2020. On the demographic impact of the climate change in Anatolia, see also Palmisano, Lawrence, et al. 2021: 22, 106739.

11. On the change in livestock, see Adcock 2020: 251, also 266; now also Haldon, Izdebski, et al. 2022: 400–401, citing Adcock's work.

12. Dibble and Fallu 2020: 1, 8–9.

13. Rose and Darbyshire 2011; Rose 2012; Kealhofer, Grave, and Voigt 2019; previously, e.g., Muscarella 1995: 94; Voigt and Henrickson 2000: 42–43. On the new data, see Manning, Kocik, et al. 2023, but see also Drews 1992: 17, with an early similar report.

14. See, e.g., Liverani 2014: 465–66, 531. Much has been written about the Phrygians, but for Gordion during this period in particular, see most recently Rose and Darbyshire 2011; Rose 2012; previously, including on the possibility of Phrygian migration into this area, see, e.g., Muscarella 1995: 91–92; Voigt and Henrickson 2000: 42–46. See also Herodotus VII.73 and Strabo VII.3.2, cited by Muscarella, for their belief that the Phrygians migrated from Thrace or Macedonian to Anatolia around the time of the Trojan War.

15. The inscription is known more formally as "TÜRKMEN-KARAHÖYÜK 1"; the survey was under the direction of James Osborne and Michele Massa. For details of the survey and the translation of the inscription, see J. F. Osborne, Massa, et al. 2020 and Goedegebuure et al. 2020.

16. Aslan 2009, 2020: 245–47; Basedow 2009; Aslan and Hnila 2015: 186–94.

17. Bunnens 2000: 16; Hawkins 2000: 73; Harrison 2009a: 171, 174, 181, 2009b: 187, 2013: 61; Bryce 2012: 60, 79–80, 2014: 100–101, 103–4, 2020: 106–7; Weeden 2013: 6; Emanuel 2015: 12; Hawkins and Weeden 2016: 9; Welton et al. 2019: 325. On the Hittites and the Bible, see, e.g., Bryce 2012, 2014: 101–3.

18. Woolley 1920: 76. See, e.g., Hawkins 2000: 73; also Bunnens 2000: 17; Bryce 2012: 55, 83.

19. See now, most usefully, the recent book by J. F. Osborne (2021). He prefers to call this group of small kingdoms by the name "Syro-Anatolian Culture Complex (SACC)"; see J. F. Osborne 2021: 1–9, 110–12, 209–19. See also, e.g., Gilibert 2011: 14–16, 55, 79–80, with references re Zincirli; Bryce 2012: 22–31, 56–57, 169–70, 2020: 108; Weeden 2013: 1–2; Liverani 2014: 448; Younger 2016: 28–30, 114–15.

20. Hogarth 1911: 8.

21. See, e.g., Hawkins 1988, 2000: 73; Harrison 2009a: 171–73; Gilibert 2011: 10–12; Bryce 2012: 19, 55, 84–85, 195–97, 2014: 101–2, 2020: 107; Marchetti 2012: 144, 146 (table 2); Aro 2013: 246; Weeden 2013: 6, 9 (table 1); Dinçol et al. 2014a: 127–28 (table 1), 130 (table 2); Hawkins and Peker 2014: 110 (table 1); J. F. Osborne 2014: 197–98, 2015: 10–11, 2021: 41–42; Hawkins and Weeden 2016: 9; Peker 2016: 49 (table 2); Younger 2016: 28–30, 116–19, 121 (fig. 3.3); Marchetti and Peker 2018: 98; Welton et al. 2019: 292–94; Millek 2020. See also Gilibert 2011: 7–8, with previous references, for the description of Syro-Anatolian city-states as typically "a capital city ruling over a belt of fortified towns and a rural hinterland of villages."

22. See, e.g., Harrison 2009a: 175; Bryce 2012, 2014: 86–87, 101–3, 2016b, 2020: 106–9; Brown and Smith 2016: 29; Younger 2016: 28–30, 144; Ilan 2019; Manolova 2020: 1195; also now J.F. Osborne 2021.

23. Sader 2014: 618; Jung 2023, with references, including remarks concerning Millek 2020–21; Millek 2021; see now also Millek 2023, which has just appeared.

24. Weeden 2013: 20.

25. The equation is not perfect and is not universally accepted; on the various discussions see, among others, Harrison 2009a, 2009b, 2010, 2013, 2014; Hawkins 2009, 2011; Bryce 2012: 128–29, 206–7, 2014: 111, 2020: 110–12; Weeden 2013: 11–18; Dinçol et al. 2015; Emanuel 2015; Brown and Smith 2016: 32–33; Hawkins and Weeden 2016: 9, 11; Younger 2016: 123–34, 144; Welton et al. 2019; Manning, Lorentzen, et al. 2020; J. F. Osborne 2021: 46–47, 63–64, 159–60; Maeir 2022d: 228–29.

26. Welton et al. 2019: 325. See also previously Harrison 2009a: 171, 174, 181 and, e.g., Harrison 2009b, 2010, 2013, 2014; also Janeway 2006–7, 2017 on Tayinat and the Aegean.

27. Welton et al. 2019: 325–26; see also Harrison 2009a: 171, 2009b: 187, 2013: 61; Sader 2014: 613–14; J. F. Osborne 2021: 62–63.

28. On all of the above, including the Taita inscription as well as the various rulers, see Harrison 2009a: 171, 173–74, 2009b: 175, 179, 2013: 62–64, 77, 2014: 396, 402–4, 409, 2016: 254, 2021: 327, 341–44; Hawkins 2009, 2011; Kohlmeyer 2009, 2011; Bryce 2012: 128–31, 206–7, 223–24, 2014: 111, 121, 2016b: 68–69, 77–78; 2020: 110–13; Aro 2013: 246–47; J. F. Osborne 2013: 776–77, 2014: 199–201, 204–5, 211n2; Weeden 2013: 12–18, figs. 2–3, and table 2; Dinçol et al. 2015: table 1 and passim; Emanuel 2015; Hawkins and Weeden 2016: 11; Younger 2016: 123–27, 133; J. F. Osborne et al. 2019; Welton et al. 2019: 294; Manning, Lorentzen, et al. 2020: 4, 24; J. F. Osborne 2021: 63–64, 117–21. See Grayson 1996: 9 (A.0.102.1) on the mention by Shalmaneser III; also now Bryce 2020: 113 and Tayinat Archaeological Project, https://tayinat.artsci.utoronto.ca/the-toronto-expedition/king-shupiluliumas-ii, on the 2012 discovery of a statue bearing an inscription of Suppiluliuma II.

29. Woolley 1920: 86; also now Gilibert 2011: 25–30; J.F. Osborne 2021: 98–99.

30. Marchetti 2012: 134–36; see also Gilibert 2011: 31–38; Middleton 2020e: 18–22; now J. F. Osborne 2021: 99–100.

31. On the inscription from 870 BC, see Hawkins 2000: 75; Yamada 2000: 72–75; Bryce 2012: 213, 2014: 117–18; Marchetti 2012: 146; Brown and Smith 2016: 25; Hawkins and Weeden 2016: 13; J. F. Osborne 2021: 148–49. On the specific Balawat bands, see Grayson 1991: 345 (A.0.101.80) and 349 (A.0.101.90), also 347 (A.0.101.85); Curtis and Tallis 2008: 32, 35, 54, figs. 11–12, 17–18, 57–58.

32. As others have noted previously; see, e.g., Gilibert 2011: 12–14, with previous references.

33. Grayson 1991: 217 (A.0.101.1); see also Bryce 2012: 213; J. F. Osborne 2021: 148–49.

34. Grayson 1991: 225 (A.0.101.2) and 275 (A.0.101.23); Radner 2011: 738–39; Schachner 2020b: 1121.

35. See Kroll et al. 2012: 6, 9.

36. Van Loon 1966: 1–2; Zimansky 1985: 1, 4, 2011: 548–49; Kuhrt 1995: 548; Radner 2011: 734–35; Kroll et al. 2012: 1; Liverani 2014: 521–22; Fuchs 2017: 250. On the bronze cauldrons and shields, see, e.g., van Loon 1966: 11–12, 84–87, 103–18; Kuhrt 1995: 560; but see now Curtis 2012; Kroll et al. 2012: 25.

37. See, e.g., van Loon 1966: 7; Zimansky 1985: 49–50, with further references; Kuhrt 1995: 550; Kroll et al. 2012: 10; Liverani 2014: 521–22; Fuchs 2017: 250, 260; and see Grayson 1991 and

1996 for mentions of campaigning in Nairi by Tiglath-Pileser I, Aššur-bel-kala, Adad-nirari II, Tukulti-Ninurtu II, Aššurnasirpal II, and also Shalmaneser III.

38. Zimansky 1985: 49; Radner 2011: 738–39; Bryce 2012: 242; Curtis 2012: 429; Kroll et al. 2012: 10; Liverani 2014: 521–22; Frahm 2017: 171, 2023: 109; Fuchs 2017: 250.

39. King 1915: 21–22; Grayson 1996: 27–29 (A.0.102.25), 140 (A.0.102.63–64).

40. See Taylor 1865; King 1915: 21; Grayson 1996: 14–15 (A.0.102.2); also now MacGinnis and Matney 2009.

41. King 1915: 21–22, pls. 1–6.

42. Translations following Grayson 1996: 16–17, 20–21 (A.0.102.2).

43. For the translation of Year 7 on the Black Obelisk, see Grayson 1996: 65–66 (A.0.102.14). For the translation of Year 15 on the Monolith Inscription, see Grayson 1996: 39 (A.0.102.6); see also MacGinnis and Matney 2009 for a variation on the translation as well as a briefer version on the Black Monolith rendered in Grayson 1996: 67 (A.0.102.14).

44. See Taylor 1865: 41–43; I owe this reference to Harmansah 2007: 184–85. See now MacGinnis and Matney 2009: 33, with illustrations, including of the actual relief at the Tigris Tunnel and on Balawat Band X; see previously Kreppner 2002: 372, 374–75, figs. 9–13; Schachner 2009.

45. For the illustration on Balawat Band X, see King 1915: 13–14, 30–31, pl. 59. For those on Bands I and II, see King 1915: 22, pls. 7–12; Grayson 1996: 141 (A.0.102.65).

46. King 1915: 27–28, pls. 37–42; Grayson 1996: 143 (A.0.102.71). On the Monolith Inscription, see Grayson 1996: 20 (A.0.102.2).

47. Van Loon 1966: 7; Zimansky 1985: 49–51; Kuhrt 1995: 552 (table 29), 554; Radner 2011: 734; Kroll et al. 2012: 10; Fuchs 2017: 251.

48. Translation of CTU 1 A 01–01, following the online Electronic Corpus of Urartian Texts (eCUT) Project: http://oracc.museum.upenn.edu/ecut/pager; also van Loon 1966: 7–8; Zimansky 1985: 50–51, 2011: 554; Kuhrt 1995: 550; Radner 2011: 736, 742, and the caption to fig. 33.1; Bryce 2012: 242; Frahm 2017: 170–71. See also van Loon 1966: 10–11 and Zimansky 1985: 59 on inscriptions left by Sarduri's successors. Note that Sarduri is called the "king of Nairi" rather than "king of Urartu," perhaps again showing the interlinked nature of the two entities. See, e.g., van Loon 1966: 7, who suggests that it was Sarduri I who "extended his power over most of the Nairi countries and founded the kingdom of Urartu" (this despite the fact that Aramu is already called "the Urartian" prior to Sarduri's reign).

49. Zimansky 1985: 50; Kuhrt 1995: 552 (table 29), 554; Grayson 1996: 14 (A.0.102.2); Radner 2011: 738–39, 745; Kroll et al. 2012: 10–14. See also Grayson 1996: 65–66, 68 (A.0.102.14) for several mentions of campaigns against Aramu and then a campaign against Sarduri, all recorded on Shalmaneser III's Black Obelisk (on which see more below). See esp. inscription CTU 1 A 04–01, which lists the first three and their relationships, on the online Electronic Corpus of Urartian Texts (eCUT) Project (http://oracc.museum.upenn.edu/ecut/pager); most of them also have a number of individual inscriptions that can be found in the same online corpus. For the list of rulers and their proposed order, which is disputed after the rule of Sarduri II, see http://oracc.museum.upenn.edu/ecut/urartianrulersandtheirinscriptions/index.html.

50. Van Loon 1966: 7; Kuhrt 1995: 554; Curtis 2012: 429; Kroll et al. 2012: 6, 22.

51. Radner 2011: 742–43; Kroll et al. 2012: 24; Frahm 2017: 170–71; see also Zimansky 1985: 69 on Urartian texts that mention vineyards, as well as orchards and grain fields.

52. See Grayson 1996: 9–10 (A.0.102.1) and 16, 23 (A.0.102.2); Bryce 2012: 219, 221, 2014: 119, 2020: 113; J. F. Osborne 2013: 776–77; Weeden 2013: 12, 15–16, fig. 4; Harrison 2014: 408–9, fig. 5; also Tayinat Archaeological Project, https://tayinat.artsci.utoronto.ca/the-toronto-expedition/king-shupiluliumas-ii.

53. King 1915: 26, pls. 31–36; Grayson 1996: 142 (A.0.102.70).

54. Gilibert 2011: 15–16, with translation given in table 8; see Grayson 1996: 10 (A.0.102.1), 16 (A.0.102.2). See also Brown 2008a: 341–44.

55. English translation following O'Connor 1977: 19, 21–22, after Donner and Röllig 2002: 13, as cited initially by Gilibert 2011: 15–16. See also Brown 2008a: 341–44; Gilibert 2011: 15–16, 79–84; J. F. Osborne 2021: 44, 74–82, 110–12, 142–43, 146, 148, 160–62, 183–84.

56. See Grayson 1996: 9 (A.0.102.1), 23 (A.0.102.2), 38 (A.0.102.6 ii 69). See also Hawkins 2000: 75, 2009: 167; Bryce 2012: 130–31, 223, 2014: 122, 125; Brown and Smith 2016: 25; Hawkins and Weeden 2016: 13; Peker 2016: 49 (table 2).

57. Peker 2016: 47–49; Marchetti and Peker 2018: 81–90.

58. See Peker 2016: 47–49; Marchetti and Peker 2018: 81–90.

59. Translation (merging the data from several inscriptions) following Peker 2016: 47–49 and table 2; Marchetti and Peker 2018: 95–97. See also Marchetti 2012: 146–47; Hawkins and Peker 2014: 108.

60. Hawkins 2000: 36, 72, 75–79, 123–24, 128–29, 131; Gilibert 2011: 12–14, 41–50; Bryce 2012; 84, 98, 280–81; Hawkins and Peker 2014: 108–9; Brown and Smith 2016: 25–26; Hawkins and Weeden 2016: 13; J. F. Osborne 2021: 78, 83, 100–102, fig. 3.7.

61. Gilibert 2011: 6, citing Bunnens 2000: 12–19; see also d'Alfonso 2020.

Chapter Five. In the Shadow of the Ruined Palaces

1. Schliemann 1880: 132–37 (no. 213).

2. See discussions in, e.g., Crielaard 2006: 278–80; Eder 2006: 550–52; M. Lloyd 2013: 112–13; Lemos 2014: 169–70; Knodell 2021: 129–31; all citing the work of Michael Wedde (e.g., 1999, 2000, 2006).

3. Deger-Jalkotzy 2008: 392. See also, e.g., I. Morris 1989: 505–6, 1999: 60–61, 65–66; Lemos 2002: 1. In archaeological terminology, this is the Late Helladic (LH) IIIC and Submycenaean periods, from ca. 1190 to 1070 BC. See also now Ruppenstein 2020a; Van Damme 2023: 172–73 and table 4; and the papers in the volume edited by Jung and Kardamaki (2023).

4. The literature on Homer is vast, even on a narrow topic such as the Bronze Age and Iron Age elements to be found in the *Iliad* and the *Odyssey*; see, for instance, some of the publications listed in the "Further Reading" section of Cline 2013.

5. See, for instance, in just the past few years, extremely important books by Murray (2017) and Knodell (2021); the volume edited by Middleton (2020a); and the two-volume set edited by Lemos and Kotsonas (2020); prior to that, we have the numerous books and articles by I. Morris, Whitley, and Papadopoulos, among others, which appeared in the 1990s and early 2000s, as well as Dickinson 2006a and the volume edited by Deger-Jalkotzy and Lemos (2006), to name only some of the most prominent publications that have appeared in English; many others have appeared in German, French, Italian, and other languages.

6. For a publication of the cemetery and grave goods at Perati in English, see Iakovides 1980; see also now subsequent discussions on Perati and the nearby site of Porto Rafti in Murray 2017: 86–89, 258–59, 2018a; Murray and Lis 2023; and briefly in Ruppenstein 2020a: 570–71.

7. Mühlenbruch 2020, with earlier references. See Maran 2006, 2016, 2023: 235–39; Papadimitriou 2006; Deger-Jalkotzy 2008: 397; Mühlenbruch 2009, 2020; Cohen, Maran, and Vetters 2010; Wallace 2010: 92; M. Lloyd 2013: 110–11; Lemos 2014: 162–64, 178–80; Middleton 2017c: 148–50, 2020c: 12, 2020e: 11–14; Murray 2017: 89–90, 258, 2018b: 226–27; Eder and Lemos 2020: 140; Manolova 2020: 1202; Maran and Papadimitriou 2020; Maran and Wright 2020; Steele 2020: 254–55; Van Damme 2023: 112–13; see also Dickinson 2006a: 60–61.

8. See LaFayette Hogue 2016 on this new evidence for a post-destruction reuse in small portions of the palace of Nestor at Pylos; also Davis and Stocker 2020: 677. See also now discussion by Maran 2023: 235.

9. See I. Morris 1999: 60–61, 2000: 78, 2006: 78; Murray 2017: 129–30, 210–11, 246, 275–81; also Deger-Jalkotzy 2008: 399–401, 406–7; Lemos 2014: 183–84.

10. Dickinson 2006b: 102, 116–17, 121; Nakassis 2020: 276. See also discussions in Deger-Jalkotzy 2008: 402–5; Wallace 2010: 88, 92–93, 102; Eder and Lemos 2020: 134–36, 149–50; also Enverova 2012 for an interesting consideration of applying the concept of heterarchy to the events of this period on mainland Greece; now also Knodell 2021: 152–53.

11. For discussions regarding *basileus* and *wanax* at this time, see, e.g., Antonaccio 2002: 13–14, 2006; Crielaard 2006, 2011; Mazarakis Ainian 2006; Palaima 2006; Eder 2007: 570, 572; Deger-Jalkotzy 2008: 403; Eder and Lemos 2020: 135–36; Maran and Papadimitriou 2020: 702; Knodell 2021: 169–70; also Boyes and Steele 2020: 12; Steele 2020: 253–54 on the loss of writing.

12. See, e.g., Weiberg and Finné 2018: 595; also Kramer-Hajos 2016: 166–79, 2020: 77, 79, 82; Finné, Holmgren, et al. 2017: 10–11; Livieratou 2020: 103–4; and Maran 2023, among others.

13. Knodell 2021: 5, 114–15; see now also Molloy 2022: 31 (online version).

14. She goes on to say, however, that the twelfth and eleventh centuries BC should be seen as the last stages of Mycenaean civilization rather than the first stretch of a Dark Age; see Deger-Jalkotzy 2008: 392. See also the very similar statements by Eder 2006: 550; also Maggidis 2020: 116–17; Dibble and Finné 2021: 59; and now also Maran 2023: 231.

15. See, in particular, Wallace 2006 (esp. 620, 641, 644), 2010 (esp. 51–104), 2017 (esp. 68, 71, 78), 2018 (esp. 325); 2020 (esp. 248); see now also comments in Pollard 2021. Imports to the island did drop, however; see Hoffman 1997 and the catalog by Jones 2000; also comments by Murray 2017: 6, 75–76, 85–86, 91, 100–101, 117; Wallace 2018: 395.

16. On the results of his archaeological surveys, see primarily Nowicki 2000, now cited by numerous scholars including, e.g., Deger-Jalkotzy 2008: 397–98; Lemos 2014: 174–77; Kourou 2016: 352; Haggis 2020: 1073; as well as Wallace 2006: 623–24, 628, 2010: 58–59; Murray 2017: 6; and others. See now also Pollard 2022. On piracy, see e.g., Samaras 2015; Hitchcock and Maeir 2019.

17. See again Wallace 2006, 2010, 2017, 2020; also Coldstream 2006: 581–82; D'Agata 2006: 400; Prent 2014: 651, 654; Hatzaki and Kotsonas 2020: 1036; Pollard 2021; Watrous 2021: 197–98.

18. Tsipopoulou 2005; see also the other papers in that conference volume. I thank Louise Hitchcock for reminding me of this fact; see also previously the brief mention in Cline 2021: 48 and previously Cline 1994: xvii–xviii, 9–11, 35, 106.

19. See Rollston 2008: 86–88, with references; also Kourou 2008a: 365–66, fig. 5, 2016: 57–58; Iacovou 2014c: 802; Bourogiannis 2018b: 250, 2021: 102; Waal 2018: 110; Richey 2019: 229; Sogas 2019: 412; Hodos 2020: 100, 185–86, fig. 6.3; Steele 2020: 263; S. P. Morris 2022: 100–101; Papadopoulos 2022: 143–44, fig. 7.1; previously S. P. Morris 1992a: 159; Hoffman 1997: 12–13, with references; Crielaard 1998: 198; Aubet 2001: 54. On the proposed "cup of x, son of y" translation, see most recently Bourogiannis 2020: 154–55, 2021: 102, both also with references.

20. See esp. Waal 2018: (esp. 86, 96, 103–8, 111–12), 2020, with references to earlier publications; see also the discussions, both pro and con, in Rollston 2019: 385–86, with references; Bourogiannis 2018a: 75–76, 2018b: 241–44, 250, 2020, 2021; see now also Kotsonas 2022, though dealing with a slightly later period. See previously Bell 2006: 90, with references; also now Hodos 2020: 194–95. Note that Mazar 1994: 54 points out that, from the Eastern Mediterranean side of things, Joseph Naveh was already stating back in 1972 that "the Canaanite/Phoenician alphabet was transmitted to the Greeks during the 11th or early 10th centuries B.C."—see, e.g., Naveh 1989, for an example of his later arguments.

21. Rollston 2010: 20, fig. 2.1, 2019: 376–77.

22. Waal 2018: 110, 2020; Bourogiannis 2018b: 235.

23. See, e.g., Hodos 2020: 197; Kotsonas 2022: 168, 177–78.

24. See Wachter 2021: 23, 25; also Knodell 2021: 215–20, 254–55; López-Ruiz 2021: 232; S. P. Morris 2022: 100–101. Previously Gnanadesikan (2009: 208–14) envisioned a similar scenario and created an imaginary scene with a Greek and a Phoenician as a possible example of the first occasion of a Greek learning about the alphabet.

25. I. Morris 2005: 8, 2000: 195–207; citing Snodgrass 1993: 37.

26. I. Morris 1989: 505–6, 1996: 1–3, 4–5, 1999: 60–62, 2000: 78, citing in various places Snodgrass 1971: 228–68, 1980, 1983, 1988; Desborough 1972; Coldstream 1977.

27. I. Morris 1989: 506, 515, 1996: 4–5, 2006: 76; see previously, e.g., Snodgrass 1971. We should note that Morris's suggestions that there was a decline in trade with the Eastern Mediterranean is now open to debate; see Murray 2017.

28. I. Morris 1989: 513, 2005: 2, 8–9, 2006: 74.

29. Coldstream 2006: 584–86.

30. Quote from Kotsonas 2019: 10. On the size and sandwiching of the Iron Age remains at Knossos, see, e.g., Coldstream 2006: 584–86; Kotsonas 2019: 2, 6; Hatzaki and Kotsonas 2020: 1034, 1036–38. On the results of the survey, see now Kotsonas et al. 2018 and Kotsonas 2019, both with previous references; also Atherton 2016; Blakemore 2016; and "Early Iron Age Knossos Was Much Larger Than Originally Thought," Sci News, January 11, 2016, https://www.sci.news/archaeology/early-iron-age-knossos-larger-than-originally-thought-03552.html. On all of the above, see also now Kotsonas 2021; also Pollard 2021 on the Early Iron Age cemeteries at Knossos.

31. H. W. Catling 1993, 1995: 124–25, 1996; see also Crielaard 1998: 187–88; Muhly and Kassianidou 2012: 124; S. P. Morris 2022: 104–5.

32. H. W. Catling 1996: 646–47; see also H. W. Catling 1995: 124, 126–27; Kourou 2008a: 363. See now also the further description and discussion in Kotsonas 2018: 15–16; Hatzaki and Kotsonas 2020: 1038–41.

33. H. W. Catling 1996: 646–47. Previously, in H. W. Catling 1995: 127, the relevant passage from the *Iliad* was quoted in full, showing the "biography" of the well-traveled boar's-tusk

helmet that Odysseus was given (*Il.* 10.261–71, citing the Penguin translation by E. V. Rieu). The boar's-tusk helmet in this North Cemetery grave at Knossos would have had a similar history, since they were no longer being made at the time this sub-Minoan warrior was buried.

34. H. W. Catling 1996: 648–49.

35. H. W. Catling 1995: 128.

36. H. W. Catling 1995: 128; see now also comments by Kourou 2008a: 363–64.

37. Quotations from Muhly 2003: 24–25 (also 2011: 49–50) and Iacovou 2007: 467 (citing also Iacovou 1999: 18); see also Iacovou 2012: 214; previously Crielaard 1998: 187–88.

38. Kotsonas 2018: 1, 9–10, 21–22; see now also Hatzaki and Kotsonas 2020: 1038–41.

39. Kotsonas 2018: 14–15, 25–26.

40. I. Morris 2006: 76. The site had also flourished previously, from the Early Bronze Age onward to the Late Bronze Age, and then continued into the Early Iron Age before finally being abandoned ca. 700 BC.

41. R.W.V. Catling and Lemos 1990. On Lefkandi overall, see, e.g., Popham and Sackett 1980: 1–3; Lemos 2006: 519–21, 2014: 171–73, 2020: 791–93.

42. On the possible sacrifice of the woman, see remarks by Antonaccio 2002: 20–21, citing previous publications by other scholars. However, as she states, "neither burial has been published fully, and further discussion of the individuals . . . must await the final publication." It has now been twenty years since Antonaccio's remarks, and forty years since the initial excavations at Lefkandi, but it is hoped that the full publication of this burial will come soon (I. Lemos, pers. comm., September 4, 2021). Study, or restudy, of the woman's bones, if they are still available, might resolve the question, if cut marks are noted anywhere on them. On all of this, either generally or specifically, see esp. Popham, Touloupa, and Sackett 1982; H. W. Catling 1993, 1995: 126; also I. Morris 1996: 3 (citing R.W.V. Catling and Lemos 1990 and Popham, Calligas, and Sackett 1993), 1999: 62, 2000: 218–22; Antonaccio 1993: 51–52, 2002; R. Osborne 1996: 41–43; Crielaard 2016: 56–59; Hodos 2020: 99–100, 104–5; Papadopoulos 2022: 145, fig. 7.2.

43. See, e.g., Popham, Touloupa, and Sackett 1982; Calligas and Popham 1993: 1–4; H. W. Catling 1993, 1995: 126, 1996: 647–48; Crielaard and Driessen 1994; I. Morris 1996: 3–4, 1999: 62, 2000: 218–19, 2006: 76, all with earlier references. See now also discussions on all of this in Lemos 2002: 162–68, 2006: 521–22, 2020: 792–93; Muhly 2003: 25; J. M. Hall 2007: 62–64; Kourou 2008a: 364–65, 2012: 39–40; Sherratt 2010: 132–35, 137–38; Crielaard 2016: 56–59; Murray 2017: 95–100; Bourogiannis 2018a: 54–55, 73–74; Hodos 2020: 163–64; Knodell 2021: 162–67; López-Ruiz 2021: 48–50.

44. Lemos 2020: 804.

45. See, e.g., I. Morris 1999: 62; Kourou 2008b: 307–8, 2012: 39–40; Sherratt 2010: 130; Bourogiannis 2018a: 54, 73–74; Stampolidis 2019: 501; Papadopoulos 2022: 149.

46. I. Morris 1989: 508, 1996: 4–5, 1999: 62, 2000: 78.

47. Kiderlen et al. 2016.

48. Snodgrass 1971: 402.

49. Smithson 1968, 1969; Liston and Papadopoulos 2004. For the quote, see Smithson 1968: 78, repeated in full by Liston and Papadopoulos 2004: 12.

50. Smithson 1968: 78–83, and the catalog on 83–116, pls. 18–33; Liston and Papadopoulos 2004: 9, 11–15; Papadopoulos and Smithson 2017: 124–76.

51. Smithson 1968: 83, quoted again in full by Liston and Papadopoulos 2004: 14 and by Papadopoulos and Smithson 2017: 982–83; see also Papadopoulos and Smithson 2017: 131.

52. Liston and Papadopoulos 2004: 15–23; see also now Papadopoulos and Smithson 2017: 3; Olsen 2020: 306–7, fig. 2.8.2.

53. Blegen 1952: 279–94, with catalog on 289–93; see now Papadopoulos and Smithson 2017: 2, 9, 104–5.

54. Blegen 1952: 279–82, 289.

55. See again Blegen 1952: 279–82, 289; see now Papadopoulos and Smithson 2017: 104–18, with catalog on 108–18. On such ritual "killing" of weapons specifically in the Early Iron Age Aegean, see, e.g., M. Lloyd 2015, 2018.

56. Coldstream 2006: 588–89; D'Agata 2006: 403; Wallace 2006: 621.

57. Hatzaki and Kotsonas 2020: 104–42, with earlier references; see also the original publication (Boardman 1967) and subsequent discussions and disagreements, including by Hoffman 1997: 17, 196–245; Kotsonas 2006; Stampolidis and Kotsonas 2006: 349–51; Prent 2014: 660; Murray 2017: 188; Sogas 2019: 412–14; and S. P. Morris 2022: 102, among many others.

58. I. Morris 1996: 1, 6. See also I. Morris 1989: 514; see also earlier discussions in I. Morris 1987.

59. Kourou 2012: 41, with earlier references; Bell 2016: 97; Bourogiannis 2018a: 65; Stampolidis 2019: 495–96; Stampolidis et al. 2019. On Al Mina, see Kourou 2012: 41–42; previously, e.g., esp. Boardman 1980, 38–40, 1990.

60. Whitley 1991: 9.

61. Note that this date is not as fixed in stone as many might expect but apparently comes to us courtesy of calculations done by Aristotle, among others; see S. P. Morris 1989: 48; Swaddling 1999: 7, 10; Crowther 2007: 5–6; Nelson 2007: 48–54; Papadopoulos and Smithson 2017: 975n14.

Chapter Six. From Collapse to Resilience

1. See Cline 2021; see also now Molloy 2022, who has discussed whether the crisis also extended up into Europe.

2. Bavel et al. 2020: 141–42, drawing on previous work by Tainter and others, state: "Although a commonly accepted definition of societal collapse is hard to come by, many scholars agree that it represents a rapid, fundamental transformation of the social, political, and economic structures of a complex society for multiple generations." See now Jackson et al. 2022; also Centeno et al. 2022: 63, who state: "If there is one central theme in the collapse literature it is that there is a notable disagreement about the meaning of the term 'collapse.'"

3. McAnany and Yoffee 2010: 5.

4. I am indebted to one of the anonymous peer reviewers of the penultimate manuscript for suggesting the concise summations in these summarizing paragraphs, though I have tinkered with the phrasing.

5. On migrations at the end of the Late Bronze Age, see again Knapp 2021 as well as Middleton 2018a, 2018b. On possible Luwian migrations, see, e.g., J. F. Osborne 2021. See also Drews 1992 on Herodotus and the Etruscans.

6. Langgut, Neumann, et al. 2014: 296.

7. For early discussions of this topic, see, e.g., Holling 1986; Holling, Carpenter, et al. 2002; Holling and Gunderson 2002; Berkes, Colding, and Folke 2003: 16–18; Redman and Kinzig 2003; Folke 2006; Walker and Salt 2006: 75–95; now also Faulseit 2016: 12–16, among others. See Weiberg 2012 for a recent application of this concept to the collapse of the Late Bronze Age Aegean; also Ellenblum 2012: 15–21; Lantzas 2016; S. O'Brien 2017; Saltini Semerari 2017: 546–48, 565–66, 569.

8. Definitions following Walker et al. 2004: 2. See also discussion in Bradtmöller, Grimm, and Riel-Salvatore 2017: 10–11.

9. See Kemp and Cline 2022; Newhard and Cline 2022.

10. See now the relevant discussions in Haldon, Chase, et al. 2020: 16–21, 31–33 and Haldon, Binois-Roman, et al. 2021: 237–38, especially if we suggest that it is a collapse of the entire system, at the same time as wondering how each of the individual pieces will have been affected and responded differently. Centeno et al. 2022: 63 state specifically that "what collapses is not necessarily an entire society or civilization, but instead the larger organizational framework."

11. I. Morris 2006: 72, 81–82, 84; see also Broodbank 2013: 506–7.

12. I. Morris 2006: 72; see also Yoffee 2006 on the concept of societal "regeneration" in this context.

13. For discussions of panarchy, the idea of which was originated by Holling in 2001, see also Gunderson and Holling 2002; Holling, Carpenter, et al. 2002; Holling and Gunderson 2002; Holling, Gunderson, and Ludwig 2002; Berkes, Colding, and Folke 2003: 18–19; Karkkainen 2005; Folke 2006; Kuecker and Hall 2011: 20; Budja 2015: 176–77; Bradtmöller, Grimm, and Riel-Salvatore 2017: 4; Saltini Semerari 2017: 546–48; Haldon, Binois-Roman, et al. 2021; also Kemp and Cline 2022; Newhard and Cline 2022. The concept of "punctuated equilibrium," borrowed from evolutionary biology and applied when we see sudden changes to a stable system, such as the Collapse at the end of the Late Bronze Age, is also relevant here, but for reasons of space I will simply refer the reader to Haldon, Chase, et al. 2020: 32; see also Cline, forthcoming, which was written independently but covers the same ground and comes to similar conclusions.

14. Note also the similarity to the discussion of complexity theory in *1177 B.C.*, in which I used the analogy of a single thrown rod wrecking the engine of an expensive car; see Cline 2021: 176.

15. See, e.g., Berkes, Colding, and Folke 2003; Walker and Salt 2006; and the various chapters in Miller and Rivera 2011 and Kapucu, Hawkins, and Rivera 2013. On the IPCC, see https://www.ipcc.ch/about/history.

16. See Kohler and Rockman 2020 on archaeology and the IPCC.

17. See Field et al. 2012. I am much indebted to Robert J. Lempert for information and for his insights regarding the various IPCC reports.

18. Lavell et al. 2012: 41.

19. Cutter et al. 2012: 296 (see also 293), with references; Handmer et al. 2012: 237, with references; Lavell et al. 2012: 42.

20. Cardona et al. 2012: 81, 86–87; Cutter et al. 2012: 300; Lavell et al. 2012: 36; K. O'Brien et al. 2012: 457, all with references.

21. The literature is immense; see previously Holling 1973 and the edited papers in Gunderson and Holling 2002; Berkes, Colding, and Folke 2003: 14–15; Gunderson 2003; Redman and Kinzig 2003; Walker et al. 2004; Redman 2005: 72–74; Folke 2006; Walker and Salt 2006: 1, 113, 119; Folke et al. 2010; McAnany and Yoffee 2010: 10; F. L. Edwards 2013: 24–25; Faulseit 2016:

12; Barnes et al. 2017; Bradtmöller, Grimm, and Riel-Salvatore 2017: 12–13; Middleton 2017b: 14–17, 2017c: 42–46; S. O'Brien 2017; Saltini Semerari 2017: 546; and now also Bavel et al. 2020: 35–37; Centeno et al. 2022: 70; Kemp and Cline 2022; Molloy 2022: 9 (online version). See also Haldon, Chase, et al. 2020: 13–15 for a discussion of collapse in the context of resilience theory, with specific points to be met.

22. The 2011 National Research Council definition can be found at doi.org/10.17226/13028: 4, 13–14; see also F. L. Edwards 2013: 29. A similar definition is used in the 2012 IPCC *SREX* publication; see Cardona et al. 2012: 75, with references; also the further discussions of resilience in Handmer et al. 2012: 238; Lavell et al. 2012: 34; K. O'Brien et al. 2012: 453, with references. The other definition cited is provided by Cox and Perry 2011: 395–96; see also most recently the relevant comments in Degroot et al. 2021: 542–43.

23. Cardona et al. 2012: 72–73, with references, including specific quote from Lavell 1999. See also originally Holling 2001: 394; now also Engle 2011.

24. Cardona et al. 2012: 73, with references; Lavell et al. 2012: 51 and table 1–1, with references. See also K. O'Brien et al. 2012: 459; Nicoll and Zerboni 2019; Bavel et al. 2020: 142–43.

25. Lavell et al. 2012: 53–54, with references; K. O'Brien et al. 2012: 443, 468, with references. See also Walker et al. 2004: 1–7 for their definitions of resiliency, adaptability, and transformability; also, e.g., McAnany and Yoffee 2010: 10–11; Barnes et al. 2017; most recently Bavel et al. 2020: 37–38; Jackson et al. 2022: 97. We might also consider the concept of "transformational adaptation," which refers to "actions that change the fundamental attributes of a system," specifically "in response to actual or expected impacts of climate change"; see Denton et al. 2014: 1121.

26. In particular, they see vulnerable groups as being more at risk from a potential disaster because of the various stressors or drivers that together threaten their "livelihoods, production, support infrastructure, and services." The question, of course, is what makes one society vulnerable and another less so, but one recent definition refers to the likelihood of a society suffering adversely when impacted by extreme events. See esp. Cardona et al. 2012: 69–72, 88, with full references to previous definitions and terminologies; Lavell et al. 2012: 34. The specific definition is "the propensity . . . to suffer adverse effects when impacted by hazard events." See now also Degroot et al. 2021: 540 on vulnerability and resilience. See also Bavel et al. 2020: 33–35 on vulnerability; their entire book, in fact, is titled *Disasters and History: The Vulnerability and Resilience of Past Societies.*

27. On fragility and society, see Dillehay and Wernke 2019: 9–10 and the other papers in the 2019 volume edited by Yoffee; Middleton 2020d; Maran 2023: 233–34, 241; also previously the relevant chapter in J. C. Scott's 2017 book *Against the Grain.*

28. Re the Phoenicians taking over from Ugarit, see, e.g., Markoe 2000: 26; Bell 2006: 101–2, 2009: 30, 2016: 102; see also more generally Aubet 2001: 113–14.

29. Redman and Kinzig 2003: 2 and fig. 3.

30. Weiberg 2012: 159.

31. See again Lavell et al. 2012: 53–54; K. O'Brien et al. 2012: 443, 468, with references.

32. Bell 2009: 38.

33. See also now the discussion in Kemp and Cline 2022.

34. See now Jung and Kardamaki 2023: 21–22; Maran 2023: 233–34, 241.

35. See, e.g., Weiberg et al. 2010; Adcock 2020.

36. See, e.g., the arguments by Wallace (2006, 2010, 2017, 2018, 2020) re Iron Age Crete, cited above. See also now Pollard 2021, 2022.

37. See, e.g., d'Alfonso 2020 regarding Anatolia and the aftermath of the Hittites, in which he briefly discusses resilience, reorganization, and transformation; also Adcock 2020: xvi, 1–4, 51–52.

38. Koch 2021: 92, 105.

39. For what it's worth, I have fluctuated between placing these southern Canaanites in categories 2, 4, and 5 during the course of writing. For the moment, I have settled on category 5 but remain open to being persuaded otherwise.

40. See Younker 1994 for a succinct summary of the various hypotheses.

41. See Mattingly 1994, with earlier references; also Finkelstein and Lipschits 2011; Finkelstein 2014.

42. Papadopoulos and Smithson 2017: 984, see also 973–74. See now also Knodell 2021: 251–52, 257; Maran 2023: 233–34; previously Weiberg 2012.

43. See now Newhard and Cline 2022. Maran 2023: 233–34 suggests other potential factors as well.

44. See Weiberg and Finné 2018: 595; also Finné, Holmgren, et al. 2017: 10–11; now Maran 2023: 237–39.

45. Maran 2023: 235–42.

46. On societal tipping points and the loss of resiliency, see Scheffer et al. 2009, 2021; Centeno et al. 2022: 66–67.

47. Adcock 2020: 54, also 59–65; Centeno et al. 2022: 64. See also Middleton 2017c: 18 and Kemp 2019; the latter poses in passing similar questions for the lower classes in the other societies at the time and concludes, "Collapse, then, is a double-edged sword. Sometimes it's a boon for subjects and a chance to restart decaying institutions. Yet it can also lead to the loss of population, culture and hardwon political structures."

48. See again Schachner 2020a, 2020b: 1109–12; also Seeher 2010; Genz 2013; Bryce 2016b, 2019; Middleton 2017c: 165, 172, 175–76; de Martino 2018; Maran 2023: 236–37.

49. Postgate 1992: 247, 249; see also Fales 2011: 13–14, 30–31, citing and agreeing with Postgate; also Younger 2017: 196; Düring 2020: 136.

50. Neumann and Parpola 1987: 171–76, table 2; Postgate 1992: 249; Düring 2020: 134.

51. See, e.g., the discussion of Assyrian society and other related details in Kuhrt 1995: 362–64, 478; Podany 2014: 100–108.

52. See Taleb 2004.

53. Handmer et al. 2012: 235. See also, e.g., Stuckenberg and Contento 2018.

54. See, e.g., Knodell 2021: 5, 114–15, as referenced above, and numerous other scholars who have touched on these topics as well, esp. Susan Sherratt and Carol Bell.

55. See Nassim Nicholas Taleb, in his book *Fooled by Randomness* (Taleb 2004: 12).

56. Eisenstadt 1988: 242; quoted also in Schwartz 2006: 6 and cited, with further discussion, by McAnany and Yoffee 2010: 5–6. See also now Centeno et al. 2022: 64–65.

57. Eisenstadt 1988: 243. Note, however, that I agree with Bavel et al. 2020: 142–43, who say specifically that ". . . we should make it clear that societal collapse was the exception rather than the rule throughout history—and even some of the so-called 'classic' collapses may be conceived of more as transitions and adaptations rather than as the destruction of all social, economic, and political structures."

58. For similar situations, see Storey and Storey 2016: 99, 111–12, 119; their discussions regarding the end of the Roman Empire and the Classic Maya collapse ring true for our examination here as well, including "that there is almost always regeneration or resiliency but not necessarily in the same place as before nor in the same cultural manifestation."

59. To quote Benjamin Porter of UC Berkeley: "Evidence . . . indicates that groups recovered at different rates and followed different trajectories of development." He also observes, "Each polity . . . followed a distinct trajectory structured by historical, geographic, and environmental factors" (Porter 2016: 385, 390). Porter is talking specifically about the Iron Age II period in the Levant, but he might just as well be talking about everyone else as well, for his observations hold true for the Aegean and Eastern Mediterranean in general in the centuries following the Collapse.

60. K. O'Brien et al. 2012: 441, with references.

61. Schwartz 2006: 5–6 (citing Yoffee and Cowgill 1988) states that "collapse usually entails some or all of the following: the fragmentation of states into smaller political entities; the partial abandonment or complete desertion of urban centers, along with the loss or depletion of the centralizing functions; the breakdown of regional economic systems; and the failure of civilization or ideologies. . . . [R]arely does collapse involve the complete disappearance of a group of people."

62. See https://www.thewoodeneffect.com/you-must-prepare-to-succeed. The original quote is often credited to Benjamin Franklin, but that may be erroneous. I am indebted to Mitchell Allen for input and discussions regarding these summative paragraphs (pers. comm., June 20, 2022).

63. Megginson 1963: 4. I thank Robert Cargill for bringing this quote to my attention.

64. On cascading failures and synchronous failures, see, e.g., Centeno et al. 2022: 68–69.

Epilogue. End of a Dark Age

1. Again, as Muhly (2011: 48) notes, "The loss of the art of writing is the defining characteristic of a Dark Age, but it remains a symptom, not the cause of such a period." See also Snodgrass 1971: 2 and now Sherratt 2020: 196–97 on the characteristics of a dark age. See also previously Tainter 1988: 4, 19–20, 193, 197; 1999: 989–91, 1030; also Chew 2001: 9–10, 60–62, 2005: 52–58, 67–70, 2007: xvi, 6–10, 13–14, 16–17nn9–10, 79–83, 94–99, 2008: 92–93, 120–21, 130–31 for his definitions and characteristics, as well as specifically on what he sees as the Dark Ages in Greece following the Collapse; relevant to this are T. D. Hall's (2014: 82–84) comments on the first edition of *1177 B.C.* For more recent relevant discussions, see also now Middleton 2017a, 2017c: 46; Scott 2017: 213–18.

2. I. Morris 1997: 97, 106, 129, also 2000: 78–106 (chap. 3). See now also the very thorough discussion by Kotsonas 2016: 239–70, who points specifically to Gilbert Murray's book *The Rise of the Greek Epic*, which appeared in 1907 (Kotsonas 2016: 242).

3. Page 1962: 22; quoted as one of several examples in Muhly 2011: 49. See also, e.g., Coulson 1990: 7, 9–10; Coldstream 1992–3: 8, 1998; Muhly 2003: 23.

4. Starr 1961: 77.

5. See, e.g., I. Morris 2000: 92–102, discussing Snodgrass 1971; Desborough 1972 (also, previously, 1964); and Coldstream 1977; see also discussions of the same in Whitley 1991 and Dickinson 2006a: 3–5. See now also Kotsonas 2020: 82–83, who credits both Starr and Moses Finley as

having "revived the concept of the Greek Dark Age(s) and passed it on to scholars like Snodgrass and Desborough, who wrote the homonymous syntheses in the early 1970s." Personally, I am not as convinced that they "revived the concept" as much as they simply continued using it.

6. On the quote, see Starr 1992: 2–3; also Coulson 1990: 7; Muhly 2003: 26–27, 2011: 50 (citing this specific quote); Sherratt 2020: 196–97.

7. Quotations taken from S. P. Morris 1989: 48, 1992a: 140 (and see also 148). See also I. Morris 1997: 98, 111, 115, 117, 122–23, 125–28, 130, 2006: 81. He cites, in particular, S. P. Morris 1992a: 140, 1992b; Papadopoulos 1993. There were some die-hard holdouts as recently as the 1990s who still regarded this period in Greece as dark and as "an age of poverty, poor communications, and isolation from the outside world" (cited by Muhly 2003: 23, who gives a few examples); see also, e.g., Robin Osborne of Cambridge University, who wrote in 1996: "The general impression that we get is of contracted horizons: no big buildings, no multiple graves, no impersonal communication, limited contact with a wider world. . . . Hence the gloom" (R. Osborne 1996: 32). However, see now also the relevant discussions by Kotsonas 2016: 262, 2020: 85; Bourogiannis 2018a: 43 (quoting Muhly 2011: 48); Murray 2018c: 19, 21–22, 28, 44, 46; Waal 2018: 109, 2020. Most recently Van Damme (2023: 112) has stated, "Originally described as a 'Dark Age,' this period [in Greece] is now acknowledged as a dynamic time of innovation and exchange characterized by an increase in social and geographic mobility."

8. Jeffers 2013: 3. Similarly, Brian Brown, in his 2008 dissertation on North Syrian urbanism from 1200 to 800 BC, notes, "The term 'Dark Age,' with its connotations of linear decline and regression, is . . . somewhat of a misnomer" and states further that recent research indicates "this term is not entirely accurate" (Brown 2008b: 2, 8–9).

9. Porter 2016: 386; Sherratt 2003: 37, see also 38–40. See also previously Niemeyer 2006: 144: ". . . in the archaeology of the Near East this 'Dark Age' currently seems to be undergoing a re-evaluation."

10. See Whitley 1991: 5; also Coulson 1990: 7–10. See also subsequent discussion by Dickinson 2006a: 1, who agrees with Whitley's statement.

11. Overall, see Papadopoulos 1993 (with rebuttals by I. Morris 1993 and Whitley 1993), 1996a, 1996b, 2014; Papadopoulos and Smithson 2017: 974–76. For specific quotes, see Papadopoulos 1993: 195; Papadopoulos and Smithson 2017: 975. On the rise of the *polis*, as well as the importance of iron, in the context of the "Dark Ages" in Greece, see Chew 2007: 105–6, 186–87, 2008: 24, 92–93, 120–21, 130–31. See also Muhly, who stated more than a decade ago, "Darkness implies disturbed social and economic conditions resulting from the breakdown of an existing political structure. That is certainly what happened in Greece by the late 12th century BC. But the cultural isolation created by such darkness is not necessarily an unmitigated disaster, for cultural isolation carries within itself the opportunities for retrenchment, consolidation and rebirth" (Muhly 2011: 48, citing also the discussions by Starr 1961). See now also Scott 2017: 213–17. On the alpha phase, see again Walker et al. 2004: 2.

12. For specific quotes, see Papadopoulos 1993: 197, 2014: 181; Papadopoulos and Smithson 2017: 974 (quoting Harland 1941: 429), 976. See also R. Osborne 1996: 37, who says that "we are obliged to conclude that the Greeks of the archaic period knew nothing about the Dark Age."

13. See also previously Cline 2014: xv, 9, 171–73 and, e.g., Bunnens 2000: 13; Kourou 2008a: 361; Bryce 2020: 106; Hodos 2022: 215.

Author's Note and Acknowledgments

1. Papadopoulos 2014: 181; his comments have been subsequently quoted and cited by a number of scholars, including, e.g., Murray 2017: 10n35. See also, e.g., Papadopoulos 1993: 194–95, 2014: 181; Iacovou 2005a: 130, 2007: 461–62; Papadopoulos and Smithson 2017: 18–19, 975–76; also Kearns 2015: 34; Murray 2017: 10n35; Saltini Semerari 2017: 551; Wallace 2018: 309; and recently the preface to Lemos and Kotsonas 2020: xxiii; Knodell 2021: 1–2, 7–8, 10–11, 13–14, 119; López-Ruiz 2021: 4–5. Although there are literally thousands of publications available for one or another of the relevant societies pertaining to either the Bronze Age or the Iron Age, there are few that attempt a synthetic approach. However, one of the briefest and most accessible accounts enumerating the transition from Bronze Age to Iron Age and the new/revised civilizations that emerge after the Collapse is a highly recommended essay by Elizabeth Carter and Sarah Morris in the volume that accompanied a wonderful exhibit titled *From Assyria to Iberia* that was held at the Metropolitan Museum of Art in 2014; see Carter and Morris 2014.

2. Cline 2007: xiv–xv. I also said there that "for every book, article, and argument that I cite here, there are dozens more that I either do not have the room to mention or have chosen not to include for one reason or another. I apologize in advance if anyone's favorite book or article has been left out." The same is most certainly applicable here. I am also fully aware that any number of other relevant books and articles will appear while this book is in press or soon after it is published, but consideration of those will obviously have to be left for a future revised edition.

REFERENCES

Ancient Sources

Foster, B. R. 2005. *Before the Muses: An Anthology of Akkadian Literature*. Bethesda, MD: CDL Press.

Grayson, A. K. [1975] 2000. *Assyrian and Babylonian Chronicles*. Reprint of 1975 ed. Locust Valley, NY: J. J. Augustin.

Grayson, A. K. 1987. *Assyrian Rulers of the Third and Second Millennia BC (to 1115 BC)*. Toronto: University of Toronto Press.

Grayson, A. K. 1991. *Assyrian Rulers of the Early First Millennium BC: II (1114–859 BC)*. Toronto: University of Toronto Press.

Grayson, A. K. 1996. *Assyrian Rulers of the Early First Millennium BC: II (858–745 BC)*. Toronto: University of Toronto Press.

Herodotus. *Herodotus*, with an English translation by A. D. Godley. 1920. Cambridge, MA: Harvard University Press.

Pausanias. *Pausanias, Description of Greece*, with an English translation by W.H.S. Jones. 1918. Cambridge, MA: Harvard University Press; London: William Heinemann.

Strabo. *The Geography of Strabo*, vol. 2, with an English translation by H. L. Jones. 1932. Cambridge, MA: Harvard University Press; London: William Heinemann.

Thucydides. *Thucydides*, with an English translation by B. Jowett. 1881. Oxford: Clarendon Press.

Modern Sources

Abulafia, D. 2011. *The Great Sea: A Human History of the Mediterranean*. Oxford: Oxford University Press.

Adcock, S. A. 2020. "After the End: Animal Economics, Collapse, and Continuity in Hittite and Post-Hittite Anatolia." PhD diss., University of Chicago.

Alaura, S. 2020. "The Much-Fabled End of the Hittite Empire: Tracing the History of a Crucial Topic." In *Anatolia between the 13th and the 12th Century BCE*, ed. S. de Martino and E. Devecchi, 9–30. Turin: LoGisma editore.

Allen, M. J. 1977. "Contested Peripheries: Philistia in the Neo-Assyrian World-System." PhD diss., University of California, Los Angeles.

Álvarez-Mon, J. 2013. "Elam in the Iron Age." In *The Oxford Handbook of Ancient Iran*, ed. D. T. Potts, 457–77. New York: Oxford University Press.

Anthony, D. 1997. "Prehistoric Migration as Social Process." In *Migrations and Invasions in Archaeological Explanation*, ed. J. Chapman and H. Hamerow, 21–32. BAR International Series 664. Oxford: Archaeopress.

Antonaccio, C. 1993. "The Archaeology of Ancestors." In *Cultural Poetics in Archaeic Greece: Cult, Performance, Politics*, ed. C. Dougherty and L. Kurke, 46–70. Cambridge: Cambridge University Press.

Antonaccio, C. 2002. "Warriors, Traders, and Ancestors: The 'Heroes' of Lefkandi." In *Images of Ancestors*, ed. J. M. Høtje, 13–42. Aarhus Studies in Mediterranean Archaeology 5. Aarhus: Aarhus University Press.

Antonaccio, C. 2006. "Religion, Basileis and Heroes." In *Ancient Greece: From the Mycenaean Palaces to the Age of Homer*, ed. S. Deger-Jalkotzy and I. S. Lemos, 381–95. Edinburgh: Edinburgh University Press.

Apostolakou, S., P. Betancourt, T. Brogan, and D. Mylona. 2016. "Chryssi and Pefka: The Production and Use of Purple Dye on Crete in the Middle and Late Bronze Age." In *Purpureae Vestes V: Textiles, Basketry and Dyes in the Ancient Mediterranean World*, ed. J. Ortiz, C. Alfaro, L. Turell, and M. J. Martínez, 199–208. Valencia: Universitat de València.

Arie, E. 2008. "Reconsidering the Iron Age II Strata at Tel Dan: Archaeological and Historical Implications." *Tel Aviv* 35:6–64.

Arie, E. 2020. "Phoenicia and the Northern Kingdom of Israel: The Archaeological Evidence." In *A Life Dedicated to Anatolian Prehistory: Festschrift for Jak Yakar*, ed. B. Gür and S. Dalkiliç, 1–19. Ankara: Bilgin Kültür Sanat.

Arkin Shalev, E., E. Galili, P. Waiman-Barak, and A. Yasur-Landau. 2021. "Rethinking the Iron Age Carmel Coast: A Coastal and Maritime Perspective." *Israel Exploration Journal* 71/2:129–61.

Arkin Shalev, E., A. Gilboa, and A. Yasur-Landau. 2019. "The Iron Age Maritime Interface at the South Bay of Tel Dor: Results from the 2016 and 2017 Excavation Seasons." *International Journal of Nautical Archaeology* 48/2:439–52.

Aro, S. 2013. "Carchemish before and after 1200 BC." In *Luwian Identities: Culture, Language and Religion between Anatolia and the Aegean*, ed. A. Mouton, I. Rutherford, and I. Yakubovich, 233–76. Leiden: Brill.

Arruda, A. M. 2015. "Intercultural Contacts in the Far West at the Beginning of the 1st Millennium BC: Through the Looking-Glass." In *The Mediterranean Mirror: Cultural Contacts in the Mediterranean Sea between 1200 and 750 B.C.: International Post-doc and Young Researcher Conference; Heidelberg, 6th–8th October 2012*, ed. A. Babbi, F. Bubenheimer-Erhart, B. Marín-Aguilera, and S. Mühl, 269–83. Mainz: Verlag des Römisch-Germanischen Zentralmuseums.

Aslan, C. C. 2009. "End or Beginning? The Late Bronze Age to Iron Age Transformation at Troia." In *Forces of Transformation: The End of the Bronze Age in the Mediterranean*, ed. C. Bachhuber and G. Roberts, 144–51. Oxford: Oxbow Books.

Aslan, C. C. 2020. "Troy and the Northeastern Aegean." In *A Companion to the Archaeology of Early Greece and the Mediterranean*, ed. I. S. Lemos and A. Kotsonas, 2:939–59. London: Wiley Blackwell.

Aslan, C. C., and P. Hnila. 2015. "Migration and Integration at Troy from the End of the Late Bronze Age to the Iron Age." In *Nostoi: Indigenous Culture, Migration*, ed. N. Chr. Stampolidis, C. Maner, and K. Kopanias, 185–209. Istanbul: Koç University Press.

Aston, D. A. 2020. "The Royal Cache: The History of TT 320." In *Bab el-Gasus in Context: Rediscovering the Tomb of the Priests of Amun*, ed. R. Sousa, A. Amenta, and K. M. Cooney, 31–68. Rome: "L'Erma" di Bretschneider.

Atherton, M. 2016. "Ancient Greek City Knossos Was Bigger and Richer Than Previously Thought, Bronze Age Relics Reveal." *International Business Times*, January 7. https://www.ibtimes.co.uk/late-bronze-age-relics-discovered-knossos-suggesting-city-thrived-under-socio-economic-crash-1536534.

Aubet, M. E. 1993. *The Phoenicians and the West: Politics, Colonies and Trade*. Cambridge: Cambridge University Press.

Aubet, M. E. 2001. *The Phoenicians and the West: Politics, Colonies and Trade*. 2nd ed. Cambridge: Cambridge University Press.

Aubet, M. E. 2008. "Political and Economic Implications of the New Phoenician Chronologies." In *Beyond the Homeland: Markers in Phoenician Chronology*, ed. C. Sargona, 179–91. Ancient Near Eastern Studies Suppl. 28. Leuven: Peeters Press.

Aubet, M. E. 2014. "Phoenicia during the Iron Age II Period." In *The Oxford Handbook of the Archaeology of the Levant, c. 8000–332 BCE*, ed. M. L. Steiner and A. E. Killebrew, 706–16. Oxford: Oxford University Press.

Aubet, M. E. 2016. "Phoenicians Abroad: From Merchant Venturers to Colonists." In *Eurasia at the Dawn of History: Urbanization and Social Change*, ed. M. Fernández-Götz and D. Krausse, 254–64. Cambridge: Cambridge University Press.

Aubet Semmler, M. E. 2019. "Tyre and Its Colonial Expansion." In *The Oxford Handbook of the Phoenician and Punic Mediterranean*, ed. C. López-Ruiz and B. R. Doak, 75–87. Oxford: Oxford University Press.

Ballard, R. D., L. E. Stager, D. Master, D. Yoerger, D. Mindell, L. L. Whitcomb, H. Singh, and D. Piechota. 2002. "Iron Age Shipwrecks in Deep Water off Ashkelon, Israel." *American Journal of Archaeology* 106/2:151–68.

Barako, T. 2013. "Philistines and Egyptians in Southern Coastal Canaan during the Early Iron Age." In *The Philistines and Other "Sea Peoples" in Text and Archaeology*, ed. A. E. Killebrew and G. Lehmann, 37–51. Atlanta, GA: Society of Biblical Literature.

Barnes, M. L., Ö. Bodin, A. M. Guerrero, R. J. McAllister, S. M. Alexander, and G. Robins. 2017. "The Social Structural Foundations of Adaptation and Transformation in Social–Ecological Systems." *Ecology and Society* 22/4:16. https://doi.org/10.5751/ES-09769-220416.

Basedow, M. 2009. "The Iron Age Transition at Troy." In *Forces of Transformation: The End of the Bronze Age in the Mediterranean*, ed. C. Bachhuber and G. Roberts, 131–42. Oxford: Oxbow Books.

Bavel, B. van, D. R. Curtis, J. Dijkman, M. Hannaford, M. de Keyzer, E. van Onacker, and T. Soens. 2020. *Disasters and History: The Vulnerability and Resilience of Past Societies*. Oxford: Oxford University Press.

Bebermeier, W., M. Brumlich, V. Cordani, S. de Vincenzo, H. Eilbracht, J. Klinger, D. Knitter, E. Lehnhardt, M. Meyer, S. G. Schmid, B. Schütt, M. Thelemann, and M. Wemhoff. 2016. "The Coming of Iron in a Comparative Perspective," in "Space and Knowledge: Topoi Research Group Articles," ed. G. Graßhoff and M. Meyer. Special issue, *eTopoi (Journal for Ancient Studies)* 6:152–89.

Bell, C. 2006. *The Evolution of Long Distance Trading Relationships across the LBA/Iron Age Transition on the Northern Levantine Coast: Crisis, Continuity and Change.* BAR International Series 1574. Oxford: Archaeopress.

Bell, C. 2009. "Continuity and Change: The Divergent Destinies of LBA Ports in Syria and Lebanon across the LBA/Iron Age Transition." In *Forces of Transformation: The End of the Bronze Age in the Mediterranean*, ed. C. Bachhuber and G. Roberts, 30–38. Oxford: Oxbow Books.

Bell, C. 2016. "Phoenician Trade: The First 300 Years." In *Dynamics of Production in the Ancient Near East: 1300–500 BC*, ed. J. C. Moreno García, 91–105. Oxford: Oxbow Books.

Bendall, L., and M. West. 2020. "Evidence from Written Sources." In *A Companion to the Archaeology of Early Greece and the Mediterranean*, ed. I. S. Lemos and A. Kotsonas, 1:55–74. London: Wiley Blackwell.

Ben-Dor Evian, S. 2011. "Egypt and the Levant in the Iron Age I–IIA: The Ceramic Evidence." *Tel Aviv* 38:94–119.

Ben-Dor Evian, S. 2017. "Egypt and Israel: The Never-Ending Story." *NEA* 80/1:30–39.

Ben-Dor Evian, S., O. Yagel, Y. Harlavan, H. Seri, J. Lewinsky, and E. Ben-Yosef. 2021. "Pharaoh's Copper: The Provenance of Copper in Bronze Artifacts from Post-imperial Egypt at the End of the Second Millennium BCE." *Journal of Archaeological Science: Reports* 38/103025:1–13.

Ben-Shlomo, D. 2014. "Philistia during the Iron Age II Period." In *The Oxford Handbook of the Archaeology of the Levant, c. 8000–332 BCE*, ed. M. L. Steiner and A. E. Killebrew, 717–29. Oxford: Oxford University Press.

Ben-Yosef, E. 2019a. "Archaeological Science Brightens Mediterranean Dark Age." *Proceedings of the National Academy of Science* 116/13:5843–45.

Ben-Yosef, E. 2019b. "The Architectural Bias in Current Biblical Archaeology." *Vetus Testamentum* 69:361–87.

Ben-Yosef, E. 2019c. "The Invisible Biblical Kingdom." *Ha'aretz Weekend*, 18 October, 6–7.

Ben-Yosef, E. 2020. "And Yet, a Nomadic Error: A Reply to Israel Finkelstein." *Antiguo Oriente* 18:33–60.

Ben-Yosef, E. 2021a. "Rethinking Nomads—Edom in the Archaeological Record." In *The Koren Tanakh of the Land of Israel—Samuel*, ed. D. Arnovitz, 282–83. Jerusalem: Koren Publishers.

Ben-Yosef, E. 2021b. "Rethinking the Social Complexity of Early Iron Age Nomads." *Jerusalem Journal of Archaeology* 1:155–79.

Ben-Yosef, E., T. E. Levy, T. Higham, M. Najjar, and L. Tauxe. 2010. "The Beginning of Iron Age Copper Production in the Southern Levant: New Evidence from Khirbat al-Jariya, Faynan, Jordan." *Antiquity* 84:724–46.

Ben-Yosef, E., B. Liss, O. A. Yagel, O. Tirosh, M. Najjar, and T. E. Levy. 2019. "Ancient Technology and Punctuated Change: Detecting the Emergence of the Edomite Kingdom in the Southern Levant." *PLOS One* 14/9:e0221967.

Ben-Yosef, E., and O. Sergi. 2018. "The Destruction of Gath by Hazael and the Arabah Copper Industry: A Reassessment." In *Tell It in Gath: Studies in the History and Archaeology of Israel; Essays in Honor of Aren M. Maeir on the Occasion of His Sixtieth Birthday*, ed. I. Shai, J. R. Chadwick, L. Hitchcock, A. Dagan, C. McKinny, and J. Uziel, 461–80. Münster: Zaphon.

Ben-Yosef, E., and Z. Thomas. 2023. "Complexity without Monumentality in Biblical Times." *Journal of Archaeological Research,* March 28. https://doi.org/10.1007/s10814-023-09184-0.

Berkes, F., J. Colding, and C. Folke. 2003. "Introduction." In *Navigating Social-Ecological Systems: Building Resilience for Complexity and Change,* ed. F. Berkes, J. Colding, and C. Folke, 1–29. Cambridge: Cambridge University Press.

Bernardini, P. 2020. "Sardinia." In *A Companion to the Archaeology of Early Greece and the Mediterranean,* ed. I. S. Lemos and A. Kotsonas, 2:1311–23. London: Wiley Blackwell.

Bickerstaffe, D. 2010. "The History of the Discovery of the Cache." In *The Royal Cache TT 320—A Re-examination,* ed. E. Graefe and G. Belova, 13–35. Cairo: Supreme Council of Antiquities Press.

Bienkowski, P. 2022. "The Formation of Edom: An Archaeological Critique of the 'Early Edom' Hypothesis." *Bulletin of ASOR* 388:113–32.

Bikai, P. M. 1978. *The Pottery of Tyre.* Warminster: Aris & Phillips.

Bikai, P. M. 1994. "The Phoenicians and Cyprus." In *Cyprus in the 11th Century B.C.: Proceedings of the International Symposium, Nicosia 30–31 October, 1993,* ed. V. Karageorghis, 31–37. Nicosia: A. G. Leventis Foundation.

Bikai, P. M. 2000. "Phoenician Ceramics from the Greek Sanctuary." In *Kommos: An Excavation on the South Coast of Crete.* Vol. 4, *The Greek Sanctuary,* ed. J. M. Shaw and M. Shaw, 302–12. Princeton, NJ: Princeton University Press.

Biran, A., and J. Naveh. 1993. "An Aramaic Fragment from Tel Dan." *Israel Exploration Journal* 43:81–98.

Biran, A., and J. Naveh. 1995. "The Tel Dan Inscription: A New Fragment." *Israel Exploration Journal* 45:1–18.

Blake, E. 2014. "Late Bronze Age Sardinia: Acephalous Cohesion." In *The Cambridge Prehistory of the Bronze and Iron Age Mediterranean,* ed. A. B. Knapp and P. van Dommelen, 96–108. Cambridge: Cambridge University Press.

Blakemore, E. 2016. "This Ancient City Was Three Times Bigger Than Archaeologists Suspected." *Smithsonian,* January 11. https://www.smithsonianmag.com/smart-news/ancient-city-was-three-times-bigger-archaeologists-suspected-180957759.

Blegen, C. W. 1952. "Two Athenian Grave Groups of about 900 B.C." *Hesperia* 21:279–94.

Bleibtreu, E. 1990. "Five Ways to Conquer a City." *Biblical Archaeology Review* 16/3:37–44.

Bleibtreu, E. 1991. "Grisly Assyrian Record of Torture and Death." *Biblical Archaeology Review* 17/1:52–61, 75.

Boardman, J. 1967. "The Khaniale Tekke Tombs, II." *Annual of the British School at Athens* 62:57–75.

Boardman, J. 1980. *The Greeks Overseas.* 2nd ed. London: Thames and Hudson.

Boardman, J. 1990. "Al Mina and History." *Oxford Journal of Archaeology* 2:169–87.

Borger, R. 1964. *Einleitung in die assyrischen Königsinschriften.* Leiden: Brill.

Borschel-Dan, A. 2021. "Ancient Cloth with Bible's Purple Dye Found in Israel, Dated to King David's Era." *Times of Israel,* 28 January. https://www.timesofisrael.com/ancient-cloths-with-royal-purple-dye-found-in-israel-dated-to-king-davids-time.

Bourogiannis, G. 2013. "Who Hides behind the Pots? A Reassessment of the Phoenician Presence in Early Iron Age Cos and Rhodes." *Ancient Near Eastern Studies* 50:139–89.

Bourogiannis, G. 2018a. "The Phoenician Presence in the Aegean during the Early Iron Age: Trade, Settlement and Cultural Interaction." *Rivista di Studi Fenici* 46:43–88.

Bourogiannis, G. 2018b. "The Transmission of the Alphabet to the Aegean." In *Change, Continuity, and Connectivity: North-Eastern Mediterranean at the Turn of the Bronze Age and in the Early Iron Age*, ed. Ł. Niesiołowski-Spanò and M. Węcowski, 235–57. Wiesbaden: Harrassowitz Verlag.

Bourogiannis, G. 2020. "Between Scripts and Languages: Inscribed Intricacies from Geometric and Archaic Greek Contexts." In *Understanding Relations between Scripts II*, ed. P. J. Boyes and P. M. Steele, 151–80. Oxford: Oxbow Books.

Bourogiannis, G. 2021. "Phoenician Writing in Greece: Content, Chronology, Distribution and the Contribution of Cyprus." In *LRBT: De l'archéologie à l'épigraphie: Études en hommage à Maria Giulia Amadasi Guzzo*, ed. N. Chiarenza, B. D'Andrea, and A. Orsingher, 99–127. Turnhout, Belgium: Brepols.

Boyes, P. J., and P. M. Steele. 2020. "Introduction: Issues in Studying Early Alphabets." In *Understanding Relations between Scripts II*, ed. P. J. Boyes and P. M. Steele, 1–14. Oxford: Oxbow Books.

Bradtmöller, M., S. Grimm, and J. Riel-Salvatore. 2017. "Resilience Theory in Archaeological Practice—An Annotated Review." *Quaternary International* 446:3–16.

Brier, B. 2023. *Tutankhamun and the Tomb That Changed the World*. Oxford: Oxford University Press.

Brinkman, J. A. 1968. *A Political History of Post-Kassite Babylonia, 1158–722 B.C.* Rome: Pontifical Biblical Institute.

Brinkman, J. A. 1984. "Settlement Surveys and Documentary Evidence: Regional Variation and Secular Trends in Mesopotamian Demography." *Journal of Near Eastern Studies* 43:169–80.

Bron, F., and A. Lemaire. 1989. "Les inscriptions araméennes de Hazael." *RA* 83:34–44.

Broodbank, C. 2013. *The Making of the Middle Sea: A History of the Mediterranean from the Beginning to the Emergence of the Classical World*. Oxford: Oxford University Press.

Brown, B. A. 2008a. "The Kilamuwa Relief: Ethnicity, Class and Power in Iron Age North Syria." In *Proceedings of the 5th International Congress on the Archaeology of the Ancient Near East, Madrid, April 3–8 2006*, ed. J. M. Córdoba, M. Molist, M. C. Pérez, I. Rubio, and S. Martínez, 339–55. Madrid: UA ediciones.

Brown, B. A. 2008b. "Monumentalizing Identities: North Syrian Urbanism, 1200–800 BCE." PhD diss., University of California Berkeley.

Brown, M., and S. L. Smith. 2016. "The Land of Carchemish and Its Neighbours during the Neo-Hittite Period (c. 1190–717 BC)." In *Carchemish in Context: The Land of Carchemish Project, 2006–2010*, ed. T. J. Wilkinson, E. Peltenburg, and E. B. Wilkinson, 22–37. Oxford: Oxbow Books.

Bryce, T. R. 2012. *The World of the Neo-Hittite Kingdoms: A Political and Military History*. Oxford: Oxford University Press.

Bryce, T. R. 2014. *Ancient Syria: A Three Thousand Year History*. Oxford: Oxford University Press.

Bryce, T. R. 2016a. *Babylonia: A Very Short Introduction*. Oxford: Oxford University Press.

Bryce, T. R. 2016b. "The Land of Hiyawa (Que) Revisited." *Anatolian Studies* 66:67–79.

Bryce, T. R. 2019. "The Abandonment of Hattuša: Some Speculations." In *"And I Knew Twelve Languages": A Tribute to Massimo Poetto on the Occasion of His 70th Birthday*, ed. N. B. Guzzo and P. Taracha, 51–60. Warsaw: Agade Bis.

Bryce, T. R. 2020. "Change and Continuity from Bronze Age to Iron: A Review." In *A Life Dedicated to Anatolian Prehistory: Festschrift for Jak Yakar*, ed. B. Gür and S. Dalkiliç, 105–20. Ankara: Gilgin Kültür Sanat Sti.

Bryer, A.A.M. 1982. "The Question of Byzantine Mines in the Pontos: Chalybian Iron, Chaldian Silver, Koloneian Alum and the Mummy of Cheriana." *Anatolian Studies* 32:133–50.

Budja, M. 2015. "Archaeology and Rapid Climate Changes: From the Collapse Concept to a Panarchy Interpretative Model." *Documenta Praehistorica* 42:171–84.

Bunimovitz, S., and Z. Lederman. 2014. "Migration, Hybridization, and Resistance: Identity Dynamics in Early Iron Age Southern Levant." In *The Cambridge Prehistory of the Bronze and Iron Age Mediterranean*, ed. A. B. Knapp and P. van Dommelen, 252–65. Cambridge: Cambridge University Press.

Bunnens, G. 2000. "Syria in the Iron Age: Problems of Definition." In *Essays on Syria in the Iron Age*, ed. G. Bunnens, 3–19. Ancient Near Eastern Studies Suppl. 7. Louvain: Peeters Press.

Bunnens, G. 2019a. "History, Anthropology, and the Aramaeans: Apropos of a New History of the Aramaeans." *Ancient Near Eastern Studies* 56:347–66.

Bunnens, G. 2019b. "Phoenicia in the Later Iron Age; Tenth Century BCE to the Assyrian and Babylonian Periods." In *The Oxford Handbook of the Phoenician and Punic Mediterranean*, ed. C. López-Ruiz and B. R. Doak, 57–73. Oxford: Oxford University Press.

Butzer, K. W. 2012. "Collapse, Environment, and Society." *Proceedings of the National Academy of Sciences* 109/10:3632–39.

Calligas, P. G., and M. R. Popham. 1993. "The Site and the Course of Its Partial Destruction and Excavation." In *Lefkandi II*. Pt. 2, *The Protogeometric Building at Toumba: The Excavation, Architecture and Finds*, ed. M. R. Popham, P. G. Calligas, and L. H. Sackett, 1–4. *BSA* Suppl. 23. London: British School at Athens.

Cantrell, D. O. 2006. "Stable Issues." In *Megiddo IV: The 1998–2002 Seasons*, ed. I. Finkelstein, D. Ussishkin, and B. Halpern, 2:630–42. Tel Aviv: Tel Aviv University.

Cantrell, D. O., and I. Finkelstein. 2006. "A Kingdom for a Horse: The Megiddo Stables and Eighth Century Israel." In *Megiddo IV: The 1998–2002 Seasons*, ed. I. Finkelstein, D. Ussishkin, and B. Halpern, 2:643–65. Tel Aviv: Tel Aviv University.

Cardarelli, A. 2009. "The Collapse of the Terramare Culture and Growth of New Economic and Social Systems during the Late Bronze Age in Italy." *Scienze dell'Antichità: Storia Archeologia Antropologia* 15:449–520.

Cardona, O. D., M. K. van Aalst, J. Birkmann, M. Fordham, G. McGregor, R. Perez, R. S. Pulwarty, E.L.F. Schipper, and B. T. Sinh. 2012. "Determinants of Risk: Exposure and Vulnerability." In *Managing the Risks of Extreme Events and Disasters to Advance Climate Change Adaptation*, ed. C. B. Field, V. Barros, T. F. Stocker, D. Qin, D. J. Dokken, K. L. Ebi, M. D. Mastrandrea, K. J. Mach, G.-K. Plattner, S. K. Allen, M. Tignor, and P. M. Midgley, 65–108. A Special Report of Working Groups I and II of the Intergovernmental Panel on Climate Change (IPCC). Cambridge: Cambridge University Press.

Carpenter, R. 1966. *Discontinuity in Mycenaean Civilization*. Cambridge: Cambridge University Press.

Carter, E., and S. Morris. 2014. "Crisis in the Eastern Mediterranean and Beyond: Survival, Revival, and the Emergence of the Iron Age." In *Assyria to Iberia at the Dawn of the Classical Age*, ed. J. Aruz, S. B. Graff, and Y. Rakic, 14–23. New York: Metropolitan Museum of Art.

Casson, S. 1921. "The Dorian Invasion Reviewed in the Light of Some New Evidence." *Antiquaries Journal* 1/3:199–221.

Catling, H. W. 1993. "The Bronze Amphora and Burial Urn." In *Lefkandi II*. Pt. 2, *The Protogeometric Building at Toumba: The Excavation, Architecture and Finds*, ed. M. R. Popham, P. G. Calligas, and L. H. Sackett, 81–96. *BSA* Suppl. 23. London: British School at Athens.

Catling, H. W. 1994. "Cyprus in the 11th Century B.C.—An End or a Beginning?" In *Cyprus in the 11th Century B.C.: Proceedings of the International Symposium, Nicosia, 30–31 October 1993*, ed. V. Karageorghis, 133–41. Nicosia: A. G. Leventis Foundation.

Catling, H. W. 1995. "Heroes Returned? Subminoan Burials from Crete." In *The Age of Homer: A Tribute to Emily Townsend Vermeule*, ed. J. B. Carter and S. P. Morris, 123–36. Austin: University of Texas Press.

Catling, H. W. 1996. "The Subminoan Phase in the North Cemetery." In *Knossos North Cemetery: Early Greek Tombs*, ed. J. N. Coldstream and H. W. Catling, 639–49. *BSA* Suppl. 28. London: British School at Athens.

Catling, R.W.V., and I. Lemos. 1990. *Lefkandi II*. Pt. 1, *The Protogeometric Building at Toumba: The Pottery*. *BSA* Suppl. 22. London: British School at Athens.

Cavanagh, M., E. Ben-Yosef, and D. Langgut. 2022. "Fuel Exploitation and Environmental Degradation at the Iron Age Copper Industry of the Timna Valley, Southern Israel." *Nature: Scientific Reports* 12:15434. https://doi.org/10.1038/s41598-022-18940-z.

Centeno, M., P. Callahan, P. Larcey, and T. Patterson. 2022. "Globalization as Adaptive Complexity: Learning from Failure." In *Perspectives on Public Policy in Societal-Environmental Crises: What the Future Needs from History*, ed. A. Izdebski, J. Haldon, and P. Filipkowski, 59–74. Cham, Switzerland: Springer.

Chadwick, J. R. 2022. "When Gath of the Philistines Became Gath of Judah." *Journal of Eastern Mediterranean Archaeology and Heritage Studies* 10/3–4:317–42.

Chapman, R. L., III. 2009. "Putting Sheshonq I in His Place." *Palestine Exploration Quarterly* 141/1:4–17.

Chapman, R. L., III. 2015. "Samaria and Megiddo: Shishak and Solomon." In *Solomon and Shishak: Current Perspectives from Archaeology, Epigraphy, History and Chronology: Proceedings of the Third BICANE Colloquium Held at Sidney Sussex College, Cambridge, 26–27 March 2011*, 137–47, ed. Peter James and Peter G. van der Veen. BAR International Series 2732. Oxford: Archaeopress.

Charaf, H. 2020–21. "The Architectural and Material Characteristics of the Late 13th–Early 12th Century BC Level at Tell Arqa, Lebanon." *Archaeology & History in the Lebanon* 52–53:46–72.

Chew, S. C. 2001. *World Ecological Degradation: Accumulation, Urbanization, and Deforestation 3000 B.C.–A.D. 2000*. Walnut Creek, CA: Altamira Press.

Chew, S. C. 2005. "From Harappa to Mesopotamia and Egypt to Mycenae: Dark Ages, Political-Economic Declines, and Environmental/Climatic Changes 2200 B.C.–700 B.C." In *The Historical Evolution of World-Systems*, ed. C. Chase-Dunn and E. N. Anderson, 52–74. London: Palgrave Macmillan.

Chew, S. C. 2007. *The Recurring Dark Ages: Ecological Stress, Climate Changes, and System Transformation*. Walnut Creek, CA: Altamira Press.

Chew, S. C. 2008. *Ecological Futures: What History Can Teach Us.* Walnut Creek, CA: Altamira Press.

Clayton, P. A. 1994. *Chronicle of the Pharaohs: The Reign-by-Reign Record of the Rulers and Dynasties of Ancient Egypt.* London: Thames and Hudson.

Cline, E. H. 1994. *Sailing the Wine-Dark Sea: International Trade and the Late Bronze Age Aegean.* Oxford: Tempus Reparatum.

Cline, E. H. 2000. *The Battles of Armageddon: Megiddo and the Jezreel Valley from the Bronze Age to the Nuclear Age.* Ann Arbor: University of Michigan Press.

Cline, E. H. 2004. *Jerusalem Besieged: From Ancient Canaan to Modern Israel.* Ann Arbor: University of Michigan Press.

Cline, E. H. 2007. *From Eden to Exile: Unraveling Mysteries of the Bible.* Washington, DC: National Geographic Books.

Cline, E. H. 2009. *Biblical Archaeology: A Very Short Introduction.* Oxford: Oxford University Press.

Cline, E. H. 2011. "Whole Lotta Shakin' Going On: The Possible Destruction by Earthquake of Megiddo Stratum VIA." In *The Fire Signals of Lachish: Studies in the Archaeology and History of Israel in the Late Bronze Age, Iron Age, and Persian Period in Honor of David Ussishkin*, ed. I. Finkelstein and N. Na'aman, 55–70. Tel Aviv: Tel Aviv University.

Cline, E. H. 2013. *The Trojan War: A Very Short Introduction.* Oxford: Oxford University Press.

Cline, E. H. 2014. *1177 B.C.: The Year Civilization Collapsed.* Princeton, NJ: Princeton University Press.

Cline, E. H. 2017. *Three Stones Make a Wall: The Story of Archaeology.* Princeton, NJ: Princeton University Press.

Cline, E. H. 2020. *Digging Up Armageddon: The Search for the Lost City of Solomon.* Princeton, NJ: Princeton University Press.

Cline, E. H. 2021. *1177 BC: The Year Civilization Collapsed.* Rev. and updated ed. Princeton, NJ: Princeton University Press.

Cline, E. H. Forthcoming. "The Collapse of Cultures at the End of the Late Bronze Age in the Aegean and Eastern Mediterranean: New Developments, Punctuated Equilibrium, and Further Questions." In *Mediterranean Resilience: Collapse and Adaptation in Antique Maritime Societies*, ed. A. Yasur-Landau, G. Gambash, and T. E. Levy. London: Equinox Publishing.

Cline, E. H., and D. O'Connor. 2003. "The Mystery of the Sea Peoples." In *Mysterious Lands*, ed. D. O'Connor and S. Quirke, 107–38. London: UCL Press.

Cohen, C., J. Maran, and M. Vetters. 2010. "An Ivory Rod with a Cuneiform Inscription, Most Probably Ugaritic, from a Final Palatial Workshop in the Lower Citadel of Tiryns." *Archäologischer Anzeiger* 2010/2:1–22.

Coldstream, J. N. 1977. *Geometric Greece.* London: E. Benn.

Coldstream, J. N. 1992–93. "Early Greek Visitors to Egypt and the Levant." *Journal of the Ancient Chronology Foundation* 6:6–18.

Coldstream, J. N. 1994. "What Sort of Aegean Migration?" In *Cyprus in the 11th Century B.C.: Proceedings of the International Symposium, Nicosia, 30–31 October 1993*, ed. V. Karageorghis, 143–47. Nicosia: A. G. Leventis Foundation.

Coldstream, J. N. 1998. *Light from Cyprus on the Greek "Dark Age"? Nineteenth J. L. Myres Memorial Lecture.* Oxford: Leopard's Head.

Coldstream, J. N. 2006. "Knossos in Early Greek Times." In *Ancient Greece: From the Mycenaean Palaces to the Age of Homer*, ed. S. Deger-Jalkotzy and I. S. Lemos, 581–96. Edinburgh: Edinburgh University Press.

Coldstream, N., and A. Mazar. 2003. "Greek Pottery from Tel Rehov and Iron Age Chronology." *Israel Exploration Journal* 53:29–48.

Comelli, D., M. D'Orazio, L. Folco, M. El-Halwagy, T. Frizzi, R. Alberti, V. Capogrosso, A. Elnaggar, H. Hassan, A. Nevin, F. Porcelli, M. G. Rashed, and G. Valentini. 2016. "The Meteoritic Origin of Tutankhamun's Iron Dagger Blade." *Meteoritics & Planetary Science* 51/7:1301–9. https://doi.org/10.1111/maps.12664.

Cook, R. M. 1962. "The Dorian Invasion." *Proceedings of the Cambridge Philological Society* 8/188:16–22.

Cordani, V. 2016. "The Development of the Hittite Iron Industry. A Reappraisal of the Written Sources." *Die Welt des Orients* 46:162–76.

Coulson, W.D.E. 1990. *The Greek Dark Ages: A Review of the Evidence and Suggestions for Future Research*. Athens: American School of Classical Studies at Athens.

Counts, D. B., and M. Iacovou. 2013. "New Approaches to the Elusive Iron Age Polities of Ancient Cyprus: An Introduction." *Bulletin of the American Schools of Oriental Research* 370:1–13.

Cowgill, G. L. 1988. "Onward and Upward with Collapse." In *The Collapse of Ancient States and Civilization*, ed. N. Yoffee and G. L. Cowgill, 244–76. Tucson: University of Arizona Press.

Cox, R. S., and K.-M.E. Perry. 2011. "Like a Fish out of Water: Reconsidering Disaster Recovery and the Role of Place and Social Capital in Community Disaster Resilience." *American Journal of Community Psychology* 48:395–411.

Creasman, P. P. 2020. "A Compendium of Recent Evidence from Egypt and Sudan for Climate Change during the Pharaonic Period." In *The Gift of the Nile? Ancient Egypt and the Environment*, ed. T. Schneider and C. L. Johnston, 15–48. Tucson, AZ: Egyptian Expedition.

Crielaard, J. P. 1998. "Surfing on the Mediterranean Web: Cypriot Long-Distance Communications during the Eleventh and Tenth Centuries B.C." In *Eastern Mediterranean: Cyprus—Dodecanese—Crete; 16th–6th Cent. B.C.*, ed. V. Karageorghis and N. Stampolidis, 187–206. Athens: University of Crete and the A. G. Leventis Foundation.

Crielaard, J. P. 2006. "*Basileis* at Sea: Elites and External Contacts in the Euboaean Gulf Region from the End of the Bronze Age to the Beginning of the Iron Age." In *Ancient Greece: From the Mycenaean Palaces to the Age of Homer*, ed. S. Deger-Jalkotzy and I. S. Lemos, 271–97. Edinburgh: Edinburgh University Press.

Crielaard, J. P. 2011. "The '*Wanax* to *Basileis* Model' Reconsidered: Authority and Ideology after the Collapse of the Mycenaean Palaces." In *The "Dark Ages" Revisited: Acts of an International Symposium in Memory of William D. E. Coulson, University of Thessaly, Volos, 14–17 June 2007*, ed. A. Mazarakis Ainian, 1:83–111. Volos: University of Thessaly Press.

Crielaard, J. P. 2016. "Living Heroes: Metal Urn Cremations in Early Iron Age Greece, Cyprus and Italy." In *Omero: Quaestiones disputata*, ed. F. Gallo, 43–78. Ambrosiana Graecolatina 5. Milan: Biblioteca Ambrosiana–Bulzoni editore.

Crielaard, J. P., and J. Driessen. 1994. "The Hero's Home: Some Reflections on the Building at Toumba, Lefkandi." *Topoi* 4/1:251–70.

Crowell, B. 2021. *Edom at the Edge of Empire: A Social and Political History*. Atlanta: SBL Press.

Crowfoot, J. W., and G. M. Crowfoot. 1938. *Samaria-Sebaste 2: Early Ivories*. London: Palestine Exploration Fund.

Crowfoot, J. W., K. M. Kenyon, and E. L. Sukenik. 1942. *Samaria-Sebaste 1: The Buildings*. London: Palestine Exploration Fund.

Crowfoot, J. W., G. M. Crowfoot, and K. M. Kenyon. 1957. *Samaria-Sebaste 3: The Objects*. London: Palestine Exploration Fund.

Crowther, N. B. 2007. "The Ancient Olympic Games through the Centuries." In *Onward to the Olympics: Historical Perspectives on the Olympic Games*, ed. G. P. Schaus and S. R. Wenn, 3–13. Waterloo, ON: Wilfrid Laurier University Press.

Cumming, G. S., and G. D. Peterson. 2017. "Unifying Research on Social-Ecological Resilience and Collapse." *Trends in Ecology & Evolution* 32/9:695–713. http://dx.doi.org/10.1016/j.tree.2017.06.014.

Cupitò, M., E. Dalla Longa, and C. Balista. 2020. "From 'Valli Grandi Veronesi System' to 'Frattesina System': Observations on the Evolution of the Exchange System Models between Veneto Po Valley Area and the Mediterranean World during the Late Bronze Age," in "Italia tra Mediterraneo ed Europa: Mobilità, interazioni e scambi." Special issue, *Rivista di Scienze Preistoriche* LXX S1:293–310.

Curtis, J. 2012. "Assyrian and Urartian Metalwork: Independence or Interdependence?" In *Biainili-Urartu: The Proceedings of the Symposium Held in Munich, 12–14 October 2007*, ed. S. Kroll, C. Gruber, U. Hellwag, M. Roaf, and P. Zimansky, 427–43. Louvain: Peeters.

Curtis, J. E., and N. Tallis, eds. 2008. *The Balawat Gates of Ashurnasirpal II*. London: British Museum Press.

Cutter, S., B. Osman-Elasha, J. Campbell, S.-M. Cheong, S. McCormick, R. Pulwarty, S. Supratid, and G. Ziervogel. 2012. "Managing the Risks from Climate Extremes at the Local Level." In *Managing the Risks of Extreme Events and Disasters to Advance Climate Change Adaptation*, ed. C. B. Field, V. Barros, T. F. Stocker, D. Qin, D. J. Dokken, K. L. Ebi, M. D. Mastrandrea, K. J. Mach, G.-K. Plattner, S. K. Allen, M. Tignor, and P. M. Midgley, 291–338. Special Report of Working Groups I and II of the Intergovernmental Panel on Climate Change (IPCC). Cambridge: Cambridge University Press.

D'Agata, A. L. 2006. "Cult Activity on Crete in the Early Dark Age: Changes, Continuities and the Development of a 'Greek' Cult System." In *Ancient Greece: From the Mycenaean Palaces to the Age of Homer*, ed. S. Deger-Jalkotzy and I. S. Lemos, 397–414. Edinburgh: Edinburgh University Press.

D'Alfonso, L. 2020. "An Age of Experimentation: New Thoughts on the Multiple Outcomes Following the Fall of the Hittite Empire after the Results of the Excavations at Nigde-Kinik Höyük (South Cappadocia)." In *Anatolia between the 13th and the 12th Century BCE*, ed. S. de Martino and E. Devecchi, 95–116. Turin: LoGisma editore.

D'Alfonso, L., E. Basso, L. Castellano, A. Mantovan, and P. Vertuani. 2022. "Regional Exchange and Exclusive Elite Rituals in Iron Age Central Anatolia: Dating, Function and Circulation of Alişar-IV ware." *Anatolian Studies* 72:37–77.

Dalla Longa, E. 2019. "Settlement Dynamics and Territorial Organization in the Middle and Low Veneto Plain South of the Ancient Adige River in the Bronze Age." *Preistoria Alpina* 49bis:95–121.

Daniel, J. F., O. Broneer, and H. T. Wade-Gery. 1948. "The Dorian Invasion." *American Journal of Archaeology* 52/1:107–18.

David, A. 2021a. "Archaeologists Find Remains of 'Royal' Garments from King David's Time—in a Mine." *Ha'aretz*, January 29. https://www.haaretz.com/archaeology/.premium-archaeologists-find-textile-shreds-with-purple-from-king-david-s-time-1.9490326.

David, A. 2021b. "Israeli Archaeologists Figure Out Where Ancient Egypt Got Its Metal after Civilization Collapsed." *Ha'aretz*, June 16. https://www.haaretz.com/archaeology/.premium-where-ancient-egypt-got-its-metal-after-civilization-collapsed-in-3200-bce-1.9903941.

Davis, J. L., and S. R. Stocker. 2020. "Messenia." In *A Companion to the Archaeology of Early Greece and the Mediterranean*, ed. I. S. Lemos and A. Kotsonas, 2:671–92. London: Wiley Blackwell.

De Buck, A. 1937. "The Judicial Papyrus of Turin." *Journal of Egyptian Archaeology* 23/2:152–64.

Deger-Jalkotzy, S. 1994. "The Post-palatial Period of Greece: An Aegean Prelude to the 11th Century B.C. in Cyprus." In *Cyprus in the 11th Century B.C.: Proceedings of the International Symposium, Nicosia, 30–31 October 1993*, ed. V. Karageorghis, 11–30. Nicosia: A. G. Leventis Foundation.

Deger-Jalkotzy, S. 2008. "Decline, Destruction, Aftermath." In *The Cambridge Companion to the Aegean Bronze Age*, ed. C. W. Shelmerdine, 387–415. Cambridge: Cambridge University Press.

Deger-Jalkotzy, S., and I. S. Lemos, eds. 2006. *Ancient Greece from the Mycenaean Palaces to the Age of Homer*. Edinburgh: Edinburgh University Press.

DeGrado, J. 2019. "King of the Four Quarters: Diversity as a Rhetorical Strategy of the Neo-Assyrian Empire." *Iraq* 81:107–25.

Degroot D., K. J. Anchukaitis, M. Bauch, J. Burnham, F. Carnegy, J. Cui, K. de Luna, P. Guzowski, G. Hambrecht, H. Huhtamaa, A. Izdebski, K. Kleemann, E. Moeswilde, N. Neupane, T. Newfield, Q. Pei, E. Xoplaki, and N. Zappia. 2021. "Towards a Rigorous Understanding of Societal Responses to Climate Change." *Nature* 591:539–50. https://doi.org/10.1038/s41586-021-03190-2.

De Martino, S. 2018. "The Fall of the Hittite Kingdom." *Mesopotamia* 63:23–48.

Denton, F., T. J. Wilbanks, A. C. Abeysinghe, I. Burton, Q. Gao, M. C. Lemos, T. Masui, K. L. O'Brien, and K. Warner. 2014. "Climate-Resilient Pathways: Adaptation, Mitigation, and Sustainable Development." In *Climate Change 2014: Impacts, Adaptation, and Vulnerability. Part A: Global and Sectoral Aspects; Contribution of Working Group II to the Fifth Assessment Report of the Intergovernmental Panel on Climate Change*, 1101–31. Cambridge: Cambridge University Press.

Desborough, V.R.d'A. 1964. *The Last Mycenaeans and Their Successors: An Archaeological Survey c. 1200–c. 1000 B.C.* Oxford: Clarendon Press.

Desborough, V.R.d'A. 1972. *The Greek Dark Ages*. London: Ernest Benn.

Dever, W. 1993. "Further Evidence on the Date of the Outer Wall at Gezer." *Bulletin of the American Schools of Oriental Research* 289:33–54.

Diamond, J. 2005. *Collapse: How Societies Choose to Fail or Succeed*. New York: Viking.

Dibble, F., and D. Fallu. 2020. "New Data from Old Bones: A Taphonomic Reassessment of Early Iron Age Beef Ranching at Nichoria, Greece." *Journal of Archaeological Science: Reports* 30:102234.

Dibble, F., and M. Finné. 2021. "Socioenvironmental Change as a Process: Changing Foodways as Adaptation to Climate Change in South Greece from the Late Bronze Age to the Early Iron Age." *Quaternary International* 597:50–62.

Dickinson, O.T.P.K. 2006a. *The Aegean from Bronze Age to Iron Age: Continuity and Change between the Twelfth and Eighth Centuries BC*. London: Routledge.

Dickinson, O.T.P.K. 2006b. "The Mycenaean Heritage of Early Iron Age Greece." In *Ancient Greece from the Mycenaean Palaces to the Age of Homer*, ed. S. Deger-Jalkotzy and I. Lemos, 115–22. Edinburgh: Edinburgh University Press.

Dillehay, T. D., and S. A. Wernke. 2019. "Fragility of Vulnerable Social Institutions in Andean States." In *The Evolution of Fragility: Setting the Terms*, ed. N. Yoffee, 9–23. Cambridge: McDonald Institute for Archaeological Research.

Dinçol, A., B. Dinçol, J. D. Hawkins, N. Marchetti, and H. Peker. 2014a. "A New Stela from Karkemish: At the Origins of the Suhi-Katuwa Dynasty." In *Karkemish: An Ancient Capital on the Euphrates*, ed. N. Marchetti, 127–31. Bologna: AnteQuem.

Dinçol, A., B. Dinçol, J. D. Hawkins, N. Marchetti, and H. Peker. 2014b. "A Stele by Suhi I from Karkemish." *Orientalia* 83/2:143–53.

Dinçol, A., B. Dinçol, J. D. Hawkins, and H. Peker. 2012. "A New Inscribed Stela from Karkemish: At the Origins of the Suhi-Katuwa Dynasty." *Near Eastern Archaeology* 75:145.

Dinçol, B., A. Dinçol, J. D. Hawkins, H. Peker, and A. Öztan. 2015. "Two New Inscribed Storm-God Stelae from Arsuz (Iskenderun): ARSUZ 1 and 2." *Anatolian Studies* 65:59–77.

Doak, B. R. 2019. "Phoenicians in the Hebrew Bible." In *The Oxford Handbook of the Phoenician and Punic Mediterranean*, ed. C. López-Ruiz and B. R. Doak, 657–70. Oxford: Oxford University Press.

Doak, B. R. 2020. *Ancient Israel's Neighbors*. Oxford: Oxford University Press.

Docter, R. F., H. G. Niemeyer, A. J. Nijboer, and J. van der Plicht. 2005. "Radiocarbon Dates of Animal Bones in the Earliest Levels of Carthage." In *Oriente e Occidente*, ed. G. Bartoloni and F. Delpino, 557–77. Rome: Istituti editoriali poligrafici internazionali.

Dodson, A. 2019. *Afterglow of Empire: Egypt from the Fall of the New Kingdom to the Saite Renaissance*. Rev. and updated ed. Cairo: AUC Press.

Dodson, A. 2023. "The Palestinian Campaign(s) of Shoshenq I." In *Weseretkau "Mighty of Kas": Papers Submitted in Memory of Cathleen A. Keller*, ed. D. Kiser-Go and C. Redmount, 297–307. Columbus, GA: Lockwood Press.

Donnelly-Lewis, B. 2022. "The Khirbet Qeiyafa Ostracon: A New Collation Based on the Multispectral Images, with Translation and Commentary." *Bulletin of ASOR* 388:181–210.

Donner, H. and W. Röllig. 2002. *Kanaanäische und aramäische Inschriften*. 5th ed., rev. and expanded. Wiesbaden: Harrassowitz.

Dothan, T. 1982. *The Philistines and Their Material Culture*. Jerusalem: Israel Exploration Society.

Doumet-Serhal, C. 2019. "Phoenician Identity in Modern Lebanon." In *The Oxford Handbook of the Phoenician and Punic Mediterranean*, ed. C. López-Ruiz and B. R. Doak, 713–28. Oxford: Oxford University Press.

Drews, R. 1992. "Herodotus 1.94, the Drought ca. 1200 B.C., and the Origin of the Etruscans." *Historia: Zeitschrift für Alte Geschichte* 41/1:14–39.

Düring, B. S. 2020. *The Imperialisation of Assyria: An Archaeological Approach*. Cambridge: Cambridge University Press.

Eder, B. 2006. "The World of Telemachus: Western Greece 1200–700 B.C." In *Ancient Greece: From the Mycenaean Palaces to the Age of Homer*, ed. S. Deger-Jalkotzy and I. S. Lemos, 549–80. Edinburgh: Edinburgh University Press.

Eder, B., and I. S. Lemos. 2020. "From the Collapse of the Mycenaean Palaces to the Emergence of Early Iron Age Communities." In *A Companion to the Archaeology of Early Greece and the Mediterranean*, ed. I. S. Lemos and A. Kotsonas, 1:132–60. London: Wiley Blackwell.

Edrey, M. 2019. *Phoenician Identity in Context: Material Cultural Koiné in the Iron Age Levant*. Alter Orient und Altes Testament 469. Münster: Ugarit-Verlag.

Edwards, A. B. 1882a. "Lying in State in Cairo." *Harper's New Monthly Magazine* 386:185–204.

Edwards, A. B. 1882b. "Recent Discovery of Royal Mummies and Other Egyptian Antiquities." *Supplement to the Illustrated London News*, February 4, 1882, 113–18.

Edwards, F. L. 2013. "All Hazards, Whole Community: Creating Resiliency." In *Disaster Resiliency: Interdisciplinary Perspectives*, ed. N. Kapucu, C. V. Hawkins, and F. I. Rivera, 21–47. New York: Routledge.

Ehrenreich, B. 2020. "How Do You Know When Society Is about to Fall Apart?" *New York Times Magazine*, November 4, 2020. https://www.nytimes.com/2020/11/04/magazine/societal-collapse.html.

Ehrlich, C. S. 1996. *The Philistines in Transition: A History from ca. 1000–730 B.C.E.* Leiden: E. J. Brill.

Eisenstadt, S. N. 1988. "Beyond Collapse." In *The Collapse of Ancient States and Civilization*, ed. N. Yoffee and G. L. Cowgill, 236–43. Tucson: University of Arizona Press.

Elayi, J. 2018. *The History of Phoenicia*. Translated from the French by A. Plummer. Atlanta, GA: Lockwood Press.

Eliyahu-Behar, A., and N. Yahalom-Mack. 2018. "Reevaluating Early Iron-Working Skills in the Southern Levant through Microstructure Analysis." *Journal of Archaeological Science: Reports* 18:447–62.

Eliyahu-Behar, A., N. Yahalom-Mack, Y. Gadot, and I. Finkelstein. 2013. "Iron Smelting and Smithing in Major Urban Centers in Israel during the Iron Age." *Journal of Archaeological Science* 40:4319–30.

Eliyahu-Behar, A., N. Yahalom-Mack, S. Shilstein, A. Zukerman, C. Shafer-Elliot, A. M. Maeir, E. Boaretto, I. Finkelstein, and S. Weiner. 2012. "Iron and Bronze Production in Iron Age IIA Philistia: New Evidence from Tell es-Safi/Gath, Israel." *Journal of Archaeological Science* 39:255–67.

Ellenblum, R. 2012. *The Collapse of the Eastern Mediterranean: Climate Change and the Decline of the East, 950–1072*. Cambridge: Cambridge University Press.

Emanuel, J. P. 2015. "King Taita and His 'Palistin': Philistine State or Neo-Hittite Kingdom?" *Antiguo Oriente* 13:11–39.

Engle, N. L. 2011. "Adaptive Capacity and Its Assessment." *Global Environmental Change* 21:647–56.

Enverova, D. A. 2012. "The Transition from Bronze Age to Iron Age in the Aegean: An Heterarchical Approach." MA thesis, Bilkent University. http://www.thesis.bilkent.edu.tr/0006047.pdf.

Eph'al, I., and J. Naveh. 1989. "Hazael's Booty Inscriptions." *Israel Exploration Journal* 39/3–4: 192–200.

Erb-Satullo, N. L. 2019. "The Innovation and Adoption of Iron in the Ancient Near East." *Journal of Archaeological Research* 27:557–607. https://doi.org/10.1007/s10814-019-09129-6.

Erb-Satullo, N. L., B.J.J. Gilmour, and N. Khakhutaishvili. 2020. "The Metal behind the Myths: Iron Metallurgy in the South-Eastern Black Sea Region." *Antiquity* 94/374: 401–19.

Eshel, T., Y. Erel, N. Yahalom-Mack, O. Tirosh, and A. Gilboa. 2019. "Lead Isotopes in Silver Reveal Earliest Phoenician Quest for Metals in the West Mediterranean." *PNAS* 116/13 (February 25): 6007–12. www.pnas.org/cgi/doi/10.1073/pnas.1817951116.

Eshel, T., A. Gilboa, N. Yahalom-Mack, O. Tirosh, and Y. Erel. 2021. "Debasement of Silver throughout the Late Bronze–Iron Age Transition in the Southern Levant: Analytical and Cultural Implications." *Journal of Archaeological Science* 125:105268.

Eshel, T., N. Yahalom-Mack, S. Shalev, O. Tirosh, Y. Erel, and A. Gilboa. 2018. "Four Iron Age Silver Hoards from Southern Phoenicia: From Bundles to Hacksilber." *Bulletin of the American Schools of Oriental Research* 379:197–228.

Eyre, C. J. 2012. "Society, Economy, and Administrative Process in Late Ramesside Egypt." In *Ramesses III: The Life and Times of Egypt's Last Hero*, ed. E. H. Cline and D. B. O'Connor, 101–50. Ann Arbor: University of Michigan Press.

Fagan, B. M. 2004. *The Rape of the Nile: Tomb Robbers, Tourists, and Archaeologists in Egypt*. Rev. and updated ed. Boulder, CO: West View Press.

Fagan, B. M. 2007. *Return to Babylon: Travelers, Archaeologists, and Monuments in Mesopotamia*. Rev. ed. Boulder, CO: University Press of Colorado.

Fales, F. M. 2011. "Transition: The Assyrians at the Euphrates between the 13th and the 12th Century BC." In *Empires after the Empire: Anatolia, Syria and Assyria after Suppiluliuma II (ca. 1200–800/700 B.C.)*, ed. K. Strobel, 9–59. Rome: LoGisma.

Fales, F. M. 2017. "Phoenicia in the Neo-Assyrian Period: An Updated Overview." *State Archives of Assyria Bulletin* 23:181–295.

Fantalkin, A. 2001. "Low Chronology and Greek Protogeometric and Geometric Pottery in the Southern Levant." *Levant* 33:117–25.

Fantalkin, A., and I. Finkelstein. 2006. "The Sheshonq I Campaign and the 8th Century BCE Earthquake: More on the Archaeology and History of the South in the Iron I-IIA." *Tel Aviv* 33:18–42.

Fantalkin, A., I. Finkelstein, and E. Piasetzky. 2015. "Late Helladic to Middle Geometric Aegean and Contemporary Cypriot Chronologies: A Radiocarbon View from the Levant." *Bulletin of the American Schools of Oriental Research* 373:25–48.

Fantalkin, A., A. Kleiman, H. Mommsen, and I. Finkelstein. 2020. "Aegean Pottery in Iron IIA Megiddo: Typological, Archaeometric and Chronological Aspects." *Mediterranean Archaeology and Archaeometry* 20/3:135–47.

Faulseit, R. K. 2016. "Collapse, Resilience, and Transformation in Complex Societies: Modelling Trends and Understanding Diversity." In *Beyond Collapse: Archaeological Perspectives on Resilience, Revitalization, and Transformation in Complex Societies*, ed. R. K. Faulseit, 3–26. Visiting Scholar Conference Volumes: Center for Archaeological Investigations Occasional Paper No. 42. Carbondale: Southern Illinois University Press.

Faust, A. 2007. *Israel's Ethnogenesis: Settlement, Interaction, Expansion and Resistance.* London: Equinox.

Faust, A. 2011. "The Interests of the Assyrian Empire in the West: Olive Oil Production as a Test-Case." *Journal of the Economic and Social History of the Orient* 54:62–86.

Faust, A. 2012. "Between Israel and Philistia: Ethnic Negotiations in the South during Iron Age I." In *The Ancient Near East in the 12th–10th Centuries BCE: Culture and History; Proceedings of the International Conference Held at the University of Haifa, 2–5 May 2010*, ed. G. Galil, A. Gilboa, A. M. Maeir, and D. Kahn, 121–35. Alter Orient und Altes Testament 392. Münster: Ugarit-Verlag.

Faust, A. 2016. "The Emergence of Israel and Theories of Thenogenesis." In *The Wiley Companion to Ancient Israel*, ed. S. Niditch. Oxford: Wiley Blackwell.

Faust, A. 2019. "'The Inhabitants of Philistia': On the Identity of the Iron I Settlers in the Periphery of the Philistine Heartland." *Palestine Exploration Quarterly* 151/2:105–33.

Field, C. B., V. Barros, T. F. Stocker, D. Qin, D. J. Dokken, K. L. Ebi, M. D. Mastrandrea, K. J. Mach, G.-K. Plattner, S. K. Allen, M. Tignor, and P.M. Midgley, eds. 2012. *Managing the Risks of Extreme Events and Disasters to Advance Climate Change Adaptation.* Special Report of Working Groups I and II of the Intergovernmental Panel on Climate Change (IPCC). Cambridge: Cambridge University Press.

Finkelberg, M. 2011. "Dorians." In *The Homer Encyclopedia*, ed. M. Finkelberg, 1:217–18. Oxford: Oxford University Press.

Finkelstein, I. 1988. *The Archaeology of the Israelite Settlement.* Leiden: Brill.

Finkelstein, I. 1995. "The Date of the Settlement of the Philistines in Canaan." *Tel Aviv* 22:213–39.

Finkelstein, I. 1996. "The Archaeology of the United Monarchy: An Alternative View." *Levant* 28:177–87.

Finkelstein, I. 1999. "Hazor and the North in the Iron Age: A Low Chronology Perspective." *Bulletin of the American Schools of Oriental Research* 314:55–70.

Finkelstein, I. 2002. "The Campaign of Shoshenq I to Palestine: A Guide to the 10th Century BCE Polity." *Zeitschrift des Deutschen Palästina-Vereins* 118/2:109–35.

Finkelstein, I. 2013. *The Forgotten Kingdom: The Archaeology and History of Northern Israel.* Atlanta, GA: Society of Biblical Literature.

Finkelstein, I. 2014. "The Southern Steppe of the Levant ca.1050–750 BCE: A Framework for a Territorial History." *Palestine Exploration Quarterly* 146/2:89–104.

Finkelstein, I. 2016. "The Levant and the Eastern Mediterranean in the Early Phases of the Iron Age: The View from Micro-archaeology." In *Assyria to Iberia: Art and Culture in the Iron Age*, ed. J. Aruz and M. Seymour, 112–22. New York: Metropolitan Museum of Art.

Finkelstein, I. 2020. "The Arabah Copper Polity and the Rise of Iron Age Edom: A Bias in Biblical Archaeology?" *Antiguo Oriente* 18:11–32.

Finkelstein, I., and A. Fantalkin. 2012. "Khirbet Qeiyafa: An Unsensational Archaeological and Historical Interpretation." *Tel Aviv* 39/1:38–63.

Finkelstein, I, and D. Langgut. 2018. "Climate, Settlement History, and Olive Cultivation in the Iron Age Southern Levant." *Bulletin of the American Schools of Oriental Research* 379:153–69.

Finkelstein, I., and O. Lipschits. 2011. "The Genesis of Moab: A Proposal." *Levant* 43/2:139–52.

Finkelstein, I., N. Na'aman, and T. Römer. 2019. "Restoring Line 31 in the Mesha Stele: The 'House of David' or Biblical Balak?" *Tel Aviv* 46/1:3–11.

Finkelstein, I., S. Weiner, and E. Boaretto. 2015. "Preface—The Iron Age in Israel: The Exact and Life Sciences Perspectives." *Radiocarbon* 57/2:197–206.

Finné, M., K. Holmgren, C- C. Shen, H-M. Hu, M. Boyd, and S. Stocker. 2017. "Late Bronze Age Climate Change and the Destruction of the Mycenaean Palace of Nestor at Pylos." *PLOS ONE* 12/12:e0189447. https://doi.org/10.1371/journal.pone.0189447.

Finné, M., J. Woodbridge, I. Labuhn, and C. N. Roberts. 2019. "Holocene Hydro-climatic Variability in the Mediterranean: A Synthetic Multi-proxy Reconstruction." *Holocene* 29/5:847–63.

Fletcher, R. N. 2012. "Opening the Mediterranean: Assyria, the Levant and the Transformation of Early Iron Age Trade." *Antiquity* 86:211–20.

Folke, C. 2006. "Resilience: The Emergence of a Perspective for Social-Ecological Systems Analyses." *Global Environmental Change* 16:253–67.

Folke, C., S. R. Carpenter, B. Walker, M. Scheffer, T. Chapin, and J. Rockström. 2010. "Resilience Thinking: Integrating Resilience, Adaptability and Transformability." *Ecology and Society* 15/4:20. https://www.ecologyandsociety.org/vol15/iss4/art20.

Fourrier, S. 2013. "Constructing the Peripheries: Extra-urban Sanctuaries and Peer-Polity Interaction in Iron Age Cyprus." *Bulletin of the American Schools of Oriental Research* 370:103–22.

Frahm, E. 2009. *Historische und historisch-literarische Texte.* Keilschrifttexte aus Assur literarischen Inhalts 3. Wissenschaftliche Veroffentlichungen der Deutschen Orient-Gesellschaft 121. Wiesbaden: Harrassowitz.

Frahm, E. 2011. "Die Inschriftenreste auf den Obeliskfragmenten aus Assur." In *Die Obeliskenfragmente aus Assur: Mit einem Beitrag zu den Inschriften von Eckart Frahm*, ed. J. Orlamünde, 59–75. Wissenschaftliche Veroffentlichungen der Deutschen Orient-Gesellschaft 135. Wiesbaden: Harrassowitz.

Frahm, E. 2017. "The Neo-Assyrian Period (ca. 1000–609 BCE)." In *A Companion to Assyria*, ed. E. Frahm, 161–208. Oxford: Wiley Blackwell.

Frahm, E. 2019. "The Neo-Assyrian Royal Inscriptions as Text: History, Ideology, and Intertextuality." In *Writing Neo-Assyrian History: Sources, Problems, and Approaches*, ed. G. Lanfranchi, R. Mattila, and R. Rollinger, 139–59. State Archives of Assyria Studies 29. Helsinki: Neo-Assyrian Text Corpus Project.

Frahm, E. 2023. *Assyria: The Rise and Fall of the World's First Empire.* New York: Basic Books.

Frame, G. 1995. *Rulers of Babylonia from the Second Dynasty of Isin to the End of Assyrian Domination (1157–612 BC).* Toronto: University of Toronto Press.

Frankenstein, S. 1979. "The Phoenicians in the Far West: A Function of Neo-Assyrian Imperialism." In *Power and Propaganda: A Symposium on Ancient Empires*, ed. M. T. Larsen, 263–94. Copenhagen: Akademisk Forlag.

Franklin, N. 2017. "Entering the Arena: The Megiddo Stables Reconsidered." In *Re-thinking Israel: Studies in the History and Archaeology of Ancient Israel in Honor of Israel Finkelstein*, ed. O. Lipschits, Y. Gadot, and M. J. Adams, 87–101. Winona Lake, IN: Eisenbrauns.

Fuchs, A. 2017. "Assyria and the North: Anatolia." In *A Companion to Assyria*, ed. E. Frahm, 249–58. Oxford: Wiley Blackwell.

Galil, G. 2010. "Most Ancient Hebrew Biblical Inscription Deciphered." EurekAlert!, American Association for the Advancement of Science, January 7. https://www.eurekalert.org/news-releases/649504. See also Science Daily, Janaury 8. https://www.sciencedaily.com/releases/2010/01/100107183037.htm.

Gambash, G., B. Pestarino, and D. Friesem. 2022. "From Murex to Fabric: The Mediterranean Purple." *Technai* 13:85–113.

Gardner, J. M. 1923. *Pharaohs Resurrected*. New York: Sorg Publishing.

Garfinkel, Y. 2017. "The Iron Age City of Khirbet Qeiyafa." In *The Shephelah during the Iron Age: Recent Archaeological Studies*, ed. O. Lipschits and A. M. Maeir, 115–31. University Park: Penn State University Press/Eisenbrauns.

Garfinkel, Y. 2021. "The 10th Century BCE in Judah: Archaeology and the Biblical Tradition." *Jerusalem Journal of Archaeology* 1:126–54.

Garfinkel, Y., and S. Ganor. 2008. "Khirbet Qeiyafa: Sha'arayimn." *Journal of Hebrew Scriptures* 8. https://doi.org/10.5508/jhs.2008.v8.a22.

Garfinkel, Y., and S. Ganor. 2010. *Khirbet Qeiyafa 1: Excavation Report 2007–2008*. Jerusalem: Israel Exploration Society.

Garfinkel, Y., M. R. Golub, H. Misgav, and S. Ganor. 2015. "The ʾIšbaʿal Inscription from Khirbet Qeiyafa." *Bulletin of the American Schools of Oriental Research* 373:217–33.

Garfinkel, Y., and M. Pietsch. 2021. "Hazor, Megiddo, and Gezer: Bronze Age Cities in Iron Age Context." *Vetus Testamentum* (July 30): 1–17.

Garnand, B. K. 2020. "Phoenicians and Greeks as Comparable Contemporary Migrant Groups." In *A Companion to Greeks across the Ancient World*, ed. F. De Angelis, 139–72. Boston: John Wiley & Sons.

Genz, H. 2013. "'No Land Could Stand before Their Arms, from Hatti . . . On . . .'? New Light on the End of the Hittite Empire and the Early Iron Age in Central Anatolia." In *The Philistines and Other "Sea Peoples" in Text and Archaeology*, ed. A. E. Killebrew and G. Lehmann, 469–77. Atlanta, GA: Society of Biblical Literature.

Georgiadis, M. 2009. "The South-Eastern Aegean in the LH IIIC Period: What Do the Tombs Tell Us?" In *Forces of Transformation: The End of the Bronze Age in the Mediterranean*, ed. C. Bachhuber and G. Roberts, 92–99. Oxford: Oxbow Books.

Georgiou, A. 2011. "The Settlement Histories of Cyprus at the Opening of the Twelfth Century BC." In *Centre d'études chypriotes 41: Actes du POCA, Lyon 2011 (Postgraduate Cypriote Archaeology)*, ed. A. Cannavó and A. Carbillet, 109–31. Paris: Édition-Diffusion De Boccard.

Georgiou, A. 2015. "Cyprus during the 'Crisis Years' Revisited." In *The Mediterranean Mirror: Cultural Contacts in the Mediterranean Sea between 1200 and 750 B.C.; International Post-doc and Young Researcher Conference; Heidelberg, 6th–8th October 2012*, ed. A. Babbi, F. Bubenheimer-Erhart, B. Marín-Aguilera, and S. Mühl, 129–45. Mainz: Verlag des Römisch-Germanischen Zentralmuseums.

Georgiou, A. 2017. "Flourishing amidst a 'Crisis': The Regional History of the Paphos Polity at the Transition from the 13th to the 12th Centuries BCE." In *"Sea Peoples" Up-to-Date: New Research on Transformations in the Eastern Mediterranean in the 13th–11th Centuries BCE;*

Proceedings of the ESF Workshop Held at the Austrian Academy of Sciences, Vienna, 3–4 November 2014, ed. P. M. Fischer and T. Bürge, 207–27. Vienna: Österreichischen Akademie der Wissenschaften.

Georgiou, A., and M. Iacovou. 2020. "Cyprus." In *A Companion to the Archaeology of Early Greece and the Mediterranean*, ed. I. S. Lemos and A. Kotsonas, 2:1133–62. London: Wiley Blackwell.

Gilboa, A. 2005. "Sea Peoples and Phoenicians along the Southern Phoenician Coast—A Reconciliation: An Interpretation of Šikila (SKL) Material Culture." *Bulletin of the American Schools of Oriental Research* 337:47–78.

Gilboa, A. 2006–7. "Fragmenting the Sea Peoples, with an Emphasis on Cyprus, Syria and Egypt: A Tel Dor Perspective." *Scripta Mediterranea* 27–28:209–44.

Gilboa, A. 2015. "Dor and Egypt in the Early Iron Age: An Archaeological Perspective of (Part of) the Wenamun Report." *Egypt and the Levant* 25:247–74.

Gilboa, A. 2022. "The Southern Levantine Roots of the Phoenician Mercantile Phenomenon." *Bulletin of ASOR* 387:31–53.

Gilboa, A., and D. Namdar. 2015. "On the Beginnings of South Asian Spice Trade with the Mediterranean Region: A Review." *Radiocarbon* 57/2:265–83.

Gilboa, A., and I. Sharon. 2008. "Between the Carmel and the Sea: Tel Dor's Iron Age Reconsidered." *Near Eastern Archaeology* 71/3:146–70.

Gilboa, A., I. Sharon, and E. Boaretto. 2008. "Tel Dor and the Chronology of Phoenician 'Pre-colonisation' Stages." In *Beyond the Homeland: Markers in Phoenician Chronology*, ed. C. Sargona, 113–204. Ancient Near Eastern Studies Supplement 28. Leuven: Peeters Press.

Gilboa, A., P. Waiman-Barak, and R. Jones. 2015. "On the Origin of Iron Age Phoenician Ceramics at Kommos, Crete: Regional and Diachronic Perspectives across the Bronze Age to Iron Age Transition." *Bulletin of the American Schools of Oriental Research* 374:75–102.

Gilboa, A., P. Waiman-Barak, and I. Sharon. 2015. "Dor, the Carmel Coast and Early Iron Age Mediterranean Exchanges." In *The Mediterranean Mirror: Cultural Contacts in the Mediterranean Sea between 1200 and 750 B.C.*, ed. A. Babbi, F. Bubenheimer-Erhart, B. Marín-Aguilera, and S. Mühl, 85–109. Mainz: Verlag des Römisch-Germanischen Zentralmuseums.

Gilibert, A. 2011. *Syro-Hittite Monumental Art and the Archaeology of Performance: The Stone Reliefs at Carchemish and Zincirli in the Earlier First Millennium BCE.* Topoi—Berlin Studies of the Ancient World. Berlin: Walter de Gruyter.

Glassner, J.-J. 2004. *Mesopotamian Chronicles*, ed. B. R. Foster. Atlanta, GA: Society for Biblical Literature.

Gnanadesikan, A. E. 2009. *The Writing Revolution: Cuneiform to the Internet.* Malden, MA: Wiley-Blackwell.

Goedegebuure, P., T. van den Hout, J. Osborne, M. Massa, C. Bachhuber, and F. Sahin. 2020. "Türkmen-Karahöyük 1: A New Hieroglyphic Luwian Inscription from Great King Hartapu, Son of Mursili, Conqueror of Phrygia." *Anatolian Studies* 70:29–43.

Goelet, O. 2016. "Tomb Robberies in the Valley of the Kings." In *The Oxford Handbook of the Valley of the Kings*, ed. R. H. Wilkinson and K. R. Weeks, 448–66. Oxford: Oxford University Press.

Gonzalez, R.A. 2018. *Inter-cultural Communications and Iconography in the Western Mediterranean during the Late Bronze Age and the Early Iron Age.* Rahden: Verlag Marie Leidorf.

Graefe, E., and G. Belova, eds. 2010. *The Royal Cache TT 320—A Re-examination*. Cairo: Supreme Council of Antiquities Press.

Grayson, A. K. 2005. "Shalmaneser III and the Levantine States: The 'Damascus Coalition Rebellion.'" *Journal of Hebrew Scriptures* 5. https://doi.org/10.5508/jhs.2004.v5.a4.

Grimal, N. 1988. *A History of Ancient Egypt*. Translated by I. Shaw. Oxford: Blackwell.

Gunderson, L. H. 2003. "Adaptive Dancing: Interactions between Social Resilience and Ecological Crises." In *Navigating Social-Ecological Systems: Building Resilience for Complexity and Change*, ed. F. Berkes, J. Colding, and C. Folke, 33–52. Cambridge: Cambridge University Press.

Gunderson, L. H., and C. S. Holling, eds. 2002. *Panarchy: Understanding Transformations in Human and Natural Systems*. Washington, DC: Island Press.

Gur-Arieh, S., and A. M. Maeir. 2020. "The Excavations in Area C." In *Tell Es-Safi/Gath II: Excavations and Studies*, ed. A. M. Maeir and J. Uziel, 117–88. Münster: Zaphon.

Haggis, D. C. 2020. "Kavousi and the Mirabello Region." In *A Companion to the Archaeology of Early Greece and the Mediterranean*, ed. I. S. Lemos and A. Kotsonas, 2:1071–87. London: Wiley Blackwell.

Haldon, J., A. Binois-Roman, M. Eisenberg, A. Izdebski, L. Mordechai, T. Newfield, P. Slavin, S. White, and K. Wnęk. 2021. "Between Resilience and Adaptation: A Historical Framework for Understanding Stability and Transformation of Societies to Shocks and Stress." In *COVID-19: Systemic Risk and Resilience; Risk, Systems and Decisions*, ed. I. Linkov, J. M. Keenan, and B. D. Trump, 235–68. Cham, Switzerland: Springer.

Haldon, J., A. F. Chase, W. Eastwood, M. Medina-Elizalde, A. Izdebski, F. Ludlow, G. Middleton, L. Mordechai, J. Nesbitt, and B. L. Turner. 2020. "Demystifying Collapse: Climate, Environment, and Social Agency in Pre-modern Societies." *Millennium* 17/1:1–33. https://doi.org/10.1515/mill-2020-0002.

Haldon, J., M. Eisenberg, L. Mordechai, A. Izdebski, and S. White. 2020. "Lessons from the Past, Policies for the Future: Resilience and Sustainability in Past Crises." *Journal of Environment Systems and Decisions*. https://doi.org/10.1007/s10669-020-09778-9.

Haldon, J., A. Izdebski, L. Kemp, L. Mordechai, and B. Trump. 2022. "SDG 13—How Societies Succeeded or Failed to Respond to Environmental Disruption." In *Before the SDGs: A Historical Companion to the UN Sustainable Development Goals*, ed. M. Gutmann and D. Gorman, 385–424. Oxford: Oxford University Press.

Hall, J. M. 1997. *Ethnic Identity in Greek Antiquity*. Cambridge: Cambridge University Press.

Hall, J. M. 2002. *Hellenicity: Between Ethnicity and Culture*. Chicago: University of Chicago Press.

Hall, J. M. 2003. "The Dorianization of the Messenians." In *Helots and Their Masters in Laconia and Messenia: Histories, Ideologies, Structures*, ed. N. Luraghi and S. E. Alcock, chap. 6. Hellenic Studies Series 4. Washington, DC: Center for Hellenic Studies. https://chs.harvard.edu/book/luraghi-nino-and-susan-e-alcock-eds-helots-and-the-masters-in-laconia-and-messenia.

Hall, J. M. 2006. "Dorians." *Encyclopedia of Ancient Greece*, ed. N. Wilson, 240–42. New York: Routledge.

Hall, J. M. 2007. *A History of the Archaic Greek World, ca. 1200–479 BCE*. Oxford: Blackwell Publishing.

Hall, J. M., and J. F. Osborne, eds. 2022. *The Connected Iron Age: Interregional Networks in the Eastern Mediterranean, 900–600 BCE*. Chicago: University of Chicago Press.

Hall, T. D. 2014. "A 'Perfect Storm' in the Collapse of Bronze Age Civilization? Useful Insights and Roads Not Taken." *Cliodynamics* 5/1:75–86.

Hallo, W. W., and W. K. Simpson. 1998. *The Ancient Near East: A History*. 2nd ed. New York: Harcourt Brace College Publishers.

Hammond, N.G.L. 1931–32. "Prehistoric Epirus and the Dorian Invasion." *BSA* 32:131–79.

Handmer, J., Y. Honda, Z. W. Kundzewicz, N. Arnell, G. Benito, J. Hatfield, I. F. Mohamed, P. Peduzzi, S. Wu, B. Sherstyukov, K. Takahashi, and Z. Yan. 2012. "Changes in Impacts of Climate Extremes: Human Systems and Ecosystems." In *Managing the Risks of Extreme Events and Disasters to Advance Climate Change Adaptation*, ed. C. B. Field, V. Barros, T. F. Stocker, D. Qin, D. J. Dokken, K. L. Ebi, M. D. Mastrandrea, K. J. Mach, G.-K. Plattner, S. K. Allen, M. Tignor, and P. M. Midgley, 231–90. Special Report of Working Groups I and II of the Intergovernmental Panel on Climate Change (IPCC). Cambridge: Cambridge University Press.

Harland, J. P. 1941. "Review of *Kerameikos I*." *Classical Journal* 36:429–32.

Harmansah, O. 2007. "'Source of the Tigris': Event, Place and Performance in the Assyrian Landscapes of the Early Iron Age." *Archaeological Dialogues* 14/2:179–204.

Harrison, T. P. 2009a. "Lifting the Veil on a 'Dark Age': Ta'yinat and the North Orontes Valley during the Early Iron Age." In *Exploring the Longue Durée: Essays in Honor of Lawrence E. Stager*, ed. J. D. Schloen, 171–84. Winona Lake, IN: Eisenbrauns.

Harrison, T. P. 2009b. "Neo-Hittites in the 'Land of Palistin': Renewed Investigations at Tell Ta'yinat on the Plain of Antioch." *Near Eastern Archaeology* 72/4:174–89.

Harrison, T. P. 2010. "The Late Bronze/Early Iron Age Transition in the North Orontes Valley." In *Societies in Transition: Evolutionary Processes in the Northern Levant between Late Bronze Age II and Early Iron Age; Papers Presented on the Occasion of the 20th Anniversary of the New Excavations in Tell Afis, Bologna, 15th November 2007*, ed. F. Venturi, 83–102. Bologna: Clueb.

Harrison, T. P. 2013. "Tayinat in the Early Iron Age." In *Across the Border: Late Bronze–Iron Age Relations between Syria and Anatolia; Proceedings of a Symposium Held at the Research Center of Anatolian Studies, Koç University, Istanbul, May 31–June 1, 2010*, ed. K. A. Yener, 61–87. Leuven: Peeters Publishers.

Harrison, T. P. 2014. "Recent Discoveries at Tayinat (Ancient Kunulua/Calno) and Their Biblical Implications." In *Congress Volume Munich 2013*, ed. C. M. Maier, 396–425. Leiden: Brill.

Harrison, T. P. 2016. "The Neo-Assyrian Provincial Administration at Tayinat (Ancient Kunalia)." In *The Provincial Archaeology of the Assyrian Empire*, ed. J. MacGinnis, D. Wicke, and T. Greenfield, 253–64. Cambridge: McDonald Institute for Archaeological Research.

Harrison, T. P. 2021. "The Iron Age I–II Transition in the Northern Levant: An Emerging Consensus." *Jerusalem Journal of Archaeology* 1:325–51.

Hatzaki, E., and A. Kotsonas. 2020. "Knossos and North Central Crete." In *A Companion to the Archaeology of Early Greece and the Mediterranean*, ed. I. S. Lemos and A. Kotsonas, 2:1029–53. London: Wiley Blackwell.

Hawass, Z. 2010. "Preface." In *The Royal Cache TT 320—A Re-examination*, ed. E. Graefe and G. Belova, 1–2. Cairo: Supreme Council of Antiquities Press.

Hawass, Z., S. Ismail, A. Selim, S. N. Saleem, D. Fathalla, S. Wasef, A. Z. Gad, R. Saad, S. Fares, H. Amer, P. Gostner, Y. Z. Gad, C. M. Pusch, and A. R. Zink. 2012. "Revisiting the Harem

Conspiracy and Death of Ramesses III: Anthropological, Forensic, Radiological, and Genetic Study." *British Medical Journal* 345:e8268. http:// www.bmj.com/content/345/bmj .e8268.

Hawkins, J. D. 1988. "Kuzi-Tešub and the 'Great Kings' of Karkamiš." *Anatolian Studies* 38:99–108.

Hawkins, J. D. 1995. "Great Kings and Country Lords at Malatya and Karkamis." In *Studio Historiae Ardens: Ancient Near Eastern Studies Presented to Philo H. J. Houwink ten Cate*, ed. Th.P.J. van den Hout and J. de Roos, 75–86. Istanbul: Nederlands Historisch- Archaeologisch Instituut te Istanbul.

Hawkins, J. D. 2000. *Corpus of Hieroglyphic Luwian Inscriptions*. Vol. 1, *Inscriptions of the Iron Age*. Berlin: Walter de Gruyter.

Hawkins, J. D. 2009. "Cilicia, the Amuq and Aleppo: New Light in a Dark Age." *Near Eastern Archaeology* 72/4:164–73.

Hawkins, J. D. 2011. "The Inscriptions of the Aleppo Temple." *Anatolian Studies* 61:35–54.

Hawkins, J. D., and H. Peker. 2014. "Karkemish in the Iron Age." In *Karkemish: An Ancient Capital on the Euphrates*, ed. N. Marchetti, 107–10. Bologna: AnteQuem.

Hawkins, J. D., and M. Weeden. 2016. "Sketch History of Karkemish in the Earlier Iron Age (Iron I–IIB)." In *Carchemish in Context: The Land of Carchemish Project, 2006–2010*, ed. T. J. Wilkinson, E. Peltenburg, and E. B. Wilkinson, 9–21. Oxford: Oxbow Books.

Heurtley, W. A. 1926–27. "A Prehistoric Site in Western Macedonia and the Dorian Invasion." *Annual of the British School at Athens* 28:158–94.

Hitchcock, L. A., and A. M. Maeir. 2019. "Pirates of the Crete-Aegean: Migration, Mobility, and Post-palatial Realities at the End of the Bronze Age." In *Proceedings of the 12th International Congress of Cretan Studies, Heraklion, 21–25.9.2016*, 1–12. Herakleio: Society of Cretan Historical Studies.

Hodos, T. 2020. *The Archaeology of the Mediterranean Iron Age: A Globalising World c.1100–600 BCE*. Cambridge: Cambridge University Press.

Hodos, T. 2022. "Globalizing the Mediterranean's Iron Age." In *The Connected Iron Age: Interregional Networks in the Eastern Mediterranean, 900–600 BCE*, ed. J. M. Hall and J. F. Osborne, 214–32. Chicago: University of Chicago Press.

Hoffman, G. L. 1997. *Imports and Immigrants: Near Eastern Contacts with Iron Age Crete*. Ann Arbor: University of Michigan Press.

Höflmayer, F., and R. Gundacker. 2021. "Sheshonq (Shishak) in Palestine: Old Paradigms and New Vistas." *Ancient Near East Today* 9/4. https://www.asor.org/anetoday/2021/04 /sheshonq-in-palestine.

Hogarth, D. G. 1911. *Hittite Problems and the Excavation of Carchemish*. London: British Academy.

Hoglund, K. G. 1994. "Edomites." In *Peoples of the Old Testament World*, ed. A. J. Hoerth, G. L. Mattingly, and E. M. Yamauchi, 335–47. Grand Rapids, MI: Baker Books.

Holling, C. S. 1973. "Resilience and Stability of Ecological Systems." *Annual Review of Ecology and Systematics* 4:1–23.

Holling, C. S. 1986. "The Resilience of Terrestrial Ecosystems: Local Surprise and Global Change." In *Sustainable Development of the Biosphere*, ed. W. C. Clark and R. E. Munn, 292–317. Cambridge: Cambridge University Press.

Holling, C. S. 2001. "Understanding the Complexity of Economic, Ecological, and Social Systems." *Ecosystems* 4/5:390–405.

Holling, C. S., S. R. Carpenter, W. A. Brock, and L. H. Gunderson. 2002. "Discoveries for Sustainable Futures." In *Panarchy: Understanding Transformations in Human and Natural Systems*, ed. L. H. Gunderson and C. S. Holling, 395–417. Washington, DC: Island Press.

Holling, C. S., and L. H. Gunderson. 2002. "Resilience and adaptive cycles." In *Panarchy: Understanding Transformations in Human and Natural Systems*, ed. L. H. Gunderson and C. S. Holling, 25–62. Washington, DC: Island Press.

Holling, C. S., L. H. Gunderson, and D. Ludwig. 2002. "In Quest of a Theory of Adaptive Change." In *Panarchy: Understanding Transformations in Human and Natural Systems*, ed. L. H. Gunderson and C. S. Holling, 2–22. Washington, DC: Island Press.

Hooker, J. T. 1979. "New Reflections on the Dorian Invasion." *Klio* 61:353–60.

Horn, S. H. 1986. "Why the Moabite Stone Was Blown to Pieces." *Biblical Archaeology Review* 12/3:50–61.

Howard, D. M. 1994. "Philistines." In *Peoples of the Old Testament World*, ed. A. J. Hoerth, G. L. Mattingly, and E. M. Yamauchi, 231–50. Grand Rapids, MI: Baker Books.

Iacovou, M. 1994. "The Topography of Eleventh Century B.C. Cyprus." In *Cyprus in the 11th Century B.C.: Proceedings of the International Symposium, Nicosia, 30–31 October 1993*, ed. V. Karageorghis, 149–65. Nicosia: A. G. Leventis Foundation.

Iacovou, M. 1999. "The Greek Exodus to Cyprus: The Antiquity of Hellenism." *Mediterranean Historical Review* 14/2:1–28.

Iacovou, M. 2002. "From Ten to Naught: Formation, Consolidation and Abolition of Cyprus' Iron Age Polities." *Cahiers du Centre d'Études Chypriotes* 32:73–85.

Iacovou, M. 2005a. "Cyprus at the Dawn of the First Millennium BC: Cultural Homogenization versus the Tyranny of Ethnic Identifications." In *Archaeological Perspectives on the Transmission and Transformation of Culture in the Eastern Mediterranean*, ed. J. Clarke, 125–34. Oxford: Oxbow.

Iacovou, M. 2005b. "The Early Iron Age Urban Forms of Cyprus." In *Mediterranean Urbanization 800–600 BC*, ed. R. Osborne and B. Cunliffe, 17–43. Proceedings of the British Academy 126. Oxford: Oxford University for the British Academy.

Iacovou, M. 2006a. "From the Mycenaean QA-SI-RE-U to the Cypriote PA-SI-LE-WO-SE: The Basileus in the Kingdoms of Cyprus." In *Ancient Greece from the Mycenaean Palaces to the Age of Homer*, ed. S. Deger-Jalkotzy and I. Lemos, 315–35. Edinburgh: Edinburgh University Press.

Iacovou, M. 2006b. "'Greeks,' 'Phoenicians' and 'Eteocypriots': Ethnic Identities in the Cypriote Kingdoms." In *Sweet Land . . . : Lectures on the History and Culture of Cyprus*, ed. J. Chrysostomides and Ch. Dendrinos, 27–59. Camberley: Porphyrogenitus.

Iacovou, M. 2007. "Advocating Cyprocentricism: An Indigenous Model for the Emergence of State Formation on Cyprus." In *"Up to the Gates of Ekron" (1 Samuel 17:52): Essays on the Archaeology and History of the Eastern Mediterranean in Honor of Seymour Gitin*, ed. S. White Crawford, A. Ben-Tor, J. P. Dessel, W. G. Dever, A. Mazar, and J. Aviram, 461–75. Jerusalem: Israel Exploration Society.

Iacovou, M. 2008. "Cultural and Political Configurations in Iron Age Cyprus: The Sequel to a Protohistoric Episode." *American Journal of Archaeology* 112/4:625–57.

Iacovou, M. 2012. "External and Internal Migrations during the 12th Century BC: Setting the Stage for an Economically Successful Early Iron Age in Cyprus." In *Cyprus and the Aegean in the Early Iron Age: The Legacy of Nicolas Coldstream*, ed. M. Iacovou, 207–27. Nicosia: Bank of Cyprus Cultural Foundation.

Iacovou, M. 2013. "Historically Elusive and Internally Fragile Island Polities: The Intricacies of Cyprus's Political Geography in the Iron Age." *Bulletin of the American Schools of Oriental Research* 370:15–47.

Iacovou, M. 2014a. "Beyond the Athenocentric Misconceptions: The Cypriote Polities in Their Economic Context." In *Basileis and Poleis on the Island of Cyprus: The Cypriote Polities in Their Mediterranean Context*, ed. M. Hatzopoulos and M. Iacovou. *Cahiers du Centre d'Études Chypriotes* 44:95–117.

Iacovou, M. 2014b. "Cyprus during the Iron Age I Period (Late Cypriot IIC–IIIA)." In *The Oxford Handbook of the Archaeology of the Levant, c. 8000–332 BCE*, ed. M. L. Steiner and A. E. Killebrew, 660–74. Oxford: Oxford University Press.

Iacovou, M. 2014c. "Cyprus during the Iron Age through the Persian Period." In *The Oxford Handbook of the Archaeology of the Levant, c. 8000–332 BCE*, ed. M. L. Steiner and A. E. Killebrew, 795–824. Oxford: Oxford University Press.

Iakovides, S. 1980. *Excavations of the Necropolis at Perati*. Los Angeles: Institute of Archaeology, University of California, Los Angeles.

Ilan, D. 2019. "The 'Conquest' of the Highlands in the Iron Age I." In *The Social Archaeology of the Levant: From Prehistory to the Present*, ed. A. Yasur-Landau, E. H. Cline, and Y. Rowan, 283–309. Cambridge: Cambridge University Press.

Ilieva, P. 2019. "Phoenicians, Cypriots and Euboeans in the Northern Aegean: A Reappraisal." *Aura* 2:65–102.

Jackson, R., S. Hartman, B. Trump, C. Crumley, T. McGovern, I. Linkov, and A.E.J. Ogilvie. 2022. "Disjunctures of Practice and the Problems of Collapse." In *Perspectives on Public Policy in Societal-Environmental Crises: What the Future Needs from History*, 75–108, ed. A. Izdebski, J. Haldon, and P. Filipkowski. Cham, Switzerland: Springer.

James, P., and P. G. van der Veen, eds. 2015. *Solomon and Shishak: Current Perspectives from Archaeology, Epigraphy, History and Chronology; Proceedings of the Third BICANE Colloquium Held at Sidney Sussex College, Cambridge, 26–27 March 2011*, 137–47. BAR International Series 2732. Oxford: Archaeopress.

Janes, S. 2010. "Negotiating Island Interactions: Cyprus, the Aegean and the Levant in the Late Bronze to Early Iron Ages." In *Material Connections in the Ancient Mediterranean: Mobility, Materiality and Mediterranean Identities*, ed. P. van Dommelen and A. B. Knapp, 127–46. London: Routledge.

Janes, S. 2013. "Death and Burial in the Age of the Cypriot City-Kingdoms: Social Complexity Based on the Mortuary Evidence." *Bulletin of the American Schools of Oriental Research* 370:145–68.

Janes, S. 2014. "An Entangled Past: Island Interactions, Mortuary Practices and the Negotiation of Identitites on Early Iron Age Cyprus." In *The Cambridge Prehistory of the Bronze and Iron Age Mediterranean*, ed. A. B. Knapp and P. van Dommelen, 571–84. Cambridge: Cambridge University Press.

Janeway, B. 2006–7. "The Nature and Extent of Aegean Contact at Tell Ta'yinat and Vicinity in the Early Iron Age: Evidence of the Sea Peoples?" *Scripta Mediterranea* 27–28:123–46.

Janeway, B. 2017. *Sea Peoples of the Northern Levant? Aegean-Style Pottery from Early Iron Age Tell Tayinat*. Studies in the Archaeology and History of the Levant, vol. 7. Leiden: Brill.

Jarus, O. 2021. "King Solomon's Mines in Spain? Not Likely, Experts Say." *Live Science*, May 4. https://www.livescience.com/king-solomon-mining-expedition-claim.html.

Jeffers, J. A. 2013. "Tiglath-Pileser I: A Light in a 'Dark Age.'" PhD diss., University of Pennsylvania.

Johnson, S. A. 2017. *Why Did Ancient Civilizations Fail?* New York: Routledge.

Johnston, P. A., and B. Kaufman. 2019. "Metallurgy and Other Technologies." In *The Oxford Handbook of the Phoenician and Punic Mediterranean*, ed. C. López-Ruiz and B. R. Doak, 401–22. Oxford: Oxford University Press.

Jones, D. W. 2000. *External Relations of Early Iron Age Crete, 1100–600 B.C.* AIA Monographs New Series, No. 4. Dubuque, IA: Kendall/Hunt Publishing.

Jung, R. 2023. "Synchronizing Palace Destructions in the Eastern Mediterranean." In *Synchronizing the Destructions of the Mycenaean Palaces*, ed. R. Jung and E. Kardamaki, 255–322. Vienna: Austrian Academy of Sciences Press.

Jung, R., and E. Kardamaki. 2023. "Introduction." In *Synchronizing the Destructions of the Mycenaean Palaces*, ed. R. Jung and E. Kardamaki, 11–33. Vienna: Austrian Academy of Sciences Press.

Kaniewski, D., J. Guiot, and E. Van Campo. 2015. "Drought and Societal Collapse 3200 Years Ago in the East Mediterranean: A Review." *WIREs Climate Change* 6:369–82. https://doi.org/10.1002/wcc.345.

Kaniewski, D., N. Marriner, J. Bretschneider, G. Jans, C. Morhange, R. Cheddadi, T. Otto, F. Luce, and E. Van Campo. 2019a. "300-Year Drought Frames Late Bronze Age to Early Iron Age Transition in the Near East: New Palaeoecological Data from Cyprus and Syria." *Regional Environmental Change* 19:2287–97. https://doi.org/10.1007/s10113-018-01460-w.

Kaniewski, D., N. Marriner, R. Cheddadi, C. Morhange, J. Bretschneider, G. Jans, T. Otto, F. Luce, and E. Van Campo. 2019b. "Cold and Dry Outbreaks in the Eastern Mediterranean 3200 Years Ago." *Geology* 47/10:933–37.

Kaniewski, D., N. Marriner, R. Cheddadi, P. M. Fischer, T. Otto, F. Luce, and E. Van Campo. 2020. "Climate Change and Social Unrest: A 6,000-Year Chronicle from the Eastern Mediterranean." *Geophysical Research Letters* 47/7. https://doi.org/10.1029/2020GL087496.

Kaniewski, D., E. Van Campo, J. Guiot, S. Le Burel, T. Otto, and C. Baeteman. 2013. "Environmental Roots of the Late Bronze Age Crisis." *PLOS ONE* 8/8:e71004. https://doi.org/10.1371/journal.pone.0071004.

Kapucu, N., C. V. Hawkins, and F. I. Rivera, eds. 2013. *Disaster Resiliency: Interdisciplinary Perspectives*. New York: Routledge.

Karageorghis, V. 1983. *Palaepaphos-Skales: An Iron Age Cemetery in Cyprus*. Alt-Paphos 3. Konstanz: Universitätsverlag.

Karageorghis, V. 1994. "The Prehistory of an Ethnogenesis." In *Cyprus in the 11th Century B.C.: Proceedings of the International Symposium, Nicosia, 30–31 October 1993*, ed. V. Karageorghis, 1–9. Nicosia: A. G. Leventis Foundation.

Kardamakis, E. 2015. "Conclusions from the New Deposit at the Western Staircase Terrace at Tiryns." In *Mycenaeans Up to Date: The Archaeology of the Northeastern Peloponnese—Current Concepts and New Directions*, ed. A-L. Schallin and I. Tournavitou, 79–97. Stockholm: Swedish Institute at Athens.

Karkkainen, B. C. 2005. "Panarchy and Adaptive Change: Around the Loop and Back Again." *Minnesota Journal of Law, Science & Technology* 7/1:59–77.

Kassianidou, V. 2012. "The Origin and Use of Metals in Iron Age Cyprus." In *Cyprus and the Aegean in the Early Iron Age: The Legacy of Nicolas Coldstream*, ed. M. Iacovou, 229–59. Nicosia: Bank of Cyprus Cultural Foundation.

Kassianidou, V. 2013. "The Exploitation of the Landscape: Metal Resources and the Copper Trade during the Age of the Cypriot City-Kingdoms." *Bulletin of the American Schools of Oriental Research* 370:49–82.

Kassianidou, V. 2014. "Cypriot Copper for the Iron Age World of the Eastern Mediterranean." In *Structure, Measurement and Meaning: Studies on Prehistoric Cyprus in Honour of David Frankel*, ed. J. M. Webb, 261–71. Studies in Mediterranean Archaeology 143. Uppsala: Åströms Förlag.

Katzenstein, H. J. 1973. *The History of Tyre: From the Beginning of the Second Millennium B.C.E. until the Fall of the Neo-Babylonian Empire in 538 B.C.E.* Jerusalem: Schoken Institute for Jewish Research.

Kealhofer, L., P. Grave, and M. M. Voigt. 2019. "Dating Gordion: The Timing and Tempo of Late Bronze Age and Iron Age Political Transformation." *Radiocarbon* 61/2:495–514.

Kearns, C. M. 2015. "Unruly Landscapes: The Making of 1st Millennium BCE Polities on Cyprus." PhD diss., Cornell University.

Kearns, C. M. 2019. "Discerning 'Favorable' Environments: Science, Survey Archaeology, and the Cypriot Iron Age." In *New Directions in Cypriot Archaeology*, ed. C. M. Kearns and S. W. Manning, 266–94. Ithaca, NY: Cornell University Press.

Kearns, C. M. 2022. *The Rural Landscapes of Archaic Cyprus: An Archaeology of Environmental and Social Change*. Cambridge: Cambridge University Press.

Kemp, L. 2019. "Civilisational Collapse Has a Bright Past—but a Dark Future." Aeon, May 21. https://aeon.co/ideas/civilisational-collapse-has-a-bright-past-but-a-dark-future.

Kemp, L., and E. H. Cline. 2022. "Systemic Risk and Resilience: Synchronous Failures and the Bronze Age Collapse." In *Perspectives on Public Policy in Societal-Environmental Crises: What the Future Needs from History*, 207–23, ed. A. Izdebski, J. Haldon, and P. Filipkowski. Cham, Switzerland: Springer.

Kiderlen, M., M. Bode, A. Hauptmann, and Y. Bassiakos. 2016. "Tripod Cauldrons Produced at Olympia Give Evidence for Trade with Copper from Faynan (Jordan) to South West Greece, c. 950–750 BCE." *Journal of Archaeological Science: Reports* 8:303–13.

Kilani, M. 2020. *Byblos in the Late Bronze Age. Interactions between the Levantine and Egyptian Worlds*. Leiden: Brill.

Killebrew, A. E. 2005. *Biblical Peoples and Ethnicity: An Archaeological Study of Egyptians, Canaanites, Philistines, and Early Israel, 1300–1100 B.C.E.* Atlanta, GA: Society of Biblical Literature.

Killebrew, A. E. 2014. "Israel during the Iron Age II Period." In *The Oxford Handbook of the Archaeology of the Levant, c. 8000–332 BCE*, ed. M. L. Steiner and A. E. Killebrew, 730–42. Oxford: Oxford University Press.

Killebrew, A. E. 2019. "Canaanite Roots, Proto-Phoenicia, and the Early Phoenician Period." In *The Oxford Handbook of the Phoenician and Punic Mediterranean*, ed. C. López-Ruiz and B. R. Doak, 39–52. Oxford: Oxford University Press.

King, L. W. 1915. *Bronze Reliefs from the Gates of Shalmaneser, King of Assyria B.C. 860–825*. London: British Museum.

Kingsley, S. 2021. "Seeking Solomon on the High Seas." *Wreckwatch* 5–6:48–58.

Kirleis, W., and M. Herles. 2007. "Climatic Change as a Reason for Assyro-Aramaean Conflicts? Pollen Evidence for Drought at the End of the 2nd Millennium BC." *State Archives of Assyria Bulletin* 16:7–37.

Kitchen, K. A. 1973. *The Third Intermediate Period in Egypt (1100–650 B.C.)*. Warminster: Aris & Phillips.

Kitchen, K. A. 2012. "Ramesses III and the Ramesside Period." In *Ramesses III: The Life and Times of Egypt's Last Hero*, ed. E. H. Cline and D. O'Connor, 1–26. Ann Arbor: University of Michigan Press.

Kleiman, A. 2016. "The Damascene Subjugation of the Southern Levant as a Gradual Process (ca. 842–800 BCE)." In *In Search for Aram and Israel: Politics, Culture, and Identity*, ed. O. Sergi, M. Oeming, and I. J. de Hulster, 57–76. Tübingen: Mohr Siebeck.

Knapp, A. B. 2014. "Mediterranean Archaeology and Ethnicity." In *A Companion to Ethnicity in the Ancient Mediterranean*, ed. J. McInerney, 34–49. London: John Wiley & Sons.

Knapp, A. B. 2021. *Migration Myths and the End of the Bronze Age in the Eastern Mediterranean*. Cambridge: Cambridge University Press.

Knapp, A. B., and N. Meyer. 2020. "Cyprus: Bronze Age Demise, Iron Age Regeneration." In *Collapse and Transformation: The Late Bronze Age to Early Iron Age in the Aegean*, ed. G. M. Middleton, 237–46. Oxford: Oxbow books.

Knodell, A. R. 2021. *Societies in Transition in Early Greece: An Archaeological History*. Berkeley: University of California Press.

Koch, I. 2020. "On Philistines and Early Israelite Kings: Memories and Perceptions." In *Saul, Benjamin, and the Emergence of Monarchy in Israel: Biblical and Archaeological Perspectives*, ed. J. J. Krause, O. Sergi, and K. Weingart, 7–31. Atlanta, GA: SBL Press.

Koch, I. 2021. *Colonial Encounters in Southwest Canaan during the Late Bronze and the Early Iron Age*. Leiden: Brill.

Kohler, T. A., and M. Rockman. 2020. "The IPCC: A Primer for Archaeologists." *American Antiquity* 85/4:627–51.

Kohlmeyer, K. 2009. "The Temple of the Storm God in Aleppo during the Late Bronze and Early Iron Ages." *Near Eastern Archaeology* 72/4:190–202.

Kohlmeyer, K. 2011. "Building Activities and Architectural Decoration in the 11th Century BC: The Temples of Taita, King of Padasatini/Palistin in Aleppo and 'Ain Dara." In *Empires after the Empire: Anatolia, Syria and Assyria after Suppiluliuma II (ca. 1200–800/700 B.C.)*, ed. K. Strobel, 255–80. Rome: LoGisma.

Kostoglou, M. 2010. "Iron, Connectivity and Local Identities in the Iron Age to Classical Mediterranean." In *Material Connections in the Ancient Mediterranean: Mobility, Materiality and Identity*, ed. P. van Dommelen and A. B. Knapp, 170–89. New York: Routledge.

Kotsonas, A. 2006. "Wealth and Status in Iron Age Knossos." *Oxford Journal of Archaeology* 25/2:149–72.

Kotsonas, A. 2016. "Politics of Periodization and the Archaeology of Early Greece." *American Journal of Archaeology* 120/2:239–70.

Kotsonas, A. 2018. "Homer, the Archaeology of Crete and the 'Tomb of Meriones'at Knossos." *Journal of Hellenic Studies* 138:1–35.

Kotsonas, A. 2019. "Early Iron Age Knossos and the Development of the City of the Historical Period." In *Proceedings of the 12th International Congress of Cretan Studies, Heraklion, 21–25.9.2016*, 1–13. Herakleio: Society of Cretan Historical Studies.

Kotsonas, A. 2020. "History of Research." In *A Companion to the Archaeology of Early Greece and the Mediterranean*, ed. I. S. Lemos and A. Kotsonas, 1:75–96. London: Wiley Blackwell.

Kotsonas, A. 2021. "Making Cretan Cities: Urbanization, Demography and Economies of Production in the Early Iron Age and the Archaic Period." In *Making Cities: Economies of Production and Urbanization in Mediterranean Europe, 1000–500 BC*, ed. M. Gleba, B. Marín-Aguilera, and B. Dimova, 57–76. Cambridge: McDonald Institute for Archaeological Research.

Kotsonas, A. 2022. "Early Greek Alphabetic Writing: Text, Context, Material Properties, and Socialization." *American Journal of Archaeology* 126/2:167–200.

Kotsonas, A., and J. Mokrišová. 2020. "Mobility, Migration, and Colonization." In *A Companion to the Archaeology of Early Greece and the Mediterranean*, ed. I. S. Lemos and A. Kotsonas, 2:217–46. London: Wiley Blackwell.

Kotsonas, A., T. Whitelaw, A. Vasilakis, and M. Bredaki. 2018. "Early Iron Age Knossos: An Overview from the Knossos Urban Landscape Project (KULP)." In *Proceedings of 11th International Congress of Cretan Studies, Rethymno, 21–27 October 2011*, ed. E. Gavrilaki, 61–77. Rethymno: Historical and Folklore Society of Rethymno.

Kourou, N. 2000. "Phoenician Presence in Early lron Age Crete Reconsidered." In *Actas del IV Congreso Internacional de Estudios Fenicios y Punicos, Cidiz, 2 al 6 de Octubre de 1995*, 3:1067–81. Cadiz: Universidodd e Cadiz.

Kourou, N. 2004. "Inscribed Imports, Visitors and Pilgrims at the Archaic Sanctuaries of Camiros." In *Χάρις Χαίρε: Studies in Memory of Charis Kantzia*, vol. B, ed. A. Giannikouri, 11–30. Athens: Archaiologiko Institouto Aigaiakon Spoudon.

Kourou, N. 2008a. "The Aegean and the Levant in the Early Iron Age: Recent Developments." In *Interconnections in the Eastern Mediterranean: Lebanon in the Bronze and Iron Ages; Proceedings of the International Symposium, Beirut 2008. Bulletin d'Archéologie et d'Architecture Libanaises (BAAL)*, n.s., 6:361–74.

Kourou, N. 2008b. "The Evidence from the Aegean." In *Beyond the Homeland: Markers in Phoenician Chronology*, ed. C. Sargona, 305–64. Ancient Near Eastern Studies Supplement 28. Leuven: Peeters Press.

Kourou, N. 2012. "Phoenicia, Cyprus and the Aegean in the Early Iron Age: J. N. Coldstream's Contribution and the Current State of Research." In *Cyprus and the Aegean in the Early Iron Age: The Legacy of Nicolas Coldstream*, ed. M. Iacovou, 33–51. Nicosia: Bank of Cyprus Cultural Foundation.

Kourou, N. 2016. "A Cypriot Sequence in Early Iron Age Crete: Heirlooms, Imports and Adaptations." *Cahiers du Centre d'Études Chypriotes* 46:51–69.

Kourou, N. 2019. "Cyprus and the Aegean in the Geometric Period: The Case of Salamis." In *Salamis of Cyprus: History and Archaeology from the Earliest Times to Late Antiquity;*

Conference in Nicosia, 21–23 May 2015, ed. S. Rogge, C. Ioannou, and T. Mavrojannis, 77–97. Münster: WaxmannVerlag.

Kramer-Hajos, M. 2016. *Mycenaean Greece and the Aegean World: Palace and Province in the Late Bronze Age*. Cambridge: Cambridge University Press.

Kramer-Hajos, M. 2020. "The Euboean Gulf." In *Collapse and Transformation: The Late Bronze Age to Early Iron Age in the Aegean*, ed. G. M. Middleton, 201–8. Oxford: Oxbow Books.

Kreppner, F. J. 2002. "Public Space in Nature: The Case of Neo-Assyrian Rock-Reliefs." *Altorientalische Forschungen* 29/2:367–83.

Kristiansen, K. 2018. "The Rise of Bronze Age Peripheries and the Expansion of International Trade 1950–1100 BC." In *Trade and Civilisation: Economic Networks and Cultural Ties, from Prehistory to the Early Modern Era*, ed. K. Kristiansen, T. Lindkvist, and J. Myrdal, 87–112. Cambridge: Cambridge University Press.

Kroll, S., C. Gruber, U. Hellwag, M. Roaf, and P. Zimansky. 2012. "Introduction." In *Biainili-Urartu: The Proceedings of the Symposium Held in Munich, 12–14 October 2007*, ed. S. Kroll, C. Gruber, U. Hellwag, M. Roaf, and P. Zimansky, 1–38. Louvain: Peeters.

Kuecker, G. D., and T. D. Hall. 2011. "Resilience and Community in the Age of World-System Collapse." *Nature and Culture* 6/1:18–40.

Kuhrt, A. 1995. *The Ancient Near East c. 3000–330 BC*. Vols. 1 and 2. London: Routledge.

Kuzucuoğlu, C. 2015. "The Rise and Fall of the Hittite State in Central Anatolia: How, When, Where, Did Climate Intervene?" In *La Cappadoce méridionale de la préhistoire à l'époque byzantine: 3e rencontres d'archéologie de IFEA, Istanbul, 8–9 novembre 2012*, ed. D. Beyer, O. Henry, and A. Tibet, 17–41. Istanbul: Institut français d'études anatoliennes.

LaFayette Hogue, S. 2016. "New Evidence of Post-destruction Reuse in the Main Building of the Palace of Nestor at Pylos." *American Journal of Archaeology* 120/1:151–57.

Langgut, D., I. Finkelstein, T. Litt, F. H. Neumann, and M. Stein. 2015. "Vegetation and Climate Changes during the Bronze and Iron Ages (~3600–600 BCE) in the Southern Levant Based on Palynological Records." *Radiocarbon* 57/2:217–35.

Langgut, D., F. H. Neumann, M. Stein, A. Wagner, E. J. Kagan, E. Boaretto, and I. Finkelstein. 2014. "Dead Sea Pollen Record and History of Human Activity in the Judean Highlands (Israel) from the Intermediate Bronze into the Iron Ages (~2500–500 BCE)." *Palynology* 38/2:280–302.

Lantzas, K. 2016. "Reconsidering Collapse: Identity, Ideology, and Postcollapse Settlement in the Argolid." In *Beyond Collapse: Archaeological Perspectives on Resilience, Revitalization, and Transformation in Complex Societies*, ed. R. K. Faulseit, 459–85. Visiting Scholar Conference Volumes: Center for Archaeological Investigations Occasional Paper No. 42. Carbondale: Southern Illinois University Press.

Larson, M. T. 2017. "The Archaeological Exploration of Assyria." In *A Companion to Assyria*, ed. E. Frahm, 583–98. Oxford: Wiley Blackwell.

Lavell, A. 1999. *Natural and Technological Disasters: Capacity Building and Human Resource Development for Disaster Management*. Concept paper commissioned by Emergency Response Division, United Nations Development Program, Geneva Switzerland.

Lavell, A., M. Oppenheimer, C. Diop, J. Hess, R. Lempert, J. Li, R. Muir-Wood, and S. Myeong. 2012. "Climate Change: New Dimensions in Disaster Risk, Exposure, Vulnerability, and

Resilience." In *Managing the Risks of Extreme Events and Disasters to Advance Climate Change Adaptation*, ed. C. B. Field, V. Barros, T. F. Stocker, D. Qin, D. J. Dokken, K. L. Ebi, M. D. Mastrandrea, K. J. Mach, G.-K. Plattner, S. K. Allen, M. Tignor, and P. M. Midgley, 25–64. Special Report of Working Groups I and II of the Intergovernmental Panel on Climate Change (IPCC). Cambridge: Cambridge University Press.

Layard, A. H. 1849. *The Monuments of Nineveh: From Drawings Made on the Spot*. London: Murray.

Lehmann, G. 2008. "North Syria and Cilicia, ca. 1200–330 BCE." In *Beyond the Homeland: Markers in Phoenician Chronology*, ed. C. Sargona, 205–46. Ancient Near Eastern Studies Supplement 28. Leuven: Peeters Press.

Lehmann, G. 2019. "The Levant." In *The Oxford Handbook of the Phoenician and Punic Mediterranean*, ed. C. López-Ruiz and B. R. Doak, 465–79. Oxford: Oxford University Press.

Lehmann, G. 2021. "The Emergence of Early Phoenicia." *Jerusalem Journal of Archaeology* 1:272–324.

Lemaire, A. 1994. "'House of David' Restored in Moabite Inscription." *Biblical Archaeology Review* 20/3:30–37.

Lemos, I. S. 2002. *The Protogeometric Aegean: The Archaeology of the Late Eleventh and Tenth Centuries BC*. Oxford: Oxford University Press.

Lemos, I. S. 2006. "Athens and Lefkandi: A Tale of Two Sites." In *Ancient Greece: From the Mycenaean Palaces to the Age of Homer*, ed. S. Deger-Jalkotzy and I. S. Lemos, 505–30. Edinburgh: Edinburgh University Press.

Lemos, I. S. 2014. "Communities in Transformation: An Archaeological Survey from the 12th to the 9th Century BC." *Pharos* 20:161–91.

Lemos, I. S. 2020. "Euboea." In *A Companion to the Archaeology of Early Greece and the Mediterranean*, ed. I. S. Lemos and A. Kotsonas, 2:787–813. London: Wiley Blackwell.

Lemos, I. S., and A. Kotsonas. 2020. "Preface." In *A Companion to the Archaeology of Early Greece and the Mediterranean*, ed. I. Lemos and A. Kotsonas, 1:xxiii–xxvi. Boston: Wiley Blackwell.

Levin, Y. 2017. "Gath of the Philistines in the Bible and on the Ground: The Historical Geography of Tell es-Safi/Gath." *Near Eastern Archaeology* 80/4:232–40.

Levy, T. E., T. Higham, C. Bronk Ramsey, N. G. Smith, E. Ben-Yosef, M. Robinson, S. Münger, K. Knabb, J. P. Schulze, M. Najjar, and L. Tauxe. 2008. "High-Precision Radiocarbon Dating and Historical Biblical Archaeology in Southern Jordan." *PNAS* 105/43:16460–65.

Levy, T. E., S. Münger, and M. Najjar. 2014. "A Newly Discovered Scarab of Sheshonq I: Recent Iron Age Explorations in Southern Jordan." *Antiquity* 341/88. https://www.antiquity.ac.uk/projgall/levy341.

Levy, T. E., M. Najjr, and E. Ben-Yosef, eds. 2014. *New Insights into the Iron Age Archaeology of Edom, Southern Jordan*. Volumes 1 and 2. Los Angeles: Cotsen Institute of Archaeology Press.

Lichtheim, M. 2019. "The Report of Wenamun." In *Ancient Egyptian Literature*, ed. M. Lichtheim, 561–68. Berkely: University of California Press.

Lipiński, E. 2006. *On the Skirts of Canaan in the Iron Age: Historical and Topographical Researches*. Leuven: Peeters.

Liss, B., M. D. Howland, B. Lorentzen, C. Smitheram, M. Najjar, and T. E. Levy. 2020. "Up the Wadi: Development of an Iron Age Industrial Landscape in Faynan, Jordan." *Journal of Field Archaeology* 45/6:413–27.

Liston, M. A., and J. K. Papadopoulos. 2004. "The 'Rich Athenian Lady' Was Pregnant: The Anthropology of a Geometric Tomb Reconsidered." *Hesperia* 73:7–38.

Liverani, M. 1988a. *Antico oriente: Storia, società, economia*. Rome: Bari.

Liverani, M. 1988b. "The Growth of the Assyrian Empire in the Habur/Middle Euphrates Area: A New Paradigm." *State Archives of Assyria Bulletin* 2/2:81–98.

Liverani, M. 2014. *The Ancient Near East: History, Society and Economy*. Translated by S. Tabatabai. London: Routledge.

Livieratou, A. 2020. "East Lokris-Phokis." In *Collapse and Transformation: The Late Bronze Age to Early Iron Age in the Aegean*, ed. G. M. Middleton, 97–106. Oxford: Oxbow Books.

Lloyd, M. 2013. "Warfare and the Recovery from Palatial Collapse in the 12th Century BC: A Case Study of the Argolid and Achaea." In *Tough Times: The Archaeology of Crisis and Recovery; Proceedings of the Graduate Archaeology at Oxford Conferences in 2010 and 2011*, ed. E. M. van der Wilt and J. Martínez Jiménez, 109–14. BAR International Series 2478. Oxford: Archaeopress.

Lloyd, M. 2015. "Death of a Swordsman, Death of a Sword: The Killing of Swords in the Early Iron Age Aegean (ca. 1050 to ca. 690 B.C.E)." *Ancient Warfare* 1:14–31.

Lloyd, M. 2017. "Why Study Dark Age Greece?" Josho Brouwers, December 6. https://www.joshobrouwers.com/articles/why-study-dark-age-greece.

Lloyd, M. 2018. "Bending in the Grave: Killing Weapons in the Early Iron Age Aegean." *Ancient World Magazine*, January 16. https://www.ancientworldmagazine.com/articles/bending-grave-killing-weapons-early-iron-age-aegean.

Lloyd, S. 1980. *Foundations in the Dust: The Story of Mesopotamian Exploration*. Rev. and enlg. ed. London: Thames and Hudson.

López-Ruiz, C. 2021. *Phoenicians and the Making of the Mediterranean*. Cambridge, MA: Harvard University Press.

López-Ruiz, C. 2022. "Phoenicians and the Iron Age Mediterranean." In *The Connected Iron Age: Interregional Networks in the Eastern Mediterranean, 900–600 BCE*, ed. J. M. Hall and J. F. Osborne, 27–48. Chicago: University of Chicago Press.

López-Ruiz, C., and B. R. Doak, eds. 2019. *The Oxford Handbook of the Phoenician and Punic Mediterranean*. Oxford: Oxford University Press.

Macalister, R.A.S. 1914. *The Philistines: Their History and Civilization*. London: Pub. for the British Academy by H. Milford.

MacGinnis, J., and T. Matney. 2009. "Ziyaret Tepe: Digging the Frontier of the Assyrian Empire." *Current World Archaeology* 37:30–40.

Maeir, A. M., ed. 2012. *Tell es-Safi/Gath I: The 1996–2005 Seasons*. Wiesbaden: Harrassowitz Verlag.

Maeir, A. M. 2017a. "Can Material Evidence of Aramean Influences and Presence in Iron Age Judah and Israel Be Found?" In *Wandering Arameans: Arameans outside Syria; Textual and Archaeological Perspectives*, ed. A. Berlejung, A. M. Maeir, and A. Schüle, 53–67. Wiesbaden: Harrassowitz Verlag.

Maeir, A. M. 2017b. "Philistine Gath after 20 Years: Regional Perspectives on the Iron Age at Tell es-Safi/Gath." In *The Shephelah during the Iron Age: Recent Archaeological Studies*, ed. O. Lipschits and A. M. Maeir, 133–54. University Park: Penn State University Press/Eisenbrauns.

Maeir, A. M. 2019. "Philistine and Israelite Identities: Some Comparative Thoughts." *Die Welt des Orients* 49:151–60.

Maeir, A. M. 2020. "A 'Repertoire of Otherness'? Identities in Early Iron Age Philistia." In *From the Prehistory of Upper Mesopotamia to the Bronze and Iron Age Societies of the Levant. Volume 1. Proceedings of the 5th "Broadening Horizons" Conference (Udine, 5–8 June 2017)*, ed. M. Iamoni, 161–70. Trieste: Edizioni università di Trieste.

Maeir, A. M. 2021. "Identity Creation and Resource Controlling Strategies: Thoughts on Edomite Ethnogenesis and Development." *Bulletin of ASOR* 386:209–20.

Maeir, A. M. 2022a. "Archaeology and Cultural History." In *Encyclopedia of Material Culture in the Biblical World: A New Biblisches Reallexikon*, ed. A. Berlejung, P.M.M. Daviau, J. Kamlah, and G. Lehmann, 29–53. Tübingen: Mohr Siebeck.

Maeir, A. M. 2022b. "Between Philistia, Phoenicia, and Beyond: A View from Tell es-Safi-Gath." In *Material, Method, and Meaning: Papers in Eastern Mediterranean Archaeology in Honor of Ilan Sharon*, ed. U. Davidovich, N. Yahalom-Mack, and S. Matskevich, 185–94. Münster: Zaphon.

Maeir, A. M. 2022c. "Jerusalem and the West—via Philistia: An Early Iron Age Perspective from Tell es-Safi/Gath." In *Jerusalem and the Coastal Plain in the Iron Age and Persian Periods: New Studies on Jerusalem's Relations with the Southern Coastal Plain of Israel/Palestine (c. 1200–300 BCE)*, ed. F. Hagemeyer, 7–21. Tübingen: Mohr Siebeck.

Maeir, A. M. 2022d. "You've Come a Long Way, Baby! Changing Perspectives on the Philistines." *Journal of Eastern Mediterranean Archaeology and Heritage Studies* 10/3–4:216–39.

Maeir, A. M. Forthcoming. "'Their Voice Carries throughout the Earth, Their Words to the End of the World' (Ps 19, 5): Thoughts on Long-Range Trade in Organics in the Bronze and Iron Age Levant." In *"And in Length of Days Understanding" (Job 12:12)—Essays on Archaeology in the 21st Century in Honor of Thomas E. Levy*, ed. E. Ben-Yosef and I.W.N. Jones. Cham, Switzerland: Springer.

Maeir, A. M., and S. Gur-Arieh. 2011. "Comparative Aspects of the Aramean Siege System at Tell eṣ-Ṣāfi/Gath." In *The Fire Signals of Lachish: Studies in the Archaeology and History of Israel in the Late Bronze Age, Iron Age, and Persian Period in Honor of David Ussishkin*, ed. I. Finkelstein and N. Na'aman, 227–44. Winona Lake, IN: Eisenbrauns.

Maeir, A. M., and J. Uziel, eds. 2020. *Tell Es-Safi/Gath II: Excavations and Studies*. Münster: Zaphon.

Maggidis, C. 2020. "Glas and Boeotia." In *Collapse and Transformation: The Late Bronze Age to Early Iron Age in the Aegean*, ed. G. M. Middleton, 107–20. Oxford: Oxbow Books.

Mahieu, B. 2018. "The Old and Middle Assyrian Calendars, and the Adoption of the Babylonian Calendar by Tiglath-Pileser I (Attested in the *Doppeldatierungen* and in the Broken Obelisk)." *State Archives of Assyria Bulletin* 24:63–95.

Manning, S. W., C. Kocik, B. Lorentzen, and J. P. Sparks. 2023. "Severe Multi-year Drought Coincident with Hittite Collapse around 1198–96 BC." *Nature* 614:719–24. https://doi.org/10.1038/s41586-022-05693-y.

Manning, S. W., B. Lorentzen, L. Welton, S. Batiuk, and T. P. Harrison. 2020. "Beyond Megadrought and Collapse in the Northern Levant: The Chronology of Tell Tayinat and Two Historical Inflection Episodes, around 4.2ka BP, and Following 3.2ka BP." *PLOS ONE* 15/10:e0240799. https://doi.org/10.1371/journal.pone.0240799.

Manolova, T. 2020. "The Levant." In *A Companion to the Archaeology of Early Greece and the Mediterranean*, ed. I. S. Lemos and A. Kotsonas, 2:1185–214. London: Wiley Blackwell.

Maran, J. 2006. "Coming to Terms with the Past: Ideology and Power in Late Helladic IIIC." In *Ancient Greece: From the Mycenaean Palaces to the Age of Homer*, ed. S. Deger-Jalkotzy and I. S. Lemos, 123–50. Edinburgh: Edinburgh University Press.

Maran, J. 2016. "Against the Currents of History: The Early 12th-Century BCE Resurgence of Tiryns." In *RA-PI-NE-U: Studies on the Mycenaean World Offered to Robert Laffineur for His 70th Birthday*, ed. J. Driessen, 201–20. Louvain-la-Neuve: Presses universitaires de Louvain.

Maran, J. 2023. "The Demise of the Mycenaean Palaces: The Need for an Interpretative Reset." In *Synchronizing the Destructions of the Mycenaean Palaces*, ed. R. Jung and E. Kardamaki, 231–53. Vienna: Austrian Academy of Sciences Press.

Maran, J., and A. Papadimitriou. 2020. "Mycenae and the Argolid." In *A Companion to the Archaeology of Early Greece and the Mediterranean*, ed. I. S. Lemos and A. Kotsonas, 2:699–718. London: Wiley Blackwell.

Maran, J., and J. C. Wright. 2020. "The Rise of the Mycenaean Culture, Palatial Administration and Its Collapse." In *A Companion to the Archaeology of Early Greece and the Mediterranean*, ed. I. S. Lemos and A. Kotsonas, 1:99–132. London: Wiley Blackwell.

Marchetti, N. 2012. "Karkemish on the Euphrates: Excavating a City's History." *Near Eastern Archaeology* 75:132–47.

Marchetti, N. 2014. "A Century of Excavations at Karkemish: Filling the Gaps." In *Karkemish: An Ancient Capital on the Euphrates*, ed. N. Marchetti, 21–43. Bologna: AnteQuem.

Marchetti, N., and H. Peker. 2018. "The Stele of Kubaba by Kamani and the Kings of Karkemish in the 9th Century BC." *Zeitschrift für Assyriologie* 108/1:81–99.

Markoe, G. E. 2000. *Phoenicians*. Berkeley: University of California Press.

Master, D. M. 2021. "The Philistines in the Highlands: A View from Ashkelon." *Jerusalem Journal of Archaeology* 1:203–20.

Matney, T., J. MacGinnis, D. Wicke, and K. Köroğlu. 2017. *Ziyaret Tepe: Exploring the Anatolian Frontier of the Assyrian Empire*. Istanbul: Cornucopia Books.

Matsui, T., R. Moriwaki, E. Zidan, and T. Arai. 2022. "The Manufacture and Origin of the Tutankhamen Meteoritic Iron Dagger." *Meteoritics & Planetary Science* 57/4:747–58. https://doi.org/10.1111/maps.13787.

Mattingly, G. L. 1994. "Moabites." In *Peoples of the Old Testament World*, ed. A. J. Hoerth, G. L. Mattingly, and E. M. Yamauchi, 317–33. Grand Rapids, MI: Baker Books.

Mazar, A. 1994. "The 11th Century B.C. in the Land of Israel." In *Cyprus in the 11th Century B.C.: Proceedings of the International Symposium, Nicosia, 30–31 October 1993*, ed. V. Karageorghis, 39–58. Nicosia: A. G. Leventis Foundation.

Mazar, A. 2022a. "Tel Rehov: The Site and Its Excavation." *Near Eastern Archaeology* 85/2:84–89.

Mazar, A. 2022b. "Tel Rehov in the Tenth and Ninth Centuries BCE." *Near Eastern Archaeology* 85/2:110–25.

Mazar, A., U. Davidovich, N. Panitz-Cohen, Y. Rotem, and A. Sumaka'i Fink. 2022. "The Canaanite City at Tel Rehov: From the Early Bronze Age to the End of the Iron Age I." *Near Eastern Archaeology* 85/2:96–109.

Mazar, A., and N. Kourou. 2019. "Greece and the Levant in the 10th–9th Centuries BC." *Opuscula* 12:369–92.

Mazar, A., and R. A. Mullins. 2022. "Facing Assyria: Tel Rehov in the Late Ninth and the Eighth Centuries BCE." *Near Eastern Archaeology* 85/2:146–51.

Mazar, A., and N. Panitz-Cohen, eds. 2020. *Tel Rehov: A Bronze and Iron Age City in the Beth-Shean Valley*. Vols. 1–5. Qedem 59. Jerusalem: Institute of Archaeology, Hebrew University of Jerusalem.

Mazar, A., N. Panitz-Cohen, and G. Bloch. 2022. "The Apiary at Tel Rehov: An Update." *Near Eastern Archaeology* 85/2:126–31.

Mazarakis Ainian, A. 2006. "The Archaeology of Basileis." In *Ancient Greece: From the Mycenaean Palaces to the Age of Homer*, ed. S. Deger-Jalkotzy and I. S. Lemos, 181–211. Edinburgh: Edinburgh University Press.

McAnany, P. A., and N. Yoffee. 2010. "Why We Question Collapse and Study Human Resilience, Ecological Vulnerability, and the Aftermath of Empire." In *Questioning Collapse: Human Resilience, Ecological Vulnerability, and the Aftermath of Empire*, ed. P. A. McAnany and N. Yoffee, 1–17. Cambridge: Cambridge University Press.

McDowall, C. 2014. "The Silver Pharaoh: Psusennes I Facing the Afterlife in Style." Culture Concept. https://www.thecultureconcept.com/the-silver-pharaoh-psusennes-i-facing-the-afterlife-in-style.

Megginson, L. C. 1963. "Lessons from Europe for American Business." *Southwestern Social Science Quarterly* 44/1: 3–13.

Middleton, G. D. 2017a. "Do Civilisations Collapse?" *Aeon*. https://aeon.co/essays/what-the-idea-of-civilisational-collapse-says-about-history.

Middleton, G. D. 2017b. "The Show Must Go On: Collapse, Resilience, and Transformation in 21st-Century archaeology." *Reviews in Anthropology*. https://doi.org/10.1080/00938157.2017.1343025.

Middleton, G. D. 2017c. *Understanding Collapse: Ancient History and Modern Myths*. Cambridge: Cambridge University Press.

Middleton, G. D. 2018a. "'I Would Walk 500 Miles and I Would Walk 500 More': The Sea Peoples and Aegean Migration at the End of the Late Bronze Age." In *Change, Continuity, and Connectivity: North-Eastern Mediterranean at the Turn of the Bronze Age and in the Early Iron Age*, ed. Ł. Niesiołowski-Spanò and M. Węcowski, 95–115. Wiesbaden: Harrassowitz Verlag.

Middleton, G. D. 2018b. "Should I Stay or Should I Go? Mycenaeans, Migration, and Mobility in the Late Bronze Age and Early Iron Age Eastern Mediterranean." *Journal of Greek Archaeology* 3:115–43.

Middleton, G. D., ed. 2020a. *Collapse and Transformation: The Late Bronze Age to Early Iron Age in the Aegean*. Oxford: Oxbow Books.

Middleton, G. D. 2020b. "Introducing Collapse." In *Collapse and Transformation: The Late Bronze Age to Early Iron Age in the Aegean*, ed. G. M. Middleton, 1–8. Oxford: Oxbow Books.

Middleton, G. D. 2020c. "Mycenaean Collapse(s) c. 1200 BC." In *Collapse and Transformation: The Late Bronze Age to Early Iron Age in the Aegean*, ed. G. M. Middleton, 9–22. Oxford: Oxbow Books.

Middleton, G. D. 2020d. Review of *The Evolution of Fragility: Setting the Terms* by N. Yoffee, ed. *American Journal of Archaeology* 124/4. https://www.ajaonline.org/book-review/4150.

Middleton, G. D. 2020e. "A Tale of Three Cities: Urban and Cultural Resilience and Heritage between the Late Bronze and Early Iron Age in the Eastern Mediterranean." *Urban History* 2020:1–25.

Millard, A. 1994. *The Eponyms of the Assyrian Empire, 910–612 BC*. State Archive of Assyria Studies 2. Helsinki: Neo-Assyrian Text Corpus Project.

Millek, J. M. 2020. "What Actually Happened in Syria at the End of the Late Bronze Age?" *Ancient Near East Today* 8/7 (July). http://www.asor.org/anetoday/2020/07/syria-bronze-age.

Millek, J. M. 2020–21. "'Our City Is Sacked. May You Know It!': The Destruction of Ugarit and Its Environs by the 'Sea People.'" *Archaeology & History in the Lebanon* 52–53:102–32.

Millek, J. M. 2021. "Just What Did They Destroy? The Sea Peoples and the End of the Late Bronze Age." In *The Mediterranean Sea and the Southern Levant: Archaeological and Historical Perspectives from the Bronze Age to Medieval Times*, ed. J. Kamlah and A. Lichtenberger, 59–98. Wiesbaden: Harrassowitz Verlag.

Millek, J. M. 2023. *Destruction and Its Impact on Ancient Societies at the End of the Bronze Age*. Atlanta: Lockwood Press.

Miller, D. S., and J. D. Rivera, eds. 2011. *Community Disaster Recovery and Resiliency: Exploring Global Opportunities and Challenges*. Boca Raton, FL: CRC Press.

Miller, J. M., and J. H. Hayes. 2006. *A History of Ancient Israel and Judah*. 2nd ed. Louisville, KY: Westminster John Knox Press.

Misgav, H., Y. Garfinkel, and S. Ganor. 2009. "The Ostracon." In *Khirbet Qeiyafa 1: Excavation Report 2007–2008*, ed. Y. Garfinkel and S. Ganor, 243–57. Jerusalem: Israel Exploration Society.

Molloy, B. 2022. "Was There a 3.2 ka Crisis in Europe? A Critical Comparison of Climatic, Environmental, and Archaeological Evidence for Radical Change during the Bronze Age–Iron Age Transition." *Journal of Archaeological Research* (August 2). https://doi.org/10.1007/s10814-022-09176-6.

Monroe, C. M. 2018. "Marginalizing Civilization: The Phoenician Redefinition of Power ca. 1300–800 BCE." In *Trade and Civilisation: Economic Networks and Cultural Ties, from Prehistory to the Early Modern Era*, ed. K. Kristiansen, T. Lindkvist, and J. Myrdal, 195–241. Cambridge: Cambridge University Press.

Montet, P. 1951. *Les constructions et le tombeau de Psousennes à Tanis*. Paris: CNRS.

Montiglio, S. 2006. Review of *Hellenicity: Between Ethnicity and Culture* by J. M. Hall. *Review of Metaphysics* 60/1:160–62.

Moran, W. L. 1992. *The Amarna Letters*. Baltimore, MD: Johns Hopkins University Press.

Morris, I. 1987. *Burial and Ancient Society: The Rise of the Greek City-State*. Cambridge: Cambridge University Press.

Morris, I. 1989. "Circulation, Deposition and the Formation of the Greek Iron Age." *Man*, n.s., 24/3:502–19.

Morris, I. 1993. "Response to Papadopoulos (I): The Kerameikos Stratigraphy and the Character of the Greek Dark Age." *Journal of Mediterranean Archaeology* 6/2:207–21.

Morris, I. 1996. "Negotiated Peripherality in Iron Age Greece: Accepting and Resisting the East." *Journal of World-Systems Research* 2/1:409. https://doi.org/10.5195/jwsr.1996.92.

Morris, I. 1997. "Periodization and the Heroes: Inventing a Dark Age." In *Inventing Ancient Culture: Historicism, Periodization and the Ancient World*, ed. M. Golden and P. Toohey, 96–131. London: Routledge.

Morris, I. 1999. "Iron Age Greece and the Meanings of 'Princely Tombs.'" In *Les princes de la protohistoire et l'émergence de l'état: Actes de la table ronde internationale organisée par le Centre Jean Bérard et l'Ecole française de Rome, Naples, 27–29 octobre 1994*, ed. P. Ruby, 57–80. Rome: École française de Rome.

Morris, I. 2000. *Archaeology as Cultural History: Words and Things in Iron Age Greece*. Oxford: Blackwell.

Morris, I. 2005. "The Growth of Greek Cities in the First Millennium BC." *Princeton/Stanford Working Papers in Classics*, no. 120509 (June 30): 2–29. https://dx.doi.org/10.2139/ssrn.1426835.

Morris, I. 2006. "The Collapse and Regeneration of Complex Society in Greece, 1500–500 BC." In *After Collapse: The Regeneration of Complex Societies*, ed. G. M. Schwartz and J. J. Nichols, 72–84. Tucson: University of Arizona Press.

Morris, S. P. 1989. "Daidalos and Kadmos: Classicism and 'Orientalism,'" in "The Challenge of Black Athena." Special issue, *Arethusa* (Fall): 39–54.

Morris, S. P. 1992a. *Daidalos and the Origins of Greek Art*. Princeton, NJ: Princeton University Press.

Morris, S. P. 1992b. "Introduction." In *Greece between East and West, 10th–8th Centuries BC*, ed. G. Kopcke and I. Tokumaru, xiii–xviii. Mainz: Philipp von Zabern.

Morris, S. P. 2022. "Close Encounters of the Lasting Kind: Greeks, Phoenicians, and Others in the Iron Age Mediterranean." In *The Connected Iron Age: Interregional Networks in the Eastern Mediterranean, 900–600 BCE*, ed. J. M. Hall and J. F. Osborne, 98–123. Chicago: University of Chicago Press.

Mühlenbruch, T. 2009. "Tiryns—The Settlement and Its History in LH IIIC." In *LH IIIC Chronology and Synchronisms III: LH IIIC Late and the Transition to the Early Iron Age; Proceedings of the International Workshop Held at the Austrian Academy of Sciences at Vienna, February 23rd and 24th, 2007*, ed. S. Deger-Jalkotzy and A. E. Bächle, 313–26. Vienna: Verlag der Österreichischen Akademie der Wissenschaften.

Mühlenbruch, T. 2020. "The Argolid." In *Collapse and Transformation: The Late Bronze Age to Early Iron Age in the Aegean*, ed. G. M. Middleton, 121–32. Oxford: Oxbow Books.

Muhly, J. D. 1980. "The Bronze Age Setting." In *The Coming of the Age of Iron*, ed. T. A. Wertime and J. D. Muhly, 25–67. New Haven, CT: Yale University Press.

Muhly, J. D. 1992. "The Crisis Years in the Mediterranean World: Transition or Cultural Disintegration?" In *The Crisis Years: The 12th Century B.C.*, ed. W. A. Ward and M. S. Joukowsky, 10–22. Dubuque, IA: Kendall/Hunt Publishing.

Muhly, J. D. 2003. "Greece and Anatolia in the Early Iron Age: The Archaeological Evidence and the Literary Tradition." In *Symbiosis, Symbolism, and the Power of the Past: Canaan, Ancient Israel, and Their Neighbors from the Late Bronze Age through Roman Palaestina; Proceedings of the Centennial Symposium, W. F. Albright Institute of Archaeological Research and American

Schools of Oriental Research, Jerusalem, May 29–31, 2000, ed. W. G. Dever and S. Gitin, 23–35. Winona Lake, IN: Eisenbrauns.

Muhly, J. D. 2011. "Archaic and Classical Greece Would Not Have Been the Same without the Dark Ages." In *The "Dark Ages" Revisited: Acts of an International Symposium in Memory of William D. E. Coulson, University of Thessaly (Volos, 14–17 June 2007)*, ed. A. Mazarakis Ainian, 45–53. Volos: University of Thessaly Press.

Muhly, J. D., and V. Kassianidou. 2012. "Parallels and Diversities in the Production, Trade and Use of Copper and Iron in Crete and Cyprus from the Bronze Age to the Iron Age." In *Parallel Lives: Ancient Island Societies in Crete and Cyprus*, ed. G. Cadogan, M. Iacovou, K. Kopaka, and J. Whitley, 119–40. British School at Athens Studies 20. London: British School at Athens.

Muhly, J. D., R. Maddin, T. Stech, and E. Özgen. 1985. "Iron in Anatolia and the Nature of the Hittite Iron Industry." *Anatolian Studies* 35:67–84.

Muhs, B. 2022. "Egypt and the Mediterranean in the Early Iron Age." In *The Connected Iron Age: Interregional Networks in the Eastern Mediterranean, 900–600 BCE*, ed. J. M. Hall and J. F. Osborne, 194–213. Chicago: University of Chicago Press.

Murray, S. C. 2017. *The Collapse of the Mycenaean Economy: Imports, Trade, and Institutions 1300–700 BCE*. Cambridge: Cambridge University Press.

Murray, S. C. 2018a. "Imported Exotica and Mortuary Ritual at Perati in Late Helladic IIIC East Attica." *American Journal of Archaeology* 122/1:33–64.

Murray, S. C. 2018b. "Imported Objects in the Aegean beyond Elite Interaction: A Contextual Approach to Eastern Exotica on the Greek Mainland." In *Change, Continuity, and Connectivity: North-Eastern Mediterranean at the Turn of the Bronze Age and in the Early Iron Age*, ed. Ł. Niesiołowski-Spanò and M. Węcowski, 221–34. Wiesbaden: Harrassowitz Verlag.

Murray, S. C. 2018c. "Lights and Darks: Data, Labeling, and Language in the History of Scholarship on Early Greece." *Hesperia* 87/1:17–54.

Murray, S. C. 2020. "The Changing Economy." In *Collapse and Transformation: The Late Bronze Age to Early Iron Age in the Aegean*, ed. G. M. Middleton, 201–8. Oxford: Oxbow Books.

Murray, S. C., and B. Lis. 2023. "Documenting a Maritime Mercantile Community through Surface Survey: Porto Rafti Bay in the Post-Collapse Aegean." *Antiquity*, April 13. https://doi.org/10.15184/aqy.2023.49.

Muscarella, O. W. 1995. "The Iron Age Background to the Formation of the Phrygian State." *Bulletin of the American Schools of Oriental Research* 299/300:91–101.

Mushett Cole, E. 2016. "Decline in Ancient Egypt? A Reassessment of the Late New Kingdom and Third Intermediate Period." PhD diss., University of Birmingham.

Mushett Cole, E. 2017. "'The Year of Hyenas When There Was a Famine': An Assessment of Environmental Causes for the Events of the Twentieth Dynasty." In *Global Egyptology: Negotiations in the Production of Knowledges on Ancient Egypt in Global Contexts*, ed. C. Langer, 3–17. London: Golden House Publications.

Na'aman, N. 1995. "Hazael of 'Amqi and Hadadezer of Beth-Rehob." *Ugarit Forschungen* 27:381–94.

Na'aman, N. 1997. "King Mesha and the Foundation of the Moabite Monarchy." *Israel Exploration Journal* 47/1–2:83–92.

Na'aman, N. 2000. "Three Notes on the Aramaic Inscription from Tel Dan." *Israel Exploration Journal* 50/1–2:92–104.

Na'aman, N. 2006. "The Story of Jehu's Rebellion: Hazael's Inscription and the Biblical Narrative." *Israel Exploration Journal* 56/2:160–66.

Na'aman, N. 2017. "Was Khirbet Qeiyafa a Judahite City? The Case against It." *Journal of Hebrew Scriptures* 17/7. https://doi.org/10.5508/jhs.2017.v17.a7.

Na'aman, N. 2019a. "The Alleged 'Beth David' in the Mesha Stele: The Case against It." *Tel Aviv* 46/2:192–97.

Na'aman, N. 2019b. "Hiram of Tyre in the Book of Kings and in the Tyrian Records." *Journal of Near Eastern Studies* 78/1:75–85.

Na'aman, N. 2021. "Biblical Archaeology and the Emergence of the Kingdom of Edom." *Antiguo Oriente* 19:11–40.

Nagy, G. 2019a. "Thinking Comparatively about Greek Mythology XVI, with a Focus on Dorians Led by Kingly 'Sons' of Hēraklēs the Kingmaker." *Classical Inquiries,* November 8. https://classical-inquiries.chs.harvard.edu/thinking-comparatively-about-greek-mythology-xvi-with-a-focus-on-dorians-led-by-kingly-sons-of-herakles-the-kingmaker.

Nagy, G. 2019b. "Thinking Comparatively about Greek Mythology XVII, with Placeholders That Stem from a Conversation with Tom Palaima, Starting with This Question: Was Hēraklēs a Dorian?" *Classical Inquiries,* November 15. https://classical-inquiries.chs.harvard.edu/thinking-comparatively-about-greek-mythology-xvii-with-placeholders-that-stem-from-a-conversation-with-tom-palaima-starting-with-this-question-was-herakles-a-dorian.

Nahm, W. 2022. "Tiglath-Pileser's River-Man." *Nouvelles Assyriologiques Brèves et Utilitaires (N.A.B.U.)* no. 3 (September): 236–37.

Nakassis, D. 2020. "The Economy." In *A Companion to the Archaeology of Early Greece and the Mediterranean,* ed. I. S. Lemos and A. Kotsonas, 1:271–91. London: Wiley Blackwell.

Namdar, D., A. Gilboa, R. Neumann, I. Finkelstein, and S. Weiner. 2013. "Cinnamaldehyde in Early Iron Age Phoenician Flasks Raises the Possibility of Levantine Trade with South East Asia." *Mediterranean Archaeology and Archaeometry* 12/3:1–19.

National Research Council. 2011. *Building Community Disaster Resilience through Private-Public Collaboration.* Washington, DC: National Academies Press. https://doi.org/10.17226/13028.

Naveh, J. 1989. *Early History of the Alphabet.* Leiden: E. J. Brill.

Nelson, M. 2007. "The First Olympic Games." In *Onward to the Olympics: Historical Perspectives on the Olympic Games,* ed. G. P. Schaus and S. R. Wenn, 47–58. Waterloo, ON: Wilfrid Laurier University Press.

Neumann, J., and S. Parpola. 1987. "Climatic Change and the Eleventh–Tenth Century Eclipse of Assyria and Babylonia." *Journal of Near Eastern Studies* 16/3:161–82.

Newhard, J.M.L., and E. H. Cline. 2022. "Panarchy and the adaptive cycle: A Case Study from Mycenaean Greece." In *Perspectives on Public Policy in Societal-Environmental Crises: What the Future Needs from History,* ed. A. Izdebski, J. Haldon, and P. Filipkowski, 225–35. Cham, Switzerland: Springer.

Nicoll, K., and A. Zerboni. 2019. "Is the Past Key to the Present? Observations of Cultural Continuity and Resilience Reconstructed from Geoarchaeological Records." *Quaternary International* 545:119–27.

Niemeyer, H. G. 2006. "The Phoenicians in the Mediterranean: Between Expansion and Colonization; A Non-Greek Model of Overseas Settlement and Presence." In *Greek Colonisation: An Account of Greek Colonies and Other Settlements Overseas*, ed. G. R. Tsetskhladze, 1:143–68. Leiden: Brill.

Nowicki, K. 2000. *Defensible Sites in Crete c. 1200–800 B.C.* Aegaeum 21. Liège: Université de Liège.

Oates, J. 1979. *Babylon*. London: Thames and Hudson.

O'Brien, K., M. Pelling, A. Patwardhan, S. Hallegatte, A. Maskrey, T. Oki, U. Oswald-Spring, T. Wilbanks, and P. Z. Yanda. 2012. "Toward a Sustainable and Resilient Future." In *Managing the Risks of Extreme Events and Disasters to Advance Climate Change Adaptation*, ed. C. B. Field, V. Barros, T. F. Stocker, D. Qin, D. J. Dokken, K. L. Ebi, M. D. Mastrandrea, K. J. Mach, G.-K. Plattner, S. K. Allen, M. Tignor, and P. M. Midgley, 437–86. Special Report of Working Groups I and II of the Intergovernmental Panel on Climate Change (IPCC). Cambridge: Cambridge University Press.

O'Brien, S. 2017. "Boredom with the Apocalypse: Resilience, Regeneration, and Their Consequences for Archaeological Interpretation." In *Crisis to Collapse: The Archaeology of Social Breakdown*, ed. T. Cunningham and J. Driessen, 295–303. Louvain: UCL Presses.

O'Connor, M. 1977. "The Rhetoric of the Kilamuwa Inscription." *Bulletin of the American Schools of Oriental Research* 226:15–29.

Oldfather, C. H., trans. 1933. *Diodorus Siculus: Library of History, Volume I, Books 1–2.34*. Loeb Classical Library 279. Cambridge, MA: Harvard University Press.

Olsen, B. A. 2020. "The People." In *A Companion to the Archaeology of Early Greece and the Mediterranean*, ed. I. S. Lemos and A. Kotsonas, 1:293–316. London: Wiley Blackwell.

Ortiz, S. M., and S. R. Wolff. 2021. "New Evidence for the 10th Century BCE at Tel Gezer." *Jerusalem Journal of Archaeology* 1:221–40.

Osborne, J. F. 2013. "Sovereignty and Territoriality in the City-State: A Case Study from the Amuq Valley, Turkey." *Journal of Anthropological Archaeology* 32:774–90.

Osborne, J. F. 2014. "Settlement Planning and Urban Symbology in Syro-Anatolian Cities." *Cambridge Archaeological Journal* 24:195–214.

Osborne, J. F. 2015. "Ancient Cities and Power: The Archaeology of Urbanism in the Iron Age Capitals of Northern Mesopotamia." *International Journal of Urban Sciences* 19/1:7–19.

Osborne, J. F. 2021. *The Syro-Anatolian City-States: An Iron Age Culture*. Oxford: Oxford University Press.

Osborne, J. F., and J. M. Hall. 2022. "Interregional Interaction in the Eastern Mediterranean during the Iron Age." In *The Connected Iron Age: Interregional Networks in the Eastern Mediterranean, 900–600 BCE*, ed. J. M. Hall and J. F. Osborne, 1–26. Chicago: University of Chicago Press.

Osborne, J. F., T. P. Harrison, S. Batiuk, L. Welton, J. P. Dessel, E. Denel, and Ö. Demirci. 2019. "Urban Built Environments in Early 1st Millennium B.C.E. Syro-Anatolia: Results of the Tayinat Archaeological Project, 2004–2016." *Bulletin of the American Schools of Oriental Research* 382:261–312.

Osborne, J. F., M. Massa, F. Sahin, H. Erpehlivan, and C. Bachhuber. 2020. "The City of Hartapu: Results of the Türkmen-Karahöyük Intensive Survey Project." *Anatolian Studies* 70:1–27.

Osborne, R. 1996. *Greece in the Making: 1200–479 BC*. London: Routledge.

Page, D. 1962. "The Homeric World." In *The Greek World*, ed. H. Lloyd-Jones, 13–25. Baltimore, MD: Penguin Books.

Palaima, T. G. 2002. "Special vs. Normal Mycenaean: Hand 24 and Writing in the Service of the King?" In *A-NA-QO-TA: Studies Presented to J. T. Killen = Minos* 33–34 (1998–99), ed. J. Bennet and J. Driessen, 205–21. Salamanca: Ediciones universidad de Salamanca.

Palaima, T. G. 2006. "Wanaks and Related Power Terms in Mycenaean and Later Greek." In *Ancient Greece from the Mycenaean Palaces to the Age of Homer*, ed. S. Deger-Jalkotzy and I. Lemos, 53–71. Edinburgh: Edinburgh University Press.

Palmisano, A., A. Bevan, A. Kabelindde, N. Roberts, and S. Shennan. 2021. "Long-Term Demographic Trends in Prehistoric Italy: Climate Impacts and Regionalised Socio-Ecological Trajectories." *Journal of World Prehistory* 34:381–432.

Palmisano, A., A. Bevan, and S. Shennan. 2017. "Comparing Archaeological Proxies for Long-Term Population Patterns: An Example from Central Italy." *Journal of Archaeological Science* 87:59–72.

Palmisano, A., D. Lawrence, M. W. de Gruchy, A. Bevan, and S. Shennan. 2021. "Holocene Regional Population Dynamics and Climatic Trends in the Near East: A First Comparison Using Archaeo-Demographic Proxies." *Quaternary Science Reviews* 252:106739. https://doi.org/10.1016/j.quascirev.2020.106739.

Palmisano, A., J. Woodbridge, C. N. Robert, A. Bevan, R. Fyfe, S. Shennan, R. Cheddadi, R. Greenberg, D. Kaniewski, D. Langgut, S.A.G. Leroy, T. Litt, and A. Miebach. 2019. "Holocene Landscape Dynamics and Long-Term Population Trends in the Levant." *Holocene* 29/5:708–27. https://doi.org/10.1177/0959683619826642.

Panitz-Cohen, N., and A. Mazar. 2022. "The Exceptional Ninth-Century BCE Northwestern Quarter at Tel Rehov." *Near Eastern Archaeology* 85/2:132–45.

Papadimitriou, A. 2006. "The Early Iron Age in the Argolid: Some New Aspects." In *Ancient Greece: From the Mycenaean Palaces to the Age of Homer*, ed. S. Deger-Jalkotzy and I. S. Lemos, 531–47. Edinburgh: Edinburgh University Press.

Papadopoulos, J. K. 1993. "To Kill a Cemetery: The Athenian Kerameikos and the Early Iron Age in the Aegean." *Journal of Mediterranean Archaeology* 6/2:175–206.

Papadopoulos, J. K. 1996a. "Dark Age Greece." *The Oxford Companion to Archaeology*, ed. B. M. Fagan, 253–55. New York: Oxford University Press.

Papadopoulos, J. K. 1996b. "The Original Kerameikos of Athens and the Siting of the Classical Agora." *Greek, Roman and Byzantine Studies* 37/2:107–28.

Papadopoulos, J. K. 2014. "Greece in the Early Iron Age: Mobility, Commodities, Polities, and Literacy." In *The Cambridge Prehistory of the Bronze and Iron Age Mediterranean*, ed. A. B. Knapp and P. van Dommelen, 178–95. Cambridge: Cambridge University Press.

Papadopoulos, J. K. 2022. "Greeks, Phoenicians, Phrygians, Trojans, and Other Creatures in the Aegean." In *The Connected Iron Age: Interregional Networks in the Eastern Mediterranean, 900–600 BCE*, ed. J. M. Hall and J. F. Osborne, 142–68. Chicago: University of Chicago Press.

Papadopoulos, J. K., and E. L. Smithson. 2017. *The Athenian Agora XXXVI: The Early Iron Age; The Cemeteries*. Princeton, NJ: American School of Classical Studies at Athens.

Pappa, E. 2020. "The Western Mediterranean." In *A Companion to the Archaeology of Early Greece and the Mediterranean*, ed. I. S. Lemos and A. Kotsonas, 2:1325–47. London: Wiley Blackwell.

Parkinson, E. W., T. R. McLaughlin, C. Esposito, S. Stoddart, and C. Malone. 2021. "Radiocarbon Dated Trends and Central Mediterranean Prehistory." *Journal of World Prehistory* 34:317–79.

Peden, A. J. 1994. *Egyptian Historical Inscriptions of the Twentieth Dynasty*. Documenta Mundi Aegyptiaca 3. Jonsered, Sweden: Paul Åströms Förlag.

Peker, H. 2016. *Texts from Karkemish I: Luwian Hieroglyphic Inscriptions from the 2011–2015 Excavations*. OrientLab Series Maior 1. Bologna: AnteQuem. http://www.orientlab.net/pubs.

Petit, T. 2019. *La naissance des cités-royaumes cypriotes*. Oxford: Archaeopress.

Podany, A. H. 2014. *The Ancient Near East: A Very Short Introduction*. New York: Oxford University Press.

Pollard, D. 2021. "All Equal in the Presence of Death? A Quantitative Analysis of the Early Iron Age Cemeteries of Knossos, Crete." *Journal of Anthropological Archaeology* 63. https://doi.org/10.1016/j.jaa.2021.101320.

Pollard, D. 2022. "An Icarus' Eye View? GIS Approaches to the Human Landscape of Early Iron Age Crete." In *Diversity in Archaeology: Proceedings of the Cambridge Annual Student Archaeology Conference 2020/2021*, ed. E. Doğan, M.P.L. Pereira, O. Antczak, M. Lin, P. Thompson, and C. Alday, 318–38. Oxford: Archaeopress.

Pomeroy, S. B., S. M. Burstein, W. Donlan, J. T. Roberts, D. W. Tandy, and G. Tsouvala. 2020. *A Brief History of Ancient Greece: Politics, Society, and Culture*. 4th ed. Oxford: Oxford University Press.

Popham, M. R., P. G. Calligas, and L. H. Sackett, eds. 1993. *Lefkandi II.2: The Protogeometric Building at Toumba; The Excavation, Architecture and Finds*. *BSA* Suppl 23. London: British School at Athens.

Popham, M. R., and L. H. Sackett. 1980. *Lefkandi I: The Iron Age (Text); The Settlement (and) the Cemeteries*. London: Thames and Hudson / The British School of Archaeology at Athens.

Popham, M. R., E. Touloupa, and L. H. Sackett. 1982. "The Hero of Lefkandi." *Antiquity* 56:169–74.

Porter, B. W. 2016. "Assembling the Iron Age Levant: The Archaeology of Communities, Polities, and Imperial Peripheries." *Journal of Archaeological Research* 24:373–420.

Postgate, J. N. 1992. "The Land of Assur and the Yoke of Assur." *World Archaeology* 23/3:247–63.

Potts, D. T. 1999. *The Archaeology of Elam: Formation and Transformation of an Ancient Iranian State*. Cambridge: Cambridge University Press.

Powell, W., M. Frachetti, C. Pulak, H. A. Bankoff, G. Barjamovic, M. Johnson, R. Mathur, V. C. Pigott, M. Price, K. A. Yener. 2022. "Tin from Uluburun Shipwreck Shows Small-Scale Commodity Exchange Fueled Continental Tin Supply across Late Bronze Age Eurasia." *Science Advances* 8/48:eabq3766. DOI: 10.1126/sciadv.abq3766.

Powell, W., M. Johnson, C. Pulak, K. A. Yener, R. Mathur, H. A. Bankoff, L. Godfrey, M. Price, and E. Galili. 2021. "From Peaks to Ports: Insights into Tin Provenance, Production, and Distribution from Adapted Applications of Lead Isotopic Analysis of the Uluburun Tin Ingots." *Journal of Archaeological Science* 134:105455. https://doi.org/10.1016/j.jas.2021.105455.

Prent, M. 2014. "Ritual and Ideology in Early Iron Age Crete: The Role of the Past and the East." In *The Cambridge Prehistory of the Bronze and Iron Age Mediterranean*, ed. A. B. Knapp and P. van Dommelen, 650–64. Cambridge: Cambridge University Press.

Pritchard, J. B. [1958] 2011. "The Journey of Wen-Amon to Phoenicia." In *The Ancient Near East: An Anthology of Literature of Texts and Pictures*, ed. J. B. Pritchard, 14–21. Reprint (with a new foreword) of the 1958 ed. Princeton, NJ: Princeton University Press.

Pritchard, J. B., ed. 1978. *Recovering Sarepta, a Phoenician City: Excavations at Sarafund, 1969–1974, by the University Museum of the University of Pennsylvania*. Princeton, NJ: Princeton University Press.

Quinn, J. C. 2018a. *In Search of the Phoenicians*. Princeton, NJ: Princeton University Press.

Quinn, J. C. 2018b. "Were There Phoenicians?" *Ancient Near East Today* 6/7 (July). https://www.asor.org/anetoday/2018/07/Were-There-Phoenicians.

Quinn, J. C. 2019. "Phoenicians and Carthaginians in Greco-Roman Literature Cities." In *The Oxford Handbook of the Phoenician and Punic Mediterranean*, ed. C. López-Ruiz and B. R. Doak, 671–83. Oxford: Oxford University Press.

Quinn, J. C., N. McLynn, R. M. Kerr, and D. Hadas. 2014. "Augustine's Canaanites." *Papers of the British School at Rome* 82:175–97.

Radner, K. 2011. "Assyrians and Urartians." In *The Oxford Handbook of Ancient Anatolia: 10,000–323 B.C.E.*, ed. S. R. Steadman and G. McMahon, 734–51. New York: Oxford University Press.

Radner, K. 2012. "The Stele of Adad-nerari III and Nergal-ereš from Dur-Katlimmu (Tell Śaih Hamad)." *Altorientalische Forschungen* 39/2:265–77.

Radner, K. 2014a. "An Imperial Communication Network: The State Correspondence of the Neo-Assyrian Empire." In *State Correspondence in the Ancient World: From New Kingdom Egypt to the Roman Empires*, ed. K. Radner, 64–93. Oxford: Oxford University Press.

Radner, K. 2014b. "The Neo-Assyrian Empire." In *Imperien und Reiche in der Weltgeshichte: Epochenübergreifende und globalhistorische Vergleiche; Teil 1, Imperien des Altertums, Mittelalterliche und frühneuzeitliche Imperien*, ed. M. Gehler and R. Rollinger, 101–19. Wiesbaden: Harrassowitz Verlag.

Radner, K. 2015. *Ancient Assyria: A Very Short Introduction*. New York: Oxford University Press.

Radner, K. 2016. "Revolts in the Assyrian Empire: Succession Wars, Rebellions against a False King and Independence Movements." In *Revolt and Resistance in the Ancient Classical World and the Near East: In the Crucible of Empire*, ed. J. J. Collins and J. G. Manning, 41–54. Leiden: Brill.

Radner, K. 2017. "Economy, Society, and Daily Life in the Neo-Assyrian Period." In *A Companion to Assyria*, ed. E. Frahm, 209–28. Hoboken, NJ: Wiley Blackwell.

Radner, K. 2018. "The City of Aššur and the Kingdom of Assyria: Historical Overview." In *The Assyrians: Kingdom of the God Aššur from Tigris to Taurus*, ed. K. Köroğlu and S. F. Adali, 2–23. Istanbul: Yapi Kredi Yayinlari.

Rassam, H. 1897. *Asshur and the Land of Nimrod*. Cincinnati, OH: Curts & Jennings.

Reculeau, H. 2011. *Climate, Environment and Agriculture in Assyria*. Studia Chaburensia 2. Wiesbaden: Harrassowitz Verlag.

Redford, S. 2002. *The Harem Conspiracy: The Murder of Ramesses III*. DeKalb: Northern Illinois University Press.

Redman, C. L. 2005. "Resilience Theory in Archaeology." *American Anthropologist* 107/1:70–77.

Redman, C. L., and A. P. Kinzig. 2003. "Resilience of Past Landscapes: Resilience Theory, Society, and the *Longue Durée*." *Conservation Ecology* 7(1):14. http://www.consecol.org/vol7/iss1/art14.

Reese, D. S. 1987. "Palaikastro Shells and Bronze Age Purple-Dye Production in the Mediterranean Basin." *Annual of the British School at Athens* 82:201–6.

Reese, D. S. 2010. "Shells from Sarepta (Lebanon) and East Mediterranean Purple-Dye Production." *Mediterranean Archaeology and Archaeometry* 10/1:113–41.

Reeves, N. 1990. *Valley of the Kings: The Decline of a Royal Necropolis*. London: Kegan Paul International.

Reeves, N. 2000. *Ancient Egypt: The Great Discoveries*. London: Thames and Hudson.

Reeves, N., and R. H. Wilkinson. 1996. *The Complete Valley of the Kings*. London: Thames and Hudson.

Regev, D. 2021. *Painting the Mediterranean Phoenician: On Canaanite-Phoenician Trade-Nets*. Sheffield: Equinox.

Reisner, G. A., C. S. Fisher, and D. G. Lyon. 1924. *Harvard Excavations at Samaria, 1908–1910*. 2 vols. Cambridge, MA: Harvard University Press.

Renfrew, C. 1978. "Trajectory Discontinuity and Morphogenesis: The Implications of Catastrophe Theory for Archaeology." *American Antiquity* 43/2:203–22.

Renfrew, C. 1979. "Systems Collapse as Social Transformation." In *Transformations: Mathematical Approaches to Culture Change*, ed. C. Renfrew and K. L. Cooke, 481–506. New York: Academic Press.

Richelle, M. 2018. *The Bible & Archaeology*. Carol Stream, IL: Tyndale House Publishers.

Richey, M. 2019. "Inscriptions." In *The Oxford Handbook of the Phoenician and Punic Mediterranean*, ed. C. López-Ruiz and B. R. Doak, 223–40. Oxford: Oxford University Press.

Roller, D. W. 2019. "Phoenician Exploration." In *The Oxford Handbook of the Phoenician and Punic Mediterranean*, ed. C. López-Ruiz and B. R. Doak, 645–53. Oxford: Oxford University Press.

Rollston, C. 2008. "The Dating of the Early Royal Byblian Phoenician Inscriptions: A Response to Benjamin Sass." *Maarav* 15/1:57–93.

Rollston, C. 2010. *Writing and Literacy in the World of Ancient Israel: Epigraphic Evidence from the Iron Age*. Leiden: Brill.

Rollston, C. 2011. "The Khirbet Qeiyafa Ostracon: Methodological Musings and Caveats." *Tel Aviv* 38:67–82.

Rollston, C. 2016. "Phoenicia and the Phoenicians." In *The World around the Old Testament: The People and Places of the Ancient Near East*, ed. B. T. Arnold and B. A. Strawn, 267–308. Grand Rapids, MI: Baker Book House.

Rollston, C. 2019. "The Alphabet Comes of Age: The Social Context of Alphabetic Writing in the First Millennium BCE." In *The Social Archaeology of the Levant: From Prehistory to the Present*, ed. A. Yasur-Landau, E. H. Cline, and Y. Rowan, 371–89. Cambridge: Cambridge University Press.

Rollston, C. 2020. "The Emergence of Alphabetic Scripts." In *A Companion to Ancient Near Eastern Languages*, ed. R. Hasselbach-Andee, 65–81. London: Wiley Blackwell.

Rose, C. B., ed. 2012. *The Archaeology of Phrygian Gordion, Royal City of Midas*. Gordion Special Studies 7. Museum Monograph 136. Philadelphia: University of Pennsylvania Press.

Rose, C. B., and G. Darbyshire, eds. 2011. *The New Chronology of Iron Age Gordion*. Gordion Special Studies 6. Museum Monograph 133. Philadelphia: University of Pennsylvania Press.

Rupp, D. W. 1987. "Vive le Roi: The Emergence of the State in Iron Age Cyprus." In *Western Cyprus Connections: An Archaeological Symposium*, ed. D. W. Rupp, 147–68. Gothenburg: Paul Åströms Förlag.

Rupp, D. W. 1988. "The 'Royal Tombs' at Salamis (Cyprus): Ideological Messages of Power and Authority." *Journal of Mediterranean Archaeology* 1/1:111–39.

Rupp, D. W. 1989. "Puttin' on the Ritz: Manifestations of High Status in Iron Age Cyprus." In *Early Society in Cyprus*, ed. E. Peltenburg, 336–62. Edinburgh: University of Edinburgh Press.

Ruppenstein, F. 2020a. "The End of the Bronze Age in Attica and the Origin of the Polis of Athens." In *Athens and Attica in Prehistory: Proceedings of the International Conference, Athens, 27–31 May 2015*, ed. N. Papadimitriou, J. C. Wright, S. Fachard, N. Polychronakou-Sgouritsa, and E. Andrikou, 569–74. Oxford: Archaeopress.

Ruppenstein, F. 2020b. "Migration Events in Greece at the End of the Second Millennium BC and Their Possible Balkanic Background." In *Objects, Ideas and Travelers: Contacts between the Balkans, the Aegean and Western Anatolia during the Bronze and Early Iron Age. Volume to the memory of Alexandru Vulpe; Proceedings of the Conference in Tulcea, 10–13 November 2017*, ed. J. Maran, R. Băjenaru, S.-C. Ailincăi, A.-D. Popescu, and S. Hansen, 107–22. Bonn: Verlag Dr. Rudolf Habelt GmbH.

Sabatini, S., and F. Lo Schiavo. 2020. "Late Bronze Age Metal Exploitation and Trade: Sardinia and Cyprus." *Materials and Manufacturing Processes* 35/13:1501–18.

Sader, H. 2014. "The Northern Levant during the Iron Age I Period." In *The Oxford Handbook of the Archaeology of the Levant, c. 8000–332 BCE*, ed. M. L. Steiner and A. E. Killebrew, 607–23. Oxford: Oxford University Press.

Sader, H. 2019a. "The Archaeology of Phoenician Cities." In *The Oxford Handbook of the Phoenician and Punic Mediterranean*, ed. C. López-Ruiz and B. R. Doak, 125–38. Oxford: Oxford University Press.

Sader, H. 2019b. *The History and Archaeology of Phoenicia*. Atlanta, GA: SBL Press.

Sagrillo, Troy L. 2015. "Shoshenq I and Biblical Šîšaq: A Philological Defense of Their Traditional Equation." In *Solomon and Shishak: Current Perspectives from Archaeology, Epigraphy, History and Chronology; Proceedings of the Third BICANE Colloquium Held at Sidney Sussex College, Cambridge, 26–27 March 2011*, ed. Peter James and Peter G. van der Veen, 61–81. BAR International Series 2732. Oxford: Archaeopress.

Saltini Semerari, G. 2017. "Towards an Archaeology of Disentanglement." *Journal of Archaeological Method and Theory* 24:542–78.

Samaras, V. 2015. "Piracy in the Aegean during the Postpalatial Period and the Early Iron Age." In *The Mediterranean Mirror: Cultural Contacts in the Mediterranean Sea between 1200 and 750 B.C.; International Post-doc and Young Researcher Conference; Heidelberg, 6th–8th October 2012*, ed. A. Babbi, F. Bubenheimer-Erhart, B. Marín-Aguilera, and S. Mühl, 189–204. Mainz: Verlag des Römisch-Germanischen Zentralmuseums.

Sass, B. 2002. "Wenamun and His Levant—1075 BC or 925 BC." *Egypt and the Levant* 12:247–55.

Sass, B. 2005. *The Alphabet at the Turn of the Millennium: The West Semitic Alphabet ca. 1150–850 B.C.E.* Tel Aviv: Yass Publications in Archaeology.

Sass, B. 2021. "Was the Age of Solomon without Monumental Art? The Frankfort–Albright Dispute, More Than Sixty Years Later." In *Travels through the Orient and the Mediterranean*

World: Essays Presented to Eric Gubel, ed. V. Boschloos, B. Overlaet, I. M. Swinnen, and V. Van Der Stede, 345–66. OLA 302. Leuven: Peeters Publishers.

Satraki, A. 2012. "Cypriot Polities in the Early Iron Age." In *Cyprus and the Aegean in the Early Iron Age: The Legacy of Nicolas Coldstream*, ed. M. Iacovou, 261–83. Nicosia: Bank of Cyprus Cultural Foundation.

Schachner, A. 2009. *Assyriens Könige an einer der Quellen des Tigris: Archäologische Forschungen im Höhlensystem des sogenannten Tigris-Tunnels.* Tübingen: Ernst Wasmuth.

Schachner, A. 2020a. "The 14th and 13th Centuries BC in the Hittite Capital City Hattuša: A (Re-)Assessment." In *Anatolia between the 13th and the 12th Century BCE*, ed. S. de Martino and E. Devecchi, 381–410. Turin: LoGisma editore.

Schachner, A. 2020b. "Anatolia." In *A Companion to the Archaeology of Early Greece and the Mediterranean*, ed. I. S. Lemos and A. Kotsonas, 2:1107–31. London: Wiley Blackwell.

Scheffer, M.E.H. van Nes, D. Bird, R. K. Bocinsky, and T. A. Kohler. 2021. "Loss of Resilience Preceded Transformations of Pre-Hispanic Pueblo Societies." *PNAS* 118/18:e2024397118.

Schipper, B. U. 2019. *A Concise History of Ancient Israel: From the Beginnings through the Hellenistic Era*. Translated by M. J. Lesley. University Park, PA: Eisenbrauns.

Schliemann, H. 1880. *Mycenae: A Narrative of Researches and Discoveries at Mycenae and Tiryns.* New York: Arno Press.

Schnapp-Gourbeillon, A. 1979. "Le mythe dorien." *A.I.O.N. Annali di archeologia e storia antica* 1:1–11.

Schnapp-Gourbeillon, A. 2002. *Aux origins de la Greèce (XIIIe–VIIIe siècle avant notre ère): La genèse du politique*. Paris: Les belles lettres.

Schneider, T. J. 2014. "Mesopotamia (Assyrians and Babylonians) and the Levant." In *The Oxford Handbook of the Archaeology of the Levant, c. 8000–332 BCE*, ed. M. L. Steiner and A. E. Killebrew, 98–106. Oxford: Oxford University Press.

Schniedewind, W. M. 1996. "Tel Dan Stela: New Light on Aramaic and Jehu's Revolt." *Bulletin of the American Schools of Oriental Research* 302:75–90.

Schwartz, G. M. 2006. "From Collapse to Regeneration." In *After Collapse: The Regeneration of Complex Societies*, ed. G. M. Schwartz and J. J. Nichols, 3–17. Tucson: University of Arizona Press.

Schwartz, G. M., and J. J. Nichols, eds. 2006. *After Collapse: The Regeneration of Complex Societies.* Tucson: University of Arizona Press.

Scott, A., R. C. Power, V. Altmann-Wendling, M. Artzy, M.A.S. Martin, S. Eisenmann, R. Hagan, D. C. Salazar-García, Y. Salmone, D. Yegorovi, I. Milevski, I. Finkelstein, P. W. Stockhammer, and C. Warinner. 2020. "Exotic Foods Reveal Contact between South Asia and the Near East during the Second Millennium BCE." *PNAS* 118/2:e2014956117. https://doi.org/10.1073/pnas.2014956117.

Scott, J. C. 2017. *Against the Grain: A Deep History of the Earliest States*. New Haven, CT: Yale University Press.

Seeher, J. 2010. "After the Empire: Observations on the Early Iron Age in Central Anatolia." In *Ipamati kistamati pari tumatimis: Luwian and Hittite Studies Presented to J. David Hawkins on the Occasion of His 70th Birthday*, ed. I. Singer, 220–29. Tel Aviv: Tel Aviv Institute of Archaeology.

Sergi, O. 2017. "The Battle of Ramoth-Gilead and the Rise of the Aramean Hegemony in the Southern Levant during the Second Half of the 9th Century BCE." In *Wandering Arameans: Arameans outside Syria; Textual and Archaeological Perspectives*, ed. A. Berlejung, A. M. Maeir, and A. Schüle, 81–97. Wiesbaden: Harrassowitz Verlag.

Sergi, O., and A. Kleiman. 2018. "The Kingdom of Geshur and the Expansion of Aram-Damascus into the Northern Jordan Valley: Archaeological and Historical Perspectives." *Bulletin of the American Schools of Oriental Research* 379:1–18.

Shalvi, G. 2018. "The Early Purple Dye Industry in Israel: A View from Tel Shikmona." In *Out of the Blue*, ed. O. Meiri, Y. Bloch, and Y. Kaplan, 65–77. Jerusalem: Bible Lands Museum.

Shalvi, G. 2020. "Tel Shiqmona: A Forgotten Phoenician Site on the Carmel Coast." In *Un viaje entre el Oriente y el Occidente del Mediterráneo / A Journey between East and West in the Mediterranean: Proceedings of the IX Congreso Internacional de Estudios Fenicios y Púnicos / International Congress of Phoenician and Punic Studies*, ed. S. C. Pérez and E. R. González. *Mytra* 5:1885–92. Mérida: Instituto de Arqueología, Mérida.

Shalvi, G., and A. Gilboa. 2023. "Between Israel and Phoenicia: The Iron IIA-B Fortified Purple-dye Production Centre at Tel Shiqmona." *Tel Aviv* 50: 75–110.

Sharon, I., and A. Gilboa. 2013. "The SKL Town: Dor in the Early Iron Age." In *The Philistines and Other "Sea Peoples" in Text and Archaeology*, ed. A. E. Killebrew and G. Lehmann, 393–468. Atlanta, GA: Society of Biblical Literature.

Sherratt, S. 1992. "Immigration and Archaeology: Some Indirect Reflections." In *Acta Cypria: Acts of an International Congress on Cypriote Archaeology Held in Göteborg on 22–24 August 1991, Part 2*, ed. P. Åström, 316–47. Jonsered, Sweden: Paul Åströms Förlag.

Sherratt, S. 1994. "Commerce, Iron and Ideology: Metallurgical Innovation in 12th–11th Century Cyprus." In *Cyprus in the 11th Century B.C.: Proceedings of the International Symposium, Nicosia, 30–31 October 1993*, ed. V. Karageorghis, 59–106. Nicosia: A. G. Leventis Foundation.

Sherratt, S. 2000. "Circulation of Metals and the End of the Bronze Age in the Eastern Mediterranean." In *Metals Make the World Go Round: The Supply and Circulation of Metals in Bronze Age Europe*, ed. C.F.E. Pare, 82–98. Oxford: Oxbow Books.

Sherratt, S. 2003. "The Mediterranean Economy: 'Globalization' at the End of the Second Millennium BCE." In *Symbiosis, Symbolism, and the Power of the Past: Canaan, Ancient Israel, and Their Neighbors, from the Late Bronze Age through Roman Palaestina*, ed. W. G. Dever and S. Gitin, 37–62. Winona Lake, IN: Eisenbrauns.

Sherratt, S. 2010. "Greeks and Phoenicians: Perceptions of Trade and Traders in the Early First Millennium BC." In *Social Archaeologies of Trade and Exchange: Exploring Relationships among People, Places, and Things*, ed. A. Agbe-Davies and A. Bauer, 119–42. Walnut Creek, CA: Left Coast Press.

Sherratt, S. 2015. "Cyprus and the Near East: Cultural Contacts (1200–750 BC)." In *The Mediterranean Mirror: Cultural Contacts in the Mediterranean Sea between 1200 and 750 B.C.; International Post-doc and Young Researcher Conference; Heidelberg, 6th–8th October 2012*, ed. A. Babbi, F. Bubenheimer-Erhart, B. Marín-Aguilera, and S. Mühl, 71–83. Mainz: Verlag des Römisch-Germanischen Zentralmuseums.

Sherratt, S. 2016. "From 'Institutional' to 'Private': Traders, Routes and Commerce from the Late Bronze Age to the Iron Age." In *Dynamics of Production in the Ancient Near East, 1300–500 BC*, ed. J. C. Moreno García, 289–301. Oxford: Oxbow Books.

Sherratt, S. 2019. "Phoenicians in the Aegean and Aegean Silver, 11th–9th Centuries BC." In *Les phéniciens, les puniques et les autres: Échanges et identités en Méditerranée ancienne*, ed. L. Bonadies, I. Chirpanlieva, and É. Guillon, 129–58. Paris: Éditions de Boccard.

Sherratt, S. 2020. "From the Near East to the Far West." In *A Companion to the Archaeology of Early Greece and the Mediterranean*, ed. I. S. Lemos and A. Kotsonas, 1:187–215. London: Wiley Blackwell.

Sherratt, A. G., and S. Sherratt. 1993. "The Growth of the Mediterranean Economy in the Early First Millennium BC." *World Archaeology* 24/3:361–78.

Shibata, D. 2022. "The Assyrian King of the Broken Obelisk, the Date of the Archive from Giricano, and the Timing of the Assyrian Calendar Reform." *Journal of Cuneiform Studies* 74:109–29.

Simon, Z. 2012. "Where Is the Land of Sura of the Hieroglyphic Luwian Inscription KARKAMIŠ A4b and Why Were Cappadocians Called Syrians by Greeks?" *Altorientalische Forschungen* 39:167–80.

Singer, I. 2012. "The Philistines in the North and the Kingdom of Taita." In *The Ancient Near East in the 12th–10th Centuries BCE: Culture and History; Proceedings of the International Conference Held at the University of Haifa, 2–5 May 2010*, ed. G. Galil, A. Gilboa, A. M. Maeir, and D. Kahn, 451–72. Alter Orient und Altes Testament 392. Münster: Ugarit-Verlag.

Sinha, A., G. Kathayat, H. Weiss, H. Li, H. Cheng, J. Reuter, A. W. Schneider, M. Berkelhammer, S. F. Adali, L. D. Stott, and R. L. Edwards. 2019. "Role of Climate in the Rise and Fall of the Neo-Assyrian Empire." *Science Advances* 5/11:eaax6656. DOI: 10.1126/sciadv.aax6656.

Smith, J. S. 2008. "Cyprus, the Phoenicians and Kition." In *Beyond the Homeland: Markers in Phoenician Chronology*, ed. C. Sagona, 261–303. Ancient Near Eastern Studies Supplement 28. Leuven: Peeters.

Smithson, E. L. 1968. "The Tomb of a Rich Athenian Lady, ca. 850 B.C." *Hesperia* 37:77–116.

Smithson, E. L. 1969. "The Grave of an Early Athenian Aristocrat." *Archaeology* 22/1:18–25.

Snape, S. 1996. "The Deir El-Bahri Cache." In *Tombs, Graves & Mummies: 50 Discoveries in World Archaeology*, ed. P. G. Bahn, 188–91. New York: Barnes and Nobles Books.

Snape, S. 2012. "The Legacy of Ramesses III and the Libyan Ascendancy." In *Ramesses III: The Life and Times of Egypt's Last Hero*, ed. E. H. Cline and D. B. O'Connor, 404–41. Ann Arbor: University of Michigan Press.

Snodgrass, A. M. 1967. *Arms and Armour of the Greeks*. Ithaca, NY: Cornell University Press.

Snodgrass, A. M. 1971. *The Dark Age of Greece: An Archaeological Survey of the Eleventh to the Eighth centuries BC*. Edinburgh: Edinburgh University Press.

Snodgrass, A. M. 1980. "Iron and Early Metallurgy in the Mediterranean." In *The Coming of the Age of Iron*, ed. T. A. Wertime and J. D. Muhly, 335–74. New Haven, CT: Yale University Press.

Snodgrass, A. M. 1983. "Cyprus and the Beginnings of Iron Technology in the Eastern Mediterranean." In *Early Metallurgy in Cyprus, 4000–500 B.C.*, ed. J. D. Muhly, R. Maddin, and V. Karageorghis, 285–94. Nicosia: Department of Antiquities.

Snodgrass, A. M. 1988. *Cyprus and Early Greek History*. Nicosia: Bank of Cyprus.

Snodgrass, A. M. 1993. "The Rise of the Polis." In *The Ancient Greek City-State*, ed. M. Hansen, 30–40. Copenhagen: Royal Danish Academy of Sciences and Letters.

Snodgrass, A. M. 1994. "Gains, Losses and Survivals: What We Can Infer for the Eleventh Century B.C." In *Cyprus in the 11th Century B.C.: Proceedings of the International*

Symposium, Nicosia, 30–31 October 1993, ed. V. Karageorghis, 167–75. Nicosia: A. G. Leventis Foundation.

Sogas, J. M. 2019. "Was Knossos a Home for Phoenician Traders?" In *Greek Art in Motion: Studies in Honour of Sir John Boardman on the Occasion of his 90th Birthday*, ed. R. Morais, D. Leão, and D. Rodríguez Pérez, with D. Ferreira, 408–16. Oxford: Archaeopress.

Stampolidis, N. C. 2019. "The Aegean." In *The Oxford Handbook of the Phoenician and Punic Mediterranean*, ed. C. López-Ruiz and B. R. Doak, 493–503. Oxford: Oxford University Press.

Stampolidis, N. C., and A. Kotsonas. 2006. "Phoenicians in Crete." In *Ancient Greece from the Mycenaean Palaces to the Age of Homer*, ed. S. Deger-Jalkotzy and I. S. Lemos, 337–60. Edinburgh: Edinburgh University Press.

Stampolidis, N. C., E. Papadopoulou, I. G. Laurentzatou, and I. Fappas. 2019. *Crete: Emerging Cities; Aptera, Eleutherna, Knossos; Three Ancient Cities Revived.* Athens: Museum of Cycladic Art.

Starr, C. G. 1961. *The Origins of Greek Civilization: 1100–650 B.C.* New York: Alfred A. Knopf.

Starr, C. G. 1992. "History and Archaeology in the Early First Millennium BC." In *Greece between East and West, 10th–8th centuries BC: Papers of the Meeting at the Institute of Fine Arts, New York University, March 15–16th, 1990*, ed. G. Kopcke and I. Tokumaru, 1–6. Mainz: Philipp von Zabern.

Steele, P. M. 2020. "Script and Literacy." In *A Companion to the Archaeology of Early Greece and the Mediterranean*, ed. I. S. Lemos and A. Kotsonas, 1:247–69. London: Wiley Blackwell.

Steiner, M. 2014. "Moab during the Iron Age II Period." In *The Oxford Handbook of the Archaeology of the Levant, c. 8000–332 BCE*, ed. M. L. Steiner and A. E. Killebrew, 770–81. Oxford: Oxford University Press.

Stern, E. 1998. "Buried Treasure: The Silver Hoard from Dor." *Biblical Archaeological Review* 24/4:46–62.

Stern, E. 2001. "The Silver Hoard from Tel Dor." In *Hacksilber to Coinage: New Insights into the Monetary History of the Near East and Greece; A Collection of Eight Papers Presented at the 99th Annual Meeting of the Archaeological Institute of America*, ed. M. S. Balmuth, 19–26. Numismatic Studies 24. New York: American Numismatic Society.

Stern, E. 2013. *The Material Culture of the Northern Sea Peoples in Israel.* Winona Lake, IN: Eisenbrauns.

Stieglitz, R. R. 1994. "The Minoan Origin of Tyrian Purple." *Biblical Archaeologist* 57/1:46–54.

Storey, R., and G. R. Storey. 2016. "Requestioning the Classic Maya Collapse and the Fall of the Roman Empire: Slow Collapse." In *Beyond Collapse: Archaeological Perspectives on Resilience, Revitalization, and Transformation in Complex Societies*, ed. R. K. Faulseit, 99–123. Visiting Scholar Conference Volumes: Center for Archaeological Investigations Occasional Paper No. 42. Carbondale: Southern Illinois University Press.

Strouhal, E. 1996. "Traces of a Smallpox Epidemic in the Family of Ramesses V of the Egyptian 20th Dynasty." *Anthropologie* 34/3: 315–19.

Stub, S. T. 2020. "The Price of Purple." *Archaeology*, November–December. https://www.archaeology.org/issues/403-2011/letter-from/9133-israel-purple-dye?tmpl=component&print=1.

Stuckenberg, D. J., and A. L. Contento. 2018. "Water Scarcity: The Most Understated Global Security Risk." *Harvard Law School National Security Journal*, May 18. http://harvardnsj.org/2018/05/water-scarcity-the-most-understated-global-security-risk.

Sukenik, N., D. Iluz, Z. Amar, A. Varvak, O. Shamir, and E. Ben-Yosef. 2021. "Early Evidence of Royal Purple Dyed Textile from Timna Valley (Israel)." *PLOS ONE* 16/1:e0245897.

Summers, G. D. 2000. "The Median Empire Reconsidered: A View from Kerkenes Dag." *Anatolian Studies* 50:37–54.

Swaddling, J. 1999. *The Ancient Olympic Games*. London: British Museum Press.

Tainter, J. A. 1988. *The Collapse of Complex Societies*. Cambridge: Cambridge University Press.

Tainter, J. A. 1999. "Post-collapse Societies." In *Companion Encyclopedia of Archaeology*, ed. G. Barker, 988–1039. London: Routledge.

Taleb, N. N. 2004. *Fooled by Randomness: The Hidden Role of Chance in Life and in the Markets*. 2nd ed. New York: Random House.

Taleb, N. N. 2007. *The Black Swan: The Impact of the Highly Improbable*. London: Penguin.

Taleb, N. N. 2014. *Antifragile: Things That Gain from Disorder*. Paperback ed. New York: Random House.

Tappy, R. E. 1992. *The Archaeology of Israelite Samaria*. Vol. 1, *Early Iron Age through the Ninth Century BCE*. Harvard Semitic Studies 44. Atlanta, GA: Scholars Press.

Tappy, R. E. 2001. *The Archaeology of Israelite Samaria*. Vol. 2, *The Eighth Century*. Harvard Semitic Studies 50. Winona Lake, IN: Eisenbrauns.

Taylor, J. G. 1865. "Travels in Kurdistan, with Notices of the Sources of the Western Tigris, and Ancient Ruins in Their Neighbourhood." *Journal of the Royal Geographical Society of London* 1865:21–56. https://www.jstor.org/stable/3268575.

Tercatin, R. 2021. "Biblical 'Royal Purple' Found at Timna Offers Look at King David Wardrobe." *Jerusalem Post*, January 29. https://www.jpost.com/archaeology/biblical-royal-purple-found-at-timna-offers-look-at-king-david-wardrobe-657082.

Thareani, Y. 2016a. "The Empire and the 'Upper Sea': Assyrian Control Strategies along the Southern Levantine Coast." *Bulletin of the American Schools of Oriental Research* 375:77–102.

Thareani, Y. 2016b. "Enemy at the Gates? The Archaeological Visibility of the Aramaeans at Dan." In *In Search for Aram and Israel: Politics, Culture, and Identity*, ed. O. Sergi, M. Oeming, and I. J. de Hulster, 169–97. Tübingen: Mohr Siebeck.

Thareani, Y. 2019a. "Archaeology of an Imagined Community: Tel Dan in the Iron Age IIa." In *Research on Israel and Aram: Autonomy, Independence and Related Issues; Proceedings of the First Annual RIAB Center Conference, Leipzig, June 2016*, ed. A. Berlejung and A. M. Maeir, 263–76. Tübingen: Mohr Siebeck.

Thareani, Y. 2019b. "Changing Allegiances in Disputed Borderlands: Dan's Political Status on the Eve of the Aramaean Invasion." *Palestine Exploration Quarterly* 151/3–4:184–201.

Thomas, Z., and E. Ben-Yosef. 2023. "David and Solomon's Invisible Kingdom." *Biblical Archaeology Review* 49/2 (Summer): 40–45.

Thompson, C., and S. Skaggs. 2013. "King Solomon's Silver? Southern Phoenician Hacksilber Hoards and the Location of Tarshish." *Internet Archaeology* 35. https://doi.org/10.11141/ia.35.6.

Thompson, J. 2015. *Wonderful Things: A History of Egyptology*. Vol. 2, *The Golden Age: 1881–1914*. Cairo: AUC Press.

Tronchetti, C. 2014. "Cultural Interactions in Iron Age Sardinia." In *The Cambridge Prehistory of the Bronze and Iron Age Mediterranean*, ed. A. B. Knapp and P. van Dommelen, 266–84. Cambridge: Cambridge University Press.

Tsipopoulou, M. 2005. "'Mycenoans' at the Isthmus of Ierapetra: Some (Preliminary) Thoughts on the Foundation of the (Eteo)Cretan Cultural Identity." In *Ariadne's Threads: Connections between Crete and the Mainland in Late Minoan III (LM IIIA2 to LM IIIC); Proceedings of an International Workshop Held in Athens, Scuola Archeologica Italiana, 5–6 April 2003 (Tripodes 3)*, ed. A. L. D'Agata and J. Moody, 303–33. Athens: Scuola archeologica italiana di Atene.

Tucker, D. J. 1994. "Representations of Imgur-Enlil on the Balawat Gates." *Iraq* 56:107–16.

Ussishkin, D. 2022. "The Function of the Iron Age Site of Khirbet Qeiyafa." *Israel Exploration Journal* 72/1:49–65.

Van Damme, T. 2023. "The Mycenaean Fountain and the Transformation of Space on the Athenian Acropolis: 1200 to 675 B.C." *Hesperia* 92/1: 111–90.

Van Loon, M. N. 1966. *Urartian Art: Its Distinctive Traits in the Light of New Excavations*. Istanbul: Nederlands Historisch-Archaeologisch Instituut.

Veropoulidou, R. 2014. "Molluscan Exploitation in the Neolithic and Bronze Age Communities at the Former Thermaic Gulf, North Aegean." In *PHYSIS: L' environment naturel et la relation homme-milieu dans le monde egeen protohistorique; Actes de la 14e rencontre égéenne internationale, Paris, Institut national d'histoire de l'art (INHA), 11–14 décembre 2012*, ed. G. Touchais, R. Laffineur, and F. Rougemont, 415–22. AEGAEUM 37. Leuven: Peeters.

Veropoulidou, R., S. Andreou, and K. Kotsakis. 2008. "Small Scale Production Purple-Dye Production in the Bronze Age of Northern Greece: The Evidence from the Thessaloniki Toumba." In *Purpureae vestes: II Symposium internacional sobre textiles y tintes del Mediterráneo en el mundo antiguo*, ed. C. Alfaro and L. Karali, 171–79. Valencia: Universitat de Valencia.

Voigt, M. M., and R. C. Henrickson. 2000. "Formation of the Phrygian State: The Early Iron Age at Gordion." *Anatolian Studies* 50:37–54.

Voskos, I., and A. B. Knapp. 2008. "Cyprus at the End of the Late Bronze Age: Crisis and Colonization or Continuity and Hybridization?" *American Journal of Archaeology* 112/4:659–84.

Voutsaki, S. 2000. "Review of *Argolis Lakonien Messenien: Vom Ende der mykenischen Palastzeit biszur Einwanderung der Dorier* by B. Eder. *Classical Review* 50/1:232–33.

Waal, W. 2018. "On the 'Phoenician Letters': The Case for an Early Transmission of the Greek Alphabet from an Archaeological, Epigraphic, and Linguistic Perspective." *Aegean Studies* 1:83–125.

Waal, W. 2020. "Mother or Sister? Rethinking the Origins of the Greek Alphabet and Its Relation to the Other 'Western' Alphabets." In *Understanding Relations between Scripts II*, ed. P. J. Boyes and P. M. Steele, 109–24. Oxford: Oxbow Books.

Wachter, R. 2021. "The Genesis of the Local Alphabets of Archaic Greece." In *The Early Greek Alphabets: Origin, Diffusion, Uses*, ed. R. Parker and P. M. Steele, 21–31. Oxford: Oxford University Press.

Waldbaum, J. C. 1978. *From Bronze to Iron*. Studies in Mediterranean Archaeology 54. Gothenburg: Paul Aströms Förlag.

Waldbaum, J. C. 1980. "The First Archaeological Appearance of Iron and the Transition to the Iron Age." In *The Coming of the Age of Iron*, ed. T. A. Wertime and J. D. Muhly, 69–98. New Haven, CT: Yale University Press.

Waldbaum, J. C. 1982. "Bimetallic Objects from the Eastern Mediterranean and the Question of the Dissemination of Iron." In *Early Metallurgy in Cyprus, 4000–500 B.C.*, ed. J. D. Muhly, R. Maddin, and V. Karageorghis, 325–47. Nicosia: Tmēma Archaiotētōn.

Waldbaum, J. C. 1994. "Early Greek contacts with the Southern Levant ca. 1000–600 B.C.: The Eastern Perspective." *Bulletin of the American Schools of Oriental Research* 293:53–66.

Waldbaum, J. C. 1999. "The Coming of Iron in the Eastern Mediterranean: Thirty Years of Archaeological and Technological Work." In *The Archaeometallurgy of the Asian Old World*, ed. V. C. Pigott, 27–57. Philadelphia: University of Pennsylvania Museum.

Walker, B., C. S. Holling, S. R. Carpenter, and A. Kinzig. 2004. "Resilience, Adaptability and Transformability in Social-Ecological Systems." *Ecology and Society* 9/2:5. http://www.ecologyandsociety.org/vol9/iss2/art5.

Walker, B., and D. Salt. 2006. *Resilience Thinking: Sustaining Ecosystems and People in a Changing World*. Washington, DC: Island Press.

Wallace, S. 2006. "The Gilded Cage? Settlement and Socioeconomic Change after 1200 BC: A Comparison of Crete and Other Aegean Regions." In *Ancient Greece: From the Mycenaean Palaces to the Age of Homer*, ed. S. Deger-Jalkotzy and I. S. Lemos, 619–64. Edinburgh: Edinburgh University Press.

Wallace, S. 2010. *Ancient Crete: From Successful Collapse to Democracy's Alternatives, Twelfth to Fifth Centuries BC*. Cambridge: Cambridge University Press.

Wallace, S. 2017. "The Classic Crisis? Some Features of Current Crisis Narratives for the Aegean Late Bronze–Early Iron Age." In *Crisis to Collapse: The Archaeology of Social Breakdown*, ed. T. Cunningham and J. Driessen, 65–85. Louvain: UCL Presses.

Wallace, S. 2018. *Travelers in Time: Imagining Movement in the Ancient Aegean World*. London: Routledge.

Wallace, S. 2020. "Economies in Crisis: Subsistence and Landscape Technology in the Aegean and East Mediterranean after c. 1200 BC." In *Collapse and Transformation: The Late Bronze Age to Early Iron Age in the Aegean*, ed. G. M. Middleton, 247–58. Oxford: Oxbow Books.

Waters, M. 2013. "Elam, Assyria, and Babylonia in the Early First Millennium BC." In *The Oxford Handbook of Ancient Iran*, ed. D. T. Potts, 478–92. New York: Oxford University Press.

Watrous, L. V. 2021. *Minoan Crete: An Introduction*. Cambridge: Cambridge University Press.

Wedde, M. 1999. "War at Sea: The Mycenaean and Early Iron Age Oared Galley." In *Polemos: Le context guerrier en Égée à l'Âge du Bronze; Actes de la 7ième rencontre égéenne international*, ed. R. Laffineur, 465–74. Aegeum 19. Liège: Université de Liège.

Wedde, M. 2000. *Towards a Hermeneutics of Aegean Bronze Age Ship Imagery*. Peleus Band 6. Mannheim: Bibliopolis.

Wedde, M. 2006. "Pictorial Evidence for Partial System Survival in the Greek Bronze to Iron Age Transition." In *Pictorial Pursuits: Figurative Painting on Mycenaean and Geometric Pottery*, ed. E. Rystedt and B. Wells, 255–69. Stockholm: Swedish Institute at Athens.

Weeden, M. 2013. "After the Hittites: The Kingdoms of Karkamish and Palistin in Northern Syria." *Bulletin of the Institute of Classical Studies* 56/2:1–20.

Weiberg, E. 2012. "What Can Resilience Theory Do for (Aegean) Archaeology?" In *Matters of Scale: Processes and Courses of Events in Archaeology and Cultural History*, ed. N. M. Burström and F. Fahlander, 147–65. Stockholm Studies in Archaeology, 56. Stockholm: Stockholm University.

Weiberg, E., and M. Finné. 2018. "Resilience and Persistence of Ancient Societies in the Face of Climate Change: A Case Study from Late Bronze Age Peloponnese." *World Archaeology* 50/4:584–602. https://doi.org/10.1080/00438243.2018.1515035.

Weiberg, E., M. Lindblom, B. L. Sjöberg, and G. Nordquist. 2010. "Social and Environmental Dynamics in Bronze and Iron Age Greece." In *The Urban Mind: Cultural and Environmental Dynamics*, ed. P.J.J. Sinclair, G. Nordquist, F. Herschend, and C. Isendahl, 149–94. Uppsala: Uppsala University.

Weinstein, J. M. 2012. "Egypt and the Levant in the Reign of Ramesses III." In *Ramesses III: The Life and Times of Egypt's Last Hero*, ed. E. H. Cline and D. B. O'Connor, 160–80. Ann Arbor: University of Michigan Press.

Welton, L., and H. Charaf. 2019–20. "The Iron Age I in the Levant: A View from the North; Prologue." *Archaeology & History in Lebanon* 50–51:2–7.

Welton, L., and H. Charaf. 2020–21. "The Iron Age I in the Levant: A View from the North; Epilogue." *Archaeology & History in Lebanon* 52–53:133–54.

Welton, L., T. Harrison, S. Batiuk, E. Ünlü, B. Janeway, D. Karakaya, D. Lipovitch, D. Lumb, and J. Roames. 2019. "Shifting Networks and Community Identity at Tell Tayinat in the Iron I (ca. 12th to Mid 10th Century B.C.E.)." *American Journal of Archaeology* 123/2:291–333.

Wente, E. F., Jr. 2003. "The Report of Wenamon." In *The Literature of Ancient Egypt*, ed. W. K. Simpson, 116–24. 3rd ed. New Haven, CT: Yale University Press.

Wertime, T. A. 1980. "The Pyrotechnological Background." In *The Coming of the Age of Iron*, ed. T. A. Wertime and J. D. Muhly, 1–24. New Haven, CT: Yale University Press.

Whitley, J. 1991. *Style and Society in Dark Age Greece: The Changing Face of a Pre-literate Society 1100–700 BC*. Cambridge: Cambridge University Press.

Whitley, J. 1993. "Response to Papadopoulos (II): Woods, Trees and Leaves in the Early Iron Age of Greece." *Journal of Mediterranean Archaeology* 6/2:223–29.

Wilson, E. L. 1887. "Finding Pharaoh." *Century Magazine* 34:1–10.

Winter, I. J. 1995. "Homer's Phoenicians: History, Ethnography or Literary Trope?" In *The Ages of Homer: A Tribute to Emily Townsend Vermeule*, ed. J. B. Carter and S. P. Morris, 247–71. Austin: University of Texas Press.

Wood, J. R. 2018. "The Transmission of Silver and Silver Extraction Technology across the Mediterranean in Late Prehistory: An Archaeological Science Approach to Investigating the Westward Expansion of the Phoenicians." PhD diss., University College London.

Wood, J. R., C. Bell, and I. Montero-Ruiz. 2020. "The Origin of Tel Dor Hacksilver and the Westward Expansion of the Phoenicians in the Early Iron Age: The Cypriot Connection." *Journal of Eastern Mediterranean Archaeology & Heritage Studies* 8/1:1–21. https://www.jstor.org/stable/10.5325/jeasmedarcherstu.8.1.0001.

Wood, J. R., I. Montero-Ruiz, and M. Martinón-Torres. 2019. "From Iberia to the Southern Levant: The Movement of Silver across the Mediterranean in the Early Iron Age." *Journal of World Prehistory* 32:1–31. https://doi.org/10.1007/s10963-018-09128-3.

Woolley, C. L. 1920. *Dead Towns and Living Men*. London: Oxford University Press.

Yadin, Y. 1970. "Megiddo of the Kings of Israel." *Biblical Archaeologist* 33:66–96.

Yadin, Y. 1976. "In Defense of the Stables at Megiddo." *Biblical Archaeology Review* 2:18–22.

Yahalom-Mack, N. 2022. "Metalworking at Tel Rehov." *Near Eastern Archaeology* 85/2:159–63.

Yahalom-Mack, N., and A. Eliyahu-Behar. 2015. "The Transition from Bronze to Iron in Canaan: Chronology, Technology, and Context." *Radiocarbon* 57/2:285–305.

Yahalom-Mack, N., E. Galili, I. Segal, E. Boaretto, S. Shilstein, and I. Finkelstein. 2014. "New Insights into Levantine Copper Trade: Bronze and Iron Ages in Israel." *Journal of Archaeological Science* 45:159–77.

Yamada, K. 2005. "'From the Upper Sea to the Lower Sea': The Development of the Names of Seas in the Assyrian Royal Inscriptions." *Orient* 40:31–55.

Yamada, S. 2000. *The Construction of the Assyrian Empire: A Historical Study of the Inscriptions of Shalmaneser III (859–824) Relating of His Campaigns to the West.* Leiden: Brill.

Yasur-Landau, A. 2010. *The Philistines and Aegean Migration at the End of the Late Bronze Age.* Cambridge: Cambridge University Press.

Yasur-Landau, A. 2019. "The Memory Machine: How 12th-Century BCE Iconography Created Memories of the Philistines (and Other Sea Peoples)." In *MNHMH/MNEME: Past and Memory in the Aegean Bronze Age; Proceedings of the 17th International Aegean Conference, University of Udine, Department of Humanities and Cultural Heritage, Ca'Foscari University of Venice, Department of Humanities, 17–21 April 2018*, ed. E. Borgna, I. Caloi, F. M. Carinici, and R. Laffineur, 413–21. Leuven: Peeters.

Yoffee, N. 2006. "Notes on Regeneration." In *After Collapse: The Regeneration of Complex Societies*, ed. G. M. Schwartz and J. J. Nichols, 222–27. Tucson: University of Arizona Press.

Yoffee, N., ed. 2019. *The Evolution of Fragility: Setting the Terms.* Cambridge: McDonald Institute for Archaeological Research.

Yoffee, N., and G. L. Cowgill, eds. 1988. *The Collapse of Ancient States and Civilization.* Tucson: University of Arizona Press.

Younger, K. L., Jr. 2016. *A Political History of the Arameans: From Their Origins to the End of Their Polities.* Atlanta, GA: SBL Press.

Younger, K. L., Jr. 2017. "Tiglath-Pileser I and the Initial Conflicts of the Assyrians with the Arameans." In *Wandering Arameans: Arameans outside Syria; Textual and Archaeological Perspectives*, ed. A. Berlejung, A. M. Maeir, and A. Schüle, 195–228. Wiesbaden: Harrassowitz Verlag.

Younger, K. L., Jr. 2020. "Reflections on Hazael's Empire in Light of Recent Study in the Biblical and Ancient Near Eastern Texts." In *Writing and Rewriting History in Ancient Israel and Near Eastern Cultures*, ed. I. Kalimi, 79–102. Wiesbaden: Harrassowitz Verlag.

Younker, R. W. 1994. "Ammonites." In *Peoples of the Old Testament World*, ed. A. J. Hoerth, G. L. Mattingly, and E. M. Yamauchi, 293–316. Grand Rapids, MI: Baker Books.

Younker, R. W. 2014. "Ammon during the Iron Age II Period." In *The Oxford Handbook of the Archaeology of the Levant, c. 8000–332 BCE*, ed. M. L. Steiner and A. E. Killebrew, 757–69. Oxford: Oxford University Press.

Zimansky, P. E. 1985. *Ecology and Empire: The Structure of the Urartian State.* SAOC 41. Chicago: Oriental Institute of Chicago.

Zimansky, P. E. 2011. "Urartian and the Urartians." In *The Oxford Handbook of Ancient Anatolia: 10,000–323 B.C.E.*, ed. S. R. Steadman and G. McMahon, 548–59. New York: Oxford University Press.

INDEX

Note: Page numbers in *italic* type indicate figures or tables.

Abbott Papyrus, 11
Abd el-Rassul, 30
Abdi-Aštart (Abdastrus), 104
Abibaal, 38, 101, 104
Abibaal Inscription, 104
Adad-nirari II, 56–57
Adad-nirari III, 77
adaptation: Assyria, 173–174; Babylonia, 173–174; civilizations, xxii, xxiv; concept of, 164; coping vs., 167–168; Crete, 140; Cyprus, 84–85, 89, 171; Egypt, 12; Greece, 137, 155; as key to survival, 194; Late Bronze Age, 109, 155; Mycenae, 133; Neo-Hittites, 119; Phoenicians, 171
adaptive cycle, 160–164, *161*, 170, 175, 198, 199
Adcock, Sarah, 114, 186
administrative structure: Assyria, 187–188, 222n19; Babylonia, 188; collapse of, 4, 188; Egypt, 13, 188; as factor in resilience, 188; Greece, 138
Aegean region, *xxxv*, 133–156. *See also* Crete and the Minoans; Greece; Mycenae
agriculture, 27, 119, 122, 137
Ahab, 31, 39, 70, 105
Ahaziahu, 73
Ahiram, 101, 105
Ahmes-Nefertiry, 29
Akhenaten, 101
Aleppo, 116, 118, 120–121
Alexander the Great, 40, 115
Allen, Mitchell, 98
alphabet. *See* writing
Amenemopet, 16, 25
Amenhotep II, 14
Amenhotep III, 86, 101
American Journal of Archaeology, 107
American Southwest, 3–4
American University of Beirut, 119
Amiran, Ruth, 36
Ammon, 21, 38, 40, 80, 119, 159, 179
Anatolia, 58, 72, 85, 98, 111–117, 121, 124, 132, 174, 186. *See also* Turkey
Angel, J. Lawrence, 151–152
anti-fragility, 84, 110, 169–170, 172–173. *See also* fragility/vulnerability; resilience
apiary, 37–38
Apollonius of Rhodes, 85
Aramaeans, 42–43, 51, 54–56, 63, 69, 72–73, 78–79, 118, 173–174
Aramaic language, 23, 42, 69
archaeology: Aramaeans, 74; Assyria, 45, 51, 57–63; Babylonia, 45, 47; Canaan, 18, 36–38; Crete, 140, 145–148; Cyprus, 88–93, 109; dangers of, 111–112; and Dorian invasion, 1–3; Edom, 25; Euboea, 148–150; Egypt, 34–35; Greece, 135–136, 143, 145–154; Hittites/Neo-Hittites, 111–112, 115–121; Israelites, 20, 22–24, 26–27, 31–32; issues of scholarship in, 45, 180, 184; Mycenae, 134–135; Phoenicians, 95, 97, 100, 105–107. *See also* historical sources
architecture, following collapse, 5

Armenia, 129
army, as factor in resilience, 188
Ashkelon Deep-Sea Project, 107–108
Aššur-bel-kala, 55, 124
Aššur-dan I, 47
Aššur-dan II, 56
Aššurnasirpal I, 112
Aššurnasirpal II, 60–67, 123–124, 128
Aššur-reša-iši, 42–43, 46, 48
Assyria: Aššurnasirpal II's reign, 60–67; administrative structure in, 187–188, 222n19; Aramaeans and, 42–43, 51, 54–56, 63, 69, 73, 173; archaeological discovery of, 45; attacks on Iron Age city-states by, 118–119; Babylonia and, 43, 48, 53, 68, 77; and Carchemish, 112; climate change in, 42–43, 52–53, 57, 78, 186; collapse of, 54–55; communication systems in, 69–70; Cyprus and, 79, 109; drought in, 48, 55, 186; Elam and, 173; food crises in, 54; historical sources available for, xxv, 43–45, 47–48; and Hittites/Neo-Hittites, 118, 123–133; in Iron Age, 42–79; Israelites and, 77, 119; in Late Bronze Age, 52; and the Levant, 39–40, 129–130; Middle Assyrian period, 55; Neo-Assyrian Empire, 55–79, 109, 116, 118, 123–133; Phoenicians and, 52, 62, 66–68, 70–71, 79, 118, 233n52; Phrygians and, 115; resilience of, 47–48, 53, 56–57, 61–79, 170–171, 173–174, 186–188; Shalmaneser III's reign, 67–76; Tiglath-Pileser I's reign, 48–54; Urartu and, 124–129, 174; writing in, 47–48, 187
Assyrian and Babylonian Chronicles, 43, 54, 56
Assyrian King List, 44
Assyrian Pressure Paradigm, 233n52
Assyrian Royal Annals, 44
Aštar(t)-imn, 104, 105
Athaliah, 105
Azarba'al Inscription, 141–142

Baal-ma'zer (Baal-azor), 104
Baal-ma'zer (Baal-azor) II, 106
Babylonia: administrative structure in, 188; archaeological discovery of, 45; Assyria and, 43, 48, 53, 68, 77; climate change in, 53; drought in, 55; and Elam, 46–47, 78; food crises in, 56; historical sources available for, xxv; Neo-Babylonian Empire, 78; population of, 47; resilience of, 47, 53, 78, 170–171, 173–174, 188
Babylonian Chronicles. See *Assyrian and Babylonian Chronicles*
Balawat gates, 57–61, 68, *69*, 71, 123, 125–127
Ballard, Bob, 107–108
Bar Ilan University, 19
Barnes, Julian, vii
Battle of Qarqar, 63, 70–72
Bavel, B. van, 246n57
bees, 37–38
beeswax, 37–38
Bell, Carol, 83, 88, 99, 172–173
Ben-Dor Evian, Shirly, 17
Ben-Yosef, Erez, 25–26, 179
Bible. *See* Hebrew Bible
Biran, Avraham, 22, 37
Black Lives Matter, xxiii
Black Obelisk, 75, *76*
Blegen, Carl, 152
Bliss, Frederick, 18
Boardman, John, 153
Book of Joshua, 19
Book of Judges, 19
Botta, Paul Émile, 45
Breasted, James Henry, 25, 31, 35
Brier, Bob, 15
British Medical Journal, 8
British Museum, 58–61, 63, 125, 131
British School of Archaeology, 105, 145
bronze, 11, 15, 57–60, 74–75, 85, 87, 91–93, 123–124, 173
Brugsch, Emil, 30
Bryce, Trevor, 66, 72
Bryn Mawr College, 1
Budge, E. A. Wallis, 59
Byblos, 38–39, 51, 52, 66, 70, 71, 83, 84, 96, 100–105, 113, 118

Ca'Foscari University, 113
Cairo Museum, 16, 17, 30
Calah inscription, 77
Cambridge University, 4, 43, 186
Canaan: assimilation of, 174, 177–178; collapse of, 20, 177–178; Egypt and, 29; foreign rule of, 119; Israelites and, 19–20, 32, 35; Philistines and, 18–19; and Phoenicians, 83; resilience of, 40–41, 83–84, 172–174, 178; and trade, 83; writing in, 27, 80. *See also* Lebanon; Phoenicians
cannibalism, 54
Carchemish, 111–114, 116–119, 121–123, 129–133, 174
Carleton College, 139
Carnarvon, George Herbert, Lord, 10
Carpenter, Rhys, 1
Carter, Howard, 10, 30
Carthage, 82, 107–108
Catling, Hector, 145–148
cattle, 114–115
cedar, 32, 51, 53, 65, 68, 95, 113
Centeno, Miguel, 186
Christie, Agatha, 60
civilizations: adaptive cycle of, 160–164, *161*; collapse of, xix–xxiv, 4–5, *5*, 157–158, 190–191, 214n9, 246n57, 247n61; resilience of, xxii–xxiii; responses of, to collapse, xxii–xxv, 191
Claremont Graduate School, 76
clay prisms, 49, *50*, 51
Clayton, Peter, 12
climate change: Assyria, 42–43, 52–53, 57, 78, 186; Babylonia, 53; contemporary manifestations, xxiii, 52, 164–171; Cyprus, 109; fragility and resilience related to, 188–189; Greece, 114; Iron Age, 159–160; Late Bronze Age Collapse, 164–171; Neo-Hittites, 114. *See also* drought
climate-society interactions, 213n3
Coca-Cola, xix, *xx*
Coldstream, Nicholas, 4, 144, 153, 196
colonialism, 45, 59, 89
Columbia Electronic Encyclopedia, 1
communications: Assyria, 69–70; Cyprus and, 108; Phoenicians and, 83–84
Conquest model, 19
Cook, Gila, 22
coping: adapting vs., 167–168; Assyria, 170–171, 173, 174; Babylonia, 170–171, 173, 174; civilizations, xxii, xxiv; concept of, 164; Crete, 140; Cyprus, 84–85; Egypt, 12, 170–171, 174–175; Neo-Hittites, 119
copper mines, 10, 17–18, 25–26, 38, 74, 86, 90–91, 109, 150
Cornell University, 83
Coulson, Willie, 4
Country Lords, 111–113, 131–132
COVID-19, xxiii, 192
Cowgill, George, xxiv, 214n9
Cranfield University, 87
Crete and the Minoans: collapse of, 140, 155, 176; cultural continuity of, 176–177; Cyprus and, 108, 232n43; disappearance of, xxi; historical sources available for, xxv; in Iron Age, 139–141, 153–154; Mycenae and, 140–141; Phoenicians and, 100, 108, 154, 232n43; population of, 144, 153–154; resilience of, 140; warrior burials on, 92, 145–148. *See also* Greece
Crielaard, Jan Paul, 93–94, 108
cultural continuity, 175–177
Curtis, John, 61
Cyprus: Assyria and, 79, 109; climate change on, 109; collapse of, 89; and copper, 26; disappearance and rise of cities in, 90–91; drought in, 109; foundation myths for cities of, 92; historical sources available for, xxv; in Iron Age, 84–94, 100, 108–110; Iron Age map, *xxxiv*; ironworking on, 85–88, 93, 110, 150, 173; population of, 89–90; resilience of, 85, 87–90, 94, 109–110, 171–173; and trade, 87, 88, 93–94, 108, 110, 173; warrior burials on, 92, 145–147

Dakar (submarine), 107
d'Alfonso, Lorenzo, 114
Damascus Coalition, 70–72

dark age, concept of, 4–5, 195–199
Darwin, Charles, 194
David, 19–26, 35
Deger-Jalkotzy, Sigrid, 139
Deir el-Bahri Cache, 8, 13, 14, 29–30
Desborough, Vincent, 196
Diodorus Siculus, 81
disaster risk management and mitigation, 164–167
disease, as factor in civilizational collapse, 10. *See also* COVID-19
Divided Kingdom (Israelites), 35
documents. *See* historical sources
Dodson, Aidan, 17
Dorian invasion, 1–3, 155, 159
Dorians, 85
drought: Anatolia, 115; Assyria, 48, 55, 186; Babylonia, 55; Cyprus, 109; Egypt, 9; Greece, 137; Iron Age, 159; Levant, 21; Mycenae, 190. *See also* climate change
Drovetti, Bernardino, 7

Eastern Mediterranean, Iron Age map, *xxxi*
economy: Assyria, 187–188; collapse of, 4–5, 158–159, 188; Egypt, 9, 10, 39; as factor in resilience, 188; Hittites, 188; Mycenae, 138–139, 185, 188; vulnerability of, 166
Edom, 21, 24–26, 29, 38, 40, 77, 80, 119, 179
Edom Lowlands Regional Archaeology Project, 25
Egypt: adaptive cycle model applied to, 175; administrative structure in, 13, 188; collapse in, 9–12, 40; drought in, 9; food crises in, 9, 12; historical sources available for, xxv; in Iron Age, 7–18, 33–40; Iron Age map, *xxxii*; and the Levant, 10, 14, 18, 33–40; Phoenicians and, 94–97; Ramses pharaonic period, 7–12; resilience of, 12, 170–171, 174–175, 188; Upper and Lower, 13–14
Ehrlich, Carl, 19
Eisenstadt, Shmuel, 190–191
Elam, 46–47, 78, 173
Elibaal, 39, 101–103
Elibaal Inscription, 102–103, *103*
Elissa (Dido), 107
Elissa (ship), 107–108
Eponym Chronicles, 44
Erb-Satullo, Nathaniel, 87
Esarhadon, 109
Eshel, Tzilla, 98
Ethbaal (king of Byblos), 101, 105
Ethbaal (king of Tyre), 105–106

famine. *See* food crises
Faruq, King, 15
Finné, Martin, 185
Floyd, George, Jr., xxiii
food crises: Assyria, 54; Babylonia, 56; Egypt, 9, 12
fragility/vulnerability, 168, 184–190, 192. *See also* anti-fragility
Frahm, Eckart, 48, 222n19
Franklin, Benjamin, 193

Garfinkel, Yossi, 26
Gath (Tell es-Safi), 18–19, 74
Gaziantep Museum, 131
Genubath, 25
Gerda Henkel Foundation, 140
Gezer, 27, 29, 31–32
Gezer calendar, 27, *28*
Gilbert, Alessandra, 113, 132
Gilboa, Ayelet, 98
Global Systemic Risk project, Princeton University, 186
Glueck, Nelson, 25–26
Goliath, 26
Gordion, 115
Gordion Knot, 115
Grayson, A. Kirk, 47, 62, 70
Greece: adaptive cycle model applied to, 161–162, *163*, 198; administrative structure, 138; burials in, 151–154 (*see also* warrior burials in); climate change in, 114; collapse in, 137; Cyprus and, 85, 108; "dark

age" period in, 4–5, 195–198, 248n7; drought in, 137; historical sources available for, 135; in Iron Age, 134–156; ironworking in, 88; migrations within, 2–3, 159; and the Near East, 100, 108, 136, 137, 139, 150, 153–154; Phoenicians and, 81, 84, 108; population of, 2–3, 137, 143–144, 155, 159; resilience of, 136–138, 143, 154–156, 162, 176; and trade, 137; warrior burials in, 92, 145–150; writing in, 80–81, 138, 141–143, 198, 241n20. *See also* Crete and the Minoans; Mycenae

Guy, P.L.O., 31

Hadad, 25, 29

Hadad-ezer, 70, 72

Haldon, John, xxii–xxiii

Hamilton (musical), xxv, 160

Hammurabi's Law Code, 46, 47

Harem Conspiracy, 7–8

Harrison, Tim, 120

Hartapu inscription, 115

Harvard University, 105; Center for Hellenic Studies, 2

Hatiba, 101

Hawkins, J. D., 120

Hayya, 130

Hazael, 23, 72–75

Hazor, 31–32

Hebrew Bible, 19, 21, 25, 31–34, 38, 42, 45, 73–74, 76, 78, 105, 116

Hebrew University, 26, 37, 105

Henuttawy, 14

Herihor, 13–14

Herodotus, 80–81, 135, 159

Herod the Great, 105

Hero of Lefkandi, 148–150

Hesiod, 5, 135, 138, 155

Hiram I, 32–33, 99, 104

historical sources: Assyria, xxv, 43–45, 47–48; Babylonia, xxv; Cyprus, xxv; "dark age" applied to periods lacking, 195, 197; Egypt, xxv; Greece, 135; Israelites, 21–22; Minoans, xxv; Mycenae, xxv; scholarly considerations concerning, 45, 180, 184. *See also* archaeology

History of Climate and Society, 213n3

Hittites, collapse of, 114, 116, 174, 177, 185–186, 188–191. *See also* Neo-Hittites

Hogarth, D. G., 117–118, 122

Homer, 135, 138, 145, 146, 155, 184, 196; *Iliad*, xxi, 82, 92, 147, 150; *Odyssey*, xxi, 82, 146

honey, 37–38

Huelva, 33, 93, 98, 106

Hurricane Katrina, 164

Iacovou, Maria, 89

Iberia. *See* Spain

information. *See* communications

Inhapy, 29

Ini-Tešub (Iron Age king), 112–114, 118

innovation: in adaptive cycle, 160, 171; Assyria, 129; Cyprus, 85, 109, 171; Greece, 2, 198; Iron Age, 159; Phoenicians, 80–81, 85, 109, 170, 171

Intergovernmental Panel on Climate Change (IPCC), xxx, 164–171, *165*, 188, 192

Invisible Israelites model, 19

IPCC. *See* Intergovernmental Panel on Climate Change

Iron Age: as a dark age, 4–6, 195–199; maps of Mediterranean region during, *xxxi–xxxvi*; scholarly opinions on, 1–6, 199

ironworking: Cyprus and, 85–88, 93, 110, 150, 173; origins of, 2, 85–88, 198; Phoenicians and, 229n16

Iš-Aštart, 104, 105

Ishbaal (Ishbosheth), 22

ISIS, 61

Israelites: Assyria and, 77, 119; conquest of Canaan by, 19–20; David's reign, 21–27; and Edom, 24–26; historical sources available for, 21–22; in Iron Age, 19–33, 178–179; settlements of, 20, 21; Solomon's reign, 30–36

Israel Museum, Jerusalem, 17

Jeffers, Joshua, 197
Jehoram, 105
Jehu, 38, 71, 73–76
Jeroboam, 35–36
Jeroboam II, 31
Jezebel, 73, 105
Joint Expedition, 105
Joram, 73
Jordan, 17, 24, 25, 119, 150
Jordanian Department of Antiquities, 25
Josephus, Flavius, 71, 104, 106–107
Journal of the Royal Geographic Society of London, 63, 127

Kaniewski, David, 90
Karageorghis, Vassos, 91
Kassianidou, Vasiliki, 86
Kenyon, Kathleen, 105
Khayyam, Omar, 190
Khirbet Qeiyafa, 26–27
King, L. W., 59
kings and regnal years, *xxvi–xxix*
Kitchen, Kenneth, 25
Klein, F. A., 24
Knodell, Alex, 139
Knossos Urban Landscape Project, 144
Koch, Ido, 177–178
Kotsonas, Antonio, 142, 144, 147–148
Kourou, Nota, 75, 93, 94, 99, 108, 232n43
Kulamuwa, 130
Kurkh Monolith, 63, *64*
Kush, 13, 39–40
Kuzi-Tešub, 112, 118

Langgut, Dafna, 21
Late Bronze Age, Great Powers in, 52
Late Bronze Age Collapse: adaptive cycle model of, 160–164, *162*, 170; alternative histories of, 189–190; climate change and, 164–171, 213n3; complex histories of, 170–178, 191–192; fragilities/vulnerabilities contributing to, 184–190; international network's dissolution after, xxiv; ironworking after, 88; lessons for today from, 192–194, *194*; migrations resulting from, 3, 159; overview of, xxi, 157–160, *189*; resilience theory applied to, 170–180, *172*, *181–183*; scholarly opinions on, 1–6; temporality of, 2–3, 137–139, 157–158, 162–163, 193, 197
Lawrence, T. E., 116–117
Layard, Austen Henry, 45, 57, 59, 64–65, 71
Lebanon, 32, 51, 53, 68, 69, 75, 83, 95, 97, 119. *See also* Canaan; Phoenicians
Lefkandi, 148–150
Leiden University, 142
Lemos, Irene, 149
Leopold-Amherst Papyrus, 11
Levant: Assyria and, 39–40, 129–130; drought in, 21; Edom and, 24–26; Egypt and, 10, 14, 18, 33–40; in Iron Age, 19–41; Iron Age map, *xxxiii*; Israelites in, 19–33; Neo-Hittites and, 121; Philistines and, 19; population of, 21; temple form in, 33
Levy, Tom, 25
Linear B, 2, 138, 142
Liston, Maria, 152
literacy, 81–82
Liverani, Mario, 53, 61
Long Wall of Sculpture, 122
Loret, Victor, 14
Louisiana State University, 194
Luwian, 37, 72, 115, 117, 120, 159

Macalister, Robert Alexander Stewart, 18–19, 27, 31
Maeir, Aren, 19
Mallowan, Max, 60–61, 66–67, 123
Maran, Joseph, 185
Marchetti, Nicolò, 111–112, 122
Marduk-nadin-ahhe, 53
Marduk-zakir-sumi, 68
Maspero, Gaston, 30
Matney, Tim, 62
Mattan I, 106
Mazar, Amihai, 37
McAnany, Patricia, 157–158

Medea/Jason (remotely operated vehicle system), 107
Megginson, Leon, 194
Megiddo, 30–32, 34–36
Merneptah, 19
Merriam-Webster's, 4, 195, 198
Mesha Stele, 24
Mesopotamia. *See* Assyria; Babylonia
Mesopotamian Chronicles, 43
Midas, 115
migrations: accompanying collapse, 3, 4, 159; Greece, 2–3, 159; Late Bronze Age Collapse, 3, 159; Mycenae, 72, 89
Minoans. *See* Crete and the Minoans
Moab, 21, 38, 40, 80, 119, 179
monotheism, 19
Monroe, Christopher, 83–84
Montet, Pierre, 14–17
Morris, Ian, 137, 143, 144, 150, 154, 161–162, 196–197
Morris, Sarah, 3, 197
Mosul Museum, Iraq, 61
Mühlenbruch, Tobias, 136
Muhly, James, 147
Murray, Sarah, 137, 139
Mushki, 115
Mutnedjmet, 16, 17
Mycenae: collapse of, xxi, 134, 137–139, 143, 155, 175–176, 190–194; cultural continuity of, 175–176; drought in, 190; fragility/vulnerability of, 184–185, 188, 190; historical sources available for, xxv; migration of, 72, 89; and the Minoans, 140–141; pottery of, 2. *See also* Greece

Na'aman, Nadav, 36, 106
Nabu-apla-iddina, 63
Nagy, Gregory, 2
Najjar, Mohammad, 25
National Museum of Egyptian Civilization, 30
National Research Council, 167
Naveh, Joseph, 241n20
Near East: Aramaeans in, 78–79; Assyrian dominance of, 55, 62; Greece and, 100, 108, 136, 137, 139, 150, 153–154; ironworking in, 88; languages in, 42, 141
Nebuchadnezzar I, 43, 46–47, 48, 53
Neo-Assyrian Empire. *See* Assyria
Neo-Hittites: Assyria and, 118, 123–133; beekeeping practiced by, 37; climate change and, 114; in Iron Age, 111–133; resilience of, 119, 132, 174; rulers and kingdoms of, 111–114, 116–118, 124–132. *See also* Hittites, collapse of
New York University, 114, 144
Nimrud, 64–66
Nowicki, Krzysztof, 140
NR-1 (submarine), 107
Nubia, 13, 39–40

obelos of Opheltas, 91–92
Olympic Games, 150, 155
Omri, 24, 31, 39, 105
Onomasticon of Amenemopet, 18, 94–95
Oriental Institute, University of Chicago, 25, 30–31, 114. *See also* University of Chicago
Osborne, James, 114
Osorkon the Elder, 34
Osorkon I, 39, 102–103, *103*
Osorkon II, 39, 70, 71, 105

Page, Denys, 196
Palestine Exploration Fund, 27
Palistin, Land of, 120–121, 129
panarchy, 162–163
Panedjem I, 14
Panedjem II, 29
Papadopoulos, John, 152, 198
Patin. *See* Palistin, Land of
Peaceful Infiltration, 19
Peleset. *See* Philistines
Pentawere, 7–8
Petrie, William Matthew Flinders, 19
Philistines, 18–22, 26, 35, 77, 119

Phoenicians: alphabet of, 80–81, 141–142, 198, 241n20; Assyria and, 52, 62, 66–68, 70–71, 79, 118, 233n52; communications system of, 84–85; contributions of, to Western civilization, 80–82; Crete and, 100, 108, 154, 232n43; Egypt and, 94–97; in Iron Age, 80–84, 94–108; and ironworking, 229n16; kings of Byblos and Tyre, 101–106; purple dye produced by, 82, 98, 110, 173; resilience of, 83–84, 88, 109–110, 169–173; self-identification of, 82; and Spain, 97–99, 106; territory of, 97; and trade, 83, 88, 99–100, 106–108, 110, 173. *See also* Canaan; Lebanon; Tyre

Phrygia, 115, 177

Piyaššili (Sharri-Kušuh), 118

P. Mayer B (papyrus), 11

population: Babylonia, 47; Crete, 144, 153; Cyprus, 89–90; decline of, accompanying collapse, 4–5; Greece, 2–3, 137, 143–144, 155, 159; Levant, 21

Porter, Benjamin, 197, 247n59

Postgate, Nicholas, 43, 186

Princeton University, xxii; Institute for International and Regional Studies, 186

Pritchard, James, 97

Psusennes I, 14–17, 25

Psusennes II, 15, 16–17, 33

Pummayon (Pygmalion), 106–107

punctuated equilibrium, 244n13

purple dye, 82, 98, 110, 173

Qarqar. *See* Battle of Qarqar

Quinn, Josephine, 82

Radner, Karen, 65

Ramses III, 7–8, 18, 117

Ramses IV, 9

Ramses V, 9–10

Ramses VI, 10, 11, 14

Ramses VII, 10

Ramses VIII, 10

Ramses IX, 10–11

Ramses X, 12

Ramses XI, 12–13, 51, 97

Rassam, Hormudz, 45, 57–61, 68, 123

Rawlinson, Henry, 127

Rehav, 36–37

Reisner, George, 105

relief sculptures. *See* wall reliefs

R.E.M. (band), xxii

Renfrew, Colin, 4, 148, 189

resilience: adaptive cycle model of, 160–164; Assyria, 47–48, 53, 56–57, 61–79, 170–171, 173–174, 186–188; Babylonia, 47, 53, 78, 170–171, 173–174, 188; Canaanites/Phoenicians, 40–41, 83–84, 88, 109–110, 169–174, 178; civilizations, xxii–xxiv; concept and theory, 160, 167–170, 184–190; Crete, 140; Cyprus, 85, 87–90, 94, 109–110, 171–173; Egypt, 12, 170–171, 174–175, 188; Elamites, 47; factors contributing to, 188–189, 193; Greece, 136–138, 143, 154–156, 162, 176; Late Bronze Age Collapse, 170–180, *172*, *181–183*; Neo-Hittites, 119, 132, 174; Phoenicians (*see* Canaanites/Phoenicians); terms and definitions related to, *169*. *See also* fragility/vulnerability

Revolting Peasants model, 19

Rib-Hadda, 101

Rich Athenian Lady, 151–152

risk management. *See* disaster risk management

rivers, 188–189

Russia, xxiii

Sader, Hélène, 119

Samaria ivories, 105

Sangara, 123, 129–132

Sapaziti, 112–113

sarcophagus of Ahiram, *102*

Sardinia, 3, 84, 86, 87, 93, 98, 106, 173

Sarduri I, 128

Sargon II, 77, 109, 118, 132

Saul, 19–22

Schliemann, Heinrich, 134

Schneider, Tammi, 76

Schumacher, Gottlieb, 35

Scott, James, 6

Sea Peoples, 7, 16, 18, 20, 85, 95, 117, 187, 190
Sennacherib, 77
settlement shift. *See* migrations
Sha'il, 130
Shalmaneser I, 124
Shalmaneser II, 112
Shalmaneser III, 39, 58, 60, 63, 67–76, *69*, 106, 121, 123, 125–131; Black Obelisk, 75, *76*; Monolith Inscription, 68, 70, 125–127, 130
Shalmaneser V, 77
Shalvi, Golan, 98
Shamši-Adad V, 68, 130
Sherden (Shardana), 18
Sherratt, Susan, 85, 197
Sheshonq I, 9, 29, 33–40, 104
Sheshonq IIa, 15, 17, 39
Sheshonq III, 39
Shipitbaal, 101–102
Shipitbaal Inscription, 102
Shishak. *See* Sheshonq I
Shitti-Marduk, 46
Siamun, 15, 16–17, 29, 33–34
Sicily, 3, 84, 87, 93, 110, 173
silver, 97–98, 106, 110
smallpox, 10
Smendes, 13–14
Smith, Elliot, 12
Smithson, Evelyn, 151–152
Snodgrass, Anthony, 151, 161, 196
Solomon, 17, 19, 24, 25, 27, 29–36
Solomon's Stables, 31, 35
source material. *See* historical sources
Spain (Iberia), 82, 93, 97–99, 106, 110, 173
Stager, Larry, 107–108
Stanford University, 137
Starr, Chester, 196–197
Strabo, 82, 85
Suhi I, 111–113, 132
Suppiluliuma I, 116, 118
Suppiluliuma II, 129
Syria, 21, 33, 51, 60, 62, 69, 72, 75, 77, 81, 83, 84, 93, 111, 116, 118, 119, 120, 121, 129, 153, 154, 174, 186
Tainter, Joseph, 2, 5
Taleb, Nassim Nicholas, 84, 229n13
Tale of Wenamun, 13, 94–97, 101
Tallis, Nigel, 61
Tanetamon, 13
Tanit (ship), 107–108
Taylor, John, 63, 125, 127
Tel Aviv University, 21, 26, 36, 106, 178
Tel Dan inscription, 22–24, *23*, 72–73
Tel Dor, 84, 95–96, *97*, 100
Telepinu, 118
Tell er-Rimah stela, 77
Tell es-Safi. *See* Gath
Temple, Jerusalem, 32–33
Terramare culture, 88
Thucydides, 1, 135
Tiglath-Pileser I, 43, 48–55, 113–116, 118, 124, 127; clay prisms of, 49, *50*, 51
Tiglath-Pileser III, 74, 77, 132
Tigris Tunnel, 127
Time (magazine), 25
Timna mines, 10, 17, 26, 217n33
Titanic (ship), 107
Tiye, 7–8
Tjekker, 18, 95
tomb robberies, 8, 10–13, 30
Tomb Robbery Papyri, 11
trade: Canaan, 83; Cyprus, 87, 88, 93–94, 108, 110, 173; Egypt, 18; Greece, 137; Levant, 37; Phoenicians, 83, 88, 99–100, 106–108, 110, 173
transformation: Assyria, 78; Babylonia, 78; Canaan, 40–41; civilizations, xxii, xxiv, 168; concept of, 164; Crete, 140; Cyprus, 84–85, 94, 109–110, 171; Edom, 179; Egypt, 9, 12; Greece, 137, 162, 176; Israelites, 178–179; Late Bronze Age, 157–158, *189*; Neo-Hittites, 119, 132; Phoenicians, 109–110, 171, 173
transition: civilizations, xxii, xxiv; Egypt, 12; Neo-Hittites, 132
Trojan War, 1, 92, 134, 135, 145–148, 196
Tsipopoulou, Metaxia, 140
Tukulti-Ninurta I, 124

Tukulti-Ninurta II, 62
Turin Judicial Papyrus, 7
Turkey, 37, 49, 62–63, 68, 78, 111, 116, 120, 124, 154. *See also* Anatolia
Tutankhamun, 10, 15, 17, 30, 86
Tyre, 32, 52, 58, 66–67, 71, 77, 82, 83, 84, 97, 99, 104–107, 118
Tyrian purple. *See* purple dye

Ugarit, 45, 84, 109, 119, 120, 140, 169, 173, 184, 190
Ukraine, xxiii
United Monarchy (Israelites), 22, 34, 35
United Nations, xxiii, 164
University at Buffalo, 151
University College London, 4
University of Akron, 62
University of Amsterdam, 93
University of Athens, 75, 93, 99
University of Bologna, 111
University of California Berkeley, 197
University of California Los Angeles (UCLA), 3, 152, 197, 198
University of California San Diego, 25
University of Chicago, 25, 30–31, 34–35, 114, 120, 186
University of Cyprus, 86, 89
University of Haifa, 95, 98
University of Lausanne, 142
University of London, 120
University of Michigan, 196
University of Oxford, 149
University of Pennsylvania, 97, 147, 197
University of Queensland, 66
University of Sheffield, 85
University of Toronto, 47, 70, 120, 129, 137
University of Waterloo, 152
Uppsala University, 170
Urartu, 58, 61, 68, 124–129, 132, 173, 177
Ura-Tarhunta, 112–113
ushabtis (statuettes), 14, 17
US National Intelligence Council, xxiii

Valley of the Kings, Egypt, 10, 13, 14
Vatican Museum, 131
Virgil, 92
vulnerability. *See* fragility/vulnerability

Waal, Willemijn, 142
Wachter, Rudolf, 142–143
Wadi Faynan, 17, 25–26, 38, 74, 150, 179
Wallace, Saro, 140, 177
wall reliefs, 44, 65
Walters Art Gallery, Baltimore, 59, 68
warrior burials, 92–93, 145–150
Warrior vase from Mycenae, *135*
Washington Post (newspaper), 52
Weiberg, Erika, 170, 185
Wenamun, 95–96, 101
Western Mediterranean, Iron Age map, *xxxvi*
Whitley, James, 154, 198
wine, 129
Wooden, John, 193
Woolley, Leonard, 117, 122
World History Encyclopedia, 195
writing: Assyria, 47–48, 187; Babylonia, 47; Canaan, 27, 80; as factor in resilience, 188; Greece, 80–81, 138, 141–143, 198, 241n20; Hittites/Neo-Hittites, 117; loss of, following collapse, 5, 195, 196; Luwian, 117; Phoenicians, 80–81, 141–142, 198, 241n20

Xenophon, 85

Yadin, Yigael, 31
Yale University, 6, 48
Yehimilk, 101–104
Yehimilk Inscription, 104
Yoffee, Norman, 157–158
York University, 19